P9-BYM-753

D0015234

BIG BLUES

BIG BLUES

The Unmaking of IBM

BY PAUL CARROLL

CROWN PUBLISHERS, INC.   NEW YORK

To Kim, with love—
all ways, all days.

Copyright © 1993 by Paul Carroll

Published by Crown Publishers, Inc., 201 East 50th Street, New York, New York 10022. Member of the Crown Publishing Group.

Random House, Inc. New York, Toronto, London, Sydney, Auckland

CROWN is a trademark of Crown Publishers, Inc.

Manufactured in the U.S.A.

Design by June Bennett-Tantillo

Library of Congress Cataloging-in-Publication Data
Carroll, Paul
    Big blues : the unmaking of IBM / by Paul Carroll.
    Includes bibliographical references and index.
    1. International Business Machines Corporation—History.   2. Computer industry—United States—History.   I. Title.
  HD9696.C64I48317   1994
  338.7'61004'0973—dc20   93-5421
                                                                    CIP

ISBN 0-517-59197-9

10   9   8   7   6   5   4   3   2   1

First Edition

ACKNOWLEDGMENTS

As you might guess, IBM didn't cooperate with this book. That's no surprise. IBM policy says the company doesn't cooperate on books. The company didn't even formally cooperate when Tom Watson, Jr.—a former chief executive, son of IBM's founder and general, all-round legend—did his autobiography a few years back.

Fortunately for this book, I've had extraordinary access to IBM executives during the seven years I've followed the company. Over that time, I've had lengthy conversations with almost all the principal characters in this book—with the only notable exception being the "father of the PC," Don Estridge, who died a year before I began to cover IBM for *The Wall Street Journal.* Once I began this project and took a leave of absence from the *Journal* in mid-1992, IBM officially stopped talking to me, but so many people from the executive ranks on down had left the company by then that there were plenty of people willing to help me. Many of the people I talked to seemed to want to bare their souls, and not just because they were mad at the way IBM had treated them or others. While the people I talked to had toed the party line while at IBM, once they had a few months' distance from IBM, they began to develop a new perspective that generated enormous frustration about the problems consuming the company they loved. They decided that only a real airing of IBM's mistakes would shake it out of its torpor.

Thanks to all those who helped. Many of the former IBMers who helped out didn't want to have their names used because they didn't want to be seen as criticizing the company, so I must thank them anonymously. Quotes not cited in the notes are derived directly from my interviews. The executives who didn't mind being identified are cited throughout the book. The one IBM name not mentioned is Bob Gilbert, who worked with me at the *Journal* before going off to become an IBM speech writer and then moving on from there; Bob explained a lot of the IBM lore to me over the years.

Thanks, too, to the senior people at Microsoft, who spent days with me recounting the history of their relationship with IBM, and who allowed me access to some of their files. Many of those I interviewed are named in the book, so I won't name them all here, but I would like to thank Pam Edstrom, in particular, for arranging sessions with Microsoft. There are numerous other people throughout the computer industry who deserve thanks for sharing their insights with me, but the list would number in the hundreds. I'll just single out Matt Fitzsimmons, who talked me through numerous technical issues, and Sam Albert, who knows everything about everybody at IBM.

At the risk of making this sound like an Oscar winner's speech, I'll thank a few other people, too, who did so much to help me shape this book. First and foremost is my wife, Kim Tarter Carroll, whose support and inspiration enriched these pages. She was my first editor, patiently listening as I told and retold the stories in this book and tried to refine them. Kim watched me while away the days early on as I worked on my inadequate golf game, all the while gently reminding me of my deadline but never once saying, "I told you so" when crunch time hit in early 1993 and I had to work all waking hours to make up for lost time. Special thanks, too, to my father, Charlie, a former journalist— and ex-*Journal* editor—whose cleverness with words was what got me interested in becoming a writer in the first place. Over the years, he has been my most enthusiastic supporter. For this book, he not only helped polish the manuscript but did some of the reporting for the final chapter to help me meet my deadline.

I benefited, too, from my numerous connections with *The Wall Street Journal*—starting with my brother Tim, a copy editor there who kept after me about meeting my deadlines and helped me make the book livelier. Then there's my good friend Tim Smith, the best writer I know. Tim held my hand back in 1991 as I was starting to think about doing the book, and he encouraged me throughout this huge project. Mike Miller and Laurence Hooper, with whom I shared the IBM beat over the past several years, provided several key insights into what was going on at IBM during my absence and let me bounce ideas off them. Thanks, too, to the management of the *Journal* for letting me disappear for a year to write this book.

Thanks, as well, to my father-in-law, Ralph Tarter, who has written a book himself, on electronics; and Terry Garnett, a friend from the computer industry. They read preliminary manuscripts and made some helpful suggestions. Jon Friedman, a friend and coauthor of a book on American Express, entitled *House of Cards*, graciously gave me access to all his material on IBM's new chief executive, Lou Gerstner, who had been a senior executive at American Express. Several people at Stanford University's Computer Industry Project—a study of the industry financed by the Sloan Foundation—broadened the book through their perspective on IBM's competitors. Particular thanks to Frank Shellenberg.

Thanks to my editor, Jim Wade, who did so much to increase the scope of the ideas in the book. Thanks to my agent, Kris Dahl of ICM. Anyone who's done a book knows that the real reason for doing it is so you can get an agent and walk around saying things like, "Well, I just talked to my agent. . . ." Reporters don't ordinarily get to do things like that. More important, though, is that Kris managed to get publishers interested in a book on the fall of IBM, written by a first-time author, long before it became clear just how quickly IBM would stumble.

Finally, thanks to my family for all their support during the sometimes-tense process of producing a book—even if some of them thought I'd never get it done.

Any errors that slipped through my network of readers and editors are, of course, mine.

PREFACE

The red was creeping up the back of Frank Cary's neck, a sure sign of trouble. The chairman of IBM was meeting with his most senior executives, the all-powerful Management Committee, just before the Fourth of July weekend in 1980 and was hearing yet again why IBM couldn't build a personal computer. Apple Computer and others had been embarrassing IBM for so many years with their hot little machines that Cary had taken to going up to executives and demanding, "Where's my Apple?" So Cary couldn't understand why IBM had repeatedly failed in attempts to respond. Why, in fact, should IBM have had to respond at all? It had identified the opportunity for a personal computer years before those kids at Apple ever got started working out of their garage in the mid-1970s, but IBM just seemed to be sinking money into development projects that never saw the light of day.

Seeing Cary mad was a rare sight around IBM; he was known for his unearthly calm. But what Cary was hearing in the Management Committee meeting was beyond the pale. Cary had been trying for years to get someone to do what he considered to be the simple job of developing a simple machine, yet all IBM had produced was a couple of lousy machines, the Datamaster and 5100 series, plus what Cary felt was a half-baked plan to buy chintzy computers from Atari— a video-game company, for God's sake—and slap IBM logos on them. Now, Cary was hearing what sounded like an excellent plan for producing a personal computer quickly—but was being told it wasn't possible because the group making the presentation didn't have the financing.

Cary narrowed his eyes behind his small wire-rimmed glasses. With his bald head reddening and his pronounced brow jutting forward, he cut off Jack Rogers, who had said he couldn't finance a personal computer because he had too many projects going in his enormous General Products Division, which was responsible for all small systems, ranging from little computers down to typewriters.

"Hearts and minds," Cary said. "This is the kind of machine that will really capture people's hearts and minds. We have to build this machine."

Rogers started to say that maybe he could find the money somewhere, after all.

"Never mind that," Cary said. "*I'll* finance it."

He turned to Bill Lowe, who worked for Rogers and who had made the presentation about how to develop the machine.

"Do you have any land off-site where you can put a development team and keep them isolated from everyone else?" Cary asked.

Lowe, whose stony manner and slicked-back graying hair reminded people of the waiters in German restaurants, showed no reaction as he started to explain that he had a small facility a little ways away from the General Products Division lab in Boca Raton, Florida, but Cary was already on to his next point.

"Take forty people and put them there," Cary said. "And pick somebody good to run it, because he'll report directly to me. You have a month. Go off and get organized and report back to me."

After years of having IBM's bureaucracy stifle its personal-computer efforts, Cary would finally get his machine.

This book is about the rise and fall of that PC and the rise and fall of IBM that went along with it. The PC kicked IBM's revenue and earnings into overdrive in the early 1980s, helping IBM produce the greatest profits any company has ever turned in. But the wild success of the IBM PC also undermined the company's core mainframe business, the one that was churning out $4 billion or more in profit each year. As mainframe profits disappeared, IBM squandered its opportunities to turn the PC or anything else into a business that would wax as mainframes waned. Thirteen years after Cary's bold decision, IBM found itself with little money coming in from mainframes and no money coming in from PCs, either.

IBM had plenty of opportunities in the PC business along the way, but it needed to change to seize them, and it couldn't. IBM reproduced the Xerox story. Throughout the 1970s, Xerox developed most of the important ideas that propelled the PC industry through the 1980s, yet it failed to capitalize because it didn't realize what it had. When Xerox finally caught on, its development groups were so unaccustomed to designing real consumer products that they came out with a pig of a PC —a huge, expensive machine that no one wanted. IBM actually got the PC right for the first few years because its overbearing bureaucracy stepped aside, but that didn't last long. Once IBM's ponderous system reasserted itself, the PC began to follow Xerox's into oblivion.

IBM's executives actually saw most of their problems coming, both in PCs and in the rest of the business. They commissioned months-long task forces with loads of smart people and forecasted the changes in the market that would cripple IBM, but IBMers couldn't quite bring themselves to do anything about those cataclysmic changes. Those in power at the time say that outsiders just can't understand how intoxicating the early 1980s were. IBM was the most profitable, the most admired, the best company in the world, maybe in the history of the world. Why change?

Instead of adapting, IBM settled into cultural gridlock. Executives spent most of their time in meetings talking to one another, using their ubiquitous overhead transparencies—or, foils—on the overhead projectors that were sometimes even built into their rosewood desks. They spoke their own language, using their three-letter acronyms and talking about "transitioning to a new environment to solution a problem and advantage the customer."

They debated new technologies, such as PCs, but the older executives who ran the company rarely dirtied their hands with the technologies enough to understand their potential and their problems. IBM had become like a music-publishing company run by deaf people.

IBM's senior executives ignored the outside world and spent most of their efforts trying to maneuver past one another, because executives felt they had vanquished competitors so completely that the only real measure of success was advancement inside IBM. Over the years, IBM's competitors in mainframes had been referred to variously as the

Seven Dwarfs, to IBM's Snow White, or the BUNCH, but the names kept having to change because IBM kept chasing companies out of the business. Remington Rand couldn't handle IBM even though it had such a head start in the computer business in the 1950s that computers were generically referred to as Univacs, the name of Remington Rand's machine. General Electric couldn't withstand IBM in the 1950s and 1960s. Of the BUNCH—Burroughs, Univac, NCR, Control Data, and Honeywell—only NCR stayed healthy past the mid-1980s, and it was eventually taken over by AT&T. This prototypical conglomerate, thought to be IBM's major competition in the United States as the 1980s began, would lose billions of dollars in the computer business. Overseas, the main Japanese companies prospered, but IBM embarrassed most of its European competitors—ICL in England, Bull in France, Olivetti in Italy. In the PC business, IBM blew by pioneer Tandy, which eventually quit the market, and almost put word-processing giant Wang out of business. Upstarts like Kaypro shot into view but faded nearly as fast. Even Apple, so totally identified with the personal computer, ran into trouble so fast that cofounder Steve Jobs was shown the door.

By the late 1980s, IBM executives would talk and talk and talk about how much they'd changed. But the will to change was long gone.

The problems showed up most startlingly in software, where IBM made a big share of its profits and considered itself to be the world leader in technology but where Microsoft, a company that consisted of only a handful of kids in 1980, snatched the PC market from IBM. Never acknowledging how bad it was at software, IBM kept dropping hundreds of millions of dollars, even billions of dollars, into losing propositions. The gridlock also showed up through all the rest of IBM, creating problems in areas from PC hardware development through the services market that IBM kept talking about wanting to enter.

IBM has already lost some $75 billion of stock-market value, going from a position several years back where its total stock value was greater than that of all the companies on all the stock exchanges in Germany put together to a spot barely in the top ten U.S. companies. The drop in value exceeded that of the second biggest company. That value has just disappeared, taking along with it the retirement hopes of hundreds of thousands of IBM employees and other investors. IBM has written off some $20 billion of assets in recent years, about twice the gross national product of Ecuador.

Yet IBM will have to spend years sorting out its problems, because IBM must change its revered culture if it is to come out of this crisis. And years sound like an eternity in a business where furious turnover of product lines means a year to eighteen months is considered to be a lifetime. The world will look very different by the time IBM pulls itself together—assuming it *can* pull itself together—and IBM will never again hold sway over the computer industry.

As IBM fades from view, it leaves behind some troubling specters. IBM has been the most important bulwark as the United States has struggled to keep Japan from attaining technological supremacy. The company led the rescue of the U.S. semiconductor-equipment and semiconductor industries in the early 1990s. IBM had produced most of the key technologies that have propelled the whole computer industry over the years, all the way from esoteric data-storage technologies for mainframes on down to the hard disks and floppy disks that are such a big part of personal computers. IBM researchers have brought the United States two Nobel Prizes in recent years. The company has spent some $7 billion annually on research and development, which is about one-tenth the total spent by corporate America each year and leads to all sorts of innovation—even if IBM often isn't the first to bring the new ideas to market.

The company has been the largest corporate contributor to non-profit and educational institutions over the years and has provided jobs for hundreds of thousands of colleges' technical students. But hiring has nearly stopped as the company has hacked away at its work force, and contributions have fallen from $189 million in 1985 to $120 million in 1992. The smaller companies that have succeeded at IBM's expense in recent years, such as Microsoft, Apple, and Sun, are young enough that they haven't yet taken up the philanthropic slack left by IBM.

"We're at a watershed," said James H. Morris, chairman of the computer science department at Carnegie-Mellon University in Pittsburgh. "The restructuring of the computer industry has put computer science at a turning point."[1]

IBM's troubles also raise questions about whether big companies can work anymore. General Motors messed up. So did Sears. In less cataclysmic ways, so have Kodak and so many other industrial giants that the Fortune 500 can no longer be counted on for job growth. If IBM, once the managerial model for big companies, can't hack it, then who can?

The shrinking of IBM, coming at the same time as other computer companies are slashing away at their payrolls, also generates concern about whether the high-tech field can be the engine of growth that the Clinton administration seems to hope. IBM will go from 407,000 employees in 1986 to perhaps 260,000 worldwide at the end of 1993, and it probably isn't through cutting. Whole towns that sprang up in New York's Hudson Valley because of IBM jobs are seeing their economies devastated. This is happening at the same time that Boston's showcase Route 128 corridor is becoming a ghost town, as Digital Equipment, Wang, Prime Computer, Data General, and many others cut back or disappear. With even Silicon Valley lamenting the loss of jobs, total employment in the U.S. computer-hardware industry has declined nearly 20 percent since its peak in 1987, and no end is in sight.[2]

Other computer companies are even less likely to generate any growth while IBM is ailing. Many have, over the years, felt that IBM was less a competitor than an environment. IBM pretty much had its majority share of the market, and everybody else fought for the rest. Most priced their products at, say, a 15 percent discount to IBM's and counted on IBM to provide a stable pricing umbrella for them. Now, the stable environment of the past few decades in the computer industry has given way to global warming. IBM has lost so much market share that it is going after everyone else's. It is even slashing its prices, trying to get close to competitors, who keep lowering their own prices in a futile attempt to sell at their normal discount off IBM's prices. Dick Munro, an IBM board member who used to be chief executive of Time Inc., told a friend in late 1992 that the company plans to use its financial muscle to maintain what he called "a last-man standing" strategy, to see how long competitors can hang on, in the hope that IBM will be the last survivor.

Even if other companies take up the slack that IBM is leaving in the U.S. economy, the problems at IBM have marked the end of a way of life in corporate America. IBM's values were formed in patriarchal times early in this century, and the company clung to those ideals even as every other major, old-style company was forced to give up on no-layoff policies and become more cold-blooded in dealing with employees. IBM finally abandoned its practice of granting people lifetime employment and began laying people off in early 1993. Even the company's revered set of beliefs—including the all-important respect for the individual—was reduced to nothing but a series of nice ideas. And with the arrival of Lou Gerstner in early 1993 as the first IBM chief executive who didn't grow up in the company, most of IBM's other cherished traditions will perish, too.

The tough part about chronicling IBM's problems is that IBM was once such a great company—great to its customers, great to its shareholders, great to its employees, great to the towns, cities, states, and countries where it operated. In many people's eyes, IBM wasn't so much a company as an institution. Yet the things that made the company so widely admired are what now make it vilified. People once referred to IBM's passion for being right, its rigorous processes, its thorough training of employees, its focus on customers' desires, its guarantee of lifetime employment. But the computer industry has moved out of the horse-and-buggy days that produced IBM's values and into a relativistic universe where everything is moving at the speed of light. So, referring to the same values IBM has always had, people talk about IBM's fear of risk, its civil-service mentality, its brainwashing of employees, its failure to make innovative products that anticipate customers' desires, its inability to adapt its work force quickly enough to react to shifts in the industry. What follows, then, is a sort of Greek tragedy. It is a very sad story.

ONE

Jack Sams, a midlevel IBM executive, was about to make the most fateful of phone calls. He had been putting together a software strategy for a personal computer in the hope that his boss, Bill Lowe, would win approval from the Management Committee for a PC project, and Lowe had told him to proceed. So, just following the 1980 Fourth of July weekend, Sams was about to call a twenty-four-year-old college dropout named Bill Gates in Bellevue, Washington. Sams knew that Gates and a childhood buddy had written languages that were being used to create programs on most of the personal computers then in use. He wanted to see whether they had a legitimate-enough operation for IBM to consider using their languages on its machine.

Gates said, "Certainly, I'd love to meet with you. How about in two weeks?"

To his astonishment, the executive from slow-moving IBM said, "How about tomorrow?"

When Sams, a balding, fatherly sort in his fifties, and a colleague flew out the next day, they went to a small bank building next to a strip mall in Bellevue, across the lake from Seattle. Sams was met at the elevator door by a waif with unruly hair and dirty wire-rimmed glasses who was wearing an ill-fitting three-piece suit. Sams assumed that this child, who could have passed for fifteen or sixteen, was the office boy. It was, in fact, the young-looking Gates.

They went through the usual rigmarole, with Gates having to sign nondisclosure agreements that said he wouldn't think of using any information IBM disclosed to him; that IBM could use whatever Gates happened to say; that Gates would, when pressed, insist he had never heard of a company with the initials *IBM* and that, even if he had, he would certainly never sue it. Gates then brought to the meeting Steve Ballmer, a college pal with a strong Nordic face and tiny icy blue eyes. Ballmer figures he was invited because his one year at business school meant that he was the only one at the company who knew how to wear a suit.

The three-hour meeting was informal, with the four just chatting about opportunities in small computers. Gates and Ballmer rocked back and forth, as they always did in those days—Gates going forward and backward, Ballmer side to side. Per procedure, Sams never let on that IBM was planning a personal computer and even used a little disinformation to make Gates think that if it produced a PC, the machine would be much more limited than the one IBM was already planning. Gates, per his usual approach, employed what would come to be known as his machine-gun style. He wanted the PC to have better graphics and a faster processor than Sams was describing. He wanted a floppy disk instead of a tape cartridge. Still, the meeting went very well. Although Gates had only thirty-one employees at that point, Microsoft was a reputable business by the standards of the fledgling PC industry, and it took Sams only a few, minutes to decide that Gates was one of the smartest people he'd ever met.

As Sams left, he tried to encourage Gates and Ballmer, but he added a word of caution: "I've been at IBM a long time, and I make a lot of proposals, but not many of them get implemented. Don't get your hopes up."

Although Gates had founded his company without any financial backing whatsoever, his was really a riches-to-riches story. His parents were William, a prominent lawyer in Seattle, and Mary, a schoolteacher whose family money and work in the community had landed her on the board of Security Pacific Bank, the national board of the United Way, and the board of regents of the University of Washington. Young Bill went to a private high school in Seattle, and, although he dropped out of college to help launch the PC revolution, the college he dropped out of was Harvard. (Even though it soon became clear what a success young Bill was making of himself, his mother took a long time to get over his dropping out. When her son got his first honorary degree from the University of Moscow, he joked that he finally had his degree from "U of M." But it wasn't until Harvard itself invited Gates back to give the commencement address for its business school that Mary Gates was mollified.)

His parents did a lot to develop the restless intellect that marked Gates. When young Bill had friends over for dinner, his parents had them play games—for instance, handing everyone a sheet of blank paper as they walked through the door and asking them to draw as accurate a map as possible of the continental United States, filling in the names of all forty-eight states. When Gates's parents had their third and final child, they informed Bill and his older sister that a newcomer was on the way by playing a game of hangman, whose solution was, "A little visitor is coming soon."[1] (The elder Gates sometimes felt they had succeeded too well in stimulating their son's thinking: They sent him to private school not because they thought they had a budding genius on their hands but because they thought he was trouble.)

Young Bill hit the hacker wave of the early 1970s with perfect timing: He reached high school at the same time that time-share computer terminals began appearing in schools. This was the first time teenagers had a shot at playing with computers, and just as kids later fell in love with video games, many high schoolers of Gates's era went for computers. Gates and his friends wound up spending all their available time in a tiny room in front of a sort of Teletype machine, holding coils of paper tape with their programs punched on them. They'd sit amid the bits of paper that had been punched out of the tapes, which made the room seem to be dusted with confetti. Gates began tinkering. He started a little software company while still in high school. He took time off from high school to write software for a large local company. In return for free computer time, he and some friends helped debug a Digital Equipment system. In a scene that IBM executives would have a hard time putting themselves in, Gates and his friends went to the Digital system's owner after hours and dug through the huge garbage containers outside, sifting through memos covered with coffee grounds to find snippets of information about how the company had its computer set up—and getting into some heavy-duty trouble when they used the snippets to hack their way through the security system and help themselves to extra time on the computer.

When Gates went off to Harvard in 1973, he had the attitude of many of the brightest students of the time: Anybody could do well in school; the trick was to do well without appearing to try. So Gates spent much of his time playing poker and hanging out in his room, being what he has called "a philosophically depressed kind of guy." Then, one cold day in December 1974, childhood friend Paul Allen came to visit. Stopping at a newsstand in Harvard Yard on his way to see Gates, Allen bought the latest issue of *Popular Electronics* and found an early personal computer called the Altair was on the cover. Allen, a painfully quiet sort whose bulk and beard make him look like a Northwest lumberjack, was worked up by the time he got to Gates's room. "Here's our opportunity!" Allen said. "If we don't do something now, we'll be too late!"

As a result, in 1975, even before IBM began putting together task forces to study how IBM could apply its mainframe technology and fabled processes to producing a personal computer, Gates began approaching the PC from precisely the opposite vantage point. The skinny, long-haired kid descended into the computer counterculture, where computers weren't refrigerator-sized demigods whose needs were tended to by a priesthood of white-coated technicians; computers were barely usable little boxes of electronics that buyers often had to solder together themselves. The tiny boxes didn't come with a keyboard or monitor; the machine was operated by using a series of toggle switches on the front. But the hackers, by playing around with the electronics and by vying to outdo one another as only hormone-ridden teenagers can do, would push advances in these computers far faster than any task force would ever be able to understand.

Gates and Allen decided they'd write software for this primitive PC, dubbed the Altair after a planet in a "Star Trek" episode. The problem was that the machines weren't yet available. What appeared on the cover of the magazine was just a mock-up. It didn't work. And it would be months before machines would be widely available. But Allen and Gates called the maker of the Altair with a bluff, saying that they were essentially done with a version of the Basic programming language that would run on the Altair, even though they hadn't started. Then they managed to simulate the workings of the little Altairs on Harvard's minicomputers and worked around the clock for eight weeks, sometimes going without sleep for days at a time. In the end, they had a version of Basic that was a technical tour de force, establishing the two as among the hottest programmers of the early PC days. It hadn't been clear that the Altair had enough processing power and enough memory to allow users the luxury of programming the machines in the humanlike language of Basic rather than having to use the native language of computers, which is written as just a string of ones and zeros. But Gates and Allen had produced an elegant Basic that helped launch the PC revolution because it made it so much easier for hobbyists to roll their own software applications.

Gates initially tried juggling work and Harvard but dropped out in January 1977 to move to Albuquerque, New Mexico, to be near the Altair's maker, MITS, which had a small office in a strip mall, next to a massage parlor.

As Gates and Allen began hiring people in their late teens and early twenties as programmers at their newly formed partnership, called Microsoft, they preserved the hacker culture that would prove to be so at odds with IBM's bureaucracy. While the IBMers they would encounter were generally middle-aged, professional executives whose first memory of a computer was of something that sat in its own air-conditioned room, the group at Microsoft came across as so young that the middle-aged secretary, hired while Gates was away on a trip, tried to stop him from entering his office on his return: She thought some sixteen-year-old was raiding the Microsoft chairman's office. While the IBMers took themselves seriously, Gates and his group treated everything as a game. Gates would sit in his office near the Albuquerque airport and wait until perhaps five minutes before his flight was scheduled to depart, then see whether he could drive to the airport fast enough to still make it. He and some programmers found they could get into a construction site nearby, and they began racing bulldozers in the middle of the night. Gates sometimes demonstrated a talent he had honed as a child—jumping out of a full-sized garbage can.[2]

Gates, in particular, maintained the intense focus that teenage boys can bring to bear on something like a video game but that most young men lose as they move into their twenties and discover how wide the world is. In the evenings, when IBM executives went home to their spouses and kids and started thinking about how to kill the weeds in their front lawns, Gates was just gearing up for a full night of work. He had disconnected his car radio and refused to own a television, to limit distractions from his work. He became known for forgetting wads of cash on his desk, losing his travelers' checks, misplacing his credit cards, and running out of gas.

Allen and Gates also created an atmosphere of intellectual ferment that once marked IBM but that disappeared there in the 1980s as success made the company cautious. In one legendary incident that shaped Microsoft's infant culture, the manager of a product came to Gates to confess that a bug in his product could wipe out users' data. The manager said he wanted to send out diskettes that would fix the bug, then confessed that the fix would cost $200,000, a sum Microsoft could barely afford in those days. Gates had been bearing in on the manager, trying to understand just what had gone wrong, but when it came to the price, all he said was, "$200,000, huh? I guess you just try to do better next time."[3]

Like most hackers, Gates generally viewed programming as an intellectual exercise, but he took a strikingly different view about the financial possibilities of software. Most hackers were holdovers from the 1960s, who viewed the personal computer as the ultimate democratizing tool. They saw PCs as a way to give power to the people by letting everyone have access to the powerful computers that had been major symbols of the corporate establishment. The hackers felt software should be shared. One person would write something and give it away. Others would improve on that software, others would improve on that, and so on—much the way artists had borrowed ideas and techniques to build on one another's work through the centuries. Gates, however, was more mercenary. In the late 1970s, he wrote a widely published letter complaining that someone had been passing out for free a version of the Gates-Allen Basic, cheating the two out of their right to make the kind of profit that would finance future work. The hacker community condemned Gates for what they saw as his base instincts, but the incident hardened him in his sense of the financial possibilities of software —a sense that would make him extraordinarily sophisticated about the business of PC software long before IBM came calling.

Microsoft got most of its business mistakes out of the way by making lots of missteps on small contracts and learning from those mistakes before doing larger deals. Microsoft accepted a fixed fee, for instance, for adapting its Basic language for use on numerous types of personal computers early on, only to realize that it could have made much more money by collecting a small royalty on each machine. Gates later ran into trouble because the new owner of the maker of the Altair was violating its contract with Microsoft by not marketing Basic to other personal-computer makers. He then almost made a fatal mistake, offering to settle if he was paid $200,000 in cash—before realizing how huge a franchise he would have given up, given how PCs took off. Gates wouldn't make those mistakes again, even if it was IBM looking to pay him a fixed fee instead of a royalty or Ross Perot offering to buy the company for a few million dollars a few years after it was founded.

As Gates began to do business with established companies, he also benefited from his appearance. His was one of the most acute minds to hit American business in decades, but he disarmed people because he didn't come close to looking the part. The executives he dealt with often had kids older than he, and Gates was so thin and had so little facial hair that he always looked almost ten years younger than he really was. He didn't comb his hair and often didn't wash it. His glasses were usually dirty. He'd try to look the part of a successful young man by wearing business suits, but they tended to be in colors that were slightly off—a little green or maybe beige. He'd wear respectable ties, but they might have a soup stain or some other kind of dirt on them.

Gates also had a distracting manner. He'd rock back and forth when he was thinking, and if someone asked him a long question, his eyes went out of focus while he thought about two or three other things and waited to respond. He could seem scatterbrained. When a *Wall Street Journal* reporter first had dinner with him, Gates asked someone with him whether she thought the chilled mint pea soup was served cold. Later, when he was supposed to have dinner with the reporter on a Sunday in April, he forgot the change to daylight saving time and so missed his flight. Too embarrassed to admit the mistake himself, he placed a call while on a later flight, then handed the phone to Ballmer and had him deliver the news.

While Allen had been nearly as involved as Gates in building Microsoft in the early days, he suddenly disappeared from the scene when he found out he had Hodgkin's disease. Even after chemotherapy beat the disease, he returned only to Microsoft's board.

In Allen's place emerged Ballmer, Gates's friend from his Harvard days. Ballmer, a tough negotiator in his own right, had joined Gates on what turned out to be exceptionally favorable terms after a year at

Stanford Business School. Gates had decided in 1980 that he needed someone with some business experience. He thought of Ballmer, who had been a product manager at Procter & Gamble before heading to business school. Ballmer demurred, but Gates flew him up to Seattle. The offer, however, turned out to be much less than Ballmer expected. In an odd combination of business and friendship, Ballmer then drove Gates to the airport so Gates could go on a long-planned sailing vacation in the Caribbean. Ballmer returned in Gates's car to Gates's house, where he was staying for a few more days, thought about the offer, and then called Gates on the yacht *Doo-Wah, Doo-Wah* to talk about the offer. A bunch of Gates's friends out on the deck of the sailboat listened in as he talked to Ballmer over single-side-band radio, occasionally shouting something like, "Give him what he wants, Bill." And Gates wound up giving Ballmer a sweet-enough deal that Ballmer has become a billionaire in his own right, too.

Ballmer is known in the computer industry as someone who's not technical. Especially in the early days of Microsoft, he was known as a B-school marketing type. His claim to fame was a clever redesign of a Duncan Hines cake box that helped the P&G product occupy more shelf space and shove aside competitors. But Ballmer, like Gates, began as a math nerd. Ballmer would go to math club after high school in Detroit, where he was the son of a Ford executive. When he and Gates were in the same dormitory at Harvard, both entered the difficult Putnam math competition and both finished among the top one hundred students in North American colleges.

"I finished sixty-seventh," Ballmer says. "Bill was ninety-ninth." He adds with a laugh, "I kicked his butt."

Ballmer complemented Gates well, and not just because he rocked side to side while Gates went forward and backward. While Gates can be intellectual about things, Ballmer is just plain ferocious. "Boom-Boom" Ballmer would pace inside his small office like a caged animal, bellowing into the phone or just roaring as he thought aloud about something. The effect was even exaggerated for visitors to the company in recent years, because, while everyone at Microsoft gets an office and Ballmer was certainly entitled to the biggest of the four sizes, he insisted on the smallest of the types of offices just to set an example. In such a tiny office, he literally bounced off the walls. He eventually developed some growths on his vocal cords that had to be surgically removed.

Afterward, he took voice lessons to learn how to roar without hurting himself.

Gates and Ballmer often seemed to be playing good cop, bad cop. Gates would agreeably set up the basics of a deal with some potential partner. Then Ballmer would get involved. He'd be in the potential partner's face, arguing over pennies. If anyone ever protested, "But Bill said . . ." Ballmer would respond, "I don't care what Bill said. This is how we're going to do it. . . ." Ray Noorda, chief executive of big rival Novell, talks of how potential Microsoft partners initially get taken to "the pearly Gates" but then are turned over to "the emBallmer."

Ballmer beat a weight problem by jogging some serious mileage even in the face of occasional back problems—he once arrived an hour late for an interview in New York City, wearing a Mickey Mouse T-shirt and covered with sweat, explaining that he had been fighting back spasms for the past two hours by lying down on the side of the road in Central Park and trying to stretch. But he still looks hulking. The prematurely bald Ballmer eats ferociously, attacking a bag of popcorn or anything else at hand if he's thinking hard about something. Visiting a reporter for breakfast in New York, he was once so intent on having a bowl of rice that he essentially reenacted the famous scene from *Five Easy Pieces* where the Jack Nicholson character just wants some toast but eventually orders a BLT and tells the waitress to hold the bacon, lettuce, and tomato. Ballmer, politer but no less insistent, told the waiter that he didn't care that rice wasn't on the breakfast menu. Rice was on the lunch menu at this hotel, which had just been bought by Japanese investors, so there had to be some around. Ballmer then ordered a fifteen-dollar lunch item and had everything but the rice held.

Critics of Ballmer's, who include people at software companies who feel Microsoft has pushed them around, describe him as a thug. Some call him the Luca Brasi of Microsoft, in a reference to the character in *The Godfather*. Those whose taste runs to more recent movies call him "Biff," in a reference to the bully in the *Back to the Future* movies. Admirers of Ballmer's point to his tenacity and intelligence.

Critics and admirers alike marvel at what best friends Gates and Ballmer call their "high band–width" communication. About the only difference in their approaches is that Gates may intellectualize a bit more, saying that losing a contract to a competitor is like losing the money twice—he loses it and his competitor gets it—while Ballmer takes a more direct approach. "Get the business!" he yells. "Get the business!"

After Sams told Gates and Ballmer not to get their hopes up, IBM went silent for a couple of weeks, but that didn't faze Gates and his people at Microsoft. They were up to their eyeballs in work for other companies, and it wasn't even clear that IBM was serious about creating a machine. Then Sams popped into view again. This time, he wanted to do a preliminary deal, so he asked to bring along several people.

"This will work great," he said. "I'll bring along my legal team to meet with your legal team. I'll bring along my technical team to meet with your technical team."

"That's fine," Gates told him, "but I don't have a legal team or a technical team. I'm it."

Gates decided early on that he wouldn't let IBM overwhelm him with people, so he scrounged up four people in an unsuccessful attempt to match the five Sams ended up bringing. One of the IBMers turned out to be someone from "corporate practices," who, in IBM's centralized system, are the KGB agents, reporting back to corporate headquarters on what happens at meetings and dictating to the executives in the meeting what they can and can't say, so Gates had to sign off on a few more nondisclosure agreements. With that out of the way, Sams told Gates a little about the PC project and reached a preliminary agreement for Microsoft to do some consulting on it.

Sams called back a few days later to talk about an operating system. (An operating system is the least-understood part of a computer because it's intangible. It's easy to see the hardware and to understand the concept of the software application, such as a word-processing package, but the operating system is a mostly invisible layer that lies between the two and that usually comes already loaded onto the hardware. The operating system is a large, complicated piece of software that translates the commands coming out of an application into the series of on and off electrical impulses that are the language the hardware speaks. It's as though applications are written in English but the computer speaks Sanskrit. An operating system translates from English into Sanskrit. It hadn't initially been clear that IBM would include an operating system with its PC. Operating systems ate up a lot of processing power as they did their translation and required so much memory that few PCs of this era contained one. But forcing people using PCs to learn the equivalent of Sanskrit was limiting their usability enough that IBM had decided to include an operating system.) Sams, however, was mistaken in thinking Gates had an operating system to sell. Gates referred Sams to a company with the fanciful name of Digital Research Intergalactic. DRI sold the CP/M operating system—for Control Program/Monitor—the most popular then available. Gates figured he could make plenty of money from developing and selling the languages, and he had an implicit understanding with DRI: They would stay off his language turf if he avoided their operating-system arena. Gates called DRI for Sams and set up an appointment for the IBM delegation for the next day in Pacific Grove, California, just off scenic Highway 1, which snakes along the coast.

But Gary Kildall, the president of DRI, committed a gaffe of epic proportions. The Ph.D. in computer science was feeling cocky, so when IBM came calling in 1980 with the business opportunity of his lifetime, he was off flying his new plane. His wife, a lawyer, was left to deal with IBM and its layers of restrictive nondisclosure agreements. She wanted no part of them. It took the better part of a day of haggling before Sams even got in the door, and the only agreement that resulted stated that the DRI people wouldn't blab about IBM's visit. The IBMers left. Sams and the others in his group tried later to come to a compromise and make a return visit but gave up in frustration. He called Gates and said it was now up to him to find or write an operating system somehow or the deal for Microsoft's languages was off.

"Then I flew back east and worried," Sams says.

In early August 1980, Bill Lowe returned to IBM headquarters in Armonk, New York, to lay out his plan to the chairman and the Management Committee. It was a dangerous place to be. The Management Committee—or, given IBMers' fondness for acronyms, the MC—ruled on issues that couldn't be resolved at lower corporate levels, so going before the committee was, to IBMers, like going before the Supreme Court. It was actually rougher, because the top IBM executives who sat in judgment were known to be brutal, especially if they thought someone was wasting their time. The best way to get an opponent to back down at IBM was to threaten to take an argument to the MC. Lowe himself had recently felt the MC's sting. He was the one who, two months earlier, had told the MC of a plan to buy PCs from Atari and put the IBM logo on them. Lowe had beaten a hasty retreat back to Boca Raton, where he told people Chairman Frank Cary had described the idea as the dumbest thing he'd ever heard.

The MC's mystique is heightened because the room where it meets is in a curious little corner of IBM—curious because it is one of the few elegant areas in a company that was so wealthy it could have been excused the occasional extravagance. The headquarters itself is a small lump of concrete so bland that Apple Computer cofounder Steve Jobs, on seeing it for the first time, decided he should charter a 747 and fly as many of his employees in from the West Coast as he could so they could relish how tasteless their big competitor was. He hadn't even seen the inside of the building. In the early 1960s, when the chairman at the time, Tom Watson, Jr., was away, someone installed squares of bright orange carpet throughout the building. On returning, Watson asked, "What is this, a fucking Howard Johnson?" But the carpet remained. In recent years, Chairman John F. Akers considered replacing it but decided that any remodeling at headquarters would send a bad signal at a time he was cutting back elsewhere. When IBM bought a lush building from Nestlé in Purchase, New York, it worried that the building was too ostentatious. Even as other companies in the 1980s were competing to see which could amass the largest art collection or fanciest buildings or biggest fleet of planes, IBM sent in work crews to rip out the mahogany chair rails and marble mantelpieces. The crews bricked over fireplaces, then plastered over the brick and painted over that.

Yet in the mystical corner where the Management Committee and directors hold their meetings, IBM management actually indulged itself. In the waiting area are imposing portraits of the former chairmen, along with some paintings from the Hudson River School that the Watson family collected over the years. Separating the area from the meeting room are walls of burnished Chinese oak, with doors that stretch all the way to the ceiling. Inside are additional expensive paintings from the Watson family collection, including a picture of fierce-eyed founding father Tom Watson, Sr., on the back wall, glaring out at whoever is addressing the Management Committee in the front of the room. The table and leather chairs are unexceptional, except for the odd V shape to the table. The shape means the IBM chairman sits at the point of the V, looking to any visitors like a Pope surrounded by his cardinals. The person making a presentation at the podium has a full array of controls to dim the lights and control the projection on a big screen at the front of the room. He also usually brings along some seventy-thousand-dollar-a-year midlevel manager to stand behind the screen and, while listening to the presentation, put overhead transparencies on a projector that shines them through the big screen for viewing by the people in the room.

The operations controlled out of that room sprawled across the world like the British empire of the nineteenth century. The sun never set on IBM's factories and offices. In an age of nuclear war, IBM had done the ultimate job of dispersal and decentralization. Its nominal headquarters had been in New York City at one time, but IBM quickly went suburban along with the rest of the world in the early 1960s. The headquarters were located in Armonk, New York, a Westchester town an hour north of New York. Probably no area had more IBM facilities than Westchester County, then and now the wealthiest county in New York State. But IBM—known as Big Blue because of its blue logos and its incredible scope—also had hundreds of other locations, carefully spread throughout the world so that no country would feel slighted and so IBM wouldn't dominate any area too completely. Just as the introduction of jet aircraft in air transport changed the way international business was conducted, the spread of IBM produced a worldwide culture, one that spoke not only IBMese but many languages—ranging from English, French, German, and Spanish to Japanese and Russian —and shared a language of profit and accountability. IBM reinforced that culture with a continuing intramural educational program that might bring employees in for weeks of training each year. It also made sure everyone marched in step by developing a lush bureaucracy that prided itself on having a higher ratio of managers per employee than any other business around.

IBM's businesses were arranged in a structure somewhat like a Mayan pyramid, with the three to six members of the Management Committee sitting at the top. The corporate headquarters that surrounded them directly controlled the service functions, such as accounting and personnel, whose costs were allocated in a fairly arbitrary fashion to the profit centers that made things and did things. Each of these businesses had its own management structure, which was ultimately responsible to the Management Committee and the chairman in Armonk. Mainframes, the huge machines in dust-free rooms that sit at the heart of major companies and governmental institutions throughout the world, have been the biggest of those businesses since the 1960s. But minicomputers sprouted into a sizable business in the 1970s. All along, IBM also sold office equipment such as copiers and, of course, the legendary Selectric typewriters. Then there were the businesses most people knew nothing about: IBM was involved from day one with NASA in its suborbital operations. Laid across those profit centers were IBM's huge sales forces, totaling more than 100,000 at the peak in the United States and about half that in both Europe and Asia. Because all IBM chairmen were historically ex-salesmen, these sales forces dominated. They were the ones who talked to customers about what products they wanted and who generated lengthy, formal lists of requirements for the products—those actually designing the products weren't allowed to talk to customers. The sales forces weren't treated as a single unit, either. There was a U.S. sales force, a Japanese sales force, a British sales force, and so on—each of which could impose its own requirements on the development of a product. The complicated structure guaranteed enough conflict that the Management Committee sat in judgment two or more days a week, ruling on everything from what a product ought to look like down to whether a customer ought to get a special price to keep a competitor from stealing him away.

As Lowe sat outside the MC room, waiting to enter this chamber of such power, he could feel the tip of the Mayan pyramid sticking up through his seat.

He thought his plans were in good shape. He even had a prototype of his PC with him, because his plans were already so completely formulated that his engineers could slap something together that at least behaved like the final product. As Lowe carefully reviewed his presentation two hours ahead of time, he did find one problem: The prototype didn't work. He and some engineers had to pull it apart and painstakingly check all the jury-rigged wiring inside until, just before the meeting was to begin, they found a wire that had jiggled loose.

Bill Sydnes, a senior engineer who made the trip with Lowe to Armonk, says that at that point "the system would do two things. It would draw an absolutely beautiful picture of a nude lady, and it would show a picture of a rocket ship blasting off the screen. We decided to show the MC the rocket ship."

The demo and the prototype drew interest and some compliments, but the Management Committee continued to see this review as just one of the numerous proposals that came in front of them each week. Lowe and his team thought of the PC as a home computer and continually referred to it that way, so it hardly seemed as if the system would be of any great interest to IBM's corporate customers. Lowe thought he might stir up some concern when he said the only way to avoid taking the two or three years that other stabs at the personal-computer market had taken was to go outside the company for almost all the parts. But, he promised, if he was allowed to do that, he could produce a machine more powerful than Apple's in less than a year.

There was a little discussion about whether using outsiders' parts would mean IBM couldn't control the direction the market would take, the way IBM controlled everything about the lucrative mainframe market. But nobody in the room had the foresight to realize either how important the personal-computer market would become or how little control IBM would, in fact, have. The MC members worried more about the possibility that outsiders would be allowed to sell the PC, because IBM wasn't sure it could make them live up to its blue-suited, white-shirted standard. Even that concern didn't really heat up until much later.

The group was also inclined to go along with Lowe's ideas because they were smarting from IBM's series of failures in the PC market. IBM's SCAMP, produced in the late 1960s, was arguably the world's first personal computer, but it was sitting in the Smithsonian, not on millions of desks. The 5110 had pretty much matched the capabilities Tandy had built into its successful TRS 80 personal computer in the mid-1970s—but IBM's machine cost ten thousand dollars, several times what other companies' machines cost. IBM thought it finally had its act together with the Datamaster, but that got nibbled to death during development in the late 1970s as various sales forces and development groups in other parts of IBM tried to impose their requirements on it, making the machine more than two years late. The biggest problem, as usual, was the software, a project that got so far out of control that the hardware had to be redesigned twice to accommodate the increasingly large operating system. (IBM's personal computers were anemic enough in 1980 that the first thing Lowe's group did after his July visit to the MC was to go out and buy a bunch of Apple IIs to do their budgets and organize their presentations, even though the group had easy access to all the IBM hardware they wanted and would have been clobbered if anyone had found the hated Apple machines around.)

Although everyone in the room agreed that relying on outsiders could eventually create some problems, no one took them very seriously. Any problems, they thought, could always be dealt with later. Cary approved Lowe's plan.

"The general attitude," says one of the Management Committee members, "was that you don't have big problems in small markets, and we thought the personal computer was a very small market."

When Lowe walked out of the meeting, nearly a dozen members of his personal-computer team were there to greet him, eager to see whether he had received financing. But Lowe, who can be so stone-faced that he has been called the Gerald Ford of the computer industry, looked glum. Then even Lowe couldn't hold back any longer and he burst into a grin. The group had a mandate.

They went out for a celebratory feast that night, at which they engaged in a little geek humor, continually changing their orders in a futile attempt to confuse their waiter. Then they flew back to Florida the next morning and hunkered down for the hardest year of their lives.

Gates, meanwhile, was trying to figure out whether he should do an operating system for IBM. His real expertise was in the languages that programmers used to write software, not in the more complex area of operating systems. Besides, he didn't think at that point he'd make much money from what would become DOS (disk operating system) and would make him a fortune; he just wanted to have his Basic language work on IBM's system, because he thought the real money was in languages. Gates and Ballmer say they didn't even think IBM's computer would do that well, adding that they wanted to work with IBM because they thought it would be cool to be known as the guys who helped IBM bring out a personal computer.

Together with his partner, Allen, and a volatile colleague named Kay Nishi, Gates agonized late into the night. Even after they decided they could handle the project and concluded it made financial sense, they wanted to hash through one more time whether they were violating their implicit understanding with Kildall and DRI that Gates and company would stay out of the operating system business.

Nishi suddenly jumped out of his chair and yelled, "Fuck 'em! Fuck 'em! Fuck 'em!"

They all looked at one another and decided to do an operating system.

Easier said than done. An operating system could take a year or more, yet IBM needed one in a few months. The problem resolved itself quickly when Allen heard through the grapevine in Seattle computing circles about a homegrown operating system called QDOS, which stood for "quick and dirty operating system." It turned out to borrow ideas and terms freely from DRI's operating system, but this was back in the days before some heavy-duty lawsuits made programmers more cautious about doing knockoffs of someone else's work. Allen called the software's author, Tim Paterson, and found that Microsoft could probably license QDOS from him.

When Gates told Sams he could probably provide an operating system, he explained all about it. Most people, including senior IBM executives at the time, think that Gates hid the source of the operating system from IBM to protect this precious find. But Sams denies that; he says Gates told him all about the system.

"The question was, Do you want to buy it or do you want me to buy it?" Sams says.

But Sams says IBM, having gotten bogged down in software so often in the past, wanted nothing to do with the operating system. The guiding principle of the PC project was that IBM would just pull pieces together from the outside, so he wanted Microsoft to have to worry about getting the operating system to work, about making sure the languages were nicely integrated with it, about doing upgrades of the operating system down the road, about handling customer inquiries, and so on.

"Besides," Sams now says, "if we'd bought the software, we'd have just screwed it up."

Microsoft ultimately bought the system, paying about $75,000. IBM, in forgoing the chance to buy what became DOS, missed an opportunity that made Microsoft's value go from a pittance back then to a stock-market value of some $27 billion today, making Gates the richest man in the United States.

Sams may be right that IBM would have bungled DOS, but IBM, in not being able to seize that chance, put itself at a horrible disadvantage in the personal-computer business because it let Microsoft set and own the standard. IBM's decision also put it on a collision course with Microsoft that, years down the road, forced it to spend billions of dollars trying to reclaim a standard that Microsoft bought for $75,000. IBM started off with 340,000 employees, $27 billion of assets, $26 billion of sales, and $3.6 billion of profits, while Microsoft began their relationship with 32 people and little else. IBM still found a way to lose.

TWO

Hal Martin, the general manager of IBM's huge plant in Rochester, Minnesota, left the cool weather on the plains of southern Minnesota and flew to Mexico City for a brief vacation as fall was approaching in 1980. Not yet fifty years old, Martin was a marathon runner seemingly in peak physical condition—until he had a heart attack and keeled over dead.

That scene on a street in Mexico City changed the course of the IBM PC. It meant that Bill Lowe left the PC business to replace the ill-fated Martin. Lowe, in turn, was replaced by Don Estridge, one of the most charismatic figures in IBM's long history.

For Lowe, leaving his history-making position in Boca Raton, Florida, was a hard choice personally. He had been in the area a long time. He liked it. He thought the PC was an exciting opportunity. But Lowe also knew how the game was played if you were on the fast track at IBM. He knew that Boca Raton was a backwater at IBM, where people were unlikely to be noticed. Before the PC came along to build it up, IBM's Boca facility was just a few buildings on the edge of a swamp in a sleepy seaside town in southern Florida. Lowe had already won big points for hatching the PC idea, so, in the IBM system, there wasn't much reason to stick around. In fact, it could be a bit dangerous. If the project flopped and he was still around, he might catch some of the blame. After a couple of encouraging phone calls from senior executives, Lowe packed up and headed off to run the seven-thousand-person Rochester site.

His replacement in Boca Raton seems obvious to all in retrospect, but he wasn't at all obvious at the time. Several early members of the team thought they should get to run the PC project and openly competed for the spot. Estridge, meanwhile, was nobody's idea of a star. He was just a midlevel manager at IBM at forty-three years old, an age when the real stars at IBM had been vice presidents for years. In fact, though this has been lost in the hero worship Estridge later won, Lowe's role in launching the PC gives him claim on some of the credit Estridge won as father of the PC. Estridge, who was six four and had a manner that reminded people of the actor Fred MacMurray, didn't even come on board until October, three months into the yearlong project. Estridge was lucky even to be around in those days, because, while few remember his pre-PC days clearly, he was close to being fired not long before he took on the PC job. (In 1990, in the damages trial that followed the airplane crash that killed Estridge, then-chairman John F. Akers testified that Estridge could have eventually become chairman of the whole company, but, assuming Akers really believed that, he appears to be the only one who thought Estridge had the remotest chance.)

Before taking on the PC job, Estridge, who had been in Boca Raton for years, had almost been pushed out the door because of IBM's Series 1, a misfit of a minicomputer that never did catch on. Estridge had drawn the assignment in the mid-1970s to do the operating system for the Series 1, but it was a mess from the start. Using the standard IBM methodology, Estridge started with some one thousand programmers. The architects, who are the inspired programmers within IBM, came in and spent months producing a minutely detailed design for the software. Then they left. In came troops of everyday programmers, who are typically less than inspired and who, in dealing with such a large system, had a hard time discerning the grand vision behind the hundreds of pages of specifications. As usual inside IBM, having a small army of people dividing the project into hundreds of closely linked pieces meant that they had to spend more time communicating with one another than actually writing code—because what might seem like a small change in one part of it could force people working on several other parts of it to make a switch akin to writing in German rather than in French.

(Oddly enough, it was a senior IBM programmer who wrote the

book—*The Mythical Man Month*—that put other companies on the road toward a good software process. The book said that to produce a baby, you need to have one woman pregnant for nine months—even though IBM seemed to want to have nine women pregnant for a month apiece. Others took that idea and turned it into a sort of artist's model for software, where a Michelangelo would stare at a piece of marble until he could see the *Pietà* inside, then cut away the marble, with assistants helping only on mundane tasks. Yet IBM clung to a construction-crew model, where a few smart people in hard hats would design the *Pietà,* then turn the work over to hundreds of assistants, each of whom would work on a tiny section of the marble in the hope that, at the end, the sculpture would resemble something. IBM might have preferred to have a Michelangelo do it all himself, but it could never be sure that the guy put in charge of a project would be a genius. Rather than chance it, IBM designed its process to allow for the lowest common denominator.)

By the time Estridge figured out how to short-circuit the process, his Series 1 operating system was, for its size, as far over budget and as far behind schedule as anything IBM has ever done. Estridge's experience left such a bad taste in his mouth that he vowed never to handle a software project again. This fact reinforced the PC group's decision to turn the operating system over to Microsoft in the early days.

Estridge's personality wasn't doing him any favors in the mid-1970s, either. He walked around in his lizard-skin cowboy boots while everybody else was wearing wing tips, generally cultivating an image as someone who wouldn't go along with the IBM system. Someone running a development project had to listen as all other parts of the company put in their two cents, knowing that any one of them could keep his product from getting out the door, but Estridge tried hard not to play along. Now that he had a flop on his hands, his bosses were wondering whether he was worth the trouble.

The only thing that kept Estridge from making his exit before he ever entered the world stage is that some IBM salesman in Connecticut sold State Farm on the idea of using thousands of Series 1's to run its insurance offices around the country. State Farm wanted the systems rejiggered to better suit its needs, and the order was so big that IBM was more than happy to comply. Estridge, as the software expert, was the logical choice. This time, he did such a slick job that IBM unloaded tens of millions of dollars of mediocre hardware.

With his reputation redeemed, Estridge and his renegade attitude fit Lowe's plans in the early fall of 1980. When Lowe disappeared from the PC business for five years to go run the Rochester operation, he turned the PC project over to Estridge, who turned out to be an excellent choice. Estridge's habit of not returning phone calls from senior people in other parts of IBM, his shunning of the hundreds of meetings to which he was summoned, and his penchant for listening to no one's dictates but his own drove other parts of IBM to distraction, but nobody could touch him—at least for a while—because he had a direct line to the chairman. Ordinarily, a midlevel manager like Estridge who ran a product development group reported to somebody, who reported to somebody, who might report to a division vice president, who reported to the division president. Even if Estridge had somehow been elevated to the position of division president, he still would have reported to the head of one of the half dozen IBM product groups, who reported to a member of the Management Committee, who reported to IBM's president, who reported to the chairman. Getting something moved up the chain of command required lengthy preparation for meetings—usually including a day of arguing over whose conference room should be used, because the executive whose room was used got a kind of home-court advantage. Then, of course, there were the lengthy meetings themselves, which often required a plane trip. It could even take days to weeks just to get a decision relayed back down. So Estridge's direct line to the chairman gave him an unbelievable amount of freedom from IBM's bureaucracy, and Estridge made the most of it. His rebelliousness shielded his little team from the pressures that made all the other attempts at personal computers too cautious. He took a group of people who had been frustrated by IBM's rules for years and told them he could personally guarantee that the rules no longer applied. The group, sometimes called the Dirty Dozen (even though it had thirteen members), responded by working harder and better than any group at IBM has before or since.

"Before I went to work on the team," says Dan Wilkie, one of the senior members, "I helped develop a printer at IBM. That printer was in development for seven years! I kept telling myself, It's coming. . . . It's coming. But the printer was hopelessly mired in design changes and bureaucracy. After a while, those layers and layers at IBM really get to you." Freed from the bureaucracy and able to tackle a project without worrying about what the rest of IBM thought, "I made more decisions in my first 30 days with the PC group than I made during my first 14 years with IBM."[1]

The group began to think of themselves as a work crew trying to lay track down fast enough to keep ahead of a train hurtling toward them at 150 mph.

People found it easy to like Estridge, who had a warm face, a goofy smile, and thick, wavy hair. He came across as a strong family man and generally solid character. When some friends were killed in a car crash, Estridge and his wife, Mary, who already had three daughters of their own, adopted their friends' daughter. After Estridge finished the Series 1 job and before accepting the chance-of-a-lifetime PC job, he took nearly three months off from IBM so he could take his family camping out west. (He was so compulsively organized that, before leaving Florida, he had his wife and kids practice setting up camp and then repacking, to be sure everyone knew their assignments and could handle them quickly.) Estridge, who grew up in Jacksonville and got his engineering degree at the University of Florida, had turned down chances for advancement because they would have meant uprooting his family and leaving Florida. He openly doted on his four strong-willed daughters, and when some hefty raises let him move the family into a new house after he succeeded in the PC job, Estridge built, by himself, a play area that he expected his grandchildren to use someday.

"I think he went to his grave with the love affair still going with his wife," says Ed Faber, the president of ComputerLand in those days. "I know that sounds corny, but you just had to see the two of them swooping around the dance floor to understand how in love they were."

Even later, when Estridge got so much publicity—and seemed to enjoy it—he never lost a sense of himself. When a bunch of industry executives lined up to speak with him after an industry conference once, he ignored them so he could talk to a fourteen-year-old boy who had approached him to ask how he could go about writing some software. Estridge avoided sitting at the head of any table. He could be autocratic, but most people didn't even mind that. They'd approach him about a decision, and he'd either say yes or no. He wouldn't commission a study, the way some IBM executives do. The person asking for a decision also always felt that Estridge heard him out.

When everybody began working long hours in the fall and winter of 1980, Estridge might wander into someone's office at eleven at night and slump his lanky frame across a couple of chairs. He'd commiserate about what a pain it was to work so hard, then maybe suggest that the person wasn't spending enough time with his or her family. He'd sometimes drive by his building late at night to see whether any lights were still on; if one was, he'd go in, wake up the engineer who was asleep at his terminal, and send him home.

While many IBM executives take themselves extremely seriously, Estridge liked to tell stories on himself. One that became a favorite as the PC group progressed had him visiting a manufacturing line in the wee hours of the morning, at a time when the PC was being produced in volume but was still in painfully short supply. He saw two seemingly complete machines being ignored by someone who was packing the PCs for shipment. When he asked why, the guy ignored him. Finally, the worker said, "UL labels," which signify that the machines meet certain safety standards.

Estridge looked, then said, "But they have UL labels."

The worker finally stopped, wiped his hands off, turned to Estridge, and said, "Listen, buster, they're on crooked."

Estridge liked to say that that worker had a better sense of the importance of quality than he did.

Occasionally, Estridge tried to fit the corporate mold, but he usually couldn't pull it off. He once used an IBM type of explanation, responding to a neighbor's question about whether he ought to have a PC by telling the person that a PC was a great "productivity tool." The neighbor gave him such a blank stare that Estridge never tried that one again.

Estridge showed a magical touch that has eluded IBM ever since he was pulled from the PC job. A devotee of the Apple II who loved to tinker with the one he had at home, he seemed to understand little machines better than the more formally trained executives who have followed him into senior positions in the PC business. When he visited the ComputerLand dealer chain, he didn't disappear into the chief executive's office and haul out an overhead projector so they could compare charts showing defect levels in the PC; he first headed for the service department to quiz the people who actually saw the problems as they developed. He seemed to understand intuitively the new counterculture era that Steve Jobs and Apple had helped usher in, one in which, as Jobs put it, you shouldn't trust a computer you couldn't lift.

One of the first big meetings Estridge faced as he took over from Lowe in the fall of 1980 was with Bill Gates and his small band from Microsoft. Estridge needed to have people push Gates hard to make sure that he could really deliver an operating system in time. Without an operating system, there would be no interesting software. Without software, the PC would make a nice paperweight.

When Gates was summoned to Boca Raton for the first time at the end of September, he and Steve Ballmer worked for days on their proposal. Jack Sams, still the IBM liaison to Microsoft, got involved, too, offering avuncular advice on how IBM meetings tended to go, how to behave, who the important players at the meeting would be, and so forth. Sams also offered some advice that IBM now may wish he hadn't: He suggested that Microsoft raise its asking price in its proposed contract with IBM. While Sams didn't know what the two were planning, he knew IBM wanted to be sure the little company supplying its operating system was healthy for years to come.

"I said, 'We know this project is going to cost more than you're willing to ask. Don't be afraid to ask me for a million dollars. Just tell me how you're going to spend it,'" Sams says.

What Sams and IBM didn't yet understand was that Gates was already much more sophisticated about PC software pricing than IBM —the twenty-four-year-old had been in the business for years and had learned plenty on some small projects.

Although Sams and IBM expected Gates to come in and ask them for a big fee up front, Gates planned to ask for a seemingly small royalty on each machine. In a crucial act of prudence, Gates also asked that IBM's license to use DOS be nonexclusive. In other words, he wanted to be able to sell rights to it to any company he chose. Even though Gates didn't think DOS would sell much, he was already sophisticated enough that he wasn't taking any chances.

Gates didn't make up his mind on exactly how to handle things until the last minute and wasn't at all sure how IBM would respond, but he was also cool enough to—as some of the IBMers put it—play a little poker. They say he came in acting as though he had a full house, and they only realized later that all he had was a pair of deuces.

The group from Microsoft took the red-eye from Seattle to Miami in September 1980, deciding along the way that, because of limited plane service, their offices near Seattle were probably as far removed from IBM's in Boca as any two points in the continental United States could be—a point that would later complicate the companies' collaboration but that seemed only a nuisance at that point. Gates and Ballmer continued refining the proposal along the way. When they landed in Miami, they discovered that Boca Raton was farther away than they'd thought and realized they'd be late for their big meeting. As they changed into their suits in the men's room at the Miami airport, they also realized that Gates hadn't brought a tie. So they drove the hour or so to Boca, then sat outside a Burdine's until it opened at 10:00 A.M. and Gates could buy a tie.

When they arrived at Estridge's tiny offices in a converted warehouse with a leaky roof, few windows, and malfunctioning air conditioning, they found the meeting room crammed with nearly twenty people, who barraged Gates with questions all day long. He looked awkward at first, sitting there in a suit that seemed to be too big, with his collar sticking up in the back. In the face of all these blue suits, this young man who looked like a teenager seemed to be under siege. One programmer harassed Gates about some work Microsoft had done for a Tandy machine, saying it wasn't up to IBM standards and that Gates had better think again if he planned to try to fob off that kind of shoddy work on IBM. The IBMers, thinking Gates was at a disadvantage, didn't even know the half of it: Gates was operating without having slept for more than thirty-six hours. But he slowly won the group over by staying cool under fire and by displaying a dazzling range of technical knowledge.

After the meeting, Estridge told Gates, Ballmer, and some IBMers a story about a recent Management Committee meeting. The incident stemmed from an encounter that IBM CEO John Opel had with Gates's mother, Mary, who was on the national board of the United Way with Opel. The determined Mrs. Gates went up to Opel to say that his company had begun doing some work with her boy, Bill, and she was sure IBM would love doing business with him. The taciturn Opel barely acknowledged the remark. But later, when Estridge went before the Management Committee to say he was taking a real risk by contracting to have his operating system done by a tiny company in Seattle, Opel said, "That wouldn't be Mary Gates's boy, Bill, would it?" Everyone in the room knew that Microsoft was golden from then on.

Gates and Estridge retired to an office to hammer out the details of their agreement alone, and, after some haggling, a contract was signed by early November 1980. Having witnessed up close the disastrous delays with the Datamaster software project at IBM, the IBMers in Boca Raton didn't really believe an upstart like Microsoft could meet its deadlines. So Estridge leaned on Gates hard enough that Gates says he felt as if he was already three months behind as he began the project. Gates quickly hired some people to handle the additional work the IBM contract provided—although IBMers say it's not clear how many people he hired and how many people he just worked to death.

Estridge went outside the company to buy almost all the parts for his PC, including a processor he got from Intel, so he managed to slap together some PC prototypes by early December to ship to Microsoft. Although Microsoft missed its initial deadline of mid-January 1981 to have an early version of the operating system up and running, it did have the system pretty much working by early February. Everybody at IBM breathed a big sigh of relief. Maybe Microsoft would work out, after all. Maybe the PC would actually happen.

Under Estridge, the PC team tried hard not to commit the standard IBM mistake of smothering a partner with affection, but he still had dozens of people working with Microsoft. The programmers at Microsoft found it odd that, even though the PC was IBM's smallest project, it still had more people writing specs for Microsoft's operating system than Microsoft had actually writing the operating system.

Estridge also dispatched people to Microsoft to make sure it was keeping its work secret. He may have been a cowboy, but even he was enough of a product of the IBM culture that he couldn't avoid the penchant for secrecy at all costs. Steve Ballmer got a call one day from an IBMer who said he wanted to arrange a visit. Ballmer said, "Sure, maybe in a few days when things settle down." Then he casually inquired about the weather in Florida. The IBMer said he didn't have a clue, because he was calling from a pay phone across the street from the Microsoft offices in Bellevue, Washington, and really wanted to come by immediately to check up on how Microsoft had filed certain documents. The call was just the first in a series of abrupt visits that would have Ballmer or someone else running down the hall, screaming, "IBM is coming." Then people would rush to hide all the documents and hardware that were supposed to be under lock and key, pushing out of the main hallway the secret hardware from other manufacturers that had been strewn there in a casual disregard of security.

IBM also gave Microsoft a hard time about Kay Nishi, partly because he was Japanese, and IBM feared its Japanese competitors most, and partly because Nishi was a wild man. He got himself and Gates the job of designing one of Japan's first PCs and Tandy's Radio Shack 100 by flying first class and accosting a Japanese executive. Nishi would fly back and forth between Japan and the United States several times a month, then sometimes lie down and fall asleep on the floor during meetings. Once, when Microsoft went to New York for a trade show, he insisted they stay at the ritzy Plaza Hotel, then showed up with some twenty Japanese who were having trouble finding hotel rooms. So someone called down for twenty cots, and they stayed in the Microsoft suite. One visitor slept in the closet, with twenty thousand dollars in his pocket.[2] Gates says the concern about Nishi mounted to the point where an IBM lawyer eventually "hauled me into a room and beat me up about him. I was signing this and signing that. They scared the hell out of me."

IBM insisted that the room where its two PC prototypes were being kept needed to have the drop ceiling modified so that the top of the room could be covered with chicken wire. That way, someone crawling over the wall from the office next door and sneaking into the room would have to cut through the wire and therefore leave a trace. (Little did IBM know that the office next door belonged to a brokerage firm, which would have loved to know about IBM's secret. Microsoft never enlightened IBM security people on that one.) The real problem occurred because IBM insisted that the door to the room with its prototypes be locked at all times. The room was just six feet by ten feet, and the prototypes each put out as much heat as a high-wattage light bulb, so the temperature in the room could get to be more than a hundred degrees. Programmers would come stumbling out of the room to get some water and pant for a while. Heat does funny things to electronics, too, especially when a system is in its early, unstable stages. So Microsoft's programmers sometimes spent days trying to fix what they thought was a bug in the software, only to find that their little sauna had made the hardware go haywire. Eventually, Microsoft just left the door open until someone sounded the warning call that Big Blue had been spotted in the neighborhood.

In Boca Raton, the team was growing to several hundred people in early 1981. The work was pretty straightforward, however, because even before Lowe went to the Management Committee for approval, the PC group had made most of the hardware decisions that would make the product a runaway best-seller. The PC group had decided to take a bit of a chance and use a relatively new Intel processor. The processor wasn't as easy to work with as older Intel processors, but it was more powerful, allowing for bigger, more complex applications to run on the system and allowing people to use floppy disks. The team did limit itself a bit, settling for a less powerful processor than they might have, for fear that the most powerful processor would scare the Management Committee into killing the project because the PC might cut into minicomputer sales. IBM, partly under the urging of Microsoft, had also decided to give its system graphic capabilities. That meant its screen would not only reproduce letters but would also allow for programs that would draw shapes—a feature that a couple of years later made possible Lotus 1-2-3, the software application that had the most to do with the PC's eventual success. (Although it's hard to remember back that far, the machines Estridge was competing against had even fewer capabilities than those he was building into the PC. His competitors were the Tin Lizzies of the PC age. Made by Apple, Tandy, Kaypro, and a host of other companies—many no longer in existence—these machines had screens that contained just a few lines. The screens could produce only characters, not images. They were so slow that even typing could overpower the processor. Even the better machines generally used tapes for data storage, so someone waiting for a bit of data had to wait while the cassette tape whirred back and forth until the processor found what it was looking for.)

At least as important, by going outside the company for the processor, most of the other chips, the floppy-disk drive, and even the operating system—all of which were available to anyone who cared to buy

them—Estridge had tapped into the industry's need for a single standard. The PC industry had been developing in a helter-skelter fashion,
with each company entering the market with its own, largely proprietary
approach—meaning that someone had to buy a Tandy monitor to go
with the Tandy processor unit, which used an operating system or
programming language tailored specifically for the Tandy system and
ran only those applications designed for the Tandy system. It wasn't
possible to mix and match a Tandy this with an IBM that and a Wang
whatever. That situation made the PC industry too restrictive for consumers. It was as though someone buying a stereo had to buy a turnta-
ble, a tape player, an amplifier, headphones, and even the records and
tapes all from the same company. Consumers insisted on being able to
play their records on their friend's systems and on being able to shop
around for the best of each type of stereo component, and the PC
industry had to provide that same kind of mix-and-match capability
before it would draw masses of buyers. The IBM PC took care of that
by succeeding well enough that competitors knew they had to follow
IBM's choices—using the Intel processor, not one from Motorola or
one they developed themselves; using Microsoft's DOS operating system, not DRI's CP/Ms, AT&T's Unix, or anything else; using programming languages that enabled applications to run on DOS; and so on.
Once IBM-compatible machines became widely available, consumers
found themselves in a comfortable, stereo industry–like setting, and the
PC industry exploded in a way that the modest advances represented by
the IBM PC never would have warranted.

Even with most of the hardware decisions made, however, things
were still chaotic. Jim D'Arezzo, a public-relations person brought
down from Armonk during the winter to prepare a communications
plan for the PC introduction, said the place was in such disarray that
he figured he'd just see how many days he could get in on the beaches
in Florida before the operation collapsed and he had to go back to the
ice and snow up north.[3] Things were happening so fast that Estridge
somehow managed to get a building erected and everyone moved in in
four months, easily a modern-day record at IBM, where three years
was considered to be fast for putting up any kind of structure.

As at Microsoft, everything in Boca was made a bit crazier because
of the push for secrecy. Lawyers and "corporate practices" people chap-
eroned Boca executives at any meetings with outsiders, administering

38

the levels of nondisclosure agreements and telling the executives what they were allowed to say. Hotel rooms were swept for bugs. IBMers flying from the local airport in West Palm Beach to Rochester, Minnesota—a common route because of close ties between the Boca and Rochester operations—were ordered not to talk business on the flights, because IBM was convinced that competitors were buying tickets on such flights just on the chance they'd overhear some interesting conversation.

One IBM executive says he stepped out of his office in Boca Raton one evening to get a cup of coffee, then returned to get plane tickets out of his desk for a flight that night. In the interim, someone from security had gone into the office and, finding the desk unlocked, put special locks on everything in the room. The guard left a form chastising the executive for a security violation and saying the locks wouldn't be removed until he showed up at the guard station to pick up the key and, no doubt, get an additional lecture. The executive would have missed his flight if he had taken the time, so he pleaded with the guards by phone. When that failed, he busted open a lock and took his tickets.

Another executive went to use the rest room on a flight, leaving some confidential PC documents behind. He thought he had covered them up on his tray table, but there apparently was a corner peeking out from under the magazines he left on top. An IBM security person was on the flight and, walking down the aisle, spotted the telltale red-and-white striped paper that especially confidential IBM documents are printed on. So when the executive returned to his seat, he found a note from the security person saying the documents had been confiscated because they weren't being cared for properly.

Michael Shabazian, one of the IBMers putting together the deal to have the PC distributed through ComputerLand, says the secrecy nearly gave his mother a heart attack. She visited him one time and found him working in casual clothes in his home—most of the time in a locked office—because IBM corporate had decided it would cause too many rumors if someone without any apparent assignment took space in one of the northern California IBM branches. (IBM had hundreds of branches throughout the United States, each of them self-contained operations that focused on a handful of major customers. The branches reported to regional headquarters, which reported to one of a dozen trading-area headquarters, all of which reported to the U.S.

marketing headquarters—all of the headquarters, of course, had sizable staffs. The structure was essentially the same in each country outside the United States, just with fewer layers of management.) Corporate headquarters especially worried that people in the branch might figure out what was going on if they started taking calls from a personal-computer dealer chain. Then one day when Shabazian was out, the phone rang. Finding the room unlocked, his mother answered the call. A voice said, in a heavy foreign accent, "Tell Michael that Mr. Jones called from GBGI to talk about Acorn in the Oak channel."

"Well, think about what that did to my Armenian mother," Shabazian says. "When I came home, she said, 'Michael, I'm so disappointed in you. How long have you been working for the KGB?'"

The PC group began using different code names when talking to the different outside companies involved in the project. That practice actually helped locate at least one leak, because shortly before the PC's introduction, someone on a weekend rafting trip told Shabazian he knew all about what IBM was going to announce; in fact, he described the product in excruciating detail. The person used enough code names that IBM security managed to have a lawyer sitting at 8:00 A.M. Monday on the front steps of the little company that had inadvertently leaked the information, ready to scare the pants off the owner. Still, all the code names began to get ridiculous. IBM executives had to halt meetings with outsiders so they could step outside and figure out whether they had been calling parts of the product "cherry" and "banana" when talking to these people before or whether they'd gone with more of a citrus theme.

As 1981 progressed, the hardware and software came together quickly. The hardware work was done by March. The operating system was finished by June. But Estridge still had plenty of headaches.

He needed to make sure he could deliver more than just operating-system software. He needed to have lots of applications available, and they needed to be good enough to make people actually want to buy the hardware—the Apple II didn't get hot until the VisiCalc spreadsheet was written for the machine in 1979, and, as things worked out, the IBM PC got its biggest boost when the Lotus 1-2-3 spreadsheet became available for it. Hardware was the tail. Software was the dog.

Estridge had to put together his controversial plan to have dealers sell the PC, marking the first time anyone other than a blue-suiter had been allowed to sell an IBM machine. Estridge also needed to build his manufacturing operation from scratch. It didn't help that he had to run his manufacturing plans through the corporate planning process, which took his group's enthusiastic prediction that they could sell 1 million machines over the three-year life of the PC and then cut that estimate to 200,000—after all, IBM only sells about 2,500 mainframes a year. Estridge hit the 200,000 mark in a little more than a year, reached 1 million right on schedule, and soon after was selling more than 200,000 a month. The miscalculation by the corporate-planning people meant that his manufacturing operation was running to catch up with demand for two and a half years.

Worn down, Estridge would rest his head in his hands, his signature sad gesture. Sometimes he even lay his head down on the meeting table, a sign to people that maybe they ought to leave the room, because when his head came back up, he might be ready to snap at somebody.

The software applications came together better than the manufacturing plan did, largely because an IBMer took a risk, and Estridge capitalized on it. Joyce Wren, an IBMer in Silicon Valley, got caught up in the hysteria over Apple and dared commit heresy: She proposed that IBM write software packages that would run on the Apple II. That idea was doomed from the beginning; IBM would never have done anything that could have helped the upstart's system succeed. But Wren and her idea did get enough attention that someone told her about the PC project and suggested she meet Estridge. Estridge suggested she set up a software business for the PC, although he didn't want her writing applications on her own; the scare he had gotten when he couldn't get the Series 1 operating system finished had convinced him IBM couldn't write software. Instead, Wren set out to buy the rights to good software packages, which she would then "publish" under IBM's label.

Wren ran around throughout 1981 putting together an eclectic mix of games and business software, including the Assistant series from Software Publishing. (She also bought the rights to sell a word processor that, unbeknownst to her, was written by someone in jail for a Cap'n Crunch scam. This person was in jail for phone fraud, having taken advantage of the fact that the whistles being given out in Cap'n Crunch cereal in those days could be used to generate free long-distance calls just by blowing it into the receiver of a phone.[4]) When the Charlie

Chaplin Tramp character began to be used in IBM's ads as the symbol for its PC in late 1981, the mainframe types around IBM sometimes derided the PC software as "Charlie Chaplin applications," but Wren's applications did the trick. Her little business soon generated $100 million of revenue a year and helped entice people to buy the PC hardware.

At the last minute, Gary Kildall and Digital Research Intergalactic resurfaced with a complaint that threatened to derail the software plan. He had decided that the QDOS that Microsoft had acquired was a rip-off of his CP/M operating system, and he was making noises about suing Microsoft and IBM for using that as the basis for DOS. But IBM knew how to play that game. Estridge sent a couple of lawyers to visit Kildall and find out what he really wanted. It turned out that he just wanted IBM to offer his next version of CP/M on its PC. Estridge was happy to oblige. To mollify Microsoft, IBM concocted an ad that showed three doors labeled DOS, CP/M and UCSD—an operating system that was made available for the PC but was never a factor. IBM had its Tramp character walking through the DOS door, which Estridge told Gates and Ballmer was designed to show that he supported DOS. The ad never ran. (But the point became moot, anyway. Kildall was months late with the version of CP/M. Then he priced it at about six times the forty dollars that DOS cost, not having learned, as Microsoft had, that the way to go was a very low price that drove volume way up. By the time he figured things out, DOS had been bundled with so many PCs and so much software had been written to work with DOS that DOS became the industry standard, while Kildall and DRI became answers to trivia questions.)

With everything finally set to go for the announcement on August 12, 1981, Estridge gathered his core team together for dinner the night before in a Manhattan hotel. Everyone was nervous, even Estridge. That day, some of Estridge's engineers discovered that dust could create a short circuit that would shock anyone touching the PC and that it could wipe out the machine. Estridge had to dispatch engineers on airplanes from Boca Raton the night before the announcement so that they could open up every PC that had already been shipped out and insert a tiny piece of cardboard to prevent the short circuit. The project had come together so fast that no one was sure that some other, catastrophic problem wouldn't jump up and bite them, too. The group in the restaurant was very excited because they believed they could sell millions of PCs—even if they hadn't been able to convince their corporate bosses of that. Still, who knew? This consumer-market stuff was new for IBM.

Estridge turned to one aide and said, "Do you really think anyone will come?"

When the next morning came, Estridge saw that all the important media had, in fact, come, but it was still a small group. Fewer than one hundred people were scattered throughout a meeting room in the Waldorf-Astoria hotel in midtown Manhattan as Estridge walked to the front and said hello. Estridge briefly explained what the little machine did. He did a quick demonstration, having the machine draw a few pictures using some software he had written himself. Then he took a few questions, thanked people for coming, and that was it.

The short accounts that appeared in the papers the next day noted that IBM had, as expected, entered the PC market, but nobody got too excited. Except for Estridge and his core group of true believers, it took a while before people realized that the age of the PC had dawned.

There was just one ominous note for the future: IBMers resisted the Microsoft group's attempts to get into the event, looking on the youngsters as just one of many subcontractors on a project whose most important feature was, after all, the Big Blue logo. Gates and his group took their exclusion as an affront. It didn't help that a few weeks later a mainframe in the bowels of IBM cranked out a form letter to Microsoft that said merely: "Dear Vendor: Thank you for a job well done."

THREE

I t took IBM executives a few months to realize what a phenomenon their PC had become, but it didn't take Matt Fitzsimmons nearly that long. Fitzsimmons, the owner of the ComputerLand franchise in White Plains, New York, knew the PC was a smash soon after he heard the gunshot outside his store. He rushed outside one afternoon in the fall of 1981, to find that a despondent homeless man had walked into the rush of people trying to get into the store. The man had pulled a gun out of a shopping bag, placed it in his mouth, and pulled the trigger. The man, who survived, later explained that he had been walking around all day looking for an audience big enough to watch him kill himself. As soon as he saw all the commotion at the store, he said, he knew he'd never find a bigger crowd.

Fitzsimmons, who had been selling just a few Apple IIs, Kaypros, and other primitive machines in the few months he'd been in business, says the only thing that kept him from selling the new IBM PCs even faster is that his store was the only place in the IBM headquarters area north of New York City where IBMers could see the little marvels. IBMers poured into his store in such enormous numbers they were sometimes standing six deep in front of the machines. Actual customers couldn't get to the PCs.

Flushed with the PC's success, Estridge and his merry band began pushing in lots of new directions in late 1981 and into 1982. They had unlimited credibility with senior management because in that first year they delivered nearly $1 billion of revenue that, not being in anyone's business plan, appeared to come out of thin air. That kind of surprise just didn't happen at IBM. Estridge's bosses looked at him as some sort of magician.

Estridge had already started working on a more advanced PC even before the original one came out, so his group had the new version, called the XT, out by early 1983. It was another coup. Throughout 1982 and 1983, the group undertook daring projects—attempting a home computer; playing around with the possibility of doing a portable long before Compaq came out with its pioneering machine; building a faster processor into a PC that would be called the AT and would push the whole PC industry to the next level; and building a chip that could have delayed the onset of the PC clones for years.

But the visibility that Estridge began receiving as the father of a new industry rankled other IBM executives, whose concern evolved into a fierce jealousy that guaranteed Estridge would eventually fall. Under quiet assault on all fronts from other parts of IBM, Estridge found himself spending most of his time fighting the internal bureaucracy, a problem that even his direct line to the chairman couldn't prevent. Ensnarled in IBM's politics, Estridge managed to surprise the personal-computer market only one more time, with the AT. After that, IBM's PC business never again showed the sort of vision or speed of execution that marked its earliest systems, the PC, the more powerful XT, and the even more powerful AT.

As Estridge slowed, he lost some of his luster. Then some of his adventuresome projects failed very publicly, hurting him even more. When he made a couple of obvious mistakes on the otherwise-successful AT, his opponents had their chance. They convinced IBM's management to yank the independent PC business back into the stultifying corporate bureaucracy. The move not only doomed IBM's PC business but eventually put Don Estridge on a plane that cost him his life.

IBM didn't start out being this bureaucratic. The politicking just sort of happened over the years as IBM vanquished its competitors so completely that the only way for its executives to measure their success was to see how far they could advance within the company. Besides, the IBM culture taught them to fight one another as hard as they could, with the idea that the arguing ensured that only the best ideas and people survived. For decades, that calculated infighting kept people on their toes; it was only later that the debating turned into bickering.

IBM actually started with a fierce young man named Tom Watson. He grew up in upstate New York as the child of Scots-Irish parents who fled the famine that afflicted parts of the British Isles in the mid-1800s. Tall, with thin lips and black eyes—always those piercing eyes —Watson seemed to want to leave his mark. As a youngster, he ran around town writing his name on anything that seemed to lend itself to graffiti. When he reached his late teens, he tried teaching, but it bored him. He tried bookkeeping, but that, too, left him cold. So the young man left the farm in the early 1890s to seek his fortune selling pianos and sewing machines off the back of a horse-drawn cart.[1]

Although initially he fumbled, he proved to be a good mimic and absorbed the techniques he witnessed at Billy Sunday camp meetings and on the Chautauqua lecture circuit well enough that he bridged the gap between the rural world of the nineteenth century and the technological, suburban world of the present. The Scottish fierceness that drove him off the farm combined with his Methodist fundamentalism to provide the backbone of IBM's character—one so competitive that the company brushed up against the antitrust laws worldwide, but at the same time one with a strong sense of morality.[2]

After achieving limited success with pianos, often taking a pig or other livestock in trade, Watson moved on to selling securities. There he worked for a flashy salesman who showed him what an impression professional dress could make on people new to the cities. He also paid Watson enough money that he no longer had to sit at the tailor shop in his shirt and shorts while his only suit was being pressed. Watson began thinking big: He had a plan to open a string of butcher shops. But the man who had him selling securities ran off with the money they had collected, not only cheating their customers but putting Watson out of the butcher business.[3]

When Watson recovered, he sought a sales job with National Cash Register and didn't accept defeat even when he was repeatedly turned down. Finally landing a job at NCR, known as the Cash, Watson picked up many of the ideas that came to be identified with IBM, starting with the way his often-enraged boss tore down Watson's personality and reconstructed it in his own image. This gave rise to the IBM sales school, which some who attended it described as a sort of brainwashing.

Watson's time at the Cash also buttressed his feeling about the importance of dress and of making the sales force feel professional, which proved to be a powerful idea in an era when the position of traveling salesman had a dubious air about it; the idea led directly to the IBM practice of having salesmen wear dark suits, white shirts, and the stiff detachable colors fashionable in that day. Watson even borrowed IBM's "Think" slogan from Eugene Patterson, the head of National Cash Register. Watson also had his first brush with an antitrust suit because of overly aggressive sales tactics that Patterson instructed him to use at the Cash. Watson was convicted and sentenced to a year in prison, but the conviction was overturned on a technicality and never pursued a second time because he had left the Cash. Although the facts of the case weren't in dispute, Watson never acknowledged guilt or showed any remorse.

While Watson is referred to within IBM as its founder, he was not. When Patterson forced him out at National Cash Register after eighteen years as too great a threat to his authority, Watson was hired as general manager in 1914 to run a conglomerate put together three years earlier by Charles Flint, a little man with a goatee and sideburns who was known as the "Trust King." Two-thirds of the company consisted of a business that made scales, coffee grinders, and cheese slicers for small shops and a business that made time clocks—which is why, for years, everyone at IBM from the lowest-level worker on up through Watson punched a time clock. The final third of what was known as Computing-Tabulating-Recording was an odd little business whose core idea, though descended from the loom, would become the basis for what people now think of as IBM. A Frenchman named Jacquard had come up with an ingenious idea to use wooden cards with slots in them to sort threads in a loom, moving them to their appropriate spots as a pattern was woven. The idea really turned the loom into a primitive computer, as a German immigrant to the United States saw. Herman Hollerith borrowed the idea. Instead of sorting threads, though, his device sorted cards holding data. Instead of making cloth, he tabulated statistics.

Hollerith's timing was good, because in the late 1800s the U.S. Census Bureau was drowning in data. By the time it started a new census, it still hadn't finished tabulating the information from the prior one. So the Census Bureau supported his business until Hollerith, a better inventor than businessman, ran into financial trouble and had to sell his primitive computer business to Computing-Tabulating-Recording.

Watson started slowly at CTR because his conviction in the antitrust suit had yet to be overturned, and it wasn't clear what would happen to the company while he served his year in prison. But Watson soon realized what a good thing he had in Hollerith's mechanical sorters and he went about setting up a force of professional-looking salesmen who could sell companies on the idea that they needed these calculators. Watson also hit on the idea of leasing the machines, which served the company so well over the decades to come. Leasing not only made the elaborate machines seem affordable by dividing their price into monthly payments; it generated more revenue over the lifetime of a machine than Watson would have received if he had sold the machine outright. Leasing also made it expensive for others to enter the business. As an established company, CTR could afford to get only a couple of percent of its machines' sales price each month, but anyone trying to horn in on the market had to be loaded with cash to be able to afford getting so little money up front while still investing enough to keep pace with the technical improvements Watson and his company kept making in their machines.

Even though he was loaded with debt, the forty-year-old Watson managed to talk his lenders into giving him more money—arguing, like the good salesman he was, that the old debt was the past, while he was talking about money that would finance the future. When a recession hit in 1921, the debt almost put CTR out of business. But the company pulled through, and in 1924, Watson renamed it International Business Machines Corporation, thinking that sounded appropriately grand. The name change seemed to signal a transformation in Watson. In his early fifties by then, he went from seeing himself as someone who'd had an up-and-down career to realizing he was someone with a destiny. He began to develop an aura.

Watson almost went broke early in the Depression because he had overborrowed to buy IBM stock; he figured that if the stock had dropped just another couple of points, he'd have been history. For good measure, the mechanically inept Watson managed to burn the family house down when he had trouble with the furnace.[4] Still, IBM kept growing right through the Depression, actually doubling in size. The company hit $40 million in annual sales by World War II. Growth slowed only briefly during the war, even though IBM switched two-thirds of its manufacturing space over to machine guns and other ordnance and sent lots of its young men off to war. (Watson continued to pay a large portion of their salaries to their families throughout the war, figuring that the young men shouldn't be penalized for serving their country—one of the stories most often told over the years as IBMers explained their loyalty to their employer.)

By the time World War II began, IBM had already become a national icon. IBMers even had their own rank in the navy; repairmen fixing the all-important calculating equipment wore a badge with an *I* in the middle, signifying that they were, say, yeomen, second class IBM. After the war, when the intercontinental ballistic missile came into being, the obvious way to abbreviate it was as IBM, but the computer giant didn't care for that, so the missile carried the more ungainly title of ICBM.

In raising his children, Watson got off to a slower start. They fondly remember the man with the fierce dark eyes, talking about how he'd sometimes amuse them on Sunday afternoons by donning one of their mother's dresses. But, as children, they rebelled at the discipline that his strict Scottish upbringing made him try to impose.[5]

Tom Junior, in particular, became a handful. Born in 1914, "Young Tom"—the name that would stick with him throughout his life, even as he headed into his late seventies—got himself suspended from school for taking what he called the "stink glands" from numerous skunks and putting them in his grade school's ventilation system, forcing the school to close for the day. Known as "Terrible Tommy" Watson, he needed six years and three schools to make it through high school. Made horribly insecure by his overbearing father, Tom Junior says he got into college only because his powerful parent imposed on the president of Brown University (a move that has since won Brown tens of millions of dollars in donations from Tom Junior). Even once he was out of college and working for IBM, young Tom spent half his day flying his plane and half in the clubs, where the tall, handsome young man flirted with models or just drank and smoked into the wee hours of the morning.[6]

Things began to change for Tom Junior when he went into the Air Corps during World War II. As a pilot, he was still a daredevil, once volunteering to act as an observer on a flight through enemy fire into Burma. When the fog got so bad they couldn't see and the altimeter showed that they should have crashed into the mountain, the pilot looked over at Tom and cackled: "What the hell! Who wants to live forever?" But Tom spent most of the war as the pilot for an Air Corps general and began, by observation and imitation, to learn about managing people. Out of his father's shadow for once, he finally developed confidence. He also got his first exposure to the computer.[7]

Right after the war, Tom went back into the family business. It grated on him that everyone at IBM treated him deferentially as the son of the chief executive, but he also realized how much this connection helped him as he started to find himself. As a young salesman flouting his father's rules against drinking, he was given a Wall Street territory so cushy that he reached his annual quota on January 2. His father moved him up through the ranks, recognizing that the war had given his son new confidence and even some discipline. Tom Senior was even entertaining the possibility of eventually letting his son run the company, but there was an obstacle: Charles Kirk, IBM's number-two executive, was just forty-two in 1947, only eight years older than Tom Junior. Then Kirk died, quite unexpectedly, of a heart attack brought on by tension, exhaustion, and a heavy but forbidden drinking habit.[8]

In the late 1940s and early 1950s, Tom Junior pressed his father to realize that computing was rapidly moving away from the mechanical sorters and tabulators that IBM had sold for decades and toward the monstrous collection of vacuum tubes and electronic parts that the U.S. military had assembled as part of its war effort in the early 1940s. Watson Senior was suspicious. Customers were hardly asking for these ungainly new devices, which included so many clicking mechanical parts that some sounded like a roomful of people knitting. He commissioned a study, which found that, over the lifetime of these new computers, all United States corporations put together would need a handful of the devices, which had less computing power than some microwaves have today. The study was right, too, to an extent—the older tabulating devices remained ubiquitous in world business through the late 1950s. But Tom Junior ignored what has been the traditional IBM approach of just listening to its customers' dictates; he insisted that there was a technological imperative at work: The new computers would way outclass the old ones; customers would figure that out soon enough; IBM had better anticipate their needs.

As Tom Senior prepared to hand the company over to Tom Junior, father and son had horrible battles. The father was so formidable that senior executives, confident men, sometimes found themselves sweating so much after a meeting with him that they had to use a handkerchief to grasp the doorknob on their way out. But Tom Junior was becoming plenty formidable himself. He once confronted his father on an airport tarmac, finally screaming, "Damn you, old man, can't you ever leave me alone?" In 1956, just a few months before dying at age eighty-two, the father finally capitulated and gave his son control of the company, which by that point was the thirty-seventh largest in the United States.[9]

Watson Senior's other son, Dick, chafed at the idea that his brother, as the elder son, would eventually run the business. So Tom Senior divided up the business, giving Dick responsibility for IBM's overseas businesses and giving Tom Junior control of the whole business, with the understanding that he would pretty much leave Dick alone. The sibling rivalry turned out to get IBM so well established overseas that its international businesses survived any number of attempts by foreign governments to limit U.S. companies' influence on their economies or to join up with other countries' computer makers to limit IBM's control of the computer market. Dick threw himself into the job, becoming fluent in French and nearly fluent in German and Spanish. He even learned enough Russian that he usually didn't need an interpreter. He made sure that IBM's English business was more English than most English computer makers were, its German business more German than German makers, so it was almost impossible to fashion a law that would slow IBM. When the Europeans banded together in the mid-1980s to form research groups aimed directly at IBM, the groups found they couldn't come up with a rule that would keep IBM itself from joining. Those overseas businesses were the only things that kept IBM from hitting the wall in the late 1980s, when its U.S. business ran into trouble. (Dick died in 1974 when he fell down the stairs at his mansion in New Canaan, Connecticut.)

When Tom Junior took over in 1956, he imposed order on a chaotic arrangement in which seemingly everyone in the company reported directly to his father and where his father made all the decisions—

surrounded by sycophants, Tom Senior told people that "loyalty saves the wear and tear of making daily decisions as to what is best to do."[10] Tom Junior's changes in the mid-1950s led to the first of the many decentralizations IBM underwent over the years. The new arrangement produced the Management Committee, which allowed Tom Junior to share a little of his authority. The new setup also produced the "contention system" that has defined IBM's management structure over the years. The idea was not only for lower-level managers to take over decision making but also for them to argue over an idea's merits so thoroughly that they were sure to be right. The process took longer, but not that much, because IBM in the late 1950s still represented just fifty thousand people and about $1 billion in sales. Over the next twenty-five years, the idea provided extraordinary discipline for IBM.

As a counterpoint to that discipline, Tom Junior ruled IBM viscerally. He'd pull someone out of a job on Friday and about half the time put him back in the job on Monday, after cooling down over the weekend. Watson and his president—big, bluff Vin Learson—once had a small misunderstanding over the rules of a sailboat race, and Watson got so mad he didn't speak to IBM's number-two executive for weeks.[11] David Kearns, who later became chairman of Xerox, said that as a young IBM executive in the 1960s he made a presentation before the Management Committee, unsure whether Watson even knew his name, and saw the famous Watson temper. Watson graciously welcomed someone arriving late for the meeting and said, "David here is making a nice presentation that you'll enjoy," then thundered, "unlike Jack, who just made a presentation and who stood right there and lied to all of us!" Kearns said he wanted to hide behind the easel that held his charts. Watson didn't just chew people out, though; he knew when to go easy on someone. He once hauled in from the field an executive whose decision had cost IBM $10 million. As the executive cowered, Watson asked, "Do you know why I've asked you here?"

The man replied, "I assume I'm here so you can fire me."

Watson looked surprised.

"Fire you?" he asked. "Of course not. I just spent $10 million educating you."

He then reassured the executive and suggested he keep taking chances.

Watson once called an assistant into his office in the early 1960s, waved a *Forbes* cover piece on 3M at him and said, "Read this! This is the sort of decentralization I want to have at the IBM company." The article described a decentralization much like the one IBM is finally moving toward today, but his staff convinced him that wouldn't be possible.

Watson, unlike some of his successors, said he tried to find "harsh, scratchy people" to put into key positions.[12] Later on, it became hard for subordinates to confess to their bosses that they had problems, but Watson, who still answered his own phone even once he became chairman,[13] encouraged people to get in his face and tell him how things really stood. He'd also happily impose his will on subordinates when he was sure he was right. For instance, when some of his executives said in the early 1960s that they didn't quite trust the durability of transistors for use in computers, he overruled them. He also gave each of the doubters one of the transistor radios just coming on the market at that time and told them to call him as soon as one failed.

In the 1950s, as the Watsons tried to figure out what to do about this new thing called the computer, Remington Rand had forged so far ahead that the general public referred to computers as Univacs, after the name of Remington Rand's machine. But Tom Junior didn't let that last long. He took what *Fortune* magazine called "the $5 billion gamble" in the early 1960s—that was about three times IBM's revenue at the time, so it would equal a $200 billion gamble today. The gamble, a bigger undertaking than the Manhattan Project, which produced the atomic bomb, was designed to produce a whole new line of mainframes, called the 360. The project was even more daring than the mere cost would indicate, because IBM under Watson did something it has never tried since: Rather than trying to protect the existing product line from the effects of the 360, IBM tried to use the 360 to wipe out all current products, including IBM's. The project looked shaky in 1965 because of software delays. IBM compounded the problem by throwing so many programmers at the project that they spent most of their time coordinating things with each other and nobody got anything done. Watson was panicky. But once the software problems got solved, the 360 let IBM go from about a 25 percent share of the computer industry in the late 1950s to more than a 70 percent one. IBM catapulted into the top ten on the list of America's biggest companies.

The magic of the 360 was twofold. It used the integrated-circuit technology that was just becoming available and moved away from the big vacuum tubes that characterized the early "electronic brains." Early machines, using vacuum tubes like those in early stereo equipment, broke down so often that during World War II the military had soldiers standing around with tubes, ready to replace one whenever it burned out. The 360 line was also the first true family of computers. To that point, any customer buying a more powerful computer from IBM or anyone else couldn't use his old software on the new machine. With the 360 line, IBM customers could start with a small machine and work their way up as their needs grew, taking all their old software along with them. That ability to run old software on new machines was a crucial feature that convinced IBM customers to write hundreds of billions of dollars' worth of software to run on IBM machines over the years.

Even as Watson was creating so much wealth for shareholders that *Fortune* magazine labeled him "the greatest capitalist in history," he did something that no self-respecting chief executive in the 1980s or 1990s would have done: He cut his own pay. His father had received a percentage of IBM's profits as part of his contract, and Tom Junior had received extensive stock options. But he decided that his options were becoming indecently lucrative, so he stopped taking them.[14]

Under the Watsons, senior and junior, IBM remained a family business. A couple of dozen members of an extended family might work together at IBM, located near one another in an IBM town in New York's Hudson Valley, seeing their friends at the IBM country club or at the family-day picnics IBM arranged. Everybody gathered for the big Christmas party. Each child walking through the door received an IBM punch card with his or her name typed on it. In what some remember as a highlight of their childhood, they were directed by the card to go to a certain table to collect some gifts—whatever, say, the Committee on Toys for Eight-Year-Olds had decided to hand out that year. (It was, oddly enough, a fear of nuclear attack that helped foster this family feeling, at least in the hamlets of New York City where IBM settled its headquarters operations in the early 1960s. Watson had convinced himself that New York City could be blown up and that IBM would therefore be destroyed if it kept its headquarters there, so he moved about fifty miles north to get out of harm's way. The other reason for the move was more realistic: Watson, living in a modest house right on the water in Greenwich, Connecticut, didn't like the hour-plus commute to central Manhattan. Armonk was just a few minutes away. To this day, at age seventy-nine, Watson still takes advantage of the shortness of the trip by hopping on his old BMW motorcycle every once in a while and checking in on IBM management.)

The Watsons fostered a sense of community by having employees start meetings by singing songs in praise of IBM. "Ever Onward" was the IBM anthem, with lyrics about how "the IBM is big, but bigger we will be." The songs, a fixture at meetings well into the 1970s, promoted reverence of senior executives—the songs carried such titles as "To Samuel M. Hastings, Chairman, Scale Finance Committee."

When Watson had a heart attack in 1970 at the age of fifty-six, he soon turned the company over to Vin Learson, who served as a caretaker for two years, then gave way to the Frank Cary era. Cary was the antithesis of Watson: professional, not visceral; calm, not fierce; a Stanford MBA, not the elder son of the former chairman. When told in 1973 that IBM lost a $350 million judgment in a suit filed by Telex that was related to IBM's mainframe near monopoly, Cary never flinched, even though this was the biggest antitrust judgment up until then and would stir up years' worth of antitrust suits against IBM. He just said to his lawyers, "Okay, what do we do now?" When IBM's chief in-house attorney, former U.S. Attorney General Nicholas deB. Katzenbach, offered to resign to give the new chairman a scapegoat, Cary merely said, "No. This is my problem, not yours."

A few years later, a brash young computer scientist named Andy Heller barged into Cary's office early one evening because he had decided to give the chairman a job evaluation. Heller told Cary that on the IBM scale of one to five, with one as the highest, Cary was a seven—the number-one ranking is known around IBM as "walks on water," so Heller, who was a half dozen or more levels down in the research organization, was telling the ultimate boss that he was drowning. Rather than throw the upstart out of his office, Cary expressed curiosity. Heller asked how Cary would rate someone who, by skimping on the people devoted to a project, was endangering a mainframe line that was IBM's most important. Cary heard him out, then politely invited him to stay and watch Bert Lance's televised resignation from the Carter administration. After thinking things over that night, Cary added 150 people to the development of what became the 3090 line of mainframes, which sustained IBM through the late 1980s. Heller went on to become a star scientist at IBM.

When a delegation of senior U.S. executives visited China in the mid-1970s, shortly after it was opened up to the West, the shrewd head of a collective farm zeroed in on Cary immediately, even though he had never before seen a Western businessman and though Cary's questions had to be relayed through a translator. When another of the U.S. chief executives asked the farmer how he dealt with competitors, the farmer replied, "There are farms and then there are farms." He nodded toward Cary and said, "Ask him. He understands."

A team of marketing executives came before the Management Committee in the mid-1970s to say that they wanted to cut some prices to match a competitor, even though the prices seemed to be so irrational that months of study by the marketing team had concluded the competitor must be losing money. Cary said, "What makes you so sure the company *is* making money? Let's leave prices where they are." Two months later, the competitor went bankrupt.

When Watson used to blow, Cary was almost the only one who dared stand up to him. When he did, there was an audible gasp as everyone in the room sucked in their breath and waited to see what would happen—but Cary almost always prevailed.

Irving Shapiro, once chairman of Du Pont and a former director at IBM, said that Cary "was one of the smartest, most capable chief executives at any company in America. He's simply a superior intellect with a lot of get up and go."

It was under Cary that IBM settled into the management style that drew such wide admiration—with its extensive training of employees, its devotion to customers, its pride in how many managers it had, and its careful screening of hundreds of thousands of people to identify and nurture those with high potential. (Those high-potential people, known as "hi-pos," prompted the joke that IBM consisted of hi-pos, lo-pos, and Alpos.)

What people on the outside didn't see was how afraid of failing Cary was underneath the calm facade and how hard he had to work to keep his bureaucracy on its toes. He didn't just rubber-stamp the responses his assistants prepared to employees' open-door complaints—which, following a Watson Senior tradition, IBM employees can send to the chairman if they think they've been treated unfairly by their managers. Instead, Cary might bore through the inch-thick material supporting the assistant's few-sentence recommendation and find something amiss with a midlevel manager he'd been watching or discover something that needed to be changed in the courses at IBM's management school. Cary didn't say much at meetings, but he had a way of asking complicated questions, such as "Who said what to you when?" Then he'd sit back and listen not only to the answer but also to the rhythms of the person's answer, to the particular words he was using, to any repetition. After processing the answer on four or five levels, Cary would ask another question that couldn't be answered simply. Pretty soon, he had cut through to the core of the issue.

Cary, like all the chairmen in IBM's history, came from a sales background, not a technical one. High school physics was as technical as Cary got; he had majored in political science in college. So Cary, like the other chairmen in IBM's annals, had to work extrahard if he wanted to govern effectively this most technologically advanced of companies. Cary, like Watson before him, decided to surround himself with people who would tell him what was really going on and weren't afraid to confront him if they thought some major project was taking the wrong approach with its technology. He wanted people who would also get in one another's faces, keeping complacency at bay. For instance, for years Cary protected Bob Evans, a senior executive with a technical background who used to blister his colleagues about their approaches on products. His colleagues would then traipse into Cary's office, complaining about what a pain Evans was and asking that he be quietly shot. Cary would just laugh and tell them they didn't understand: It was Evans' job to be a pain. It wasn't that Cary thought Evans was always right. He actually confessed to colleagues that he thought Evans had a lower hit rate than a few of his technical colleagues. Cary just wanted to keep things stirred up.

Under Cary, IBM researchers saw early on that personal computers would become possible in the 1970s. That was pretty simple. The electronics on chips were shrinking rapidly, so the computers containing the chips could shrink, too. What wasn't so easy was getting a machine out the door. IBM's General Products Division, based in Atlanta, would propose some grand plan for a small computer, then, a few years later, come out with a machine like the Datamaster or one of the 5100 series. Those failures are why Cary kept at the issue so hard. He finally decided that the assumptions behind those machines were the problem. His executives were all assuming that the systems would use only IBM technology, that they'd be sold only by IBM salesmen, that they'd carry all the standard IBM service policies. Those assumptions were all near and dear to the hearts of every IBM product group, but once Cary identified them as the problem, he had no trouble tossing them out.

Cary couldn't sustain the growth rates that Watson produced, but nobody could have. (Cary did joke once about how he might have been able to keep pace with Watson. He walked into an IBM computer facility in England, where IBM had acres of mainframes and disk drives, seemingly being used by just a couple of operators. "Jesus," Cary said. "If we could just get other people to use computers the way we do, our sales would be bigger than the U.S. GNP.") Besides, Cary had to spend much of his time fighting a federal government antitrust suit that lasted from 1969 until 1982 and that limited the sorts of things IBM management could discuss. The government collected more than 760 million documents from IBM during that stretch. The case had everyone working so hard that one lawyer for IBM billed twenty-seven hours in a single day (by taking a flight from New York to the West Coast and picking up three hours because of the time change).[15] IBM's top executives were afraid to put anything down on paper for fear the government would subpoena the document. Lawyers, who were developing a stranglehold on the business, decided what could be said at meetings. No one could talk about IBM's market share, or if they did, they'd talk in meaningless terms, describing the market for word processors as though it included everything from the supercomputer on down to paper and pencils. Executives couldn't do any competitive analysis. Developers weren't allowed to buy a competitor's machine; they were just supposed to know what was in it.

Cary was actually prepared to break the company in two, which is why in the mid-1970s he created the grab bag General Products Division, which included many of the nonmainframe businesses and eventually spawned the personal computer. (Under pressure from the government, he looked at breaking the company up more, but when the lawyers produced their charts showing where each part of IBM sold its products, IBM appeared to ship products only to itself. Cary and his advisers decided it would be just too hard to break IBM up further.) As the government case began to fade in the late 1970s, the Justice

Department lawyers offered to drop the case if IBM gave them a face-saving solution, so house counsel Katzenbach did offer to split off a piece of IBM. But it was just the small, money-losing Satellite Business Systems. The government lawyers took the offer as an insult. They said, "Don't call us, we'll call you," and they never called back.

Probably the biggest mistake that happened in the Cary era was Future Systems, an attempt to make the sort of breakthrough that the 360 line made in the 1960s. This time, though, the idea was too bold. FS, as the system was called, required too many leaps forward in technology all at once—many of the ideas are just now appearing in computers. There shouldn't have been any real harm done. In the early 1970s, the U.S. economy pulled out of the recession that had hurt sales enough to make IBM rethink its mainframe strategy in the first place, and IBM sailed merrily on. But FS had cost so much money and had been such a flop that it made it hard to take risks from then on. That was especially true because the person who bore the brunt of the problems with FS was John Opel, who became the next chairman.

When Opel succeeded Cary in 1980, he seemed to be just an extension of Cary. Operating behind a stand-up desk that looked like a podium, the stiff, bespectacled Opel seemed even more professional, even more cerebral. Opel was so low on the charisma scale that he barely registered; one director called him "plain vanilla."[16] But his passion for reading and the arts, combined with his penchant for pondering deep questions, made him seem like the philosopher king, a fitting symbol for a company reigning over its field the way IBM did in the early 1980s.

When Opel joined IBM soon after World War II as a salesman in Missouri, embarking on a path that took him to the top of the company, his mother scolded him by saying, "With all your background and education, it seems to me you could have found something more permanent."[17]

Opel shunned personal publicity, saying that all the awards he was receiving as man of the year in places as far away as Brazil weren't warranted. On the rare occasion when a reporter called Opel at home, if his wife answered, she'd politely promise to go fetch him, then put the phone down and not return.[18] But the reticence just fueled the idea that Opel was the dispassionate "brain" of IBM.

Looks were deceiving. Opel didn't, in fact, have Cary's intellect. As a result, he got carried away with IBM's success and set the company up for much of the trouble to follow.

Opel was taking over a company very different from the one that existed when he joined in the late 1940s. Electric typewriters were the exotic technology in business machines after World War II. Only a handful of computers even existed. In many industries, such as mining or steel, the lifetime of a technology lasts about as long as the career of an executive, so the top official of such a company doesn't have to adjust to many new ideas. But at IBM, which was in an industry where the technology turned over every few years, Opel was having to deal with technologies that were ten or more generations beyond those in the machines he started selling in Jefferson City, Missouri, as the soldiers came back home from the war.

Opel worried about IBM's leasing policy. He thought that some other company could come up with a technology that would pass IBM's mainframes by. Customers would cancel their leases with thirty days' notice, and IBM would then be stuck with a pile of useless metal and sand. So Opel changed IBM's pricing policies to encourage customers to buy rather than lease. Suddenly, instead of getting a couple of percent of each machine's purchase price each month, IBM was getting the whole shebang. Revenue and earnings soared. Then when the PC came along in 1981 and really kicked in in 1982 and 1983, revenue took off. Revenue for all of IBM went from $29 billion in 1981 to $46 billion in 1984. Earnings doubled from $3.3 billion to $6.6 billion—still the largest profit any company anywhere in the world has ever achieved. IBM settled in as the most admired company in *Fortune*'s annual survey of U.S. businesses. IBM's stock-market value more than doubled, reaching about $72 billion at the end of 1984, making it the most valuable company in the world.

As the surge from the shift began to dissipate. IBM even changed its normally ultraconservative accounting policies so that it could treat some of its new leases as sales, counting all the revenue and profit up front rather than a bit at a time as the money actually came in. IBM also began to defer until later years more than three-quarters of the expenses from some big software projects, making results in the early to mid-1980s look better than they really were. The new policies artificially inflated results even more than the shift to leasing already had.

IBM settled into a feeling that it could be all things to all customers.

Much like Ford's River Rouge plant, it would receive at one door the rawest of materials—sand, metal, and plastic—and pump multimillion-dollar machines out another door. IBM would develop all the technologies it needed, make all the parts of all the products, sell all its machines itself, help customers finance the purchases, install the machines at customer sites, fix them on-site, and so on. Under Opel, the company also settled into a golden age in dealing with employees. IBM —which seemed to stand for "I've Been Moved" during this era—took extraordinary care when moving someone, providing a large relocation allowance, guaranteeing a price for the sale of the person's home, finding a job for the person's spouse, even if it required extensive retraining.

Everything might have been fine if Opel and his crew had realized how much the shift from leasing to selling pumped up results and how vulnerable the loss of the leasing business left them. Instead, Opel bragged internally about how IBM's growth meant it was creating each year a new Digital Equipment, the second-biggest computer company after IBM. Opel predicted the company would reach $100 billion in revenue by 1990 (he came up more than $30 billion short). In giving up on leasing, Opel relinquished a security blanket that meant he began each year having already achieved 80 percent of his revenue target. Yet Opel invested as though he was guaranteed at least 15 percent growth a year. He increased expenses an unsustainable 13 percent a year.

"There were lots of analyses about what would happen if the growth rates didn't last, but no one believed them," says Dean Phypers, a Management Committee member during this era.

Opel also made more subtle mistakes. He feared the major Japanese companies so much that he decided IBM's biggest problem was matching their expertise in low-cost manufacturing. That's why he spent so much on building automated factories that IBM has been spending the past few years dismantling. When Steve Jobs, the Apple Computer cofounder, was given a tour of Opel's prize, a heavily automated type-writer and printer plant in Lexington, Kentucky, he came away saying the technology was great, "'but they're building the *wrong* printer." Having already spotted the possibilities for laser printers, Jobs correctly surmised that IBM's noisy, slow impact printers were on their way out. Sure enough, after two decades as the highly profitable center of IBM's typewriter and printer businesses, Lexington began to see results worsen, and IBM later dumped the business. The new owners have ripped out much of the IBM automation. While Opel worried about Japanese companies so much that he was focusing on ways to cut out the few percent of his costs that came from human labor, IBM put a lot of odd-looking products on the market or came out late with good ones. And the computer market was becoming less forgiving; IBM studies have found that in recent years 90 percent of a computer's profits are made in the six months after someone first brings the product to market.

Opel would muse about the possibility of problems, saying all the favorable publicity he was receiving embarrassed him, because he was sure that he, like everyone else, had feet of clay if someone chose to look hard enough. He also acknowledged that he should probably decentralize more, to put decision-making authority into the hands of lower-level people who lived in the real world of the marketplace rather than in the rarefied atmosphere of "galactic headquarters" in Armonk.

"If I were to take IBM and divide it up into a lot of little companies and put them on the market and offer investors the opportunity, I could probably quadruple the market value of IBM," he said in an interview all the way back in 1985.

But he quickly added: "It's just a thought I had." He couldn't quite convince himself he ought to act, because he thought he had already put IBM through more change than it could handle for a while. Some sort of breakup probably would have been a good idea. When AT&T agreed to be broken up in early 1982, it and its successor companies started out with stock-market value of $47.5 billion. A decade later, they had surpassed $180 billion, nearly a fourfold increase. When IBM beat back the federal antitrust suit in early 1982 and avoided being broken up the way AT&T was, IBM had a stock-market value of $34 billion. By early 1993, IBM's stock market value had fallen to around $25 billion. The fourfold increase Opel saw as possible would never happen.

While the changes he made in the company were minimal by to-day's standards, even trivial, as he prepared to leave office in 1985, he talked of "the enormous change we've been trying to manage. . . . I suppose I've had more change to manage in a shorter period of time [than his predecessors], all sort of telescoped . . . because there's an acceleration in the industry." He said that during his four years as chief executive "we have done the unexpected—reorganizations, acquisitions, price cuts, new marketing tactics." He added, almost condescendingly, that "these changes have yet to be clearly absorbed in our company around the world, and over the balance of this decade just getting that in place is going to absorb one heck of a lot" of his successor's time. Little did he know.

Opel described it as a big deal that he expected half of IBM's hardware revenue from the following five years to come from products that weren't on the market at the time he was speaking—even though the industry was about to enter a stage where aggressive companies like Sun turned over almost their entire product lines every year. Every hardware system more than a year old was called Gramps. Five years was forever.

With the success at IBM in the early 1980s, IBMers took on a new arrogance. With competitors seemingly vanquished, the only way for those inside IBM to measure their success was to see how high they could rise within the company. Like civil servants, they referred to themselves and each other by their salary levels: "I'm a fifty-seven, but she just became a sixty-one." People learned that the way to get ahead wasn't necessarily to have good ideas. That took too long to become apparent. The best way to get ahead was to make good presentations. People would say of comers: "He's good with foils," referring to the overhead transparencies that began to dominate IBM meetings. People began spending days or weeks preparing foils for routine meetings. They not only made the few foils they actually planned to use but made a huge library of backup foils, just in case someone had a question. Presentations became so important that it was no longer acceptable to be stumped by a question, to say, "I'll get back to you." Foils—sometimes referred to as "slideware"—began innocently enough. They stemmed from Tom Watson Senior's habit of keeping a roll of butcher paper by his desk so he could jot down thoughts. But they became such a part of the culture that senior executives began having projectors built into their beautiful rosewood desks.

IBM's odd accounting system contributed to the air of unreality that took hold in the early 1980s. A huge percentage of IBM's costs were treated as general overhead, which a group of accountants apportioned to IBM's various businesses. A product group finding itself getting 80 percent of its costs assigned to it each year didn't need to worry about keeping costs down; it needed to prepare good foils so it could argue to the accountants that some other IBM product group should carry more of the overhead. IBM's accounting system also generally assigned all of a technology's development costs to the first business that used the technology in a product. Typically, that meant the hugely profitable mainframe division paid the development bill. Everyone else got a free ride, making it hard to spot problems in, for instance, the PC business until much too late. Until the mid-1980s, there was just a single profit-margin goal for the entire company, rather than a variety, depending on how competitive a market segment was. That single goal made it hard for IBM to get into businesses, such as personal-computer printers, that would have initially provided modest profits but that turned out to be strategically important.

IBM's sales policies reinforced some of the problems. Salesmen, for instance, lost their commission if a product they sold was ever replaced by something else. That was fine in principle. It meant that anyone cramming a mainframe down a customer's throat lost the commission when the unhappy customer returned it. The commission policy was also meant to make salesmen work extrahard to shut out any competitors who might try to supplant IBM equipment. But the commission policy tended to make salesmen work to keep existing equipment in place even if that meant ignoring more innovative IBM products, like the PC, and even if the success of those products turned out to be crucial to the future of the whole company. Who wanted to give up the commission on a $15 million mainframe in exchange for a commission on a $500,000 minicomputer or a dozen $5,000 PCs? Nobody.

IBM's shift from leasing computers to selling them also seemed to change the attitude of the sales force. It used to be that leases gave each salesman 80 percent of his quota at the start of the year, as long as the customer stayed happy with the equipment that was already there. The effect was to make the salesmen focus awfully hard on keeping the customer happy. With leasing gone, though, the salesmen had to start from scratch each January 1. They had to push so many boxes at customers that they no longer cared so much about existing equipment. The change was so subtle that it took IBM a few years even to realize that it had a problem, but the change was serious enough that the company spent the final years of the decade and the early part of the 1990s trying to figure out how to restore those precious ties with its main corporate customers.

Under Opel, IBM became lazy. It had only a few hundred customers to really care about—the managers of the computer operations at the world's biggest companies, who bought the bulk of IBM's mainframes and minicomputers. So IBMers learned the birth dates of their clients' kids, played golf with them, and generally encouraged them to believe that no one was ever fired for buying from IBM. IBM had also become so entrenched in corporate America that it could usually have an executive ride to the rescue if some salesmen actually lost a sale. A study in the late 1970s found that more than half the chief information officers at Fortune 500 companies were IBM alumni, susceptible to pressure from friends at IBM if they should ever consider committing an act of disloyalty. More than sixty of the Fortune 500 companies either had someone on IBM's board or had an IBMer on their boards. Matt Fitzsimmons, when he was chief information officer at Burns International Security in 1980, tried to buy some disk drives from Memorex after IBM was repeatedly late in filling an order. The next thing he knew, he got an angry call from the chairman of Burns, who was phoning from a golf course, where an IBM executive tracked him down to complain. Later, when Fitzsimmons bought the ComputerLand franchise in White Plains, New York, he had some business with Texaco suddenly dry up. He was told that Texaco's chairman had killed the modest-sized contract and had decided Texaco should buy direct from IBM—at the urging of IBM Chairman Frank Cary, a Texaco board member.

The complacency seeped into top management at IBM, where Opel —having suffered through the FS project—wasn't inclined to take many risks. He also couldn't abide the kind of loud arguments that Cary let technical expert Evans carry on. Instead, IBMers began to focus on winning arguments without "breaking glass"—which meant offending colleagues. Harsh, scratchy people disrupted things and just didn't seem necessary. After Evans carried on a three-year-long harangue about the importance of using a new technology, Opel finally blew up at a Management Committee meeting in 1984. Although Evans turned out to be spectacularly right and IBM's slowness closed off some important opportunities, in particular in the workstation market, Opel said coldly that he'd heard about enough. He fired Evans.

The only thing IBM really needed to worry about in those days was stranding a customer by not delivering on a promise. The customer's boss didn't know enough about computers—in fact, he found them intimidating—to know whether IBM was providing a good deal, but he would be able to tell if some crucial product was delayed. So IBM came up with development processes that, above all else, delivered products on time. The processes often turned one-year development projects into three-year ones, but who really cared? People writing software had their work checked for bugs, because the customer would notice those, but not to see whether the software was fast enough to really sizzle. IBM had a monopoly on the market for software for its big systems, so who cared about speed? Besides, the slower the software, the more it would slow the customer's systems—and the more mainframes he'd buy from IBM.

Under Opel, what had been a series of understood processes became *the process*. While the white shirts and blue suits had long been a part of IBM's culture because it made the salesmen look and feel professional, by Opel's time the look had become a religious issue. Someone coming to IBM's school for new salesmen while wearing a shirt that wasn't white would be publicly humiliated with the question, "Do you have a laundry problem or an attitude problem?" Salesmen, always an upbeat group, were trained so hard to be optimistic that realism ceased to be an option. They were actually told in sales school that if they were run over by a car and were lying in the mud by the side of the road about to die, when someone came up and asked how they were doing, the only appropriate response was, "Super."

Part of the reason the "process" appeared was because problems like those with the 360 software scarred IBM enough over the years to make it cautious; it caught on, too, because IBM's success made people feel that they must be doing everything right, so why change anything? Everything that could have a rule established for it, did. Even the speech writers, a generally unruly group, found themselves caught up in the rules. Their motto was "Humor at IBM is no laughing matter." Executives took it so seriously that speech writers wouldn't write jokes into speeches; they would just leave a big blank spot open for a joke and write in the spot, "Humor to come." They'd then give the executive several jokes to choose from and would mark his choice in an official joke data base. Anytime a joke was used, it wasn't supposed to be used again for a certain period, which varied depending on the rank of the person who used it.

Most of the two hundred single-spaced pages that make up the data base are hopelessly dull jokes about people trying to play tennis in wing tips. Only one is worth repeating. It shows surprising self-awareness on someone's part about IBM's burgeoning bureaucracy. The joke has an executive, presumably from IBM, arriving home drunk at 3:00 A.M., to find his angry wife waiting for him at the door. He takes one look at her and says, "In light of the circumstances, I believe I'll dispense with my prepared statement and proceed directly to the Q and A."

One day about a year after the introduction of the PC, when the morning packet of press clippings landed on the desk of Paul Rizzo, Opel's vice-chairman, Rizzo went ballistic. The PC, as usual, dominated the press clippings, a fact that had been driving IBM's senior management nuts. The PC accounted for roughly 0 percent of IBM's revenue and profits, yet it had struck such a chord with the public that that's all the press wanted to cover. Here IBM made these enormously profitable mainframes that were on the cutting edge of technology, yet all anybody wanted to write about was a toy machine. And there was Don Estridge's face plastered all over the clips, as though this midlevel manager was the most important at IBM. Rizzo slammed the press packet down on his desk and bellowed that he never wanted to see Estridge's face in the paper again.

Estridge drew that reaction throughout IBM. The more coverage he drew, the more he angered people in other parts of the company. They thought he was grandstanding and was, in fact, hurting IBM by not trying to tie his products into the rest of the company's, by not working with the IBM sales force, or by not being willing to buy his parts from IBM. The people who made memory chips at IBM hated Estridge; he apparently never placed a single order with them. Even people who managed to get a deal with Estridge were angry with him because he drove such a hard bargain and, unlike many IBM businesses, wouldn't let his internal suppliers mark up their prices if they had a problem and ran over their budget. Sales executives couldn't get Estridge to show up at their meetings, even if they were trying to solve a problem for a traditional large customer.

If having enemies wasn't enough, Estridge also was in danger of being smothered by affection. All the high-potential types at IBM wanted to be touched by the PC's magic, so tons of professional managerial people began trying to migrate south to Boca Raton. Senior management encouraged the movement because it wanted its senior people to have their tickets punched in all the many major areas at IBM. After *Time* magazine named the PC its "Machine of the Year" for 1982, John Akers—newly appointed by Opel as president—joked to Estridge that if his business continued to be such a blockbuster, IBM would have to move its headquarters from Armonk to Boca Raton.

Senior management began sending hundreds and thousands of people Estridge's way. The corporate staff figured he might be able to find a use for lots more people, and with some of IBM's office products, such as typewriters, running into problems in the early 1980s, the company needed a dumping ground for people. (IBM couldn't, of course, cut the people loose, because that would violate the company's full-employment policy.)

Fans of Estridge's among his bosses began talking as early as March 1982 about trying to bring him back into the fold simply because they thought he'd done a great job and hoped his business could touch some other parts of IBM with its magic. "You couldn't have a business that might account for 25 percent of your revenue not be tied into the formal system," says one Management Committee member from that period. Estridge's superiors also thought that pulling him back into the regular structure would integrate his organization better with some of the research and development in operations in other parts of IBM. They assured him this would be for the best because it would give him access to technologies that would let him improve the performance of his machines faster than he could if he relied just on what his bosses saw as the inferior, off-the-shelf parts that he had cobbled together in his initial machine.

With everybody after him, try as he might, Estridge couldn't avoid going to Armonk a couple of times a week and getting caught up in corporate politics. Pretty soon, layers of management appeared beneath him. Developers who used to have easy access to Estridge found they couldn't even get through to him on the telephone. He wanted to stay independent. He wanted to expand the PC line both up and down—a concept he called "PC Plus"—to take on other parts of IBM. But he lost the battle and, on August 1, 1983, his informal little business became the Entry Systems Division.

Estridge had started out with a lean and mean group in an ugly little concrete-block building with a flat roof in a remote corner of

IBM's Boca Raton site. Even once he started expanding, he just moved across the road to a small building near a shopping center. Now he found himself with two headquarters buildings, complete with fountains and atria.

The decision to make the business a division occasioned remarkably little debate. All the senior executives appeared to think the idea made good sense. They seemed to feel that a couple more layers of staff would help Estridge catch the sorts of mistakes that were starting to happen on products like the PCjr. They couldn't yet see that Estridge was succeeding precisely because he'd been freed from following IBM's thousands of rules. Nor did they understand that the only big product successes IBM would have in the 1980s and early 1990s would come when some group disdained the IBM rule book.

When the PC business became a division, Estridge picked up enough extra staff that he went from an already-bloated four thousand people to ten thousand overnight. Estridge also lost his direct line to the chairman. Now he had to wade through three or four layers of management before reaching the top of IBM. It always takes a while for problems to appear in a high-tech business, because operations can coast for a while on the development work that is in progress, but the change to division status meant the problems were now sure to come.

The trouble didn't start right away. The XT, whose development was begun months before the PC was even announced, appeared in early 1983, only about a month behind schedule. Part of the delay came because Microsoft, in revising DOS to accommodate the XT's biggest innovation—a hard disk—ran into snags. IBM was furious when it heard about the problem, but the delay turned out to be minor. All was forgiven. The XT (which stood for "extended technology") once again put IBM in the forefront of PC technology. Like the PC, it sold like crazy. By now, IBM had captured 75 percent of the business market for PCs.

Besides the XT, Estridge's group began another project at about the time the original PC was announced. This one was aimed at the home market and would ultimately be called the PCjr. The original plan seemed to make sense. The PC had turned out to be more of a business machine than one for the home, so why not take another shot at the home market? Let people buy a cheap system through truly low-end distribution channels, including department stores such as K Mart. Let them build up the system as required by adding peripheral devices, so they can eventually make their PCjr the equivalent of a PC. Let people run all the software that the PC could, so they can do the same things at home and at work. The Junior was supposed to be announced in July 1983, in plenty of time for the Christmas season.

The idea fit in well with some things senior management was considering at the time, including the possibility of getting into the consumer electronics market, perhaps trying to put computer-network cabling into homes or doing something with interactive television. The idea may, in fact, have fit in too well, because the Junior drew a lot of attention from the Management Committee. The original idea began to change.

Much of the talk was the standard IBM discussion: Should a new product be allowed to cut into an existing line's sales, as a Junior would cut into the PC if it was as powerful and compatible as the plan indicated it would be. The MC apparently never ordered Estridge to change his plans, but the product began to be scaled back. There was initially supposed to be a full-sized keyboard for the Junior, but that got knocked out. In its place went a keyboard with tiny keys, which eventually drew such scorn as to be called the "Chiclet" keyboard. Critics complained that the keyboard could only have been intended for children with tiny fingers—and, although few people realize it to this day, they were right. The Chiclet keyboard was initially intended only for grade schools and young children. Dozens of peripheral devices that would have allowed the Junior to be upgraded to a PC were scrapped. Prices were raised. The plan to sell through the K Marts of the world was scrapped. It was bad enough that IBM products were being sold through computer dealers, but the idea of a blue-light special on Big Blue products couldn't survive the review process.

IBM went from the idea of a full-featured, cheap product sold like television sets to a crippled, expensive product sold like mainframes— yet manufacturing plans were scaled back only modestly. The Junior also came out just late enough to miss the Christmas season. Suddenly, IBM couldn't find anybody willing to buy the thing.

After more than a year, IBM tried some price-cutting, added back some features, let department stores carry the product—and actually generated some interest. Some marketing people put together what they thought was a cute advertising campaign, which would have been done entirely in lowercase letters and would have involved changing the name PCjr to pcjr. But the campaign raised enough hackles that it wound up in front of the MC. The MC had recently formed a corporate-image group, so it kicked the campaign over to that group for more study, and the idea eventually died. The Junior quickly lost steam again, too. It just had too bad a reputation, and competitors had come out with products that were more compelling.

IBM announced in 1985 that the PCjr "will fulfill its manufacturing schedules." In IBM-speak that meant the patient had died.

Although Estridge had spent little time focusing on the Junior—he had it built by a contractor because he wasn't willing to devote any of his own resources to it—it still had to count against him as his first real blunder. The flurry of publicity surrounding the Junior's untimely death scarred senior management so deeply that, until a couple of years ago, executives said in private that they were gun-shy about trying new things because they feared they'd take another beating like they had with the PCjr.

Even before Compaq came out with its revolutionary portable personal computer in 1982, Estridge and company had also started playing around with a portable—which, at thirty pounds, was far heavier than today's laptop and notebook computers but at least came as a single piece that could be lugged around in a case with a handle on it. IBM saw the technology trends as well as anybody, so its technologists understood the inexorable move toward smaller systems. But IBM consistently underestimated how quickly costs would fall, so it also consistently underestimated how big a market would become—a five-hundred-dollar product sells a whole lot more units than a one-thousand-dollar product. IBM's difficulty was that it had to rely on the price estimates of the groups producing the parts internally, who carried all the IBM overhead and expectations of profitability, while the upstart PC manufacturers dealt with fledgling parts suppliers who were inclined to ignore profitability while they tried to establish themselves.

"Our competitors weren't always burdened with all the facts we had at our disposal," as one senior IBM executive put it.

IBM was also so secretive that it couldn't get much feedback from customers on products before they were introduced. And customers, having never seen a portable, weren't too likely to tell IBM that what they really wanted were systems that could be closed up and lugged to another site. Sony customers didn't say that what they really wanted was a tiny portable radio and tape player in various sizes, shapes, and colors, maybe in some cool colors, or waterproofed so they could go running in the rain while carrying the device. Sony trusted the technology trends, did a few prototypes, showed them to customers, got an enthusiastic response, and produced the Walkman. IBM did a few portable prototypes, showed them only to other IBMers, got an indifferent response—and *Compaq* produced a portable that not only secured its future but showed legions of other companies how to compete with IBM.

Even once Compaq brought out its portable, IBM was so sure it understood the technology that it didn't buy a single Compaq system to see whether there was anything to be learned from it. When IBM brought its system out more than a year after Compaq, in February 1984, the system was too heavy and the screen was fuzzy. It died quickly. IBM didn't come out with a decent portable until years later, in 1990, long after the PC market had moved to the much smaller laptops and was well on its way toward the even smaller notebook computers. By being so slow to get started on the path toward portables and then laptop and notebook computers, IBM relegated itself to a tiny slice of what became a $6-billion-a-year market by the early 1990s.

Going on all fronts at once, Estridge also began work in 1982 on his next really big system, the AT (which stood for "advanced technology"). The idea here was to get to market as fast as possible with the next-generation Intel processor. But Estridge, as part of his growing involvement with the rest of IBM, found himself with some additional agendas.

For one thing, under pressure, he began moving toward the slow, more formal way of developing products at IBM. The AT also marked the period when IBMers up and down the line began to realize that just slapping a Big Blue logo on a PC didn't guarantee IBM the sort of control over the PC market that it enjoyed in mainframes. In mainframes, IBM produced all the technology inside the boxes, but in PCs, it bought its chips from Intel, its operating system from Microsoft, and its monitors, floppy-disk drives, and hard-disk drives from a whole assortment of other companies. Because IBM's rivals could buy those outsiders' PC parts just as easily as IBM, IBM began to realize it might actually face some competition for once. IBMers, from Estridge's subordinates on up through the Management Committee, began taking a series of scattered shots aimed at the two companies that increasingly controlled the PC standard: Microsoft and Intel.

Although it's not generally known, IBM actually tried to customize the Intel processor that would be the heart of the AT. The work would have solved a fundamental problem with the chip (known as the 80286), and IBM would have been the only one with access to its version of the chip. No clones, at least for a long time. IBM, not Intel, would have also controlled the most important part of the AT generation of technology.

The AT chip was becoming known in the industry as brain-damaged, and for a very good reason. It operated in two different modes, but it wasn't possible to move back and forth between them. The chip was like a car that would start in first gear and could move up to fifth gear, but once it got into fifth gear, it couldn't go back down to first. All the software available for the PC at that point would run in the AT chip's version of first gear. All the software that would take advantage of the chip's fancy new features—its additional speed and ability to deal with much greater amounts of memory—would run in fifth gear. A customer, however, needed to be able to move between first and fifth gears. Otherwise, he'd have to make a hard choice. He'd either have to throw out all his existing software and operate only in fifth gear or keep his old software and operate only in first gear, forgoing any new software that would quickly become available for fifth gear.

Estridge's engineers produced a slick way of attacking the AT chip's problem. They borrowed an idea from Intel, which, when testing its chips, placed an extra pin on the bottom (the pins are used to plug the chip into the circuit board inside a PC, much as the prongs on an electrical plug fit into a wall socket). Estridge's engineers found that, using a special connection akin to Intel's, they could let the AT chip switch back and forth between its two modes. Because IBM's size and influence had won it a special deal with Intel, providing IBM access to Intel's basic technology, together with the right to tinker with the technology, the extra pin would have been hard for other PC manufacturers to duplicate. But the pin didn't work. IBM's engineers could never make their revised chip fast enough to satisfy people using old applications. These people, used to having their applications running in first gear at fifteen mph, would find the system with IBM's new chip inching along at three or four mph.

IBM might still have tried to introduce products using its customized chip, but a Microsoft programmer came up with a slick way of solving the AT chip's problem in software. That meant there was no need for IBM's special hardware. The person who solved the problem was the sort of programmer whom Microsoft and other software companies craved in the early PC days but who never would have lasted at IBM. Gordon Letwin—short, burly, bearded, given to wearing T-shirts and working around the clock—came to Bill Gates's attention when Gates tried to sell some of his early software to the company that then employed Letwin. He found Letwin lying in wait, spoiling for a fight. Letwin sees the world in stark terms: He's right, you're wrong, and, politeness be damned, why try to hide it? It's possible to prove him wrong but not to argue him down. Letwin raged in front of his bosses, with some reason, that software he had done on his own was better than what Gates was peddling. Letwin lost that fight but won the war, because Gates hired him as one of Microsoft's first dozen programmers, and Letwin received stock now worth many tens of millions of dollars. Letwin's idea about the AT chip came to him while playing around on his own. If the AT chip started in first gear but couldn't get back to it later, then every time he wanted to return to first gear, he'd turn the computer off and start it up again—much like turning a car off at forty-five mph to switch from fifth gear down to fourth. The plan was complex, because a computer's processor loses all the work it's doing when it's shut off, but Letwin found a way to manage that problem. Because IBM had code-named the AT Salmon and had used marine names for associated projects, Microsoft called his trick Fish Magic.

Even with the idea of the extra pin dead, Estridge still wasn't out of tricks as the development work headed into 1984. He'd borrow one from the mainframe business. Estridge took advantage of IBM's close relationship with Intel and bought up all the AT-type chips available. If he owned them, no one else could buy them. If no one else could buy them, nobody else could make PCs competing with his machines. The idea actually worked for a while. It was some months after the August 1984 AT introduction before competitors began announcing their own AT-class PCs, and it took rivals almost a year to produce the machines in volume. Estridge did create a problem for himself, though, because a funny thing happens to chips as they move into high-volume production: They not only become cheaper to make as the producer removes the kinks from the extremely complicated manufacturing process but they become radically cheaper to manufacture, and the manufacturer even learns how to make them run faster. As clone makers began to come out with their own versions of the AT, Estridge found himself stuck with a mountain of chips that were both more expensive and slower than those competitors were using. Estridge managed to wave his hands over the problem fast enough that consumers didn't defect to competitors in great numbers, but the problem was still significant, because it marked the first time that competitors had managed to get out in front of IBM in using PC technology.

Estridge the risk-taker created a bigger problem for himself by ignoring standard IBM discipline, which requires that there be two suppliers (whether internal or external) for every part of a system, in case one supplier develops a problem. Estridge contracted with only one company for hard drives for his AT and one for the chips that control the workings of the hard drives. The suppliers developed problems. The AT came out in August 1984, but then customers started having their disks crash—making a sickening sound like a needle on a record player scraping across a record. Customers lost data, perhaps the worst thing IBM could do to a customer. Even if the disks didn't crash, problems with the controller chips sometimes corrupted customers' data—not much, but enough to throw off a couple of numbers in a spreadsheet. IBM had to stop putting disk drives in its ATs until it figured out what was going on. Estridge dug himself an even deeper hole because he didn't realize how severe his suppliers' problems were, even though IBM's management system required that problems be immediately quantifiable. Estridge kept flying to Armonk and heading to Management Committee meetings in the sacred corner of IBM to insist that his problems were almost over. Instead, the problems dragged on for nine months.

On a lark, a local Boca Raton company placed an ad asking customers to send it all the crashed disk drives they had. It got so many that they filled a barge, which the company floated off the Boca shore and sank, filling a hole in the reef—and getting the company a lot of publicity at the expense of an IBM that had hoped the issue would just disappear quietly.

The problems with the AT left Estridge naked to all those factions inside IBM that resented the fact that he didn't return their phone calls and that he soaked up all the press coverage. With the PCjr fiasco still resounding in everyone's minds, the AT trouble meant he actually had to pay some attention to what other parts of IBM thought. By late 1984, he began to get more malleable, even buying parts from other units of IBM.

Two things saved Estridge, at least for a while. One was that competitors hadn't yet figured out that IBM had set a PC standard they needed to follow. The Wangs and Digital Equipments of the world were still trying to sell systems that couldn't run software written for the IBM PC—not realizing that they were, in effect, trying to sell Beta in a VHS world. Other companies, such as Tandy, thought it was enough to be fairly standard, so they'd argue that they were 90 percent IBM-compatible. To consumers, that sounded like being pretty much VHS-compatible—sort of like saying, the picture is generally okay but it may go fuzzy during the movie's sex scenes. The other thing that saved Estridge was that IBM still seemed to control the industry enough that many companies were inclined to wait to see what IBM would do with any new generation of Intel chip, so competitors couldn't bring out their AT-class systems until IBM did.

Competitors were slow enough that the AT still qualified as a raging success. PC revenues hit $4 billion in 1984, meaning the PC business would have been the seventy-fourth-largest industrial company in the United States and would have been the country's third-largest computer maker, after only the rest of IBM and Digital Equipment. Still, IBM's MC members began to wonder about their feeling that it wasn't possible to have big problems in a small market. The PC market was beginning to look very big indeed. And when Estridge ran into the delays on the AT that let competitors move into the void IBM had left, IBM found itself facing a new term, *clones*, which eventually undermined the entire company.

As problems began to surface in IBM's PC hardware and PC operating-system areas in 1983 and 1984, IBM added to the trouble by botching application software. IBM had had a promising start, publishing software made by others, but once the "process" intervened, it smothered the Estridge group's efforts.

Software Publishing, for instance, had brought out its Assistant series of business software on IBM's PC and planned to continue enhancing the software, but IBM began taking forever to review the upgrades to make sure they met its standards. IBM, believing it could impose order on the chaos it found in the PC world, once decided that Software Publishing had to knock a feature out of its word processor— such as the fairly straightforward ability to hyphenate words when they are wrapped from one line to the next. The reason was that IBM planned to reserve that feature for another word-processing product, but the feature was so widely available in competitors' products that IBM merely hurt sales of its products. Conforming to IBM's standards once forced Software Publishing to take a product that it thought was ready for the market and spend a year reworking it. Software Publishing, then a little start-up company, couldn't afford that sort of delay, so it released the product for competitors' hardware, giving them access to a piece of the popular Assistant series and helping them win credibility in their struggles against IBM. When IBM continued to dither, Software Publishing even brought out its new Assistant series software for use on IBM's hardware, but under a different name—meaning IBM got none of the royalties it was entitled to receive from sales of the Assistant series.

IBM crippled its own Displaywrite word-processing package by limiting its ability to handle electronic mail, which became a hugely popular application. This was back in the days when IBM still thought of typing as something to be done on a mainframe or minicomputer, and the mainframe people wanted to protect their mainframe-based e-mail system, called PROFS, by keeping e-mail off PCs. In addition, mainframe executives argued that the hundreds of thousands of secretaries who had gotten used to PROFS and the mainframe version of Displaywrite didn't really want any new features.

Joyce Wren, who started the software business for Estridge in 1980, found herself spending two to three days a week in Armonk throughout 1982, 1983, and 1984. Those were two or three days that she used to spend with customers or looking at competitors' applications, but she found herself caught up in jurisdictional disputes. For instance, Wren says she once needed a graphics program done in a hurry, so she found a couple of brothers, put them in a hotel in Fort Lauderdale for eight weeks, and got her program. Wren then found herself hauled up to Armonk because the IBM graphics people in Hursley, England, had somehow found out what she had done. They climbed all over her for not consulting them first.

"My goodness," Wren says, "it would have taken them six weeks just to respond. It was like we were on completely different timetables. They didn't understand how fast we had to respond."

In the midst of all the confusion that the infighting created, IBM wound up ignoring one of the greatest opportunities that ever crossed its doorstep. Although only a handful of people know it, even inside IBM, in the summer of 1982, Mitch Kapor, the founder of Lotus Development, practically begged IBM to take exclusive marketing rights to his Lotus 1-2-3 spreadsheet. If IBM had gone for that, it would have collected billions of dollars of revenue over the years from the spreadsheet. More important, 1-2-3 would have filled in the only missing piece in IBM's strategy in those days. IBM's competitors still assumed that IBM set the industry standard for hardware design; together with Microsoft, IBM controlled the operating system; and if IBM had taken Kapor up on his plea, it would have owned the one application that was so significant that it accounted for the biggest burst ever in PC sales. IBM would have had the whole PC industry under its thumb.

Kapor wasn't the most impressive of supplicants at the time. A former cabdriver, stand-up comedian, and teacher of transcendental meditation, he was portly and, even in those days, given to wearing Hawaiian shirts. Still, he had won some impressive backing from Sevin Rosen and Kleiner Perkins, venture-capital firms that would finance Compaq and most of the other successes in the early PC days. Kapor also had a dynamite business plan that produced the greatest first-year sales that any company in history had yet seen.

Kapor didn't like the idea of dealing with IBM, but Jim Lally from Kleiner Perkins convinced him to spend much of his dwindling budget on a trip to Boca Raton. Kapor initially tried to see Estridge himself. When that failed, it took two tries to set up an appointment with someone a level down. Kapor and Lally arrived in Boca on a brutally hot, humid day in July 1982, only to find that the person they were supposed to see had no interest in seeing them. They were bucked down another level.

When they tried to brief that executive on their product plans, he said he wasn't allowed to listen. Independent software companies such as Microsoft and Borland would find ways to make exorbitant sums of money over the years based on the fact that their visibility attracted programmers who wanted help marketing their products. But back in 1982, IBM was too cautious to use its far greater visibility. So many start-up companies had sued IBM for creating products that resembled their ideas that the IBM executive was allowed to hear from Lotus only information that was already public knowledge. That meant he couldn't hear anything from Lotus.

Kapor says he lied and insisted that the whole briefing he was about to give was widely known. Even then, the IBM executive just listened politely for a few minutes. At the end, he told Kapor and Lally that he had some neat demos of new IBM equipment; would they be interested in viewing them? After half an hour, Kapor and Lally were shown the door. They arrived back at the airport so early for their departing flight that they just sat in the coffee shop in the tiny Boca Raton airport, shaking their heads and wondering how they had failed utterly to make their case.

Lally, now a rich man because of Lotus's success, says today, "They prevented us from making a fatal mistake. So we're forever in their debt and hold them in the highest possible regard."

By 1985, Wren had left the PC applications business in frustration. Her replacement decided it was unprofitable and killed it.

With problems mounting, Estridge was losing his sense of humor. Among other times, he blew when he saw an Apple Computer poster that showed Kapor, Bill Gates, and Fred Gibbons of Software Publishing saying innocuously nice things about Apple's new Macintosh in early 1984. Apple cofounder Steve Jobs had come up with a cute idea, putting the three up on the stage at a gathering in Hawaii to introduce the Mac to his employees. (As it happened, Estridge was staying at the hotel on vacation and bumped into Jobs in the lobby. They recognized each other and chatted briefly about nothing in particular.) Jobs's idea was to simulate the "Dating Game" TV show, with the three software leaders telling people why they wanted to go out with a Mac. Afterward, Jobs did a point-of-sale poster along the same lines.

At about the time the poster came out, Kapor found himself in Boca Raton—having become such a star by now that he had no trouble getting attention. He was surprised to find himself pulled out of a meeting to go see Estridge, whom Kapor had never met. As soon as Kapor walked into Estridge's office, before he could even sit down,

Estridge lit into him about the poster. With two imposingly large lieutenants standing by his desk, Estridge accused Kapor of utter disloyalty. Didn't he understand that IBM was the one responsible for Lotus's success? Didn't he realize that he was in a partnership with the IBM company? Why was he messing around with Apple? Kapor—normally very confident and, in this case, sure he had done no wrong—found himself reeling, edging backward toward the door, apologizing all the way, just hoping to escape this onslaught.

Gibbons, who was fortunate enough not to visit Boca during this stretch, nonetheless picked up the phone one day, to find Estridge on the other line, giving him a similar earful. Only Gates didn't get beaten up over the poster, for reasons that he can't explain; he just says he and Estridge always got on well, so maybe Estridge cut him some slack.

Despite the problems that had begun to take root in the PC business, though, the aura of success continued to float around Estridge's head. Not only did his employees worship him but most of IBM's competitors began wooing him. Apple courted him to be its president, offering him $1 million a year. Sun came after him. In less than a decade, Estridge had gone from almost being fired by IBM for messing up the Series 1 operating-system project to a position where almost any job in the industry could have been his. But he never listened to a competitor for long. He had always thought it was neat to be able to tell people, "I work for IBM,"[19] then watch the admiration in their eyes.

However, IBM's senior managers weren't quite so wild about Estridge anymore. In IBM lore, the Watsons always encouraged "wild ducks"—people who weren't inclined to fly in formation—but it was no longer possible to stay outside the formation for very long. Estridge was pulled from his job running the PC business in early 1985. He was replaced by Bill Lowe, the same Bill Lowe who had turned the PC project over to Estridge back in 1980.

As usual, IBM disguised the demotion. The announcement said Estridge was being put in charge of worldwide manufacturing, which IBM management insisted was an attempt to broaden Estridge's background to prepare him for bigger and better things. In reality, he had been relieved of responsibility for perhaps the most exciting business in IBM's history and had been given a fancy title that carried little real responsibility. Estridge wondered privately to friends about why he had been shot and talked with a few about maybe even leaving IBM. Publicly, he insisted he welcomed the chance to prove himself in a new way, and he worked hard to make an impression.

When he said good-bye to an assembly of the group in Boca Raton in March 1985, the group rose to its feet twice for long ovations. Estridge tried to rise to the occasion, but, with his hair now gray and his face lined from four and a half years of extraordinary pressure, the teary-eyed Estridge was just too tired.[20]

Estridge never really fit in at the Armonk headquarters during the few months he had the new job. He wasn't one of these polished executives with years of experience in different product areas or different countries. He had to educate himself on manufacturing processes and had much to learn about sitting in meetings all day—after all, he had spent a career trying to avoid the bureaucracy that now engulfed him. People working with him at the time say Estridge failed to make an impression on his bosses. Having been put in what IBMers call the "penalty box," he was never coming out.

Estridge finally took his wife on a long-promised vacation, to unwind after the turmoil of the job change. They wound up on a Delta flight that tried to land in Dallas in stormy weather on August 2, 1985. As the plane came in for its landing, just seven hundred feet above the ground, a powerful downdraft knocked the plane toward the earth. The pilots fought back, but the plane was out of control. The wind shear was making the plane speed up or slow down as much as twenty knots a second. In seconds, the plane had spun out of control and smashed into the ground. The crash killed 137 people, among them Don and Mary Estridge.

At the Estridges' funeral, which drew hundreds of people, there were red roses on the caskets. Dan Wilkie, one of the original PC crew in Boca Raton, was reminded of something Estridge once did to motivate his troops. Estridge had seen some red-rose lapel pins and, on a whim, had bought a bunch. When someone did something special or was especially down, Estridge gave the person a pin and told him to wear it with pride, as a member of a team that was shaking up IBM and the whole industry. As Don Estridge's casket was about to be lowered into the ground, Wilkie took his rose pin out of his lapel, walked over, and laid it on the casket. Seven others followed in silence, leaving a tiny circle of eight rosettes as everyone said their good-byes.[21]

FOUR

ven though Bill Lowe was the godfather of the IBM PC, there was such a to-do surrounding Don Estridge in the early 1980s that Lowe's wife once asked him, "Bill, why aren't you as good as that Estridge guy?" Now that Lowe had replaced Estridge, Lowe would get to see just how he stacked up.

Lowe was certainly well seasoned in the IBM tradition of professional managers. An engineer by training, he had spent thirteen years working his way through some equipment-testing operations, then got an early break in 1975 when he wound up on the staff at the Atlanta headquarters of the General Products Division, the grab bag of low-end businesses. He got a bigger break when he moved to Boca Raton a year later with the mandate to try to find a way to get into the high-profile personal-computer business. After he presented the Management Committee with the idea for the stupendously successful PC in 1980, Lowe had what IBMers call "a star on his forehead"—he was destined to do well.

When he went off to Rochester, Minnesota, in the summer of 1980 after getting the PC operation going, he earned credit for launching a successful minicomputer, the System 34. Finally, he headed to headquarters in Armonk for a staff job that got him acquainted with all the major players in the company and let him see how the big boys played politics. Along the way, he learned plenty about IBM's myriad procedures.

As early as 1982, when a midlevel executive named Sam Albert mentioned Lowe's name in front of then-president John F. Akers, Akers perked up. "You know what Bill Lowe is?" he asked rhetorically. "Bill Lowe is a stud."

Even though Lowe met all the standard IBM criteria, he was hardly an inspired or inspiring choice. A decent golfer and sometime poker player, Lowe was friendly in private, but he never figured out how to make a big audience feel any of that warmth. When speaking in public, Lowe didn't seem to have a neck; if he moved his head, he'd swivel his shoulders. (Perhaps the only time he managed to do something out of the ordinary was years later when he left his wife and went to Georgia with his thirtyish executive assistant, whom he married in 1992.)

Lowe never demonstrated any of the vision that Estridge had of a world full of PCs operated by the common man. Lowe barely touched his own PC, except for electronic mail.

"Bill doesn't have a clue what a PC is," says Stewart Alsop, editor of the *InfoWorld* trade publication and a friend of Lowe's (and son of the political writer of the same name).

If Estridge was a true believer in PCs, then Lowe was an agnostic. He was trained in the IBM system that said a professional manager could manage anything, from the smallest group making the smallest computer on up through the armies of people who produce the mainframe behemoths.

Arriving in the PC job in Boca Raton in spring 1985 with a mandate to bring the business to heel, Lowe quickly put in place the typical mechanisms. Where Estridge discouraged memos, saying, "We don't have time to write memos," Lowe wanted a complete paper trail. Estridge told people they didn't need approval from anyone else for a decision after they had talked to him. Lowe always asked, "Has corporate (i.e., Armonk) seen this memo?" "Has manufacturing seen this?" Most important, "Have the lawyers seen this?" Even as the PC business became more bureaucratic in Estridge's later days, most anyone in the PC business could just wander into Estridge's office. But when Lowe moved into the large office with the plush peach carpet, he set up two rows of secretaries outside, forming a gauntlet that anyone wanting to see him would have to run.

As Lowe settled into his job, one of the first things he had to do was figure out what to do about that little software company named Microsoft up near Seattle that seemed to be doing so well at IBM's expense. In deciding how to handle Microsoft, he ended up getting considerable guidance from the sidelines from his boss, Mike Armstrong, who was an exceptionally effective executive but who was a marketing expert who turned out to have as little feel for the technology as Lowe did.

Armstrong was a forceful presence. He was a vicious tennis player in a business where most executives preferred the more sedentary game of golf. While some executives had themselves driven around in limos during the week and tooled around in their Mercedes on the weekends, Armstrong might hop on his Harley motorcycle. A trim, prematurely bald man with a twinkle in his eye, Armstrong was known as a "nice tough guy," one senior ex-IBMer said.

"He's the type of guy who would not just tell you to jump out the window," the ex-IBMer added. "He'd show you where the window was and help you jump out. And on your way out, you'd find yourself thanking him." The ex-IBMer quoted a friend as describing one of the first meetings Armstrong had with his senior management team when, years later, he left IBM to run Hughes Aircraft. Armstrong described the draconian cutbacks he planned to make through the whole company and said that, to set an example, he had decided to cut the group in the room in half. "The funny thing," the executive from Hughes said, "is that as I walked out of the room I was thinking that he was doing the right thing."

Armstrong could be unusually direct, too, even when it came to accepting culpability. He says, for instance, that the decision to pull the independent PC business back into the fold in 1983 was a group decision and that there were some good reasons for the move. But Armstrong, who had general responsibility for overseeing IBM's low-end businesses, including PCs, from 1983 through 1986, adds, "Eventually I guess you have to say I made the decision, if you want to assign blame."

By 1985, Armstrong had amassed all the usual points that a senior executive at IBM had to have if he wanted a shot at the top job some day. He had been a slick salesman, then moved up through the ranks into more senior marketing jobs, where he set pricing, determined what requirements the product groups had to meet in defining various products, and so on. Although not especially technical, he had then been given the mainframe business to run, because any hot prospect thinking of becoming chairman of IBM needed a strong dose of the mainframe mentality. Armstrong had, of course, succeeded at everything he had done. It didn't hurt him, either, that he was known as a crony of Akers, who had ascended to the chief executive's job in 1985. The two had bumped into each other during their first trip to IBM's school for salesmen in the early 1960s and had climbed through the ranks together, staying friendly enough that they once took a raft-trip vacation together.

Armstong and Lowe knew they faced a smart negotiator in Bill Gates. Estridge used to tell his senior software executives, "Don't ever let me get into a meeting with Bill Gates alone. I don't know how to respond to what he says." But as Lowe and Armstrong headed to the negotiating table in mid-1985, they felt confident that the weight of IBM's power and the discipline that IBM had instilled in its executives would give them plenty of control over Gates, with whom IBM was once again having to negotiate over a joint operating-system strategy.

In fact, Lowe and Armstrong were at a horrible disadvantage. Although IBM's marketing training was exceptional at teaching executives how to devise complicated product plans and pricing strategies to hold on to customers, that schooling really only prepares people to milk old markets and products. It doesn't help anyone recognize a new market. The IBM marketing mantra—"We'll do whatever the customer wants" —also tends to make executives willing to fiddle with plans as soon as a market begins to shift, no matter what that does to product development or to partnerships. That indecisive quality can leave IBM vulnerable—as it did repeatedly in Lowe's and Armstrong's dealings with Gates.

Lowe had inherited from Estridge a group of people still struggling to come to grips with their relationship with Microsoft—Estridge's software people had spent much of 1984 in task forces, trying to figure out a coherent strategy and to decide how Microsoft fit into it. The problem was that the relationship was turning out to be very different from anything these mainframe-trained IBM executives had seen before. They were used to treating all outsiders as suppliers. That still worked on the hardware side, but software was more subjective. Building hardware was akin to erecting a house, but working on software in a joint venture was more like writing a novel together.

The executives didn't come to a clear conclusion. It would have been lovely to leave Microsoft behind and devise their own operating system, but IBM's failure on earlier software projects made Lowe and others cautious about trying something on their own. Instead, the IBM committees decided that IBM should merely start doing *some* of the software writing itself, rather than just telling Microsoft what was needed and letting Microsoft do all the work. It was an issue of manhood: IBM shouldn't have to rely on these upstarts to do this software work for it. IBM would also demand "rights equivalent to ownership" over the code that was to be produced jointly, to affirm its control over the process.

While IBM studied, Gates acted. He knew all along what his prime directive was and he never wavered. He would maintain the IBM relationship at all costs. Then he would leverage that relationship as hard as he could. Gates, because he didn't have the dubious benefit of IBM's years in the business, also understood the new PC market far more clearly than they did. He saw how quickly faster processors and graphical user interfaces would become crucial. Gates, by dealing with all the computer manufacturers, also had begun to see how quickly the clones would catch on—a fact that Lowe and Armstrong wouldn't have been willing to accept even if they had foreseen it.

Lowe and Armstrong were also hamstrung by the smugness still prevalent among IBMers at the time. IBM's sales executives had become complacent in the early 1980s because the computer industry had turned out to be like the movie *Field of Dreams* for IBM—IBM just had to build something and customers would come. That feeling continued to be true in the corporate world through the mid-1980s because IBM's few hundred major customers all believed the old saw that "no one was ever fired for buying from IBM." What Lowe and Armstrong didn't realize is that, in the PC world, consumers spending their few hard-earned dollars are much sharper buyers than big companies spending millions of dollars drawn from seemingly bottomless corporate coffers. The IBM executives also didn't understand that this brave new consumer-driven world could be understood much better by a kid like Gates than by corporate chieftains.

As the passionate Gates and Ballmer prepared to meet the professional Lowe and Armstrong in the spring of 1985, both sides had to deal with some difficult recent history.

In 1983, Estridge's software team had taken a fancy to an idea produced by a researcher in IBM's Yorktown Heights facility, a futuristic glass complex rising up through the trees along the winding Sawmill River Parkway north of New York City. The idea would have let people use more than one program at once by allowing them to divide their screens into various windows. The idea would also have reduced complexity by giving them menus of commands to choose from, meaning people could start forgetting all the arcane DOS commands they'd had to memorize.

As the months went on, however, IBM began to botch its latest software project for all the usual reasons—it put too many people on the project, the work took too long, the software operated too slowly, and it turned out that customers wanted something much glitzier than IBM provided. The product soon became known to the world as Top-View but was dubbed "TopHeavy" by customers and became one of the biggest flops in the history of IBM's PC business.

IBM wound up giving away most of the copies of TopView that it produced after its introduction in 1984, but the financial bath it was starting to take on the project was only the beginning. IBM's tight relationship with customers meant that once it declared a product strategic and made a promise to customers, it had to keep it at all costs. Other companies didn't have to do that. In later years, after IBM and Microsoft produced an operating system called OS/2, Microsoft could say to customers, "OS/2, OS/2, OS/2," then say, "Oops! Never mind. We meant Windows, Windows, Windows." Customers would applaud Microsoft for recognizing the error of its ways and putting the error behind it. But IBM's big customers staked their jobs on their trust in IBM, so once IBM wound up with a dog like TopView, it had to stick with it to the bitter end. IBM kept trying for years to make TopView work and couldn't abandon it until customers lost interest.

Even before IBM embarked on its TopView failure, Gates and Microsoft were taking a more difficult but ultimately successful route that complicated their dealings with IBM more than anything else ever would. Steve Jobs of Apple had shown Gates in 1981 an early version of the Macintosh computer, in hopes that Gates would do some applications to run on the Mac. As soon as Gates saw the Mac, he fell in love with the slick way it used icons to let users pick programs or perform basic functions; the way it let people move the cursor around on the screen with a mouse; and the way the Macintosh let people have more than one window open on a screen at a time, making it easy to flip back and forth between different programs and to move information easily from one file to another. Gates quickly decided that, down the road, everyone would want to interact with their computers through a graphical user interface like the Macintosh's. Jobs and Gates turned out to be very right. Customers who were beginning to get used to the fast, sharp graphics of video games in the mid-1980s wanted their computers to be vivid and quick, too; nobody wanted their PCs to look like IBM's dumb terminals, with just a few characters on them, as happened with TopView. (A little editorial comment here: One of the great scams of the 1980s, abetted by IBM and its mainframe mentality, was that people needed to become "computer-literate." Paranoid parents immediately rushed out to buy computers, fearing that Junior would be left behind if he didn't quickly unlock a computer's secrets. In fact, computer literacy was just a way for computer makers to make users feel that they needed to adapt to computers. The fundamental insight that Jobs had first and that Gates had a bit later was that the situation should be reversed—that computer makers must go to the trouble of adapting their machines to the users. The way Jobs put it was that even IBM wasn't big enough to ship a mother with each personal computer it sold, so the trick was to figure out how to build motherhood into the machine.)

By late 1981, Gates had a team working on a project for the PC world that would become known as Windows. In late 1982, at the huge Comdex trade show in Las Vegas, Gates saw a competing product called VisiOn, which, unlike Windows, was far enough along that it was being demonstrated. But Gates then got lucky—something that has happened to him more than once. VisiCorp, the maker of VisiOn, began to self-destruct in 1983 because of lawsuits that senior executives filed against one another. Gates didn't even announce Windows until the Comdex show in late 1983—where he was already important enough that he gave the keynote address at the huge trade show, but where he was still such a low-budget operation that he had his father run his slide projector during the speech. Even after the announcement, Gates's project was delayed so many times that it prompted the coining of the term *vaporware*—a now-common term in the industry that is used to describe a product that has been announced but that seems to exist only out in the ether somewhere. Despite the problems, though, Gates applied such enormous pressure that his Windows team kept plugging away and stayed ahead of any competitors who were wrestling with the problems of doing a Macintosh-like interface for IBM-compatible PCs. Unlike the complacent executives at IBM, Gates had always lived in fear that someone would come along and do something better than he had if he let his guard down for a second, so he put the Windows group on what they called a death march. Windows finally made it out the door in 1985.

Gates and Estridge learned they were on different paths when Gates flew to Boca to show Windows to Estridge in late 1983. At that point, Gates got a shock, because Estridge showed him TopView. Gates decided that IBM would never be interested in Windows.

In the ensuing months, the two even talked about having Microsoft kill Windows so the companies could focus on jointly developing a next-generation operating system, but that conversation never went very far. Gates thought he was onto something with Windows, and it would turn out to be a runaway best-seller, so he wouldn't have given it up easily. Besides, Estridge couldn't very well tell another company how to run its business. That was the kind of thing that would bring the Justice Department snooping around, and even though IBM had won the anti-trust suits against it, it wasn't in a hurry to face any new ones. Without any way to resolve the Windows-TopView conflict, the two companies seemed to be headed in different directions.

After Lowe took over in 1985, there were plenty of reasons for him to meet Gates, but it was a cartoon that finally brought them together. *InfoWorld,* a big trade publication, ran a drawing of the two of them dressed as gunfighters, with pistols drawn and aimed at each other. Gates, always looking for a way to improve his relationship with senior IBM management, called Lowe to suggest that maybe they should meet to clear the air. Lowe agreed, and Gates hopped on a plane to Boca Raton.

The two hit it off. Gates found Lowe to be smart and appreciated how direct he was. Lowe found Gates to be exceptionally bright and energetic. Gates, despite his nerdy image, travels extensively and reads widely on noncomputer subjects, giving him a base of knowledge that he can use to be interesting and thoroughly charming when he so chooses.

After a few more conversations, they settled down to discussing whether to continue their work together—which was not at all a foregone conclusion. It turned out that Lowe didn't really want much, though. He mainly wanted a share in the development work on the next generation of operating systems. After all, he had to find something to do with the seventy or so programmers who were left with little to do following the Datamaster operating-system debacle in the late 1970s and the AT operating-system failure in 1984. Gates was happy to oblige —even though both sides should have seen the difficulties that joint development would cause. The "rights equivalent to ownership" that Lowe wanted was a little tricky to negotiate, but even that wasn't too tough.

When it came to royalties on DOS and future operating systems, Lowe made his real mistake, letting Gates once again run roughshod over his elders at the negotiating table. Lowe owned some 80 percent of the market for personal-computer sales to businesses and, like so many other IBMers who thought their company was the center of the universe, assumed he was entitled to that sort of share. After all, with mainframe revenue cooking along nicely in 1985 as the whole company nearly matched its 1984 record profit, Lowe's mainframe colleagues maintained more than an 80 percent market share. So Lowe's main objective was to get as low a price as he could for DOS on his machines. He cared little about the 20 percent sliver of the PC market that other manufacturers had claimed.

Once again, Gates was happy to oblige, sure he was beginning to see the future more clearly. A sort of generation gap had developed between the older executives at IBM, who couldn't believe that the computer-industry equivalents of rock and roll and long hair would catch on, and the kids of the industry, like Gates, who knew that rock was the wave of the future. While IBM—which was used to selling just a couple of thousand mainframes a year—had decided at the time of its PC announcement in August 1981 that it would sell just 200,000 PCs over the next three years, Gates had told a PC magazine shortly thereafter that IBM would sell that many in 1982 alone. Gates turned out to be right. He was now once again expecting the PC market to grow much faster than mainframe-oriented IBM believed to be possible. He could also see the growing role of the clones. So Gates told Lowe, sure, no sweat, you can have DOS for your machines essentially for nothing. All Gates wanted in return was the right to collect all the royalties from *other* manufacturers of PCs, such as Compaq and Tandy. Lowe agreed, and the two signed a Joint Development Agreement in June 1985.

Pretty soon, the shares began shifting. Today, they're reversed. IBM has less than 20 percent of the IBM-compatible market, while the rest of the PC world—the world to which Lowe gave Gates the rights to sell DOS—has more than 80 percent. Lowe's IBM-centric view of the world wound up costing IBM any claim on what turned out to be a huge hunk of the highly profitable, perhaps $2 billion market for PC operating systems.

His lack of insight also meant that the Joint Development Agreement did nothing to address the Windows question, an oversight that eliminated any chance that IBM would maintain its leadership of the PC market. Lowe had missed the significance of graphical interfaces and dithered about how strong a relationship to have with Microsoft. If he and IBM hadn't been tainted by their experience with mainframe customers who were locked into IBM equipment and cared not at all about how computer screens looked, they could have seen graphics coming and included a graphics system on their own or as part of what would have been a partnership with Microsoft. Slick color had been around in televisions since the 1960s, it had hit video games by the early 1980s, and it would soon arrive so thoroughly in computers that scientists would begin talking about virtual reality—where people wore goggles that used little screens to generate seemingly real worlds in which the goggles' wearer could exist. But IBM still felt customers would be happy interacting with their computers through screens with a few words printed on them. So Gates was allowed to pursue on his own a project that, while hopelessly unrealistic at its inception because Windows required more processing power than PCs had in its early days, would win because the vision behind it was right. Consumers in the video-game era not only wanted to forget DOS commands and not only needed additional capabilities; they wanted fancy graphics and pretty colors. It took Gates almost nine years to get a good version of Windows on the market, but Lowe and IBM were so slow on the uptake that they gave Gates all the time he needed and let him get Windows well entrenched among customers. By the time IBM figured out what was going on and put out a product that could compete with Gates's, the money Gates earned from the royalty payments from DOS sales to clone makers had made Microsoft wealthy enough that it could afford to stand up to IBM. Microsoft's seizing of the leadership of the PC industry from IBM contributed to IBM's stunning loss of share in the market for PC hardware, which eventually cost it more than $15 billion a year in revenue.

Before signing the Joint Development Agreement with Microsoft in mid-1985, Lowe and IBM had plenty of leverage over Microsoft. Afterward, they had none, and they would never get it back.

FIVE

As usual, Dick Hanrahan was talking about purple pine trees. The IBM software executive was in a meeting with Bill Gates and Steve Ballmer from Microsoft in early 1986 and was giving them such a hard time, they were stunned. He was the first really high-level software guy who had been brought to bear on IBM's PC software, and he brought with him the attitudes he had built up in his twenty years in the mainframe business. His message to Microsoft that day was: For the life of me, I can't figure out why we're doing business with you. What do you bring to the party? Gates scrambled to explain, but Hanrahan cut him off with his favorite expression: "purple pine trees."

This time, Hanrahan was using the absurd image as a question of loyalty. "What if I tell you to paint purple pine trees?" Hanrahan asked. "Would you paint purple pine trees just because the IBM company told you to?"

When Gates started to explain, Hanrahan cut him off again.

"See," Hanrahan said, "you wouldn't. And if you won't put purple pine trees in a program just because IBM says to, then I can't trust you."

When the meeting broke up, Gates and Ballmer went outside the IBM building in White Plains, New York, a small city forty-five minutes north of New York City that is surrounded by major corporate head-quarters. They paced furiously up and down the sidewalk on the edge of the bad part of town, across the street from a strip mall full of abandoned stores. The area seemed all the grayer as dusk settled in on a miserably cold day. Tired from a long cross-country flight and unable to figure how to respond to Hanrahan and his purple pine trees, Gates and Ballmer just kept pacing.

"This is it," Gates said. "We're dead. Our relationship with IBM is history."

If true, that parting of the ways would have at least minimized the damage that Bill Lowe had done when he signed the Joint Development Agreement with Microsoft in mid-1985. Breaking off the relationship might also have made IBM learn some of the hard lessons about personal-computer software that it didn't learn until too late.

Pacing some more, the agitated Gates found himself near a pay phone on the street corner. He tried to call Lowe, Hanrahan's boss, to complain that Hanrahan seemed to want to kill the operating-system work that Microsoft and IBM had begun under their 1985 agreement. Lowe wasn't there. More pacing. Gates and Ballmer piled back into their car and drove off, pondering how to patch things up with IBM.

Hanrahan's pointed concerns about purple pine trees in early 1986 brought to a head some tensions that had been building since early 1983, way before Lowe got the top PC job and before the introduction of the AT in 1984. Early in 1983, IBM had begun thinking about doing an operating system that would take advantage of the power of the new processor that was the heart of the AT. IBM didn't talk to Microsoft about its plan, though, because it had decided this was its chance to break free from the little company in Seattle, who numbered four hundred or so by now, a more than tenfold increase from the time IBM had first approached Gates in mid-1980. Although Don Estridge had become friendly with Gates in 1981 and 1982, even making frequent pilgrimages across country to the Seattle area to see him, Estridge decided that he would try to do a layer of operating-system software that would sit on top of DOS and provide lots of additional capability —such as the ability to run more than one program at once. If he succeeded, Microsoft would control only boring old DOS, while Estridge would control the sexy new features and could control future development. He'd be able to can Microsoft. Microsoft, at only a few million dollars in sales, would have been in no position to fight IBM— if only IBM had been able to get the software to work.

Estridge also saw that while PCs were typically isolated machines at that point, they would increasingly be hooked into networks of PCs and bigger machines, so he commissioned some software that would help link the machines up in networks. Both projects were to be finished in about a year and a half, in time for the introduction of the AT in the summer of 1984.

But IBM made all its typical mistakes. It put far too many programmers on each project, making them spend more time communicating than programming. In addition, IBM management kept letting various parts of the company pull the developers in different directions. The mainframe people insisted that they owned networking, so the PC programmers had to play by mainframe software rules. IBM's marketing groups, which were organized by geography, insisted on variants tailored to all their markets—even if it would take someone a year of work to customize the software for the Turkish market and even if IBM had no hopes of selling anything there.

The PC developers couldn't just shrug off these demands, either. In the bureaucracy that had developed, everybody had a vote on everybody else's project. Essentially, IBM had turned into a company where everyone could say no, and no single person could say yes, and IBMers were considered wimpy if they didn't say no at least a few times on each project—in the IBM lingo, someone disagreeing "nonconcurred." The objections had to work their way up through the ranks until, after weeks or months of meetings, they finally reached someone senior enough to resolve them. Then the answers flowed back down through the chain of command. By late 1983, Estridge's operating system and networking projects were already six to nine months behind schedule. He committed a mercy killing on them. The fact that these projects failed is what opened the way for the disastrous OS/2 software project that by the late 1980s and early 1990s sent Microsoft soaring and IBM reeling.

As Estridge pursued his operating-system and networking projects on his own, Microsoft had continued to do some contract work for IBM related to DOS, but IBM kept changing its mind about whether to make just some small changes and get something to market or to start all over with a much more powerful operating system. By early 1984, IBM had gone into heavy-duty task-force mode. A new software executive named Bob Markell had arrived on the scene to work for Estridge, and, under some corporate pressure, was revising his whole software strategy, including whether to continue to use Microsoft. Rather than have to lie to people at Microsoft about the reevaluation, rumors of which had reached plenty of ears at Microsoft, Markell and his people simply stopped talking to Microsoft for several months in the middle of 1984—even as Microsoft was polishing up an operating system that it thought IBM wanted to bring to market toward the end of 1984. The wasted effort made people at Microsoft from Gates on down wonder whether the executives at IBM had even a clue about what they were doing.

The reevaluation lasted six months but never really went very far. There were a couple of proposals floating around for doing operating systems separate from Microsoft, but it was always pretty clear that IBM would follow the path of least resistance. IBM had been working with Microsoft, and the operating system Microsoft had produced seemed to be doing just fine, so why change? Besides, the failures of the IBM AT software projects made some IBMers gun-shy about trying something entirely on their own—Estridge chief among them, because of his disaster on the Series 1 operating system.

By the end of 1984, Estridge and his boss, Mike Armstrong, had decided to throw out the operating-system work Microsoft had nearly completed and had signed off on the idea of doing a much broader rewrite of DOS, a project that later became known as OS/2. It would let people run more than one program at once—continuing to write a letter, for instance, while printing one in the background. The new version would also take a stab at hiding from the user some of the arcane DOS commands that had turned many early PCs into what people were calling "closet computers"—that is, an angry user would stash the PC in a closet, never to use it again. The new operating system would not have a Macintosh-like graphical interface, though, because Estridge and Armstrong hadn't yet recognized the need. The IBM plan was to bring the new operating system out in mid- to late 1986, which they thought would be in plenty of time to let customers take full advantage of the AT's processor—after all, IBM's mainframe business often brought out new versions of an operating system years after the introduction of the mainframe line they were designed to take advantage of. Armstrong decided that the AT was powerful enough that, with this new operating system coming, it would be the PC business's strategic machine. It would be upgradable whenever better hardware or software became available. Thinking in terms of the seven-year lifetime of a line of mainframes rather than the one-and-a-half-year lifetime that PC products would soon see, Armstrong began describing the AT as a machine that would be around for years and years. Salesmen then sold customers on buying thousands and thousands of ATs, making one of those promises that IBM then couldn't break: that the AT would be at the core of IBM's PC strategy for years to come.

"I made calls on hundreds of customers," Armstrong says. He says that once the AT got rolling, he felt he had to reassure corporate customers about the future of "the absolutely huge installed base of ATs," but adds, "Some people say I made the wrong call. I stand accountable."

With Armstrong and Estridge now staking everything on the future of the AT, the operating-system work got started in late 1984. But, with the bad blood that had developed between IBM and Microsoft, the work began haphazardly. It didn't begin in earnest until Lowe arrived in early 1985, went through the feeling-out process with Gates, and signed the Joint Development Agreement with Microsoft in June of that year. So IBM's work on a new operating system, begun in early 1983, didn't get restarted until more than two years later.

Markell, Estridge's senior software executive, had actually tried to get started earlier by trying to swipe one hundred programmers from an ailing workstation project called the RT, which was part of the PC business. He had sold Estridge on the idea, mainly because Estridge felt the RT would flop and wanted to kill it. But when Lowe came on the scene in early 1985, he decided that IBM procedure called for another task force to study the situation. The programmers stayed put while Lowe vacillated once again. Eventually, he came up with a compromise. He would slowly starve the RT, which could ill afford any more problems, while giving Markell just a handful of people at a time. Markell says that by the end of the first three months of the project, when he was supposed to have sixty or seventy people, he had five. These were just the beginning of the problems that made the birth of OS/2 so difficult.

This latest task force introduced another complication, too, because the programmers Markell got had to stay in Austin, Texas, nowhere near the two main sites where development would be done—Boca

Raton and Redmond, Washington, a suburb of Seattle where Microsoft had by now moved its headquarters. Adding another site helped turn the project into a hodgepodge that never really did get straightened out. Although tiny teams of people living on top of one another were known in the industry to be the best way to create software, the new OS/2 operating system wound up involving more than seventeen hundred programmers working under two separate management structures at four sites on two continents. The problem was so obvious, it should have raised a red flag with *somebody*—with Lowe, with Armstrong, with the Management Committee, with Gates. But Microsoft just wanted IBM's business; it would live with whatever development structure IBM cared to set up. Because of IBM's mainframe heritage, the company was used to dealing with big development teams in different cities, even different countries.

This is a case where IBM's good-citizenship policy hurt it. It wanted to spread its development operations and factories throughout the world and to maintain good relations with the states and countries where it operated. In addition, IBM never wanted to have too many people in one spot, for fear that it would dominate a city too completely, leaving the community vulnerable were it ever to scale back or pull out. This policy, so astute politically, hurt IBM's development operations because it meant that managers had to get used to dealing with little teams of people spread out throughout the IBM empire. The other issue at work here was IBM's success. It had a monopoly on the operating systems that were used to run software applications on its mainframes, letting it charge whatever it wanted for the operating system and making it the largest and most profitable software company in the world. IBMers got confused. They assumed their profitability meant that they wrote good software. In fact, all the earnings meant was that IBM had a monopoly. Once IBM found itself in a hypercompetitive marketplace like the PC business, it took the company a long time to realize that its development process was too slow. To this day, lots of IBMers insist that the company writes great software, even though the company doesn't have a single successful PC software product.

Even in the past couple of years, IBMers who talk about the importance of small, focused teams grouped in one spot tend to talk about the idea as a revelation from on high. Back in 1984, IBMers were so comfortable with the idea of sprawling development operations that no one gave the complicated development arrangement with Microsoft a second thought.

Exacerbating the difficulty in the OS/2 development was the cultural conflict between Microsoft and IBM programmers, which quickly turned into an all-out war. In sharp contrast to the dignity and order at the IBM facility in Boca Raton, the Microsoft people landed in Boca en masse and threw themselves at a problem. They worked around the clock for days at a time, then retired to a condo Microsoft had rented and collapsed, dormitory-style, perhaps six to a room. The Microsoft people dressed casually. They threw Frisbees in the halls at the IBM facility in Boca. A football once crashed into a fire alarm and set it off. Mrs. Fields cookie wrappers littered the hallway near the offices where the Microsoft programmers holed up. They kept coffee machines in their offices, in open defiance of IBM's rules prohibiting them as a fire hazard.

To the IBMers, the group from Redmond, Washington, was scruffy and out of control. The Microsoft programmers seemed to belong in a college dorm, holding "keggers," rather than in the sober offices of IBM. That included Gates and Ballmer, who began having what programmers referred to euphemistically as "car trouble." The two once rushed off to Boca separately and rented cars, then returned to the airport together and somehow forgot about the other car. A couple of weeks later, a representative of Avis called Microsoft and politely asked about the fate of its car.

Another time, Ballmer bumped into an IBMer in Boca who was griping that, as hard as he worked, one guy was always at the office when he got there at 5 A.M. and was still there when he left at midnight. The IBMer wondered who this guy was who worked so hard.

"See that car," he said, pointing to the parking lot. "It's always here. It drives me nuts."

As Ballmer looked at the car, his eyes opened wide. He realized he had rented it a month before and left it there. He slapped himself on the forehead.

"So that's where it went," he said.

Things once got really confused when Ballmer forgot to get his driver's license renewed, so Gates rented a car for Ballmer to drive. Ballmer then misplaced the car. This time, when the rental-car company called Gates to ask about the car he had rented, he really had no idea where it was because Ballmer was the one who had lost it and

Gates didn't remember renting the car for him. Another time, Ballmer's car broke down while he was rushing to the Seattle airport for a flight, so he abandoned the car by the side of the road, flagged down a van, and hitched a ride to the airport.

Gates angered the IBM programmers with his tendency to go way over their heads. Because of the split responsibilities in the IBM-Microsoft work there was no clear way of determining who would win an argument. So if Gates ever got an answer he didn't like about part of the project, he essentially said, Let me talk to someone important. He quickly went to the software executive reporting to Lowe or even to Lowe himself. Eventually, Gates even went over Lowe's head.

Gates won so many battles that the IBM programmers decided that IBM stood for "Intimidated by Microsoft." They also took shots at their bosses in Somers, New York, where Lowe and his staff had offices. The programmers noted the I. M. Pei–designed glass pyramids on the roofs of the Somers buildings, rising above the wooded hills and visible for miles in any direction, and said it was a good thing the pyramids were there—to make room for all the pointy-headed IBM executives.

The IBMers complained, with justification, that the Microsoft programmers were cowboys who had been raised in the early Wild West days of the personal-computer business, saying that they had better start adjusting to a little law and order. The Microsoft programmers weren't big on following the accepted rules of programming. They used whatever tricks they could to get some feature to run fast. Never mind that the trick might be obscure, meaning that someone trying to write an application program using that feature of the operating system might not understand how the trick worked and might write some code that crashed the system. Never mind that the poor programmer who in later years tried to update the operating system might get confused and wreak unintentional havoc. The Microsoft group also didn't bother documenting their work much. One programmer inserted the initials of friends as headers for the sections of code he was writing, to remind himself what the different sections were supposed to accomplish; he knew what the initials stood for and how he had used them, and he didn't much care whether anyone else did. The Microsoft programmers didn't go in much for testing, either. They thought they did, but their testing wasn't up to the standards IBM had developed in its mainframe work over the years.

The IBMers got annoyed, too, when the Microsofties didn't show up for meetings. At IBM, part of the clean-living culture of the company is that meetings start early, at 7:00 or 8:00 A.M. But the programmers at Microsoft might not have knocked off for the night until 6:00 or 7:00 A.M., so if they ever made it to an early IBM meeting, it was only because they had stayed up all night.

Mark Zbikowski, a Microsoft programmer, says that IBMers sometimes called him during their early-morning staff meetings in 1985 and 1986 to ask a question. He'd say, "I'm sorry, but I'm asleep," then cut them off.

The Microsoft programmers returned the IBMers' disdain. They thought that the people from IBM weren't very smart. The group from Microsoft decided IBM stood for "Incredible Bunch of Morons" or "Install Bigger Machines." The Microsofties also found IBM paranoid. They complained that IBMers followed them into bathrooms, lest they overhear some trade secret in there. Several also point to a defining incident that occurred one night when a bunch of them took the long flight to Boca from Seattle, determined to pound away at a whopping problem. When they arrived late in the afternoon, they set up their computers in a cafeteria and settled in for the long haul. But late in the evening, their IBM chaperon left them to use the bathroom and get a cup of coffee. By the time he got back, a security guard had seen that the cafeteria was full of non-IBMers. Even though the cafeteria was hardly full of industrial secrets, even though the Microsoft programmers were wearing visitor badges, and even though they had a plausible story that could easily be checked, the guard noted that no one wearing an IBM badge was present, and so he evicted them all before their chaperon returned. The Microsoft group said, Nuts to this, and went back to their condo to sleep.

Zbikowski says IBM lawyers were everywhere, even as late as 1985, years after the federal antitrust suit ended. When he was chatting about work with an IBM programmer, a lawyer approached them and said they couldn't talk about work on their lunch hour. Zbikowski once went out and had a few beers with some of the IBM programmers after work. The next day, a lawyer lectured the programmers about going out after work with "a vendor." Zbikowski heard one of the programmers yelling into his phone the next day, "Fuck you! What I do on my time is my own fucking business." But when that programmer later invited Zbikowski to a Super Bowl party, a lawyer told the IBMer to uninvite him, and Zbikowski and his IBMer friend complied rather than cause a fuss.

The group from Microsoft complained about IBM's approach to programming, which didn't seem to allow for creativity. The IBM system didn't measure quality because that was too subjective. The system didn't measure speed, either, until the whole project was finished. (IBM tried to focus on speed at the end of the project, but that doesn't work very well—it's hard to make a novel a potboiler if it's been written in pieces by one hundred people in one hundred different styles and nobody has had them concentrate on putting sexy scenes and titillating language into the novel from the beginning.) The IBM system mainly measured how many lines of code someone wrote, which actually encouraged programmers to write inefficient software. (This would be like paying authors by the word, an approach that would have forced you to wade through a lot more words than you're now reading.) Big pieces of software run slowly because they overtax the PC's processor. It's like a lawn mower trying to cut thick grass. It'll eventually work, but it's a pain. Large amounts of software also require computers with lots of memory for storing all the code—which turned out to be a crucial problem in the case of OS/2, because memory chips were very expensive in the mid- to late 1980s when OS/2 was struggling to catch on.

One of the biggest fights the IBM and Microsoft developers had came when a Microsoft developer took a piece of IBM code that required 33,000 characters of space and rewrote it in 200 characters, $1/160$th of the original space. That was considered rude. Other Microsoft developers then rewrote other parts of IBM's code to make it faster and smaller. That was even ruder. IBM managers then began complaining that, according to their measurement system, Microsoft hadn't been pulling its weight. Measured in lines of code, they said, Microsoft was actually doing *negative* work, meaning Microsoft should have been paying IBM for the condensing it was doing.

Microsoft also complained about IBM's unwillingness to change things when problems became apparent. IBMers simply denied that problems existed. Often, the Microsoft programmers said, the IBMers seemed to believe more in the overhead transparencies, or foils, they had prepared to predict the behavior of some software than they did in tests of the software's actual behavior when it was run on a machine. In fact, the real problem was the IBM culture of optimism, which was set by the salesmen who run IBM and those who, as they are groomed for top jobs, run many of the business units within the company. Those salesmen, taught that things always have to be super, eventually discouraged even the typically blunt developers from acknowledging any problems.

Although IBM has some exceptionally sharp developers, it also has more than its share of clunkers. The problem stems from IBM's long-cherished full-employment policy. While programmers at most personal-computer software companies in the mid-1980s were youngsters trained in new languages such as C, most of IBM's good programmers were longtime employees who had initially specialized in older languages, such as Cobol. That's like telling someone who is proficient at languages to switch from translating English into French to translating English into German. That's certainly possible, if the person is given enough time to learn German, but that person will probably never be as good as someone raised to understand the nuances of German. Besides, IBM had also watered down the quality of its programming staff by using it as a dumping ground for people in IBM plants whose jobs had been eliminated. That's like taking an assembly line worker at General Motors and telling him he's going to learn to translate Proust's *Remembrance of Things Past* from French into Swedish. Even if the worker is the smartest person in the world, that's going to be hard.

Encountering these new or newly retrained programmers at IBM shocked people like Zbikowski, the Microsoft programmer who was awakened by IBM phone calls in the morning and who typified the breed Microsoft was sending to Boca Raton in 1985 and 1986. He came from the Gates-Ballmer model of competitive intellects; in fact, he and Ballmer had known each other since they met as thirteen-year-olds at math camp. Unlike the IBM programmers who came from other types of jobs or who were having to be retrained in the new computer languages of the time, Zbikowski had been schooled at Harvard in the latest computer tongues. In the same way that baseball players tend to hit their prime at age twenty-eight or twenty-nine, Zbikowski, who was in his late twenties, was hitting his. He'd been in the business long enough to know the rules but not so long that his base of knowledge had become outdated. He didn't care about IBM's process—he didn't even understand it much—he just cared about the challenge of doing good software. He also cared about getting home and knew that IBM's slowness was resulting in his spending weeks at a time in Boca Raton at a time when he and his wife back in Seattle were trying to have a child.

"Microsoft's model is only good people," says Ed Iacobucci, who was IBM's design manager on the OS/2 project at this point. "If you're not good, you don't stick around. IBM's is more a masses-of-asses kind of program."[1]

The Microsoft programmers began to revolt, complaining to Gates and Ballmer throughout 1985 and 1986 that IBM was too stupid to do business with. Gates and Ballmer held to their prime directive, that they had to keep IBM's business at any cost. So programmers coined the term *Bogu*, which they would call out to Gates and Ballmer anytime they were preparing for a meeting with IBM. The word *Bogu* stood for "bend over and grease up." The term eventually was directed primarily at Ballmer and became *Bogus*, for "bend over and grease up, Steve."

"Steve [Ballmer] went on a real kick to try to get us all to think that the IBM programmers were just like us. It was just that they wore suits," says Gordon Letwin, a senior Microsoft programmer who early on decided that he could never work with IBM again. "I thought that was entirely the wrong approach. It would have been like the U.S. telling its soldiers in World War II that they were just like the Nazi soldiers, except in different uniforms. Meanwhile, the Nazis are committing these horrible war crimes [in their concentration camps]."

By the second half of 1985, the clones also started coming between IBM and Microsoft. Clone makers had begun getting access to the Intel processor chips that were the core of IBM's AT, and IBM was slow to come up with a new trick. Although IBM didn't have a clue yet how serious the problem would be, it did know it hated the idea of clones—and anyone who helped to make them. Microsoft was helping to do that. In the early PC days, Microsoft had been so intimidated by IBM that when Hitachi approached Microsoft about doing a clone, Microsoft steered it toward doing a different sort of system. But Gates, having been far-seeing enough in his early dealings with IBM to make sure he could sell DOS to all comers, was now cheerfully helping any and all PC makers ensure that the same DOS operating system that ran on IBM machines could also run on theirs.

As the tension grew, IBM continued to explore ways of divorcing Microsoft. For instance, a senior IBM scientist surfaced in 1985 with a plan to give up on doing an operating system for the AT generation of hardware that was the target of the work Lowe and Gates were doing jointly and stake out a position with an operating system for the next-generation Intel chip, known as the 80386. That sounded too risky to Lowe. (Something like the scientist's plan could have worked. Doing its own PC operating system from scratch would have required, of course, that IBM be able to produce an acceptable one—a skill that IBM has yet to demonstrate. But setting up an Estridge-like operation that was allowed to break all the rules of software development and bash something together could have succeeded. Even if it hadn't, some-one trying new things and looking outside IBM to see how the rest of the PC world did software might have uncovered the flaws in IBM's operating system work long before IBM recognized that it even had a problem. As it was, IBM didn't make any fundamental changes in its software work until 1991, six years after the scientist's proposal.) Ru-mors of the scientist's plan and the other IBM attempts to distance itself from Microsoft always seemed to find their way back to Redmond, Washington, setting Gates to rocking back and forth even more than usual.

Gates went on the offensive by pushing Windows against IBM's TopView, the incipient OS/2, and all other contenders. He needed IBM's support for Windows because, even though he had finally man-aged to get the product out the plant door in late 1985, Windows didn't seem to be going anywhere. The product was so late that, when it finally became available, some industry luminaries held a roast at the fall Comdex trade show in Las Vegas, turning up the heat even beyond the ninety-degree temperatures outside the convention center. One joked that Windows took so long to produce that the bald Ballmer, who had been losing his hair for ten years, had had a full head of hair when the project began. Gates decided Windows could benefit from the sort of boost IBM gave DOS, so he sent letters, made speeches, called people at IBM, all pushing the idea that his Windows would make a great interface for this fancy new version of DOS that was to come out soon. Finally, toward the end of 1985, the tension eased. IBM had shown a glimmer of interest.

In early 1986, Gates finally convinced Lowe and Armstrong of the importance of all this touchy-feely "gooey" stuff—"gooey" being the way people pronounce *gui*, which stands for "graphical user interface." Lowe and Armstrong didn't see just how quickly the PC world would move toward graphical interfaces, but they did know that the clones were giving them fits and that they were desperate for a way to make their PCs look different. They told Gates: Give us some of that gooey stuff.

Things were not, of course, that simple. IBM had made a public commitment to TopView, so it couldn't just trash the project even though it was already apparent that it was a bad idea. Lowe's software executives insisted that Windows be redone so it could run programs written for TopView—never mind that that's like saying a CD player's laser has to be redesigned to play records. IBM and Microsoft trusted each other so little at this point that IBM wouldn't help Microsoft figure out TopView, and Microsoft didn't want to buy any rights from IBM. When an IBMer joked that maybe Microsoft should go buy itself a TopView clone, Ballmer did. He spent $3 million to buy a little company with a TopView clone called Mondrian. (Even this turned out to be golden for Microsoft. While TopView disappeared as an issue within months, meaning Microsoft had no use for its $3 million TopView clone, the dozen people at the little company included some who now hold senior positions at Microsoft and whom Gates has described as among the company's best hires ever.)

Once Microsoft got going on combining TopView with Windows, the cast of characters at IBM started to change once again as software executive Ed Kfoury arrived on the scene. Just a few weeks after Gates won a preliminary endorsement of Windows that might have smoothed over the differences between IBM and Microsoft that would cost IBM so dearly, the IBM position began to shift one more time. Kfoury is an affable sort, full of stories about sailing and other adventures outside IBM. He is short, round, and bald, with a snort of a laugh and a gravelly voice that make him resemble the cockney detective played by Bob Hoskins in the movie *Who Framed Roger Rabbit?* Gates and Ballmer liked Kfoury when they had dinner with him and Lowe in early 1986 in a suite on the top floor of La Reserve Hotel, a fancy establishment in White Plains with a view out over the rolling hills that hold the bedroom communities north of New York City. The catch was that Kfoury, like many of the executives now being run through the IBM PC business, came from "big iron," the mainframe business. When he heard all this talk about graphics, he thought of his IBM friends in Hursley, England, who developed mainframe graphics and, in IBM's territorial world, assumed that meant they owned *all* the graphics IBM produced. Suddenly, Microsoft found that Windows might not be used as the interface for IBM and Microsoft's new OS/2 operating system. Gates and Ballmer had to compete with Hursley for the right to supply the graphical interface.

Gates and Ballmer kept after Kfoury about some technical issues in early 1986 and after a few weeks got what Ballmer calls "a verbal handshake," saying they'd won the business to do the interface for what became OS/2. But Hanrahan—he of the purple pine trees—quickly arrived on the scene as a senior executive, and IBM's position changed again. Hanrahan, another mainframe type, proceeded to grill Gates and Ballmer so thoroughly that he set them to pacing in the cold wind outside his office in White Plains. He, more than anyone else, kept calling into question whether IBM should even be messing around with Microsoft.

Gates had to really pick up his selling—more trips to White Plains, more letters, more phone calls. Finally, after a few weeks, Hanrahan decided he, at least, wouldn't throw Microsoft out on its ear. But Kfoury felt he needed to renegotiate part of the Joint Development Agreement, even though it was less than nine months old. Lowe had finally realized that the clones were going to be a bigger presence than he had thought. Kfoury wanted to renegotiate the royalty structure to give IBM a bigger share.

Gates erupted. Why, he wanted to know, did IBM want to toss a grenade into the middle of an already-complicated relationship that was straining to produce a complex operating system?

Kfoury remained adamant. He began to hold the joint development work hostage until Gates conceded on the royalty issue. But Gates, who knew he had the better end of the joint venture, was in no hurry to cave in.

So in the spring of 1986, IBM went back into task-force mode on its operating-system strategy for the third time since 1980, and the IBM-Microsoft relationship went into what Microsoft called the "Black Hole"—nobody at Microsoft heard from IBM for months. It didn't help that Microsoft had its initial public stock offering during this period, making Gates, Ballmer, and some other senior Microsoft executives rich beyond the comprehension of the executives on the IBM side. Gates alone became worth $311 million on the first day the stock traded publicly, and the figure only increased from there. Even lower-level people became wealthy, and they flaunted their good fortune by wearing buttons that said FYIFV—which stood for "fuck you, I'm fully vested." The IBM executives couldn't understand. They felt sure they were more important than anyone from this little company way off in the Pacific Northwest. Some IBM executives also felt they had created Microsoft and wondered why they hadn't become wealthy, too. The IBMers couldn't see that being smart wasn't enough, getting a big office at IBM wasn't enough, working hard and following the rules wasn't enough; the only way to succeed the way Gates and the others at Microsoft had was to be willing to take risks the way they had.

The biggest problem for the relationship occurred, though, as Earl Wheeler grew in influence throughout 1986. Wheeler, another big-iron software executive who was running IBM's multibillion-dollar software business, had no direct involvement in the PC business; he had his own business, which was just on a par with PCs in the IBM structure. But Wheeler had wide influence and was about to find a way to impose on the PC business what IBMers describe as a semimystical vision for the future of IBM's software and hardware development.

The vision became reality because of an advertisement. Hated rival Digital Equipment kept running an ad that shouted, "Digital Has It Now!" as a way of proclaiming that, while it was notoriously hard to get IBM equipment to talk to other types of IBM equipment, it was easy to get Digital's machines to talk to one another. IBM, the ads would say, talked a lot about improved networking abilities for its machines, but "Digital Has It Now!" Whenever IBM was making some networking announcement, the ads appeared: "Digital Has It Now!" When IBM hauled its biggest corporate customers off to a meeting in Orlando, Florida, to talk about product plans, DEC took out double-page ads in the local paper every day. "Digital Has It Now!" IBM was sick of it, and Wheeler thought he had a solution.

The drab Wheeler is a caricature of the IBM executive. He is tall and carries himself as stiffly as he did when he spent two years in the air force in the late 1950s. In meetings, he is gentlemanly but cold. He is demanding—some of his staff refer to him as "Earl Wants." Wheeler, more than any other senior IBMer, talks in the IBM code of three-letter acronyms. When talking to outsiders, at least those without degrees in computer science, he requires a translator. He has little sense of humor.

Once, when he was being interviewed by a *Business Week* reporter, he did get himself a little worked up, describing a piece of software as a power nozzle on a vacuum cleaner that would pull all kinds of data into the mainframe. The *Business Week* reporter, a wise guy, said, "Earl, I think your analogy sucks." Everyone in the room burst out laughing, except Wheeler, who got red in the face and asked if he'd done anything wrong.

Wheeler joined IBM as a junior engineer in the mid-1950s. He actually got to learn some programming skills in the air force, where he spent two years to fulfill an ROTC obligation.[2] Once back at IBM, he began to make his reputation when he came up with a quick and dirty way to get a major piece of software out the door after others had become bogged down in trying to do it. Wheeler's software turned out to work too slowly even for the taste of IBM salesmen, who rather liked selling slow software because it made customers need more main-frames. The software was eventually rewritten, but Wheeler had already earned some praise and moved on to the next project. That project turned out to be the 360 mainframe line that Tom Watson, Jr., brought out in the mid-1960s and that made IBM golden for decades. Although the operating system for the 360 was so late that Watson thought the company might go down the tubes, Wheeler wasn't senior enough at that point to catch the blame. He then began slowly working his way up the ladder, almost the way a politician would. He worked hard so that anytime there was a senior opening in a research or software position, he influenced who filled it—for instance, Wheeler had a lot to do with putting Hanrahan into his position as the vice president for software in the PC division. That way, by the time he got to the senior software position at IBM, he had a whole network of important execu-tives who felt beholden to him, not only in his big software business but in the development labs of the various other businesses—mainframes, minicomputer, personal computers, communications equipment, and so on. He didn't have any clear influence with the sales force in the countries around the world where IBM operated. He also didn't have anyone beholden to him at corporate headquarters. But he even had considerable power with the salespeople and with the corporate bosses for a reason incomprehensible to anyone who has ever heard or seen how bad a public speaker he is—he drones on in excruciating detail about the joys of CICS, LU6.2, or MVS/ESA. But he was known around

IBM as a good speaker. Essentially, he was able to take complex ideas and distill them to a few simple ones. In a company run by salesmen who didn't understand the technical complexities and needed relatively easy concepts to grasp, that ability was incredibly important—even though there was no guarantee that Wheeler had boiled things down to the right ideas and little way for his salesmen bosses to check.

Wheeler built up so much authority over IBM's software operations that he could afford to be one of the most direct of IBM's senior managers. One former executive says, for instance, that when Wheeler ran a project that became the 8100 mainframe, he worked ruthlessly to kill competition. When the former executive, much more junior than Wheeler, went to talk to him armed with a folderful of all his technical information supporting a rival project, Wheeler demanded the folder and never gave it back. When listening to proposals for software projects that didn't fit his vision, he didn't just work behind the scenes to have them mysteriously killed. He told the person flat out, "No, I'm not going to let you do that." End of discussion.

In responding to the Digital ads, Wheeler boiled things down to the point where he argued that he could solve IBM's networking problems by adding a thin layer of software on top of some IBM operating systems and by disciplining the software writing process—a powerful idea, if he could pull it off.

Wheeler had, however, boiled the problem down to the wrong issues. For one thing, he had taken a typically IBM-centric view of the world. He was running around trying to figure out ways to make IBM machines talk to one another over dedicated lines, when customers wanted something much broader: They wanted their IBM machines to talk to their Digital machines, their Hewlett-Packard machines, their Sun workstations, and so forth. (When, in 1986, customers were for the first time invited to address a planning session of IBM's senior management, one put up a slide that showed his far-flung computer operations. IBM equipment was in almost all the key spots controlling the network, but the network also included all sorts of non-IBM equipment. The executive told the IBMers that he was going to tie it all together with or without them but would rather do it with them. People in the room talk of the revelation that seemed to hit everyone simultaneously—there really was a lot of non-IBM equipment even in big IBM accounts, and IBM needed to deal with that reality. But the idea that IBM needed to help hook alien equipment up to its machines took a long time to sink in, especially for members of the old guard, such as Wheeler.) Instead of focusing just on an internal problem, Wheeler should have been working to adopt industry-standard ways of letting machines talk to one another.

The plan Wheeler pushed also tended to smother any development project, because it forced IBM equipment to the lowest common denominator. Even if some IBM hardware system was constructed in such a way that programmers could take shortcuts in writing software for them, the Wheeler blueprint made people take the long way around— other IBM hardware might not allow for those shortcuts, and Wheeler wanted to make software writing techniques identical on all systems. The blueprint needed to be all-inclusive, so Wheeler's people got bogged down in trying to deal with old technologies, such as the dumb terminals that mainframe customers used to use. Never mind that the terminals were disappearing fast and that Wheeler's schemes could have allowed for much faster communication and more powerful software if they could have been tuned to fit newer, PC-based technologies.

Wheeler's blueprint, called Systems Application Architecture—or SAA, given that there had to be a three-letter acronym—also took far too long to unfold. He concocted the idea in 1985, but it took him a year to sell it internally and another year to get it ready to unveil. When the announcement came in 1987, it was merely a promise to deliver some documents with specifications on how software would be developed. Those weren't ready for almost another year. It took years more to churn out additional inches-thick development manuals in gray binders.

By now, lots of the manuals have been finished, but the world looks very different from what it did when Wheeler got started. Customers have IBM shifting away from its proprietary approaches and toward the industry's standard ways of hooking machines together. In the meantime, SAA's dogmatic approach has helped ruin some development projects, such as the IBM-Microsoft OS/2 venture. The original reason for SAA—Digital and its in-your-face ads—has long since ceased to be a factor. But nobody could tell Wheeler that back in early 1986. He had so much clout that he was referred to as the eight-hundred-pound gorilla at corporate, who could sit on anyone he chose.

Wheeler used his weight to kill even TopView, despite its having been declared strategic as recently as 1984 and despite IBM's aversion to breaking promises. Wheeler decided that, as part of SAA, the world would go "gooey"—with interfaces vaguely resembling the graphical approach of the Macintosh—so TopView and its menus of text weren't good enough anymore. While killing TopView was a good move, Wheeler still tried to carry far too much baggage with him into the new world of graphical interfaces. He decided he needed to allow for all the dumb terminals IBM customers used, so he felt he had to design SAA to use their severely limited way of dealing with graphic images. That meant Wheeler decreed Microsoft and its Windows were out again, and, as of mid-1986, IBM's Hursley group was back in.

Word filtered back to Gates that he had a problem. He didn't realize just how severe it was, but, in his forceful way, he started selling again. He wrote letters to Lowe and most anyone else he could think of, arguing that Windows was the way to go for a graphical interface, that IBM and Microsoft had shaped the industry together, and that IBM shouldn't do anything to jeopardize their joint success.

Then Gates got a break. Chairman John F. Akers told a group of securities analysts that he'd get out of the PC industry if it ever became a "commodity" business—meaning one in which it wasn't possible to use IBM's technological prowess to differentiate its products from competitors and in which manufacturers competed primarily by cutting prices. The ever-opportunistic Gates wrote a letter to Akers in mid-1986 saying that PCs needn't be commodities, if IBM would only use its semiconductor expertise in Burlington, Vermont, and Fishkill, New York, to differentiate its chips from those Intel was making available to the clones and if the company would produce operating-system improvements fast enough to take advantage of whatever special features IBM could build into its chips. Gates offered to meet with Akers to explain in greater detail what he meant. Akers liked Gates, especially early on in their relationship. He, in fact, had asked Gates whether he'd like to follow his mother onto the national board of the United Way, then had gotten Gates placed on the board. So Akers agreed to have lunch with Gates.

This forced Lowe's hand. It was one thing for IBM to be keeping people from talking to Gates on the IBM-Microsoft joint development project, but it was another thing for Gates to have lunch with the IBM chairman thinking that the relationship would continue, when it was, in fact, mostly over. So Lowe asked Gates to come by and meet with him the day before the Akers lunch, in early July 1986.

The meeting with Lowe was one of the crucial moments in the IBM-Microsoft relationship. Gates and Ballmer went to meet Lowe at the main IBM building in White Plains. The building was typical IBM: low and blocky, buried in the middle of the town. Lowe had moved the PC headquarters there so he would be just a few miles down the road from headquarters in Armonk, a decision that completed corporate headquarters' attempts to bring the PC group into step with the rest of the business. So many people shared this building that several talk of the epiphany that occurred when there was a fire drill around this time and the full one thousand or so people in the building wound up standing outside together in the cold. All these blue-suit, white-shirt types, knowing they were on the fast track because they had headquarters jobs, stood there and stared at one another, wondering, Who are all these guys?

When Gates and Ballmer arrived, they went into a modest conference room with light veneer pine paneling next to Lowe's office. Lowe, with a few assistants watching, took an hour and a half to say that Wheeler's SAA blueprint required that Hursley's graphics approach be used up and down the whole IBM product line and that tying Hursley's approach together with the Windows approach to graphics wouldn't work. Lowe delivered his devastating conclusion: Microsoft had lost the business of doing the graphical interface that would let users interact with what everyone in the room expected would be the next generation of PC operating system.

Microsoft, he said, could continue to do some piecework on the base operating system. But it would be locked out of doing the most innovative piece of the new system. In addition, IBM for the first time would be heading off on its own, which meant it probably wouldn't need Microsoft again.

Lowe called for a break in the meeting to give Gates a chance to think about how to respond.

John Sabol, the Gates assistant who took notes in the meeting, says, "Bill didn't immediately realize that we'd lost the whole goddamn war, so he was just thinking away. Ballmer was panicky."

The meeting reconvened after forty-five minutes. Gates was on edge. He said later that his message to IBM was: "We're flexible guys! We're flexible guys! Test our flexibility!" But he stayed under control enough to lay out a complicated scheme that showed how to overcome the technical problems in combining the Hursley and Microsoft approaches to graphics. Gates also explained how his approach should prevent developers from deviating from IBM's SAA blueprint.

Despite his nervousness, "Bill was completely rational in explaining how to deal with the problem," says Sabol, who described the approach as the slickest riff of technical improvisation he has ever seen Gates pull off. "Bill Lowe, being a thoroughly rational guy, too, said that sounded okay."

The lunch with Akers the next day, which Lowe had supposed would seal Gates's fate, instead turned into a love-in. Rather than be locked into just part of the market for PC operating systems, Gates got the chance to develop products for the whole market, an opportunity he seized to turn Microsoft into a powerhouse controlling the entire PC software business. Lowe followed up later by flying out to the Seattle suburbs for a pleasant dinner with Gates at his home on the shores of Lake Washington. Gates, seemingly just thinking out loud, soon raised once again the prospect that he would wipe out Windows and just focus on the work with IBM.

The reprieve didn't last long. IBM's developers decided that Hursley/ Windows really spelled Hursley, while Gates and Ballmer decided it spelled Windows. Ballmer said publicly that any future operating systems from IBM and Microsoft would run applications written for Windows, essentially promising that Windows would survive the compromise intact. Nathan Myhrvold, a senior Microsoft developer, was so sure that the Hursley approach would fall by the wayside that he told people he'd rig the new operating system so that if anyone ever did something that used the Hursley approach, a little window would appear on the person's screen providing Myhrvold's home number and instructing, "Call Nathan collect."[3] But Wheeler, "the eight-hundred-pound gorilla," had begun sitting on people. He was going to make the Hursley approach stick because, by God, that was what SAA called for.

So many other fights erupted between IBM and Microsoft that Gates began referring to his relationship with IBM as "riding the bear."

Perhaps the greatest friction occurred because it was turning out that designing OS/2 to run on PCs that used the AT processor built some severe limitations into the OS/2 operating system. The largest of the problems was that many of the software applications designed to run on DOS wouldn't run on machines using OS/2, and so many customers had bought so many DOS-based applications that it would be hard to convince people to throw those away just for the pleasure of using OS/2. By late 1986, Gates wanted to solve the problem by skipping the AT processor and designing OS/2 to run on PCs using the next-generation processor, the 80386. An OS/2 designed for the 80386 would have run all DOS applications just fine because it was a much better-designed chip than the AT processor. But Armstrong couldn't go along with Gates. He had given customers one of those grand IBM promises about the strategic importance of the AT, so he couldn't do anything innovative that excluded the AT.

As 1986 progressed, the tension rose. At one meeting with IBM, Ballmer wrote notes to himself in the margins of some printed material, saying things such as, "Bill [Gates] to calm down" and "Shut up, Steve [Ballmer]?" Ballmer also warned himself that IBM "will personalize. [This] can get personal." He added that "Jay is superpissed," a reference to an IBM executive named Jay Martinson, who was widely disliked at Microsoft.

Eventually, IBM and Microsoft produced an awkward compromise. They designed OS/2 to run on the AT, as IBM wanted, but they added something called the "compatibility box," which was designed to help OS/2 run old PC applications built to run on DOS. It didn't work. OS/2 wouldn't run lots of the old DOS applications. In addition, the compatibility box would run only one DOS application package at a time—which tried-and-true DOS already did. Why bother switching to OS/2? Armstrong wound up with the worst possible outcome. In fulfilling his promise to customers about the strategic value of the AT, he generated an operating system that didn't run well enough on the AT to keep those customers happy and didn't work well on more advanced PCs, either. The focus on the AT turned out to be the biggest problem for OS/2.

Even within IBM, scuffles broke out in mid-1986 over the misguided operating-system strategy. Markell, who had been brought in as a senior software executive of Lowe's, told Lowe and Armstrong that adding a graphical interface to OS/2 was too radical a step to take right away. Markell and some other IBM software executives said that they should be allowed to finish what they were doing, get something out into the marketplace, and only then start contemplating doing a graphical interface. The software executives contended in a months-long series of meetings, full of overhead transparencies, that IBM was confusing its customers and independent software companies by continually giving them early versions of OS/2 so they could start developing applications that would run on OS/2, only to tell them repeatedly to throw out the work they'd done because IBM had decided to start over again on OS/2 to make it newer, better, and more advanced. Markell and the other software executives argued in mid-1986 that it would take another year or so to finish work on the new operating system, then it would take years more for corporate customers to write software using it. The confusion would also delay the writing of applications by independent software companies, Markell and the others warned, and the degree of availability of good applications would determine whether OS/2 succeeded. Look what happened with Apple's Macintosh, they said. They contended that writing applications using a graphical interface was so complicated that a lack of software meant the Mac was only now beginning to catch on in 1986, even though it had been in the market for two and a half years. If IBM wasn't careful, Markell and the others warned, it could wind up having little useful new software until the late 1980s for a PC—the AT—that had been available since 1984.

Although even Markell turned out to be wildly optimistic—little interesting software had appeared for OS/2 as of mid-1993—Armstrong didn't buy the arguments. As a marketing guy, he just knew that the market had changed, so IBM needed to immediately follow the market toward graphical interfaces—given that IBM once again had failed to anticipate customers' needs and had to play catch-up with more prescient competitors. The Mac argument didn't faze Armstrong, either. It was doing just fine by mid-1986. IBM, he said, should learn from Apple's mistakes and help application writers get software out faster than Apple did. The unspoken theme of Armstrong's argument was the standard "IBM owns the future" attitude. Customers would wait for IBM to complete its operating system, Armstrong seemed to think. They always did.

The clincher for Armstrong and Lowe was that, with the clones coming on, they had to find some way to differentiate their hardware from the clones. IBM had a multibillion-dollar business to protect. Armstrong and Lowe thought that having a nice graphical interface to their operating system would help. They also planned to do some pieces of the new operating system on their own, apart from Microsoft. Those pieces would let users of IBM PCs set up data bases and communicate with networks of IBM PCs and mainframes. Armstrong and Lowe planned to make customers wonder just how well the pieces would run on clones' hardware.

Markell argued that it wasn't possible to differentiate hardware by using software. If the software ran on IBM computers, he said, it would run on all the clones, too. So where was the advantage?

"It's probably my greatest failing that I couldn't convince people that this would be a disaster," Markell says. "I got so upset that I got out [in 1987]."

Armstrong acknowledges now that he spent too much time trying to make OS/2 "enterprise-attractive" rather than "desktop-competitive." (Translation: IBM was trying too hard to tie PCs into the network of IBM mainframes at the core of most businesses, rather than just focusing on what users wanted on their desktop computers.) Back in 1986, though, he and Lowe insisted that their programmers restart their work on OS/2. So what started out in 1983 as a simple project to produce an operating system by the 1984 introduction of the AT had been rethought in 1984, restarted in 1985, and now started again in 1986.

Important customers were confused. Application software companies were mad. Gates and Microsoft were both confused and mad. That wasn't the end of the trouble, either. Throughout all the jousting between IBM and Microsoft over the new graphical interface, IBM was allowing Microsoft to proceed with a limited form of the new operating system, which would at least get something on the market that would use some of the AT's capabilities. IBM was pretty sure it no longer wanted that version, but IBM, still trying to get Gates back to the bargaining table to talk about royalties, continued to hold such information hostage. Armstrong and Lowe also didn't entirely trust Microsoft, so they didn't tell Gates and Ballmer much about plans for new PCs coming in 1987 that wouldn't be able to run the operating-system version Microsoft was producing. So Microsoft kept pounding away at the software, testing it, tuning it for speed. The plan was for a December

1986 introduction, but IBM killed that version shortly before the planned introduction. Microsoft's vain efforts meant that, because IBM couldn't figure out whether Microsoft was an enemy or a friend, the Microsoft portion of the work on OS/2 would now have to begin anew in 1987.

All the delays and friction between IBM and Microsoft postponed the full version of OS/2, with its graphical interface, until late 1988, and customers paid no attention even once it finally reached the market. The product, designed for use even by people doing catalogs of CDs or whatever at home, required a shelf of manuals and had to be shipped to customers on more than a dozen diskettes, intimidating even the technical people at companies and computer dealers who tried to install OS/2. Rather than pricing OS/2 cheaply—the way Microsoft had made DOS ubiquitous—IBM charged $340. The product required so much memory that people also had to buy two thousand dollars' worth of extra memory just to let it run. In fact, the product turned out to be too slow actually to run on AT-class machines, so anyone planning to use OS/2 either had to have a more powerful, 80386-based system or trash his less powerful computer and spend several thousand dollars on a new one. IBM and Microsoft had started out trying to build a fighter jet of an operating system, but they disliked and distrusted each other so much that they wound up with a sort of *Spruce Goose*. They produced the world's heaviest PC operating system. It could fly, but just barely, and was more likely to wind up in a museum someplace.

Software applications running on OS/2 didn't trickle into the market until 1989 and 1990. Those, too, turned out to be dogs. Customers disdained the extra pieces of software IBM did on its own for OS/2, which IBM called the Extended Edition of OS/2, and IBM eventually dropped the Extended Edition. IBM didn't get a reasonably usable version of OS/2 out until spring 1992—nine years after the work began. The world was so different by then that, despite having decent technology, the product couldn't possibly succeed.

IBM and Microsoft compounded the problem by making bold predictions at the announcement of OS/2 in April 1987 and in the following months about how the system would quickly supplant DOS, capturing 90 percent of the PC operating-system market within a few years. The companies would be held to those predictions in the days to come, leaving OS/2 with the smell of failure. IBM got OS/2 off to an awful start, too, because Lowe, insisting on a return on all the investment he'd pumped into OS/2, pushed to get some version on the market as soon as possible. The version was so preliminary that Brian Proffit, an OS/2 manager at IBM at the time, says no other company would have tried to sell it to customers. He says the version, called OS/2 1.0, should have been labeled a developer's kit and sent around for free to programmers at corporations and at software companies to help them do applications that ran on OS/2.

"If we sold thirty copies of that version of OS/2 I'd be amazed," Proffit says.

With market researchers swarming over anything IBM did, the world quickly figured out that OS/2 was off to a bad start. Philippe Kahn, president of Borland, a large and influential software company, labeled OS/2 as "BS/2."[4]

If IBM had divorced Microsoft at any number of points along the way, it might have initially had problems, but it also might have figured out how to address them. If IBM had embraced Microsoft, it might have created a decent product. Instead, IBM made a halfhearted divorce and offered a halfhearted embrace. IBM wound up with a bad product and an angry partner.

The problems with OS/2 were getting costly, too, even for a company like IBM with seemingly bottomless pockets. By early 1987, IBM had more than one thousand programmers on the project, meaning it was spending more than $125 million annually. (This is straightforward math. The rule of thumb for years had been that a programmer costs a company $100,000 to $125,000 a year, when salary, benefits, office space, and equipment such as a workstation are all included. IBM has always been at the high end of that range. Thus the math: $1,000 \times \$125,000 = \$125$ million.) Although the initial plan had been for a modest software project, IBM had already spent several hundred million dollars on its false starts.

Gates continued to try to convince the world that everything was fine in his relationship with IBM, that somehow IBM's announcement of OS/2's graphical interface meant it was endorsing his struggling Windows project. In fact, Gates, not someone from IBM, wound up on the cover of *Business Week* the following week, even though the real news was that IBM had rethought its entire PC strategy and Gates was just a small part of that. The *Business Week* headline proclaimed Gates the

BILLION-DOLLAR WHIZ KID, and the story said he had sold IBM on using Windows as the basis for OS/2. But that wasn't true. Gates continued to sell as hard as he could to make it true, but the Windows problem would expand over the years to the point where it split IBM and Microsoft apart—and IBM, not Microsoft, would lose.

In addition to all its other blunders, IBM, in the midst of all its dealings with Microsoft, also made the single-most-expensive mistake that its PC business ever made. The mistake came in mid-1986 when Gates offered to let IBM buy a piece of Microsoft. He thought that might tie the two companies together more closely, because Microsoft would feel more beholden to IBM, and IBM would benefit if Microsoft prospered. Maybe that would stop the endless bickering.

Gates and Lowe never got very specific, but the general idea was that IBM buy 10 percent of Microsoft. Lowe initially seemed interested. There was even a precedent, because IBM had bought similar stakes in Intel and Rolm. But following the initial Gates-Lowe conversation, Lowe came back and said he'd pass. The sting of the U.S. antitrust suit was still great enough that Lowe didn't want to be seen as throwing IBM's weight around too much by gaining some control over Microsoft. Completely misunderstanding how the PC market would develop, Lowe said IBM didn't want to be seen as dominating the PC market too thoroughly.

If IBM had bought 10 percent of Microsoft at mid-1986 prices, that would have cost it less than $100 million—small change for a company that earned more than $6.5 billion in 1985. That 10 percent would today be worth nearly $3 billion, so the investment would have earned IBM more than it has earned over the entire history of its PC business.

SIX

In late 1986, *Computer Reseller News,* a trade publication, did a survey of its readers and found that 15 percent of them said they owned an IBM PC 2 personal computer. The thing was, the PC 2 didn't even exist, nor would it ever.

The readers could be forgiven their confusion; the press had spent so many months speculating about when IBM would bring out a new generation of PCs—dubbed "PC 2"—that the new machines had begun to seem real to lots of people. As everybody remotely associated with the PC industry knew, IBM had to do *something* to its line of PCs. It had been more than two years since IBM had announced its workhorse AT. In the meantime, while IBM had once seemed to own the PC market, the onslaught by the clones that started in late 1985 had cut IBM's share of PC sales to business customers from more than 70 percent to less than 40 percent. In September 1986, little Compaq had slapped IBM in the face by coming to New York City, in the middle of IBM country, to stage an extravagant announcement of a PC that used the next-generation Intel 80386 chip and that operated several times as fast as IBM's most powerful machine, the AT. As lasers flashed around the room in a Manhattan disco, it was clear that customers loved the additional horsepower in the Compaq machines and that Compaq would steal lots of sales from IBM. More important, it seemed that Compaq might be stealing the technology leadership of the PC industry from IBM. Everyone in the audience was cautious because they knew that the computer industry landscape had been littered over the years with the corpses of companies that had dared to challenge IBM, only to have IBM quickly produce a better product and steal all the upstart's customers. But as the weeks and then months went by without even the hint of a response from IBM, everyone involved in the computer industry began to wonder when IBM would finally *do* something. Whatever new PCs IBM produced would not only determine IBM's future in the business but would also define the future of the PC hardware business for years to come.

Guessing when IBM would act had become the great spectator sport in the industry, with analysts trying to establish their prescience by picking the date. One said January 1987; another, February; a third, April. All sounded positive, although, of course, they couldn't disclose their sources. Some guesses were absurdly specific. One analyst had the announcement pegged for halftime at the Super Bowl.

In fact, everybody was wrong. IBM had planned to get the new line out so fast that "we'd take the market by storm," says Mike Armstrong, the boss of Bill Lowe, who ran the PC business. Armstrong says the initial plan was to announce a new line of PCs in August 1986 and have huge volumes available for the Christmas buying season. If IBM had succeeded, it might have taken competitors by storm, but all the usual problems set in.

Lowe was trying to use mostly IBM technology in his new line—in sharp contrast to the approach he had advocated when he described to the Management Committee his plan for the original PC back in 1980. Lowe had now decided that IBM needed to start drawing on its corporate research capabilities so it could step up the pace of progress in the PC industry and move its own products beyond the capabilities of what IBM saw as the rinky-dink, off-the-shelf parts available from outside suppliers. (Lowe somehow ignored the fact that throughout the 1970s IBM had fallen on its face in the PC business because it had been too slow to turn its technology into products to *match* the pace of those outside suppliers, let alone to outrace them.) Lowe also felt he needed to make his PC business adopt more of the discipline of the processes used in the mainframe business.

"We concluded as a team that prevailing in PCs was not that different from prevailing in the rest of the computer business," Armstrong says.

Once Lowe introduced the mainframe mentality into the PC business, however, the heavy schedules of meetings and turf battles that resulted ensured that progress slowed. Development of the new line of PCs lagged on so many fronts that Lowe wasn't even close to making his August 1986 announcement timetable. He rescheduled part of the announcement for late January 1987—the product manager did, in fact, buy advertising time during the halftime show of the Super Bowl, hoping to recreate the attention Apple had received with its "Big Brother" ad introducing the Macintosh three years earlier. Lowe came closer to meeting that schedule but decided at the last minute to pull the ad so he could have a task force study whether to include some circuitry known as the Micro Channel in all the new PCs or just some of them.

His attitude was that he'd rather be right than be early. Besides, customers would wait for IBM to decide what it wanted to do. They always had. Lowe would find out soon enough, however, that the PC business wasn't at all like the mainframe business. It was better to be early than to be right. And no customer would wait for any manufacturer, not even IBM.

Lowe's predecessor in the PC job, Don Estridge, had a very different plan back in late 1984 and early 1985. Rather than get fancy and try to outmarket the clones, he wanted to beat them on raw speed. He began pushing a plan that would have rendered everyone's PC product line obsolete, including his own. Estridge always wanted to be first to reach the market with new technology, as he had been with the original PC and with the AT, so he wanted to bring out a line based on the seductive next-generation Intel 80386 processor, which would soon be available in sample quantities. He figured he could announce machines using the new chip so fast that clone makers would take several quarters to recover. By the time they caught up, he figured he'd be working on something else.

Estridge planned to take advantage of his most-favored-nation status with Intel to get access to early samples and to get the sort of technical help he needed if he was to develop a machine well ahead of the pack. He also planned to buy up the early production of the 80386 to gain the sort of time that his big purchases of the prior-generation chip had given him on the AT. Estridge told colleagues in Boca Raton that, from the day of his new line's announcement forward, he wanted the world to understand that all earlier PCs, including IBM's, were now just toys.

However, having become the head of an official division in 1983, Estridge was no longer as free to do whatever he wanted as he had been when he ran the original PC project. Instead of having a direct line to the chairman as he had had in the early days, by late 1984 Estridge reported to Armstrong, who reported to a member of the Management Committee, who reported to the president, who, finally, reported to the chairman, John Opel. By the time Estridge worked his way through all those levels, it was much harder to win approval for a radical notion like his plan for the 80386.

The early versions of the 80386 chip cost hundreds of dollars apiece, so it was easy to see designing them into high-end PCs that cost close to ten thousand dollars. But it was another thing to plan a complete line around the 80386, including low-end machines that cost $2,500—given that the processor is just one sliver of silicon in a system that includes not only dozens of other chips but also expensive devices ranging from the disk drives to the monitor. The processor alone would have accounted for more than a quarter of IBM's costs in manufacturing a low-end PC. Armstrong and Estridge's other bosses decided that the profit margins on his 80386 machines would be unacceptably thin and so they killed the plan.

The senior executives, all ex-salesmen, preferred the less disruptive approach that was more conventional around IBM and that had helped it wring such extraordinary profits out of the mainframe business. The executives wanted to milk the existing product line as long as possible. After all, all the expensive work that goes into designing PCs had already been paid for. So why not just sit back and keep producing PCs that cost IBM about half what customers would pay? Only when IBM couldn't delay any longer would it pay to design and bring out products using new technology. (What Armstrong and Estridge's other bosses didn't realize was that by the time Estridge's line would have been available, the low-end PCs were carrying similarly minuscule profit margins, anyway. Armstrong and his peers in the senior ranks of IBM had become spoiled. IBM earned $6.6 billion after taxes in 1984, a remarkable 14 percent of its revenue of $46 billion, and IBM's senior managers still naïvely demanded that all parts of the business be able to earn that kind of spectacular margin.) Estridge's 80386 plan was still barely breathing when he was pulled out of the PC job in early 1985 and replaced by Lowe, but Lowe, more attuned than Estridge to the desires of his bosses, quickly smothered it.

The powerful Intel 80386 chip resurfaced from time to time as the PC group put together its three-year plans—which resembled the five-year plans of the old Soviet Union and were a legacy from IBM's mainframe business, where change occurred so gradually and could be managed so carefully by IBM that long planning horizons were possible. But the 80386 processor never made it into IBM's product plans. While the chip was undeniably fast, Intel had had enough trouble getting the bugs out of the prior-generation AT processor back in 1984 that Lowe's technical advisers didn't believe Intel would get the next-generation chip out as rapidly as it was promising. Better to wait and see what would happen.

IBM's minicomputer business also had expressed concern about the 80386, thinking it was powerful enough that PCs built around it could eat into sales of the highly profitable minicomputers. Lowe knew it would be virtually impossible to sell the Management Committee on a product that could cannibalize the sales of a powerful fellow business unit.

Besides, Lowe and his team still naïvely thought they controlled the PC standard, so they didn't think any major competitor would introduce a product based on the Intel 80386 before IBM. If someone did jump the gun, IBM thought it could make that rival pay a heavy price just by fiddling around with a little circuitry inside IBM's PCs when it came time for IBM to introduce systems using the 80386. Just a few changes in wiring could ensure that peripheral devices—such as hard-disk drives, modems, and circuit boards containing memory chips—that could be plugged into an IBM 80386-based PC couldn't be plugged into the rival's 80386 PC. Because makers of peripheral devices had historically always first tried to make circuit boards that augmented the capabilities of IBM's PCs, Lowe assumed that they would concentrate on getting their products to work with his 80386 PCs and ignore competitors'. That would really hurt a competitor if a peripheral maker did something innovative, such as produce circuit boards that let a PC send and receive faxes. If fax capabilities were available just for IBM's PCs, the competitor who jumped the gun would have to waste time redesigning its products to fall back into line with the IBM standard way of doing things.

Even if Intel got to market on time with the 80386, Lowe didn't think he needed to bother moving too quickly to use it. He was wrong —and his errors left him naked. When Compaq Computer announced an 80386-based machine in September 1986 and staked its claim to an immensely lucrative market for the next generation of PCs, Lowe did not even own a single copy of the new Intel chip. It took Lowe almost a year to catch up with Compaq, giving Compaq plenty of time to build up its financial strength and establish itself in the minds of customers as the new technology leader in the PC business.

In the same way that Lowe's indecision in dealing with Microsoft cost IBM its leverage over that company, Lowe's slowness to adopt the 80386 chip lost him his influence over Intel, the only other company that might rival Microsoft as the standard setter of the PC business. Together, the losses closed off to Lowe any opportunity to turn the PC business into something that would carry IBM once its mainstay mainframe business ran into trouble—or even to make a modest profit off PCs.

Intel always had a certain glow about it, because it was founded in part by Robert Noyce, one of two men who developed the first integrated circuit. Until the late 1950s, a circuit consisted of numerous discrete pieces—resistors, transistors, capacitors, and so on—that were wired together by hand to control the flow of electricity inside, for example, a radio. Noyce and Jack Kilby, working separately, found ways to make entire circuits in one piece, on a slice of silicon. Their methods eliminated the need for all the slow hand-wiring. In addition, because the electronic parts no longer needed to be big enough for fat human fingers to handle, they could be shrunk to the point where millions of electronic devices now fit on a single fingernail-sized computer chip. The Noyce-Kilby work ushered in a wave of miniaturization the likes of which had never been seen. During the Depression, radios required so many vacuum tubes that they filled a whole corner of a living room. Radios were pieces of furniture, occupying the center of attention the way a baby grand piano might catch someone's eye now. Once transistors came along, radios, freed of the need for vacuum tubes, shrank to the size of paperback books by the late 1950s. Once integrated circuits became possible, radios shrank to the point where they now take up space about half the size of a credit card in someone's Sony Walkman. The miniaturization opened the way to everything from the development of a more worldwide culture through international air travel to the threat of nuclear destruction—a modern jet would be so heavy, it couldn't even get off the ground if all its miniature circuitry were done using the old vacuum-tube, hand-wired technology, and neither could missiles carrying nuclear warheads. The forces of miniaturization swept along everything they touched—including, just to pick a name at random, IBM, which became a global institution because tiny electronic circuitry made mainframes possible and which is now fading because of the even smaller electronics in PCs.

By the early 1960s, Noyce was known as one of those who did the most to unleash the already obvious, almost mystical powers of miniature electronics. He generated additional attention when he led a group of Fairchild Semiconductor employees—known in the industry as "Fairchildren"—in a breakaway to form Intel. The group, known as the "traitorous eight," meekly told the world that Intel was a shortened version of INTegrated ELectronics, but everybody in the industry knew that the brash company's name was short for INTELligence.

Intel produced another breakthrough in the early 1970s because of a bit of luck. While Intel attacked some basic technology questions, it agreed to do a little contract chip design. It happened that one agreement was done with a Japanese company seeking to build a new sort of calculator. Then, when engineer Ted Hoff was sitting on a topless beach in Tahiti, with the smell of suntan lotion filling his nostrils, for reasons known only to him he came up with a revolutionary way to tackle the project for a Japanese maker of calculators. The idea required what became known as a "computer on a chip" and led the way to the microprocessors that today are the brains of all personal computers and workstations.

The idea was akin to those of Noyce and Kilby—although neither was on a topless beach when his inspiration struck. Hoff came up with a way to combine all the basic elements of a processor onto a small chip, at a time when processors were typically huge things inside refrigerator-sized mainframes. The processors were so big because they consisted of several parts—a core chip that actually massaged the data, some logic chips that prepared data for use by the core chip, a little memory, and so on. The only tiny processors that existed in those days were the ones inside calculators, which were designed for just a few mathematical functions and couldn't be reprogrammed to handle word processing, graphics, or any of the other things that microprocessors can now manage.

By combining all the pieces of a processor onto a single chip that could then be miniaturized, Hoff opened the way for today's world of ubiquitous, disposable electronics. While the Manhattan Project pulled together huge numbers of mathematicians to crank through the extensive calculations needed to determine how to make an atomic bomb, most any household appliance these days—from a microwave oven to a CD player—includes sophisticated electronics that could be programmed to do the same calculations in a fraction of the time it took some of the best minds of the century. With all the chips in car radios, air-bag sensors, antilock brakes, fuel-injection systems, and so on, many cars these days contain much more processing power than the IBM 360 mainframes that made the company such a force in the 1960s. (Of course, the microprocessor also opened the way to talking greeting cards and many of the other evils of modern times.) The fundamental rule of electronics has proved to be that everything gets smaller and cheaper—very fast. So once Hoff found a way to combine all the pieces of a processor onto one chip, the forces of nature took over and made processors so small and cheap that it is nearly impossible to repair, for example, a radio anymore, and it's almost certainly not worth the expense. Better to just throw out the radio and spend twenty dollars on a new one—a thought inconceivable to someone fiddling with one of the twenty knobs on his closet-sized radio during the Depression. The processing power of computers became so widely available that acquiring it was about as cheap and easy as buying electricity. That ubiquity of processing power repeatedly changed the landscape of the computer industry and, by the early 1990s, made things awfully hard for old-line companies like IBM. IBM kept telling customers to buy from it because its brand of electricity was better than everyone else's and described in great detail the technology it used to make its electricity. But customers learned that IBM's electricity was no different from anyone else's.

When Hoff approached Noyce with his radical notion for a microprocessor, Noyce—rather than going off and studying this breakthrough idea, as IBM spent years investigating its novel technologies—

simply listened for a few seconds. Noyce had a mysterious look in his eyes, as though he had always known that the microprocessor would become possible. Then he said, "Do it."

As things turned out, microprocessors didn't interest Intel much initially. Even as the 1970s progressed, the chips were mainly used in devices like the Altair computer, which were too forbidding to operate to achieve wide acceptance among anyone other than hobbyists. Selling processors for the Altair was like selling clarinets—not a bad business but not a big one, either, because clarinets are too hard to learn to play. Intel's marketers projected that it might sell ten thousand or so processors a year—not the fifty thousand a *day* that Intel now sells. Motorola seemed to own whatever future there was for microprocessors as the 1980s began. The one big seller among PCs of the time, the Apple II, used a microprocessor from Motorola. In addition, Motorola's new 68000 family of processors was generally acknowledged to be far superior to Intel's.

Still, Intel had jumped on microprocessor technology so early that it was positioned to get lucky, and it did. Back in 1980, when Lowe and then Estridge put together the original PC plan, their engineers came from a project that had played around with early Intel processors, and their familiarity with Intel's chip layout meant that they could build a machine around an Intel chip faster than they could a Motorola chip. In addition, some of the early software for PCs, such as Microsoft's languages, had been written for Intel processors, which meant that software would already be available for the PC when it hit the market. IBM had plenty of technology of its own, so it could have done its own processor, but Estridge never considered that seriously. IBM had been too slow in turning earlier processor technologies into products, so they had bombed when they were introduced. (In the computer industry, the speed of the development process largely determines the speed of the chip. If companies building chips have access to the same basic technologies—as usually happens—whoever can use them in a new chip first has the fastest chip on the market.)

When IBM expressed interest in Intel, Intel thought that was fine, but its executives, like those at Microsoft, treated the decision as just a small design win. After all, the processors IBM was buying cost only about nine dollars apiece, roughly what IBM was spending on solder in each PC to attach parts to circuit boards. Intel also had other things on its collective mind. By the early 1980s, Japanese competition in memory chips—Intel's main business at that point—had picked up so much that Intel would lose $114 million in the 1983 third quarter alone. After years of trying, Japanese companies had finally figured out the tricky business of making memory chips and were now producing them so efficiently that Intel's position became tenuous. IBM invested nearly $400 million in Intel in 1983 and 1984, just to make sure its processor supplier stuck around a while; in return, IBM got almost a 20 percent stake in Intel. IBM also gained the right to buy 10 percent more.

Still, once Intel recognized what a hit the PC was, and then how fast IBM would sell its next-generation computer, the AT, Intel consolidated its position so quickly that it went from being a beggar at IBM's door to a company that, in some years, earned more than IBM and whose stock-market value surpassed IBM's in the early 1990s. IBM spent years putting together task forces to study how to proceed with its hardware. But IBM also kept changing its collective mind as different factions pulled projects in different directions in a vain attempt to keep all IBM's customers happy all the time and as the crosswinds in the marketplace made it hard for the sales executives who ran IBM's businesses to stick with one plan. Intel, by contrast, was so focused on its narrow slice of the chip market that it quickly put together a single strategy that changed little over the years: the plan that let it build on the IBM relationship to the point where it could become largely independent of IBM—and get rich.

When it came to the chip that was the core of the AT, IBM still dominated Intel enough that it insisted Intel license the rights to the chip to others. That way, if Intel ran into trouble making the chips, IBM had a second source. From Intel's viewpoint, though, that licensing created competitors, which forced the processor's price down to the point where Intel couldn't make much money.

With the dawn of the next-generation chip, the 80386, Intel decided to take an extraordinary series of gambles. A maker of computer processors is in a peculiar position. It doesn't sell a product that a U.S. Steel, say, would know what to do with. So a maker of processors has to rely on the kindness of strangers in a world where only a few strangers can help—those being the handful of major customers, such as IBM, who sell huge volumes of PCs that might use the processors. When IBM showed little interest in using the 80386 soon, Intel was faced with the choice of either finding someone else to champion the chip and bring it to market in a PC or sitting around and waiting until IBM adopted the 80386—all the while making little money from the prior-generation processor because of the heavy competition in that part of the market. Intel had special incentive to try to find a new champion, because it had a monopoly on the 80386. The sooner it moved the market to the more powerful processor, the sooner Intel could escape the withering competition it faced with the older processor. So Intel turned to Compaq, despite the risk of annoying its most important customer, IBM.

When that gamble paid off and Compaq's successful machines began accelerating a customer move toward the new Intel 80386 chip, Intel still had to deal with IBM. Intel had made enough money from its processors by late 1986 that it could now resist IBM's efforts to have Intel license the rights to the chip to another manufacturer, so that IBM would be guaranteed a second source. But Intel did mollify IBM by granting IBM the rights to make 80386 chips for its own use— even though that decision could have cut heavily into Intel's sales. Intel also agreed to let IBM modify the 80386 however it liked. That decision could have devastated Intel, because IBM has world-class processor technology and could have come up with more powerful variants of the Intel chip and rendered the 80386 obsolete. IBM executives say they actually tried twice to do versions of the 80386 that would have been far more powerful. IBM just couldn't get them done in time.

One version was tried by Glenn Henry, a senior IBM scientist, who hoped to combine the Intel 80386 with a workstation chip that IBM was developing. That way, the chip would have run all the programs designed for the PC but would also have let IBM control the future. Because Henry's hybrid chip would also run programs designed for IBM's powerful workstation chip, IBM could have weaned customers off their dependence on machines that used Intel's chips by interesting them in the software done specifically for the IBM workstation chip. If IBM could have switched customers' attention to the workstation software, IBM, not Intel, would have set the standards for the hardware inside IBM-compatible machines. IBM, not Intel, would have reaped all the profits that setting a computer standard grants. The results of Henry's experiment were promising, but things bogged down. Henry says he eventually wound up spending three or four days a week travel-ing to brief others inside IBM on his work and to generate support. That left him only one or two days to do actual work on the project. He eventually gave up and left IBM in frustration, going to a major competitor, Dell Computer. It wasn't until 1991 that IBM even used a homegrown variant of the 80386 in its PCs, and the chip represented a small-enough advance that it hurt Intel not at all.

Having won the gambles it took in 1986, Intel found itself with a monopoly on the 80386 chip and made a killing. The only thing that still hung over Intel's head was the 20 percent stake owned by IBM. Intel wanted IBM to sell that stake to make other PC manufacturers more comfortable dealing with Intel. IBM did. It sold the stock in 1986 and 1987 for some $625 million, earning an impressive 50 percent-plus return over three years on its $400 million investment—but also passing up another opportunity to make more money than it has through all its efforts in the PC business. The stock IBM bought would have been worth $5.4 billion if the company still held it today, giving IBM a $5 billion gain on its small investment. IBM also never exercised its right to buy an additional 10 percent of Intel, passing up a further $2.5 billion.

With all obstacles out of Intel's way, a subtle thing began to happen in 1986 and 1987. Customers, analysts, and the press began talking about PCs in terms of the Intel processor at the heart rather than talk about them as IBM machines, Compaq machines, or whatever. The change was barely noticeable at first, but the IBM logo had begun to lose its value. IBM no longer owned the future. Intel and Microsoft did.

With Lowe worrying about Intel and the clones, he focused so narrowly that he missed scads of strategic opportunities elsewhere in the PC market. Customers in the mid-1980s became so interested in upgrading their PCs with additional memory, disk drives, and so forth that multi-billion-dollar markets developed, but IBM chose not to participate. Culturally, IBM saw itself as a seller of systems, not as a mere supplier of parts. So, although IBM invented the technology for both floppy disks and hard-disk drives, it was the Seagates and Conners of the world that made their fortunes by selling disk drives to intrepid individual users and to clone makers. IBM is the largest chip maker in the world, but it was the Japanese companies that built their businesses by selling memory chips to clone manufacturers, learning, along the way, how to make chips more inexpensively than IBM could, meaning that IBM's competitors often had a cost advantage over IBM when it came to buying memory chips.

Lowe's group did try building a modem and selling it through dealers, but they did it badly. Hayes, a little company in Atlanta, had succeeded so well with its modem that it had defined the standard way for PC's modems to talk to one another. But IBM could never accept that someone else had set a standard, so its modem would talk only in IBM's modem language, not Hayes's. That meant an IBM PC using an IBM modem could talk only to another IBM PC, but not to any of the millions of other machines out there. To PC users, that didn't make any sense. They wanted to talk to everybody. So the IBM modem bombed.

The biggest opportunity IBM missed in the mid-1980s was in printers, which were part of a business separate from Lowe's. The printer business, based in Lexington, Kentucky, actually had plans to do PC printers from very early on. The executives there studied and studied to figure out how the Japanese were doing so well and came up with a way to match Japanese products' capabilities and even beat the Japanese on costs. There was just one problem: The products would carry roughly 8 percent pretax profit margins. That was about what the Japanese were making, but that didn't matter to IBM's Management Committee. Those were the days when IBM was earning margins two to three times that great across its entire business—thanks, in particular, to the higher margins IBM earned on overseas sales, where prices might be twice as high as in the United States. IBM's senior executives, under Chairman John Opel, still thought of IBM as one business, rather than several, so there was just one profit-margin goal for the entire company, and 8 percent pretax just didn't measure up.

Ed Lucente, who ran the typewriter and printer business at the time, would travel to Armonk, foils in hand, to argue his case. He'd sit outside the quiet, august corner of headquarters where the Management Committee meets. Then he'd go in to describe what he thought was an opportunity that would pay off handsomely in the long run. Then he'd be met with derision.

What did the Lexington group think it was doing talking about such slim profit margins? he'd be asked. Did it want to ruin the entire business?

The plan was sent back to Lexington for more study. When the results were the same, the Management Committee kicked the plan back again.

Lexington eventually caved in and came up with a product plan that contained prices that were too high for the products to sell well but that met the Management Committee's profit-margin expectations. Once IBM got into the business, the prices even came down some once it became clear that customers weren't exactly snapping up IBM's printers. Still, IBM's culture continued to stifle sales.

A team of marketing executives had gone around to talk to computer dealers about how to market printers, and they got all sorts of good advice, says Kathy Vieth, an executive in Lexington at the time. She says dealers warned the IBMers that printers weren't bought the way PCs were; they were bought as an afterthought. So IBM couldn't expect the brand loyalty in printers that it had in PCs. Instead, IBM would need to work with dealers, providing higher profit margins, easier payment terms, and so forth, to entice them to recommend IBM printers.

The IBMers nodded their heads and went home. But it's hard at IBM to do anything that hasn't been done before. New things tend to get shot down, or at least be debated to death as IBM's marketing forces and related product groups raise objections—arguing, for instance, that giving dealers high profit margins and flexible conditions would set dangerous precedents for other IBM products sold through dealers. Anyone at IBM wanting to do something with any kind of speed finds himself using old ideas, because they've already run the gauntlet at IBM and survived. So when IBM fixed its dealer profit margins and other terms on its PC printers, they turned out to be exactly the same as the terms on PCs, which dealers had said wouldn't fly. They didn't. The ProPrinter bombed.

"We went back to the dealers to ask what happened, and they said, 'We told you why this wouldn't work,'" Vieth says. She laughs and adds, "We told them, 'Well, tell us again.'"

The ProPrinter eventually turned into a nice little business for IBM, but when IBM tried to turn that into a nice big business, it focused on the wrong issues. Senior IBM executives throughout the 1980s would confess in private moments that the Japanese companies were the ones that had them lying awake nights worrying about the future of IBM. Given that the Japanese's secret seemed to be huge factories churning

out inexpensive products, Opel in the early 1980s had become fascinated with the possibility that robotics would help him cut his labor
costs. He invested $350 million in automating the Lexington facility
that produced IBM's printers and used it as a showcase with customers
and the press to demonstrate that IBM manufacturing was state-of-the-
art. The problem was that human labor costs were just a couple of
percent of the cost of each machine. Even if automation cut those costs
in half, that would only cut expenses by perhaps 1 percent. What really
mattered was designing the right products, and Lexington missed big-
time in PC printers.

Laser printers began to sweep through the PC industry in the mid-
1980s, but the people in Lexington thought they knew more than the
companies that were looking into doing laser printers. Lexington produced expensive high-speed laser printers for mainframes and knew
that just one of the mirrors that reflects the laser onto a page to form a
character cost thousands of dollars more than a PC laser printer could
probably afford to cost. Smug in their detailed cost analysis and culturally unable to go outside for a fresh perspective, Lexington decided a
laser printer wasn't yet possible.

Canon, unburdened by IBM's wealth of information, went ahead
and built an inexpensive laser-printer engine—the mechanical guts of
the machine. Even then, Lexington could have bought the Canon engine and produced a printer, but—the original PC experience notwith-
standing—IBM didn't like to rely on some outside supplier for such a
central piece of a product's technology. Hewlett-Packard, a conservative company in its own right but one not struggling with IBM's culture,
went ahead and bought the Canon engines, slapped some covers on
them, built in some software, and stole the market. HP now has 60 to
70 percent of the laser printer market, producing more than $2 billion
a year in revenue and the sort of profit margins IBM would love to
have, even though HP still buys the guts from Canon.

IBM eventually gave up on all the lovely robotics and, deciding that
Lexington was a marginal business, sold it in 1991.

Lowe did pursue a couple of Estridge projects, building a laptop computer and a faster version of the XT, but those quickly bogged down in
IBM's elaborate development processes. IBM's laptop plans had been
comparable to those of competitors when IBM began contemplating

designing one. But senior PC executives at competitors didn't have to fly all over the country constantly to spend half their workweeks in meetings, briefing other parts of their organizations on their plans. Competitors' development executives didn't have to compile inches-thick books that daily incorporated reams of paperwork—so that any-time a boss asked to see it, the book would be up to date on exactly where even the tiniest detail of the project stood. Competitors didn't have to worry about satisfying the demands of sales forces in 160 countries before they could proceed with their development. Competitors didn't have to deal with IBM's formal "escalation" process, under which dozens of disagreements between the development group and other parts of IBM were appealed upward, where, after weeks of preparing foils and arguing, someone decided the issue and sent an answer back down through the bureaucracy.

IBMers, however, had to deal with all those problems and more, and the IBM system made the laptop late, very late. The Convertible laptop was obsolete the second it went out the door. It was almost a full generation behind competitors when it appeared in April 1986. It was criticized as being too heavy, as lacking enough processing power, and as having a screen that was unacceptably hard to read. The Convertible didn't even have a modem, even though the main point of a portable computer was that someone could take it on the road and communicate with the office over a modem. The product manager couldn't bring himself to put a Hayes modem in the computer, and IBM didn't yet have a modem available. He arrogantly assumed customers would wait until IBM finished its modem. He was wrong. Lowe immediately put people to work fixing the problems in mid-1986, but the IBM "process" strangled those efforts, too, by late 1986. Lowe wound up six to nine months behind competitors with his next version of the Convertible and never did catch up. Because of the problems first with the portable in 1984 and then with the laptop, IBM missed out on a market that now totals several billion dollars a year.

The Convertible eventually became such a joke that even the wooden Lowe was willing to poke fun at it. At a June 1988 press conference, when asked how the Convertible was selling, Lowe gave a weak smile and said, "If you'd like one, I'm sure we can get you one."

The version of the XT was even worse. The project initially looked like a trivial exercise in engineering, because it was using old technology. The plan was to bring it out sometime in early 1985 as a less expensive variant of the AT. But the work bogged down so completely that the XT 286 didn't see the light of day until August 1986. The technology in it was so old by that point that it was even worse off than the Convertible. The XT 286 was obsolete *before* it went out the door.

Almost as bad, despite all the studying Lowe's group did on the XT 286, they made a horrible oversight. Circuit boards designed to plug into its sister machine, the AT—to add extra memory, a hard disk, or something else—were too high to fit inside the XT 286. Anyone wanting to use one of those boards had to take the covers off his machine and leave the PC's innards naked to the world. The XT 286, like the Convertible, became what IBMers call a "boat anchor," meaning it should be dropped over the side of a ship.

As Lowe was pondering whether to "refresh," in IBM parlance, his existing product line in 1986 or bring out a whole new line to beat back the clones, he was told about a bit of engineering that a group had done on an obscure piece of PC hardware in order to address, in part, a problem with radio-frequency emissions from PCs. The group, facing increasing trouble meeting FCC guidelines designed to keep PCs from interfering with radio broadcasts, had found a solution. It involved changing the "bus," a series of circuits inside a computer that carries data from one part of the machine to whatever part needs the information. The solution also involved altering the layout of the pins that protruded from the ends of circuit boards, allowing them to be plugged into the computer's main circuit board. Changing the layouts of the pins would mean that all the memory cards that had been sold for use with earlier PCs wouldn't fit into the slots in PCs using the new bus— it would be like having three-prong electrical plugs in a world where all the electrical sockets were built for two-prong plugs, and adapters weren't available. The engineers didn't mind, though. They had come up with a clean solution to the radio emission problem, and engineers like clean solutions.

Lowe, as it turned out, didn't mind, either. Customers had gone along when IBM put a different bus in the AT from the one in the original PC, so Lowe figured they'd go along again. In addition, Lowe and his immediate boss, Armstrong, saw the new bus as giving them an opportunity to play an old mainframe trick: IBM had found that if it kept changing the innards of its machines fast enough, then those trying to copy it always stayed nine to eighteen months behind. If the clones really wanted to make machines exactly like IBM's, then they'd have to come up with a way to copy the complicated circuitry in this bus. Maybe, Lowe thought, the new bus would give him some breathing room.

Initially, the plan was just to put the bus into the new high-end machine, based on the Intel 80386 chip. But, after yanking the announcement planned for halftime at the Super Bowl in 1987 and studying things some more, Lowe decided to go even further with the new bus, called the Micro Channel. Lowe decided to put the Micro Channel into his midsized machines, which used the aging AT-class chip. Even though selling a computer based on its bus is like selling a house based on its plumbing, as long as the Micro Channel was the main difference between IBM's hardware and the clones Lowe figured he might as well use it in as many machines as possible, even if it meant a few months' delay to reengineer some of the machines.

Lowe knew that the Micro Channel required some selling, because it wouldn't benefit users at all in the short term, but he figured he could hold their interest with a vision of how benefits would show up in the long term; that had always worked in mainframes, where IBM executives would lay out a technology strategy that might take them ten years to implement.

As part of his marketing, Lowe decided that he needed to show the world just how serious he was about the Micro Channel. So he killed the AT. It was his biggest seller and the best product in PC history up to that point. It also let customers use the plentiful circuit boards that they had become used to when adding memory or a disk drive. But Lowe felt he couldn't let customers choose between the old standard and the Micro Channel—not if he wanted to make the Micro Channel the new standard.

In yet another fateful move, Lowe also decided that the whole new line would use three-and-a-half-inch floppy disks, rather than the five-and-a-quarter-inch ones that were then standard. The three-and-a-half-inch floppy disks were clearly superior—they held more data than their older cousins and, because they came in a hard plastic case, they weren't as susceptible to damage as the flimsy five-and-a-quarter-inch disks were in their cardboard covers. The question wasn't whether the smaller disks would become standard; the question was when. Lowe felt he could use IBM's clout to let customers know that the time was now.

With the main hardware decisions finally set, Lowe just had to prepare an appropriately extravagant announcement in early April 1987. His marketing people rented out the Miami Convention Center so they could bring thousands of big customers and computer dealers down to the warm weather while it was still cold up north and keep people around for a couple of days of briefings. When the big day came, they used fireworks and a laser light display to help create a jazzy feel, and customers seemed excited. Lowe also held a press conference in the auditorium of the art gallery in the basement of IBM's main building in New York City, and it overflowed with reporters.

Everybody in the industry talked about the IBM announcements as a defining moment in the history of the computer business. Software developers, competitors, and customers all figured that they had to adapt to IBM's plans—and the betting was that many competitors wouldn't live to tell their tales of battling IBM.

The new machines were called the PS/2 line, for Personal System/2—the new chairman, John Akers, had himself insisted that the machines be called systems, to make them sound more substantial, more like mainframes than like the Charlie Chaplinesque original PC. They had some sharp new graphics that let IBMers do slick demos with TV-quality images of homes set back among trees or of metal balls precisely reflecting images of things surrounding them. Lowe also had people doing demos to show how he had used IBM's manufacturing prowess to prepare him to take on the clones: executives pretended to be assembly-line workers and put a PS/2 together in less than a minute, showing how IBM planned to cut labor costs in producing the new systems.

While the machines themselves were only mildly interesting, Lowe and IBM built up so much excitement that it seemed they now had to worry only about keeping cloners at bay. This time, Lowe thought IBM was prepared.

He was set to file a barrage of patent applications that covered all parts of the design of the Micro Channel. Anyone trying to clone it would require a year or more, he told people at the time. Lowe even had two surprises awaiting anyone who tried to copy the new designs. The first was that he could increase the speed of the Micro Channel—

and would as soon as anyone matched the speed of the first version. The second was a gift from his lawyers. They had told him that companies making AT clones had violated some key IBM patents. Although it would be hard to enforce those in 1987, years after competitors began violating them, anyone wanting to license the new patents was going to have to pay up on the old ones, too. IBM had also changed its patent-licensing policy. In the past, licensees had had to pay IBM only 1 percent of the price of the product using the IBM patent, but Lowe was now going to demand as much as 5 percent of the price of each clone sold—adding as much as $150 to the price of a $3,000 clone in a market that depended heavily on low prices.

Lowe thought he was in a great position. All he had to do now was wait for the clones to come to him.

SEVEN

The clones never came.

Bill Lowe spent all of 1987 and 1988 waiting for Dell or Tandy or Toshiba or *somebody* to launch a successful clone. Initially, he sounded tough. He said anybody trying to copy the Micro Channel architecture in his new PS/2 line had better either have some pretty slick engineers or an awful lot of good lawyers. As the months went by and competitors shunned the Micro Channel, Lowe said that, well, maybe he'd be willing to license the Micro Channel under the right terms. Then he became willing to license under just about any terms. By the end, Lowe was practically begging other companies to adopt the Micro Channel. How could IBM claim to own the new standard if nobody else used it?

The clones almost came. IBM had created enough confusion and still seemed to have enough control over the industry standard that big competitors talked about doing clones. Even IBM archrival Compaq did most of the engineering work it needed to do to produce a clone. But, first, IBM had to show that customers really wanted the Micro Channel—and Compaq resolved not to let that happen.

The debate began almost immediately following the IBM PS/2 announcement in spring 1987. It was terribly civil, with Compaq and IBM executives sharing seats on panels all over the world and talking politely of their opponents, but the debate consumed the PC industry for more than a year and a half. By the end of the debate, it became clear that IBM had staked the future of its PC business on an irrelevancy—a piece of hardware, the bus, that mattered little to a PC's performance and that few people even knew was in a PC.

IBM argued that the Micro Channel carried data faster than the standard bus. That was clearly true, but Compaq insisted that it didn't matter. Compaq said IBM had built itself a fast road in a world full of slow horses. The AT-style bus wasn't being used at anywhere near capacity, Compaq argued, so there was no need for a faster bus just yet. Maybe some day, but the new bus certainly wasn't worth the 50 percent or so premium that IBM charged for its machines compared with the clones.

Compaq tried to seize the moral high ground by claiming that the Micro Channel broke faith with IBM's customers. Compaq stressed that corporate customers couldn't plug into IBM's new PCs the circuit boards they had bought over the years to add extra memory, modems, and so on to their AT-style PCs. Customers had to buy new circuit boards, at several hundred dollars a pop, that had been redesigned so they could plug into the Micro Channel. Compaq insisted that the only one that would benefit from the Micro Channel was IBM because IBM would regain control over the direction the industry would take. That control, Compaq said darkly, would let IBM turn the PC world into something more like mainframes, where captive customers had to pay just about any price IBM chose to charge because there was so little competition. Compaq now claimed to be the keeper of the flame, vowing that it would continue to use the old AT-style bus and saying it, not IBM, was now the industry standard.

IBM caucused and, a few weeks later, rebutted Compaq. Compaq responded with some more technical concerns, which IBM eventually contested, but IBM was being so slow to respond that Compaq was scoring heavy points. Although the argument quickly descended into technical minutiae, Compaq seemed to be winning the argument on merit, too. Some companies began advertising themselves in the trade press as Compaq-compatible.

As the debate dragged on, a *Wall Street Journal* front-page story (not written by this reporter) neatly summed up people's positions. The story said Micro Channel was IBM's version of Colgate toothpaste's MFP, a mystery ingredient that no one understood but that was supposed to be magic. The story embarrassed IBM by quoting knowledgeable customers and industry executives as saying they had no clue what

IBM was talking about. Ed Belove, a senior technical executive at software giant Lotus Development, was quoted as saying that the Micro Channel had to do something, because IBM said it did. But he didn't have any idea what it was. Score more points for Compaq.

Customers gradually got up in arms, too, in 1987 and 1988 over Lowe's decision to insist that the PC world immediately shift to three-and-a-half-inch disks. Corporate customers, in particular, wanted to move to the new style of disk at their own pace and didn't want IBM or anybody else dictating to them. A theme was developing here. It was Big Blue as Big Brother. That played all right in the mainframe world but not in PCs, where customers had a choice.

Once customers got to kick the tires on the new IBM PS/2s in the spring of 1987, they quickly decided that they wanted one of two types of machines. They wanted PCs based on the powerful new Intel 80386 chip or they wanted good old reliable machines along the lines of IBM's AT. Lowe offered neither as of mid-1987. He had killed the AT. (Interestingly, Lowe's longtime boss, Mike Armstrong, moved to Paris at the end of 1986 to run IBM's European operations and decided to continue making and selling the AT. It continued to be a huge success.) Lowe had also been so slow to see the potential of the 80386 that he didn't get a PS/2 to market based on the 80386 until late 1987, more than a year after Compaq. Even then, Compaq had been so closely identified with machines built around the 80386 that it continued to outsell IBM by three or four to one in what turned out to be an exceptionally lucrative market for these new high-end PCs.

IBM's market share, nearly 80 percent in the halcyon days, had already fallen to less than 40 percent under assault from the clones. Lowe had assured his bosses that the PS/2 strategy would reverse that decline. Instead, the share slipped again in 1987 and fell further in 1988.

As 1987 progressed, Lowe was slow to realize what trouble he was in. He had somehow convinced himself that his PS/2 line offered the best ratio of price to performance of any machines on the market. He had believed the foils, or overhead transparencies, that his executives had shown him concerning all sorts of obscure measures about the speed of individual pieces of a PS/2, such as how fast a hard disk yielded up a bit of information. But nobody outside IBM cared about those foils. Customers cared only about how fast a PC was when it came to real-world applications, such as recalculating a spreadsheet, and customers understood that the only significant difference between IBM's machines and competitors' was that IBM wanted a 30 to 50 percent price premium. Lowe had staked so much on the PS/2 introduction in April 1987 that he was able to come out with only a few new models in 1987 and 1988, and they were minor variants on the initial machines. In typical IBM fashion, Lowe decided that there was nothing wrong with his strategy that some marketing pressure couldn't solve. So he lived out of an airplane in 1987 and 1988, traveling across country to evangelize customers and industry executives about how they really needed the PS/2 and its dandy, swift bus. Lowe spent only three full days in the office in one eighteen-month stretch, leaving the PC business to essentially run itself and ignoring the problems that were brewing in IBM's relations with Microsoft.

Finally, one day in the summer of 1988, Compaq Chief Executive Rod Canion and Senior Vice President Mike Swavely picked up the phone to see whether other PC companies were willing to take IBM on head-on over the Micro Channel. They were. Canion and Swavely quickly lined up eight other big PC makers, including Tandy and two others that had said they might build PCs using the Micro Channel.

Compaq had actually been pretty sure that it would find support, largely because of what it had learned from IBM's old friends Intel and Microsoft. Canion would gripe to Microsoft's Bill Gates and Intel's Andy Grove about what a silly idea he thought the Micro Channel was. Gates and Grove routinely talked to more senior people in the PC business than anyone else because they supplied the basic parts of a PC to everyone in the IBM-compatible part of the market, and they had heard plenty of other grousing. While they didn't mean to foment a rebellion against IBM, they did tell Canion and Swavely that other conpanies shared their distaste for the Micro Channel.

Reassured by Microsoft and Intel, Compaq had done most of the engineering on an alternative to the Micro Channel even before Canion and Swavely placed the phone calls. So Compaq could already demonstrate it could make a bus that was as fast as IBM's while—the crucial distinction—being able to use all the old-style circuit boards that people already owned and didn't want to have to throw away. Canion and Swavely continued to argue that customers wouldn't need a faster bus for years, but they wanted customers to know that Compaq could provide one should the need arise. Once customers were reassured about the future, Canion and Swavely felt certain, IBM and its Micro Channel would lose all claim to setting the industry standard and making customers follow its lead.

In 1981, just seven years before Compaq mounted its attack on IBM's control of the PC business, Compaq was only an idea in the minds of some executives at Texas Instruments. They were seemingly unexceptional executives. Their idea was bad. And they shouldn't have been able to line up much financing from venture capitalists. Other than that, the future Compaq was in great shape.

The executives, led by Canion, had become frustrated by Texas Instruments' ineptitude in trying to get into the incipient personal-computer market and unwillingness to try again after an earlier, expensive failure. TI had been one of the pioneers in electronic calculators and couldn't see how fast the profits would disappear from that market. It also was doing well making memory chips and couldn't imagine how quickly the Japanese would dominate that market, to the point of forcing TI out of the business for a time. So TI in the early 1980s was feeling comfortable in the same way that IBM felt throughout the 1980s and wasn't inclined to take another risk. (By the end of the decade, TI would be a shell. It would make all its money off the sales of rights to its patents and would lose money on the rest of its operations. Having missed its chance to enter the PC business, TI would have made more money if it could have dispensed with the business of actually making and selling things and just stripped itself down to a handful of lawyers negotiating patent-licensing agreements.)

Canion hardly seemed daring. He appeared washed-out. He was tall, thin, and pale, with short straight brown hair and a tinny, almost whiny, voice. Apparently bothered by his contacts, Canion blinked a lot. He looked as though he didn't get outside much to enjoy the Texas sunshine. Canion and his three cofounders were hardly radicals working out of some garage in California. They were "organization men" every bit as much as the typical IBMer—years later, one Compaq annual report had a photo of the top nine executives at Compaq, all of them white males and all of them coincidentally dressed in black suits, white shirts, and red ties. But Canion and the others were unlike IBMers in the most important respect: They were willing to stick their necks on the line for an idea they believed in.

When Canion approached the venture-capital firm of Sevin-Rosen, which provided the financing for many of the most successful start-ups in the early PC days, he got little encouragement. L. J. Sevin didn't care much for Canion's initial idea, which was to do an add-in component for the IBM PC; this would have been a disaster because so many other people had the same idea. Sevin also told Canion that his business plan didn't measure up to the strict rules that Sevin and his partner, Ben Rosen, had established for themselves after some misadventures. But Sevin and Canion were friends, having met through mutual contacts in the semiconductor industry in Texas, so Sevin said he'd see what he could do.

When Sevin talked to Rosen, Sevin said he had a friend who didn't measure up to their criteria but who was probably worth a shot, anyway. Rosen said it was funny Sevin should say that because he, too, had a friend like that. The two agreed to trust their instincts about their friends, so they put up much of the money for Canion and Compaq. (Rosen's friend did just as well for Sevin-Rosen. He was Mitch Kapor, who founded Lotus.)

Sevin discarded Canion's idea for an add-in card, so Canion and some of his engineers drew another idea on a napkin at the restaurant where they were dining. The idea was pretty simple: It was an IBM-compatible PC with a handle on it. But the idea for a portable computer was also powerful. It let Compaq sell a product that IBM didn't have, which insulated Compaq from competition from IBM. The idea also let Compaq enter the market for IBM-compatible computers in 1982, long before most of the established companies understood that IBM's introduction of the PC in 1981 had set such a strong standard that customers would demand that any PCs they bought from other companies be able to run all the software written for IBM's machines and be able to use all the peripheral devices that had been designed to plug into the IBM PC. The Compaq portable was ungainly, at some thirty pounds, but it did the trick. Once Compaq had established its beachhead, it became bolder, and it was the first company to clone the IBM AT after that machine debuted in August 1984. When that worked out, too, Compaq grew so fast that it became the youngest company ever to reach the Fortune 500 and then to hit $1 billion in annual sales.

Compaq could easily have fallen into the sort of complacency that existed at IBM. But Canion and Compaq didn't just sit back and wait for customers to say what they wanted, the way IBM often did. Canion and his engineers focused at least as much on what technology was making possible—a crucial point because it meant Compaq could be first to market with products that customers didn't know enough to ask for because they didn't know the products were possible. Compaq was not only first to market, in 1986, with a machine based on the Intel 80386 chip; it also came out with the first good laptop, the first top-notch notebook computer (again first sketched on the back of a napkin), and the first "server," an increasingly important, powerful form of PC that stores data for use by anyone in a departmental network of PCs or that controls the networked PCs' access to laser printers, fax machines, and so on.

Compaq also benefited from a healthy sense of fear, an emotion that never seemed to trouble anyone at IBM. Especially in Compaq's early days, Canion and his group knew IBM could put them out of business at any time just by coming out with comparable products. The IBM brand name was so powerful and its marketing forces so strong that Compaq needed to make its machines much better than IBM's just to stay even. Canion also knew that any number of Compaq's competitors could beat him to market if he dawdled, and that he might never catch up. Canion's investors also kept the heat on, because venture capitalists want a quick return on their investment; they don't have the deep-pockets mentality that made IBMers smug.

So Canion and his team didn't tolerate anything like IBM's deliberate "process" of determining what product to build—in which teams of marketing people canvassed customers and put together lists of customer requirements, which were handed to development people, to be reviewed by senior management and then to be debated to death among various marketing forces and product groups, most of which had a vested interest in avoiding radical change. At Compaq, some engineers would sketch an idea on a scrap of paper, get a boss to nod his head, and then go attempt it. Some ideas would be clunkers and get killed along the way. Some would be so-so products, such as the server, which was a couple of years ahead of its time. But Compaq had an exceptional hit rate, and at least the products got out the door in time to have a chance of succeeding.

Compaq also speeded up the actual development of a product by shunning the IBM system—under which a final list of customer requirements was sent to development, which did a prototype and sent that to manufacturing, which then figured out how to make products in volume and relayed its plans back to the sales organization, which then determined a marketing plan. Compaq turned everybody loose on the problem at once. The process was as messy as a food fight, but it cut months out of the time it took to get a product on the market.

Compaq differed from IBM, too, because it had an independent chairman, venture capitalist Rosen. Unlike at IBM, where the chairman and chief executive are the same person and no board member who hadn't been an IBM executive knew anything about the computer business, Rosen brought enormous perspective to the Compaq board. He was a techie, trained as an engineer at Cal Tech. He became a securities analyst following the semiconductor industry at Morgan Stanley, but in the late 1970s he became fascinated with the early personal computers. He bought them all and played with them, and, with his background in the semiconductor field, he could see just how quickly the inevitable move toward miniaturization would make them better. Rosen started what became the most prominent personal-computer industry newsletter and began a conference, the PC Forum, that became a must for all the big shots in the industry—people found that they could learn more and do more deals just by hanging out by the pool at Rosen's conference for three days than they would during the rest of the year. Rosen then decided that the real opportunity was in investing, so he and old friend L. J. Sevin set up what became the most successful fund in the history of venture capital. Once Compaq got rolling, Rosen did little on a day-to-day basis there. By the mid-1980s, he was known in the industry as much for his antics as his acumen. The white-haired, balding Rosen would juggle, spin a pizza pan on his finger, balance a chair on his nose, dress up as a drum major and march through a meeting—anything for a laugh. He'd organize vicious games of charades at industry conferences, the point of which seemed to be to make PC executives make obscene gestures as they acted out their clues. (The movie *Octopussy* was, for instance, famous for the way someone acted it out.) Rosen stayed in touch with all the powers in the industry, but as long as things were going so well at Compaq, he was content to go into semiretirement, working on his golf game at the country club in Mt. Kisco, New York, an hour north of New York City. But when, in the early 1990s, Compaq eventually got fat and happy the way IBM had, Rosen didn't hesitate for a second. He pulled aside two midlevel Compaq people and sent them on a secret mission to pretend that they were setting up a PC company and find out what the costs would be. He then compared that business plan with Compaq's and saw just how much Compaq was overspending on parts and processes. Despite the ten phenomenal years of work that Canion had produced, Rosen had no qualms about confronting him at a board meeting in late 1991—even though he and Canion described themselves as good friends, they weren't chummy in the way that IBM senior executives become pals as they move up the ranks together. When Canion resisted change, Rosen forced him out. Compaq bounced back.

The value of an outside perspective can't be overestimated, especially in the computer business, where the technology changes so fast that letting a management problem fester for even six months can leave a company with a line of products a whole generation behind competitors. When Apple ran into trouble in the mid-1980s, cofounder Steve Jobs might have run it into the ground if not for venture capitalist Mike Markkula. Markkula, a computer industry veteran, knew enough to figure out quickly what the problems were and still owned enough of the company that he had the incentive to move fast, even if it meant hurting his friend Jobs. Markkula leaned on Apple's new president, John Sculley, to do something about Jobs in 1985, and Apple recovered quickly. When Hewlett-Packard ran into milder problems in the early 1990s, cofounder David Packard suddenly reappeared on the scene, wandering the halls to figure out what the problems were and helping right the company. At Digital Equipment, by contrast, the board didn't contain anyone who could stand up to founder Ken Olsen. So he was allowed to take the extraordinary success that he had achieved by the mid-1980s and turn it into a mess; he was finally pushed aside in 1992.

By early September 1988, Compaq and the other rebels were ready to make their stand. They began calling other companies to line up as many supporters as they could, and they quickly came up with more than sixty. Responses came in so fast that between the time the list of supporters was printed the day before the announcement and the time of the actual announcement, more than twenty additional companies had called to say they wanted to be counted in. It seemed that nobody wanted to take the IBM bus.

Compaq—joined by such major clone makers as Tandy, AST, and Zenith—self-consciously staged its announcement in a Manhattan hotel just across town from where IBM was holding a PC announcement of its own; this group of rebels reveled in the boldness of their attempt to take the industry's leadership from hated IBM. There wasn't really much to announce. The rebels just said that they were going to work together on some technical specifications for the bus, a mundane bit of circuitry that never would have interested anyone if IBM hadn't made its Micro Channel such an issue. Still, the mood was giddy as each of the founding nine members got to say a few words on the hastily arranged stage. When the mutineers answered questions following their brief presentation, Canion took the opportunity to say that he had called Bill Lowe to tell him what the group was doing.

"Bill was cordial," Canion said, "but he declined to join." Canion smiled.

After the questions ended, people milled about in the packed ballroom. The group was as impressive a gathering as had happened in a long time, with many senior executives and prominent analysts and consultants in the room, but nobody was in a hurry to leave. Everyone just wandered around marveling at the audacity of what they had just witnessed and wondering whether Compaq and the others could get away with it. People wondered, too, about the fact that Intel was going to make the chips that would control their rival bus. Intel, once so dependent on IBM and so agreeable to IBM's wishes, was by 1988 so successful that its executives just responded with shrugs when asked whether the company's relationship with the rebels wouldn't endanger its ties to IBM.

In effect, the Intel executives said, we're just a supplier of bullets. What IBM, Compaq, and the others do with the bullets is their business.

The founding group behind the mutiny, who were quickly dubbed the "Gang of Nine," all happened to be at a Salomon Brothers PC conference the next day in another Manhattan hotel ballroom, where Tandy's chief executive, John Roach, in his Texas drawl, referred to fellow panel members as "Gangster Rod Canion," "Gangster Safi Qureshey" of AST Research, and so forth. Lowe, the luncheon speaker, packed the room because everyone in the industry wanted to hear how he would respond to the rebels. But, wooden as ever, Lowe simply read a standard speech that didn't even acknowledge what happened across town the day before. Then, without taking any questions, he left.

As the autumn of 1988 progressed, it became obvious that Compaq and the rebels had carried the day. Even now, six years after IBM began telling customers that what they really needed was a faster bus right away, PC customers buy four or five machines with an old AT bus for every one they buy with a faster bus, whether from IBM or the Compaq-led group.

By choosing to build his clone-killer strategy around the bus, an irrelevancy, Lowe not only cost IBM its role as the technological leader of the PC business; he also lost a lot of customers. His attempts to cram the Micro Channel down people's throats, together with his insistence on OS/2, an operating system that no one wanted, cost IBM some twenty additional points of market share by the end of the decade. That translates to close to $10 billion a year in revenue. The loss also took IBM from its position as the clear leader to one where its market share roughly equaled Apple's and Compaq's. IBM would just be one among equals, leaving it vulnerable to the price wars that crippled its business as the years went on.

Lowe's PC strategy had been a torpedo below the waterline at IBM. No one knew it by the end of 1988, but IBM was sinking. Lowe's days at IBM were almost over.

As Lowe was fumbling his clone-killer strategy in 1987, the rest of IBM was going through a rough stretch, too. Mainframe sales were slow, partly because all the customers who had been waiting with bated breath for a new line that IBM began selling in 1985 had by 1987 bought all the machines they wanted and partly because the PC revolution was finally beginning to take its toll. Not only were corporations using PCs to handle new applications, such as supplying more stock-market information to brokers on Wall Street; some companies found PCs so inexpensive that they were even dumping some mainframes and replacing them with PCs.

That was the most ominous of signs for IBM. Its biggest asset has long been the millions of lines of software that customers had written for its mainframes to handle payroll, accounting, and so forth. Rewriting that software to run on PCs is phenomenally expensive and time-consuming for customers, so they generally avoid doing it. Rewriting is also risky, because new software on a new machine never works as well as a long-used and fully tested program. Performing any given task on a mainframe is maybe one hundred times as expensive as on a PC, but,

even if the expense of rewriting the software could be justified, customers always wonder whether they really want to risk having the new
software crash, thus losing a big hunk of, say, customer orders. If some
customers were beginning to take a chance and move their software off
mainframes and onto PCs, then IBM had a real problem, because
mainframes accounted for around half of its revenue and two-thirds of
its profits.

Digital Equipment, a major foe since the mid-1960s, was also hammering IBM in minicomputers in 1987 with its "Digital Has It Now"
ads. While Digital had a single line of Vax computers, all of which
talked nicely with one another and could run each other's software,
IBM had five minicomputer architectures, none of which could talk
easily with the others and none of which could run another's software.
Digital's Vaxes were actually so good at talking even to other manufacturers' computers that some consultants told customers that the easiest
way to get two IBM machines to talk to each other was to put a Vax in
the middle and have both of them talk to the Vax. IBM had mounted
one of its typically huge projects in the early 1980s to solve the communication problem, but the project, called Fort Knox, got pulled in so
many directions that it collapsed—after four thousand people wasted
four years working on it.[1] With so much development time lost, IBM
had little way to respond to Digital and its user-friendly Vaxes.

In late 1986, IBM did launch a more limited product, which IBM
marketers referred to internally as the "Vax killer." But the system,
called the 9370, got off to a horrible start. As IBM's director of investor
relations was walking out of a securities analysts' briefing on the day of
the announcement, he mentioned to a couple of analysts that IBM was
worried about its European business. Analysts had been concerned
about Europe, IBM's mainstay at a time when demand for IBM products in the United States had been frighteningly soft for more than a
year, so they quickly issued warnings that sent the stock tumbling. The
newspaper accounts the next day then said that IBM had a major
problem in Europe and that its stock had fallen drastically—and, oh,
by the way, IBM did introduce some kind of large computer. The 9370
eventually began to recover from its bad start, but once customers had
finished their test drives, they came up with a harsh verdict. The 9370
was overpriced, underpowered, and too complicated to use. IBM had
trotted out United Airlines at the announcement, saying it would build

a whole travel-agent network around thousands of 9370s, but even United Airlines eventually canceled its plans to use the 9370—a very public embarrassment.

In PCs, of course, IBM was losing share to Compaq and the other makers of IBM-compatible systems at the same time it was wasting money on the operating-system mess it was concocting with Microsoft as they grudgingly cooperated to get the full version of OS/2 out by the end of 1988. Still, the PC business's costs stayed so high that when Compaq did a competitive analysis of IBM, it decided that IBM could be making at most only a 3 to 4 percent pretax profit in PCs and might even be losing money. The Compaq analysis didn't even include the costs of OS/2 development or the costs that Lowe's business was incurring as it tried to get a workstation business going, seven years after Apollo's pioneering workstation reached the market. IBM's accounting system, however, continued to tell Lowe and his superiors that PCs were, at least, a nicely profitable business even if IBM was losing market share.

When the whole company bogged down in 1987, it was beginning to look like something more might be going on than the normal fluctuations that afflict computer companies as products get hot, then quickly cool off as technology rages past them. This would be two lousy years in a row, following what IBM considered to be a so-so year. IBM earned $6.56 billion in 1985, the second-highest profit any company has ever earned, a number larger than the sales of the second-largest computer maker that year. But IBM had itself set the record the year before by earning $6.58 billion, so to IBM 1985 looked like a down year. Then came 1986, a real down year, when earnings slid 27 percent. Revenue increased less than 3 percent, a real comedown from the 15 percent-plus days of the early 1980s and far less than IBM's grandiose plans. As 1987 began, IBM was again optimistic. Its executives predicted that interest in some faster versions of the mainframe line, sales of the new 9370 minicomputer, and the pent-up demand they were so sure existed for the new PS/2 line of PCs would kick in in the second half and save the year. When none of those dreams came true, earnings rose only marginally from the difficult 1986 results and revenue climbed less than 6 percent—again not nearly enough to support the sort of 13 percent annual cost increases that John Opel had set the company up for after he succeeded Cary as chief executive in 1980.

Opel had finally given way, though, to John F. Akers—ceding the title of chief executive to Akers in 1985 and then the chairman's title in 1986. The timing appeared to be perfect, because IBM seemed to be having enough trouble that it no longer needed a philosopher king like Opel. Instead, IBM needed a man of action—just what ex-navy fighter jock Akers looked to be.

Akers always had a regal aura about him. Before he was named to the top job at IBM, a professor showed a Harvard Business School class some videotapes of half a dozen senior IBMers, and the class almost unanimously picked Akers as the one who would ascend to the top job. He was a forceful speaker who had a firm voice and command of his audience. If an executive, a stockholder at the annual meeting, or a reporter asked what Akers thought was a silly question, he didn't hem or haw; he just said it was a stupid question and moved on. Slow decision making seemed to make him nervous. When some executive suggested studying an issue further, Akers might snap, "Study? We do, we make, we buy, we sell."[2] When Akers became national chairman of the United Way, he complained to friends about how hard it was to keep board members from talking him to sleep. He occasionally said something such as, "Look, do you want to make a decision on this? Or do you just want us all to drive home tonight and feel bad about it?"

Though of only average height, he had a firm jaw and sniper gray eyes, which reminded people of his past as a navy fighter pilot, coolly landing his jet on aircraft carriers bobbing up and down on twenty-foot ocean waves. He was still trim at fifty-one, a result of spending many early mornings on an exercise bicycle at home as he pondered the future of his company. He carried himself with a confidence born of total success in any job he'd ever had.

"He was the CEO from central casting," says Irving Shapiro, the former chairman of Du Pont and an IBM director in the early 1980s. "There was never any question about whether he would get the job."

John Fellows Akers was born in 1934 in Needham, Massachusetts, just outside Boston, to Kenneth Fellows and Mary Joan Reed Akers. His father had been a civil engineer, trained at MIT, but lost his job. "They didn't want to build too many bridges during the Depression," Akers has explained. Akers's father then became a sales manager at an insurance company; his mother, who didn't go to college, had been a secretary when she met his father. Later, when the family needed money, she founded a small real estate brokerage firm. Akers went to the public high school in Needham and did well enough to get into Yale. At Yale, though, he was remembered more for his scrappiness than for his intellect. Friends from the time say that as a student, well, he was a pretty good hockey player. On the ice, "Johnny" was known not only as very competitive but as disciplined; when the game ended, win or lose, he was already thinking about the next game.

When Akers got his degree in industrial administration in 1956, he went off to serve on active duty as an ensign in the peacetime navy for four years, long enough to let him become a carrier pilot. After finishing with the navy, he joined IBM as a salesman and quickly became one of the all-time greats at the job. He had a politician's knack for remembering names, he knew the product, he knew how to close the sale, and he could schmooze with the best of them—telling Ivy League stories, chatting about sports, or talking about his days landing his fighter plane on a short landing strip that kept moving up and down in the waves. Akers was tabbed as one of the highest of the "hi-pos," always getting one of the top rankings among his peers in the elaborate grids that IBM's personnel people put together as they tried to figure out who among IBM's hundreds of thousands of employees had what it took to move to the top tier.

Akers was known in those days as gruff because he didn't tolerate people who weren't as quick as he was. But even then he was smooth enough to impress his bosses. IBM counsel Nicholas deB. Katzenbach remembers being struck by Akers as he briefed Akers and a group of other midlevel executives in the early 1970s on how to handle themselves as the corporation fought the federal anti-trust suit. Katzenbach said he had no idea who Akers was but was impressed with his series of penetrating questions about the essence of the government's position. Katzenbach also noted that, while Akers had obviously prepared extensively for the meeting, he was slick enough to have memorized his research so he wouldn't have to use notecards and seem overeager in front of his peers. Katzenbach decided he would remember Akers, because he was sure that Akers would rise through the ranks and become a force at IBM.

It took Akers seven years to become a manager, but once he did, he moved up rapidly. Four years later, still topping the charts, Akers won a chance to be an administrative assistant to a senior executive, a test to see whether he really had the right stuff. It was Akers's good fortune to wind up with Frank Cary, who at that point was just a senior vice president. Cary got a good look at Akers's polish and discipline and liked what he saw. Cary sometimes beat up on Akers, calling him "John Boy"—as in, Get in here, John Boy, and let's talk about this. (Cary continued the habit even after he became chairman and Akers became one of his senior executives.) But the relationship became strong enough that Akers even felt comfortable kidding Cary about his rise to power. Akers noted that soon after he arrived, Cary, a longtime senior vice president, became an executive vice president, and then, while Akers was still his administrative assistant, became president, a promotion that anointed him as the next chief executive. Akers jokingly tried to take credit for Cary's promotions.

Years later, Akers's hockey coach at Yale asked him how he rose to the top of IBM and he says Akers responded, "By being nice to everybody."

When Akers finished his year working for Cary in Armonk in the early 1970s, he had done well enough to win a job as a regional sales manager. There he became known as a good motivator in the IBM tradition of hokey kickoff meetings and company songs. Akers, a decent golfer, tennis player, and skier, often used sports stories to come across as one of the guys. One year, he made a film in which he congratulated his team of salespeople on making their quota the year before despite some tough times. Then he held up a football and said, "But this is what we did last year." Someone tossed him a football that was four times normal size, and he added, "This is what we have to do this year." The crowd loved it.

When Akers made a huge jump and was named the head of the U.S. marketing force, he made just a short, modest acceptance speech in front of his new team. "My appointment just shows that anything is possible at IBM," he said.

When in the mid-1970s he became president of the mainframe division, the kingmaker at IBM, employees marveled at how the young star kept his workday under control. He got in around 8:00 A.M., not terribly early by IBM standards, and could always be seen striding toward his car by 5:30 or 6:00 P.M. When someone would stop him and ask how he could be leaving so early, or whether he was at least taking some work home with him, Akers would respond, "If an executive has trouble finding enough time to spend at home with his family, then either there's something wrong with him or there's something wrong with his job." Then he'd keep marching off to his car.

Akers became known as a natural leader, one who would make the decisions but who listened to subordinates and could count on their support.

James F. MacDonald, who worked for Akers at IBM before becoming president of Gould, an electronics firm, says, "I'd walk into a meeting, lose the argument, and still walk out smiling, thinking it was a good meeting."[3]

Akers's military bearing and punctuality accentuated his aura of leadership. If he said he wanted something by 4:30 because he was going home early that day, someone arriving at 4:32 found him gone. Like many senior executives, he built up a staff that kept him constantly busy and on schedule: While someone met with him, someone else was waiting to talk with him while walking to the elevator, where another person would join Akers and ride with him to the airport, where someone else would meet him for the plane ride.

Akers never had to engineer a turnaround at some part of IBM and never had any experience outside the United States, but by the late 1970s his charisma had made him everyone's choice to become chairman. Irving Shapiro, the IBM director and former chairman of Du Pont, says that Cary and Opel both chastised him for missing a small dinner at a board meeting in Paris in the late seventies because that was to be his introduction to Akers. Even though this was years before outsiders knew Akers would succeed Opel, his two predecessors had decided it was time to continue his grooming by having him start meeting the board. While Akers was always known as a Cary protégé, he continued to be at the top of every list that personnel put together of the four or five candidates to be the next chief executive. Not only did Akers seem to have the talent but he was also young enough that he would have a full nine years to shape IBM before hitting the mandatory retirement age of sixty at the end of 1994.

When Opel named Akers president in 1982, making it certain that Akers would win the top job, Akers was typically unassuming. Akers would kid about going home that night and telling his three children at the dinner table about the promotion. Much to his surprise, he told friends, his teenaged daughter got excited. "Why," he asked, "do you care about this promotion when you've never cared about any of the others?" She noted that IBM executives typically have convoluted three-line titles, then exclaimed, "President of IBM! Finally a title that my friends can understand."

Akers changed little despite the promotion. He drove a Mercedes, but an old one from 1977. He lived on six acres hidden from the street by a thick copse of trees on top of a hill in Westport, Connecticut, one of the wealthy communities of senior executives that dot the Connecticut coast near New York City. However, the two-story, four-bedroom home was modest and was, in any case, where he had lived long before he hit the top of IBM. His one real indulgence was a home on Nantucket, which had belonged to an eighteenth-century whaling captain and had been lovingly restored. Akers is proud enough of the house that he sometimes opens it to local tours. Usually, boys from Needham don't wind up in Nantucket.

His wife, Susan, a tall, elegant lady, took an approach similar to her husband's, coming across as a gracious hostess who hadn't lost her sense of herself even though her husband had risen high in the world. When she and Akers flew with other couples on the corporate jet, she got the drinks and served the hors d'oeuvres; there wasn't any staff of flight attendants as there are on some companies' planes. While many of the spouses of IBM executives treated the corporate staff as their own, pestering people for help catering events or getting engagement announcements involving their children placed in *The New York Times*, Mrs. Akers made herself conspicuous by never asking for any sort of assistance.

As the Akerses settled in as IBM's first couple in 1985 and 1986, they seemed comfortable. He was taking over a company that was capturing perhaps 70 percent of the entire computer industry's earnings in the boom times of the early 1980s and that had generated more than $50 billion in profit over a history as illustrious as any company had ever had. When in 1985 Akers addressed an IBM annual meeting for the first time, he said, "IBM's prospects have never been brighter than they are today." So Akers sat contentedly in his corner office, overlooking the remnants of an old orchard behind the headquarters building in Armonk, wearing his monogrammed white shirts and using his reading glasses to devour all the reports he was receiving about IBM's successes.

He had a bronze statue of basketball player Jerry West on a bookcase as a reminder of his interest in sports. He had a picture of himself with Ronald Reagan on his desk, a reminder of his Republican convictions. He kept a computer terminal on his credenza, a reminder of IBM's livelihood—and an unintentional symbol for why IBM hit the wall almost as soon as Akers settled into his office chair. This was a dumb mainframe terminal with no intelligence inside, not one of the PCs that had already reached millions of desktops worldwide and had begun to erode the mainframe underpinnings from IBM. In addition, the chairman of the largest computer company in the world rarely used the terminal. While all the young guns in Silicon Valley spent hours each day hovered over their PCs, shooting off e-mail, studying reports, or just tinkering with the system to understand the technology better, Akers had assistants who handled his memos for him. He liked to get his reports on paper, not on a computer screen. If some analysis needed to be done on a computer, Akers had staff to handle that for him. He never played around with the system. He didn't feel very comfortable with computers.

The mediocre years IBM experienced in 1985 and 1986 troubled Akers. He had constantly reassured the world through press releases, speeches at the annual stockholders meeting, and sessions with securities analysts that IBM was about to get things going again and surpass the earnings record it had set in 1984. Akers even indicated that he expected the company to surpass $180 billion in revenue by 1993—a goal that he missed by, oh, $120 billion. As 1987 began, Akers knew he had embarrassed himself by underestimating the problems IBM faced during the two previous years. Once the prospects for 1987 began to fade, making him realize he was going to produce three bad years in a row in his first three years as chief executive, Akers felt his backbone stiffen. He had succeeded at everything he'd ever attempted. He had risen to the top of the most powerful company in the world. Through sheer force of personality, he was going to make sure he succeeded now.

But Akers, who looked so decisive, had never had to engineer a turnaround before. His response to his problems was to commission a series of task forces. Hundreds of people holed up for months in specially outfitted, windowless basements of buildings in some of the more remote outposts in the headquarters area, such as a small IBM building overlooking the harbor in Stamford, Connecticut. Special badges were needed to enter the task-force area. Hidden entrances made it hard for other employees even to see who was arriving or leaving.

By mid-1987, the task forces' results were in, and they weren't encouraging. IBM wasn't just facing an early frost. The problems were the beginning of an ice age. Akers's senior staff had concluded that the mainframe business was fading. It could be counted on for only 5 to 8 percent growth a year, far below what was needed to support IBM's recent 15 percent-plus increases in revenue. The study urged a shift away from hardware, which accounted for 71 percent of IBM's revenue but which would grow more slowly than software and professional services. The study cited the opportunities in systems integration—putting together large hardware systems for customers and writing the software to go with them. (The emphasis on systems integration echoed the recommendations of a 1984 task force, which Akers's predecessor, Opel, had ignored.) Akers's study also warned that most growth would come overseas, while IBM had more than 60 percent of its 400,000 people in the United States and did the vast bulk of its research and development in this country.

Akers, hardly one to back away from a problem, accepted the challenge and began saying all the right things. He proclaimed that IBM would get more than half its revenue from software and services by the early 1990s.

By IBM standards, Akers became an activist. A former assistant says that in his first year as chief executive, he took twice as many "major personnel actions" as Opel had the prior year—major personnel actions being things such as closing a big parts-distribution facility in Greencastle, Indiana. After having helped Opel build IBM up since the early 1980s to a peak employment of 407,000 in the spring of 1986, Akers also announced the first of a series of attempts to slim back down. He announced a package of early-retirement and severance offers in the United States—euphemistically called the FAP, for Financial Assistance Package—that took ten thousand jobs out of the IBM work force in the United States.

The polished Akers did all this very much within IBM's tradition of lifetime employment and respect for the individual. The several hundred employees in Greencastle were not only offered jobs elsewhere at IBM in 1987; they were recruited heavily. Other sites sent representa-

tives to Greencastle to try to get the best employees at job fairs that
were held in the Greencastle auditorium, where the sound system
blared out such songs as, "The Future's So Bright I Gotta Wear
Shades." Employees expressing interest in jobs elsewhere in IBM were
flown around the country to be wined and dined by their prospective
bosses.

Akers's other program, designed—unlike the Greencastle approach
—to get people to leave the company, was entirely voluntary. Akers
offered a generous package to all but those in a handful of "skills
categories," such as programming, where IBM felt it needed all the
people it had. The company offered lengthy counseling to people on
whether it made financial sense for them to leave and assured them
they could change their minds about leaving right up until the deadline.
IBM also provided access to a placement service to help them find new
jobs on the outside. Departing employees could look for another job on
IBM time and use IBM facilities for as long as six months. Akers was
sending employees out into the non-IBM world without a sign saying
FIRED around their necks as he would later. He was essentially placing
want ads for them, saying, "Valued employee seeks new opportunities
elsewhere."

Akers got another shock, though, when the results of the severance
program came in: A huge number of IBM's best people took the severance packages and left. One executive who was running a product group
at the time said that, with the support of several division presidents, he
went to Akers to say that the corporate lawyers had told him IBM didn't
need to offer the buy-outs to everyone. IBM could use the opportunity
to clear out the deadwood that inevitably accumulates in any institution
of 400,000 people. Why take the chance of losing the best people?
Akers assured him that IBM's top-rated employees would all stay because they'd feel they had the most opportunities inside the company.
Akers held a so-called Distribution A meeting—of roughly the top
seventy-five people in the company, the ones on the A distribution list
—to insist that everyone in the company be given equal access to the
severance offers. Akers didn't want any manager steering certain people
toward taking the offer and telling other people that the offer wasn't
meant for them. As it turned out, according to the man who confronted
Akers, of the ten thousand people who took the severance packages,
eight thousand were rated "one." There were just 22,000 people so

rated in the U.S. work force of 220,000 at the time, so Akers's program cleared out more than one-third of his best people in the United States. (There was a rule of thumb about midlevel IBM executives in those days that said no one should hire them right out of IBM. They had too many bad habits caused by too many years in a bureaucracy handling carefully circumscribed duties, so common wisdom had it that their first job in the real world would bewilder them and they'd mess up. It was better to be the second one to hire them. IBM did, after all, hire some of the best people, and after one failure, the midlevel executives had usually lost their bad habits. The rule of thumb meant that the bureaucrats at IBM had few opportunities on the outside. It was only the entrepreneurial types, the best and the brightest, who took the wad of cash from IBM and trusted that they could find their fortunes elsewhere.)

With so many of his best people heading for the hills and with the company's earnings staying weak throughout 1987, Akers began to realize that he had to start changing the company's culture. But it was hard for him to change. He was, after all, a product of this overpowering culture. As such a smart, forceful, optimistic, politically astute graduate of IBM's dominant sales force, Akers was one of the purest examples of that culture that was ever produced. So, rather than overthrow everything he knew and loved about IBM, he mainly just *talked* about changing. One of the most trumpeted of Akers's actions, for instance, was his declaration that 1987 was the Year of the Customer and his addition of "enhancing our customer partnerships" as one of IBM's hallowed corporate goals, which no one had altered in years. The pronouncement didn't do anything fundamental to restore the close relationships IBM had with its customers in the early 1980s. Akers just *told* his sales force and product designers to restore those ties. He assumed that was enough.

The one fundamental change Akers attempted to make at IBM in 1986 and 1987 came straight out of the old IBM playbook. He would, in the IBM vernacular, "fill the skies with blue suits." Akers and his marketing lieutenant, Ed Lucente, concocted a plan to solve the sales weakness in the United States by flooding the streets with new salesmen drawn from plants and staff operations where they were no longer needed. The decision eventually involved moving so many people around that

IBM called it the biggest movement of people since the end of World War II.

Lucente was known as a tough guy. He had an angry face with a broad forehead, piercing little eyes, strong jaw, and pointy nose. He always seemed impatient, ever ready to jump up and challenge someone in his big voice. Lucente had started in the sales force in Pittsburgh and, like almost all senior IBM executives, made his way up through the marketing ranks, although he hadn't lost the rough edges that got polished off most of his peers along the way. He came across as more arrogant than most. Memos sent to him would come back with one- or two-word responses: "Yes," "No," "See me." One young staff member talks of being told to go see Lucente to have him review some documents before the AS/400 minicomputer announcement in 1988. The time for his meeting came and went without any acknowledgment from Lucente or his secretary, even though the patiently waiting staff member could see that Lucente was in his office. After an hour and a half, Lucente came out of his office, and the staff member got up the nerve to confront him.

Lucente, still without acknowledging he was late, just said, "What am I supposed to do?"

The young man told him.

Lucente picked up the several-hundred-page stack of documents, flipped through it with his thumb in a few seconds, and, having read not a word, wrote, "OK. Ed" on the top sheet. He turned and marched back into his office.

Lucente bought into the IBM bureaucratic ways so completely that he had an overhead projector built into his beautiful rosewood desk and had a screen behind his desk that he could lower at the touch of a button. He was always ready to review or make a presentation with some of the standard IBM foils.

One acquaintance of Lucente's describes him as a devout Catholic who worried about whether his realignment of the sales force was ripping apart people's lives. The acquaintance would see Lucente out jogging before 6:00 A.M. in New Canaan, Connecticut, and Lucente might stop to chat, even acknowledging his worries. But once he got to the office, his guard went up. Because he supervised cuts of about 15,000 people total in 1987 and helped wipe out 8,200 staff jobs and 16,000 manufacturing jobs, he became known as "Neutron Eddy"—a reference to the neutron bomb, meaning that Lucente had left all the buildings standing but had killed all the people. (The Neutron Eddy reference, when it first appeared in *The Wall Street Journal,* did not amuse IBM. Akers summoned the reporters on the beat as well as several layers of editors to Armonk for lunch with him and his Management Committee. While Akers initially seemed to shrug off attacks on him personally in the mid-1980s and even ignored most shots at IBM as a company later in his tenure, it turned out that he just wanted to complain about the Neutron Eddy reference, plus a couple of only slightly more substantive things. He repeatedly asked why the *Journal* insisted on getting so personal. As it turned out, his concerns about personal references even extended to favorable stories. When *Business Week* once published a glowing portrayal of IBM vice president Lucie Fjeldstadt, Akers complained internally. Part of the reason was that the piece treated her as a hero accomplishing wonders despite the straitjacket placed on her by the IBM bureaucracy. Akers, as the keeper of the bureaucracy, took that as an indirect shot at him. Part of the reason, too, was that *any* personal publicity makes IBM nervous. The general feeling is that the Watsons were fairly publicity-shy despite building the company from scratch into a colossus, so how dare any of the current caretakers pose as heroes, especially as long as Tom Junior was still alive? Akers was much more comfortable having outsiders view IBM as a faceless team, not a collection of stars and screwups.)

Lucente had few options as he went about expanding the U.S. sales force, because IBM's tradition of lifetime employment meant that he couldn't simply hire from the outside. He had to take the people whose programming and manufacturing jobs were being eliminated and retrain them as salesmen. That meant months of schooling and many months more for these people to get comfortable in their new jobs. Even then, senior ex-IBM marketing executives now acknowledge, the quality of the sales force suffered. They say salesmen are born, not retrained. Even if someone was the best plant foreman ever, it didn't mean he'd ever learn to close a sale. While IBM says it doesn't keep statistics on how many of those put into the sales force are still with the company, the senior ex-IBMers say that the vast majority of those retrained at such expense have left as the sales force has imploded in recent years.

With Lucente working on beefing up the sales force—known as "wing-tipped warriors"—Akers called a rare press conference in January 1988 in the boardroom high up in the forty-two-story IBM building in midtown Manhattan. Sitting at the head of a square table that filled the huge, hushed room, Akers looked like a blue-suited King Arthur surrounded by his knights. With the old Tom Watson, Sr., library with its THINK sign and portrait of a glowering Tom Senior, just down the hall, Akers spoke with an assurance that came from a real sense of history. He said that the computer market had changed fundamentally and that, to adapt, IBM was going to go through its biggest change in management structure since Tom Junior took over in the mid-1950s. Akers hinted that the changes might even be more radical than the contention system Tom Junior put in place.

The idea was that the Management Committee would push decisions down into the organization so that Akers would no longer have to referee disputes among different divisions of IBM and so that the MC would no longer have to decide on such minutiae as whether a customer would get a special price on a product. The different IBM products were also to be cut loose to compete against one another without having senior management try to protect profitable, old products such as mainframes. Akers declared that IBM henceforth would be known as a company of risk-taking entrepreneurs.

He gave the job of implementing the new structure to Terry Lautenbach, everybody's favorite senior executive. Lautenbach is a beefy man with truck driver–like forearms and with the ability to match anybody scotch for scotch. He has a warm smile and often laughs at himself. A former speech writer says one of Lautenbach's favorite stories had him meeting a former schoolmate. The friend wondered how Lautenbach had done so well in business despite being an indifferent student. Lautenbach responded, "It's easy. If I can make something for three dollars and sell it for seven, well, that gives me a nice four percent profit margin."

The silver-haired Lautenbach—who some people say looks like Dick Van Dyke on steroids—was also easy to like because, even though he was just fifty when he got his elevated new position, he was only briefly mentioned as a candidate to succeed Akers in the top job. In the competitive politics of IBM's senior executives, that was important. The reason Lautenbach wasn't taken more seriously was that he had a heart problem that had required a bypass in the early 1980s and it resembled a problem that had killed an older brother when he was in his early fifties. While Lautenbach had seemed to recover fully from the heart trouble, his health was enough of an issue that those competing for the top job didn't have to worry about climbing over him on their way up.

Lautenbach had plenty of admirers for other reasons, too. He had earned good credentials climbing up through the marketing ranks and had turned around IBM's network-equipment business. He was also known as exceptionally decisive. He would get in at 7:30 A.M., answer his own phone until his secretary arrived, and just plow through business.

"He is the most impressive combination of management skills, decisiveness, and energy I've ever seen," says John Sabol, a Microsoft executive who was once Lautenbach's administrative assistant at IBM.

Joe Zemke, now the chief executive of IBM competitor Amdahl, says that when he worked at IBM, he was initially indecisive when Lautenbach once offered him a transfer. "I said, 'I've got to think about this. I've got five kids and I'm not sure I want to relocate.' Terry looked up at me and said, 'I have six. You'll take the job. I have some files in an office down the hall I'd like you to look at.' Being around Terry was like being caught up in a hurricane."

Lautenbach won points as an open-minded manager because he set himself up as the mentor for Ellen Hancock and kept promoting her as he moved up the ranks. That was a good call, because Hancock—a techie who joined the company as a programmer—has done well running IBM's network-equipment business. It also let Lautenbach make a statement. Even though IBM is still very much a boy's club at the top, he helped make Hancock a senior vice president and, given the size of the business she now runs, probably the most senior woman executive in the history of American business.

Lautenbach was a testament to Tom Watson, Sr.'s feeling that nepotism was good for business. He and three of his brothers were sort of the Kennedy family of IBM. They would get together for family holidays and compete on all sorts of levels, not least of which was their advancement inside IBM. Husky brother Dan eventually ran one of IBM's big marketing areas in the United States, while Ned—the one small, quiet, mousy brother—and Terry became senior vice presidents.

Such nepotism could get complicated. Terry Lautenbach once had

Ed Lucente's brother Angelo reporting directly to him, while Ed Lucente was Ned Lautenbach's immediate boss. When Terry and Ned later got promoted in 1988, Ned should have reported directly to Terry. Akers had to jury-rig a structure that allowed Ned to report to someone else. But IBM management had always figured that if nepotism meant attracting families like the Lautenbachs and gave IBM a family-business feel, then complications could be tolerated.

Under the new structure Akers announced in early 1988, Terry Lautenbach's charter was to have essentially all of IBM reporting to him, except for the marketing operations outside the United States. The idea was that he could make decisions faster than the Management Committee could and would free it to focus on other things. He was also supposed to delegate his authority.

It didn't happen. Lautenbach was too much a product of the IBM culture to willingly delegate authority. Instead, he built himself another organization, with another big staff. Decisions got made no faster than they had under the old system. Businesses such as the PC and workstation units still had to fight to get the right to go after their more profitable older brothers, the minicomputers and mainframes. Akers had once again *talked* about a change that would have helped solve his problems, but IBM was no better off than it had been before. Actually, the company was worse off, because it lost precious time focusing on a false solution.

The only thing that saved IBM from disaster in 1988 was a project that, like the PC, began in a little skunk works set up on the sly. While IBM had tried a frontal assault on the minicomputer market for years, throwing many thousands of development people at huge projects, the problem was solved by five people working in a vacant lab in Rochester, Minnesota.[4] They came up with a way to combine two of IBM's incompatible minicomputer lines—the System 36 and System 38—while preserving the best features of both. The little group sold their managers on the idea and, with the group for once protected from the "process," developed the product in two years. That was about half the normal time for such a project at IBM. The marketing people even got into the swing of things and gave up on maintaining secrecy. They got hundreds of customers and software developers involved early on, meaning that the new minicomputer was dead on target and had loads of useful software available from day one.

Somehow, though, the new minicomputer's success would not convince IBM management that it should finally junk the convoluted development processes that had kept thousands of people from solving a problem that five people handled nicely. IBM's senior executives seemed to learn some marketing lessons from the new computer, the AS/400, but, mainly, they just reveled in the successes it brought. The AS/400 quickly grew into a $14-billion-a-year business, meaning that it would have been the second-largest computer maker in the world if it had been independent and would have been one of the forty largest companies in the United States. At least as important, the AS/400— AS stands for "application system"—also sent arch minicomputer competitor Digital Equipment and its snotty ads crashing to earth. The IBM line helped cut Digital's stock-market value by more than three-quarters, forced it to lay off tens of thousands of people, and got the Digital board to dump founder Ken Olsen.

With the AS/400 helping IBM's earnings finally to increase again in 1988, after three tough years, Akers relaxed once more. He reverted to his talk-talk-talk approach to solving problems. He decided he would cut corporate bureaucracy by starting a campaign to get people to "Just Say No" to requests from higher-ups for unnecessary paperwork and he acted as though that solved the problem—even though budget planners still wrote reports about coming reports, even though official design monitors still sat in on all product meetings to make sure all the steps in the official design process were followed, and even though the bureaucracy was still so dense that a corporate vice president, one of the top fifty people at the company, was seven levels below Akers in the reporting structure. There are companies with more than $1 billion a year in revenue whose lowest-level worker isn't seven levels below the chief executive.

Still, thinking that he had hacked through the red tape, Akers seemed comfortable at the end of 1988 that he had things under control. Although he had committed to keeping a low profile until he had good news to deliver, there he was at the end of 1988 granting a series of major interviews about the turnaround at IBM.

"The things we set out to do are in fact happening," he said.

The one area that still worried Akers was the United States, where revenue fell again in 1988 despite the thousands of additional salesmen created in the "back to the sales force" movement. Lucente, as the top U.S. marketing executive, had to take responsibility. He also had developed such a reputation as a hatchet man while rearranging the sales force that he had lost some of his ability to manage, so Akers replaced Lucente. In the process, he set in motion a series of changes that ushered in the next era in IBM's PC business.

Akers gave Lucente a "special assignment," an unusually obvious way of letting the world know that Lucente had been put in what IBMers call the "penalty box." (His stay in the penalty box was, however, extraordinarily short. After just a few months, he was sent to Japan to run IBM's huge Asian operations. Given Lucente's lack of international experience up to that point, many people saw the job as a way of grooming him to succeed Akers. In any case, the appointment left people wondering why Lucente hadn't had to follow the normal route and produce some sort of success in order to earn his way out of the penalty box.) To succeed Lucente in late 1988, Akers tapped Lowe's relatively new boss, George Conrades, who was the general manager of a product group that included PCs, workstations, and a few other things.

For Lowe, that finally created the opening he wanted. He'd been a division president running the PC business for three and a half years, a long time in one job for someone who saw himself as a rising star, so he was impatient to get to the next level. But Lowe was passed over. Akers gave the job to Dick Gerstner, who had been running IBM's Asian operations (and who is the older brother of Lou Gerstner, who became IBM's chief executive in 1993).

Lowe decided that, in the IBM vernacular, he had run out of runway. He left in December 1988 to take a job at Xerox. He actually seemed relieved. The press had been brutal in chronicling all the failures of the IBM PC strategy, in criticizing Lowe personally, and in noting that he had been passed over for a promotion. Now he was going to nice, quiet Xerox. Maybe he could avoid the press, stop spending so much time on the road, and actually get some work done. Let someone else deal with the pitiless media spotlight on the IBM PC business.

EIGHT

Back in the 1970s and early 1980s, IBM executives had imposing, macho nicknames: Spike and Buck and Bo and Blackjack. When Jim Cannavino left as head of the mainframe division and arrived on the PC scene at the end of 1988 to take over from Bill Lowe, though, he seemed to usher in an age of friendly diminutives: Jimmy, Bobby, Nicky, Davey. The group, in their early to mid-forties, were sometimes referred to as the "Kids." The assumption was that they'd grow up to run the company someday.

To stake his claim to the crown, all Jimmy Cannavino needed to do was pull off a miracle in the PC business, where IBM executives were beginning to realize that every mistake that could have been made had been made. The PS/2 line of PCs wasn't selling. The OS/2 operating-system software was a mess. The strategy on selling software applications was nonexistent; so was any strategy for selling PC peripheral equipment. Intel and Microsoft had been given the opportunity to take control of the direction of the industry, and they had seized it. IBM was nowhere.

Cannavino, having largely grown up on the mainframe side of the IBM house, had once sneered that if God had meant for man to have personal computers, He would have built them into our wrists. So Cannavino had to learn quickly what PCs were all about—as IBMers say, he had to drink out of a fire hose.

One of the places he started was with Bill Gates. Gates, ever-attentive to his relationship with IBM, called to see whether he could spend some time with the new guy, and Cannavino agreed. The two decided to have a couple of brief meetings in early 1989 to get acquainted before they even started to talk business. Gates was going to be east a couple of days after they talked on the phone, so they agreed that he'd stop by Cannavino's office in White Plains for an hour and a half or so of friendly chatting.

It didn't work. They managed to stay cordial for the first few months as they felt each other out, but by the late summer of 1989 their feelings had hardened into strong dislike, and things went downhill from there.

Gates came across as a smart aleck. He kept offering advice, telling Cannavino that he really ought to cut programmers in one spot, focus them differently on another problem, and so forth. Gates didn't let up, either. He sat there, rocking back and forth, with his arms folded across his stomach, firing off ideas in his machine-gun style.

Other IBMers shrugged off Gates's manner. As seasoned IBM executives, they just saw him as a bright kid with more ideas than he could control. Cannavino, though, found it hard not to be irritated. He had never gone to college, and while that made everyone else view his success as all the more extraordinary, his lack of formal education always made him sensitive to people who talked down to him. That was especially true if the person perceived himself as more intellectual than Cannavino. Gates didn't have a college degree, either, but he had, after all, dropped out of Harvard. Cannavino had merely spent time at a technical institute while working at a grocery store and a pizza parlor.

Cannavino appeared to Gates to be a windbag. He'd talk about his horses or his cars. Maybe he'd go on about how IBM was showing American manufacturers how to stand up to the Japanese. The edgy Gates always wanted to move on to some point or other, so he chafed as Cannavino waxed philosophical.

When the two disagreed, Cannavino never said anything threatening. He would just mutter everything through clenched teeth, and his body language seemed to say, I'm going to make you an offer you can't refuse. The tough-guy pose put off the wispy Gates.

As the months passed and the summer of 1989 approached, Cannavino learned enough to know he had a conflict with Microsoft. Gates, having almost given up on Windows at least a couple of times, now saw enough potential that he was straining to get a new version out the door. That work seemed to Cannavino to undermine the IBM-Microsoft work on OS/2 because the two operating systems competed for the same users. Any success for Windows also benefited only Microsoft, because Bill Lowe had turned down Microsoft's repeated requests to make Windows a joint project and had rejected the opportunity to buy into Microsoft. Cannavino didn't like the way the situation felt.

Cannavino also began to realize what a sweetheart deal Lowe had given Microsoft by letting it collect all the royalties from operating systems sold to clone makers. Cannavino insisted that the royalty arrangements be redone so that IBM and Microsoft split all DOS operating-system revenue fifty-fifty. His position was that the two had formed a partnership whose intent was to split things down the middle, no matter what the letter of the contract specified. Gates's position was: Tough. And he had the contract on his side.

Finally, in one meeting in early summer in 1989, Cannavino began to press Gates hard, especially about his plans for Windows. The early versions of Windows had gone nowhere since they became available in 1985, and Cannavino hadn't been aware just how serious Gates was about doing a new version of Windows for release in the spring of 1990. He felt Gates had been deceiving him. Cannavino wanted to know why Gates was pushing the graphical Windows so hard when he was supposed to be endorsing OS/2 as the new graphical-interface standard. When Gates seemed evasive, Cannavino bore in.

Gates began rocking forward and backward so hard that Cannavino thought he was going to bang his head on the table. Then Gates began to sweat. Cannavino told people who worked for him that the sweat just poured out, not only from under Gates's armpits but from his forehead, his neck, his back, his chest. The IBMers say Cannavino could smell the fear in Gates. (Gates says this is ridiculous. What matters, though, is what Cannavino thought, because he based so much of what he did later on the reading he took of Gates.)

Cannavino decided he couldn't trust Gates anymore. So he went back to his office and requested time with the Management Committee. In essence, he told Chairman John Akers and the various other bosses at the meeting: I know you all think that Bill Gates and Microsoft are great and that they make a terrific partner, but, let me tell you, he doesn't feel like a partner to me.

At that point, IBM management decided that they either needed to break off the relationship with Microsoft or bring Microsoft to heel. The question was how.

Cannavino grew up in West Melrose Park, Illinois, a tough ethnic neighborhood about fifteen miles west of Chicago where childhood friends say the schools taught sex education before algebra. He had his first child at age seventeen and married his high school sweetheart when he graduated. He supported his young family by getting by on three or four hours of sleep a night and working the sorts of hours that became a personal trademark. He worked odd hours in the family pizza parlor while taking on all the work he could find at the local supermarket. Cannavino became manager of the produce department, then, when the meat manager left, he asked whether he could take on that job, too—and the second salary. The supermarket management agreed. Soon, another manager left, and Cannavino wound up with that job, too, along with a third salary. It meant he was working 6:00 A.M. to 10:00 P.M. most days, but it made for a reasonable living. To top things off, Cannavino started going to the DeVry Technical Institute near Chicago to learn about electronics.

Then one day, the supermarket was unionized, and management no longer could pay one person three salaries. Cannavino decided he'd better look for a new job. Because his car was in the shop and he didn't have any great ideas about where to look, he boarded a bus headed toward Chicago. He figured that better jobs would be available as he got closer to the city. The route ended in Oak Park, a nice suburb just west of the city, and, as it happened, the bus dumped Cannavino right in front of an IBM branch. He had heard of IBM, so he decided to go inside and introduce himself.

Cannavino told the receptionist he had an appointment. When she asked with whom, he fumbled for a few seconds and she filled in the blank.

"Mr. Thompson?" she asked.

"That's right," Cannavino said, "Mr. Thompson."

Thompson happened to be the branch manager. The receptionist seemed dubious about whether Cannavino really had an appointment, so he said, "Okay, if Mr. Thompson will just come down here and tell me he forgot my appointment, I'll go away."

IBM isn't really set up to deal with fast-talking hustlers, so the receptionist called Thompson. The manager, trained to be polite in the IBM way, came out of his office to apologize for having misplaced the note about the appointment. He set Cannavino up to take an aptitude test for repair technicians, then ushered the teenaged Cannavino into his office.

Cannavino aced the test, but when Thompson asked him about his educational history, Cannavino admitted he had only a high school degree. With typical moxie, Cannavino then insisted that he could become the manager's best repair technician within six months. If he didn't, he would willingly give up his job and return all his paychecks. Thompson just laughed.

He hesitated. Cannavino didn't meet the normal standards, so it was hard to justify hiring him. But these were desperate times at IBM back in the early 1960s. IBM was preparing to launch the 360 line of mainframes in a $5 billion gamble that would make or break the company and it needed to hire thousands of people to help provide service for the machines. Thompson took a chance. Cannavino got his job.

After about three months, Thompson barged out of his office and screamed for Cannavino. "Get your ass in my office!" he shouted for all to hear.

Cannavino stared blankly at his fellow workers in the repair shop and said, "I guess I'm out of here. I don't know what I did, but I must be gone."

Thompson growled that someone from accounting had called to yell at him, complaining that some records were all screwed up because a technician named Cannavino wasn't cashing his paychecks.

"Are you trying to get me fired?" Thompson demanded.

Cannavino said he was just sticking to his end of their bargain.

"What bargain?" Thompson yelled, his exasperation rising.

When Cannavino explained, a little smile crept over Thompson's face as it all came back to him. He said he had assumed Cannavino was just kidding.

"Oh, no," Cannavino replied. He'd been saving all the checks in a shoe box in case he had to return them.

Thompson finally laughed and said, "Oh, that's right, you're the interview I forgot about."

Cannavino figured that as long as Thompson was laughing, he ought to go ahead and confess that he'd made up the interview, just to get that one off his chest.

Thompson kept laughing. He said Cannavino should by all means cash the checks.

Cannavino said that would help, because he could now quit the pizza parlor job he had continued on the side to support his wife and son until he started getting paid by IBM. Cannavino quickly took on additional responsibility, especially for problems with the mainframe operating system. Cannavino, who had two more sons by the time he was twenty-one, moved from doing mechanical repair into programming, becoming the first person in his family to work outside a trade. (His father was a repair technician, his mother a bank clerk. His brother is a machinist. One sister is a housewife and the other helps run a family restaurant.) Cannavino holed up in his office for days at a time, surrounded on the floor by piles of computer printouts, candy bars, crackers, and a sleeping bag, when he had a tough problem to solve. In the process, he and another young programmer developed such a good reputation for fixing bugs that colleagues dubbed them the "Change Team" ("engineering changes" being the IBM euphemism for fixing bugs that could crash whole systems). That name actually then helped Cannavino get far greater exposure because of a fortuitous bit of miscommunication.

O. M. Scott, a senior executive from headquarters, visited Chicago one time in the late 1960s and decided to meet with all the major teams in the area. He'd heard someone mention the Change Team and, not knowing that it was a nickname for just two people, had his secretary schedule a lunch with them.

Cannavino's colleague was out sick that day, so the lunch was just Scott and Cannavino. It took the two a while to figure out what was going on. Cannavino had just been told to have lunch with Scott, not why. He kept waiting for Scott to get to the point. Scott kept wondering who this guy Cannavino was and when Cannavino was going to take him to the meeting of the full Change Team.

When they finally straightened things out, they laughed and laughed.

Cannavino took the opportunity to ask for a promotion. Even as a teenager on his first day on the job at IBM, he was brash enough that he started keeping a notebook that he filled with the decisions he would make if he was running IBM. He wanted to test his judgment, against the day when he might run the company. Scott asked whether he could keep Cannavino in Chicago by giving him more responsibility. Cannavino said he might go along with that. He asked whether he could give up his salary and just be paid a piece rate, per bug fixed.

Scott asked how much Cannavino would want per bug.

"It doesn't make any difference," Cannavino responded. "Make the price as low as you want. You have an unlimited supply, and I fix them fast, so I'll make plenty of money no matter what the price."

But Scott couldn't get any of his bosses to go along with a plan to throw out the whole IBM salary structure, so he decided that the only thing left to do was to send Cannavino to Poughkeepsie, New York, the heart of IBM's mainframe development. That way, the youngster could get involved in actually writing the software, not just slapping Band-Aids on it.

Once Cannavino reached Poughkeepsie in the late 1960s, he stirred things up once again. He came up with a method that he thought would let many applications run drastically faster on IBM's new mainframes. When he couldn't convince his bosses to let him monkey with a key part of the system to test his idea, he decided to do it on his own. He discovered that three departments in his facility had one of the new mainframes on order and figured that one didn't need the machine for a few months. So he sneaked into the area where mainframes were readied for shipment and changed a mailing label so that one of the machines was sent to a vacant lab. Cannavino then appropriated the lab as his own for the next several months. With help from two colleagues who would work well into the night, Cannavino quickly effected his change. The results were better than expected. Lots of software applications now ran more than twice as fast on the new mainframes.

Now that Cannavino could prove his results, his bosses loved the idea. Not knowing that the machine was stolen, they started bringing people from other operations through Cannavino's makeshift lab, unaware that it, too, had been appropriated without any authorization. The bosses bragged about what a smart young fellow they had in Cannavino. He still had to deal with a moment of panic when the rightful owner of the machine figured out what had happened to it and called Cannavino in to chew him out. But Cannavino got off with just a stiff warning—essentially being told he'd be fired if he ever did something that bright again.

By now, Cannavino was working so much that he didn't see his wife or three sons often, so his marriage broke up after just seven years. The flip side of that was that he had begun to catch the eye of some very senior people. Carl Conti, who eventually became a senior vice president and the general manager of the product group that included mainframes and mainframe disk drives, took a chance on Cannavino and asked him to become lab director down the road in Endicott, New York, even though Cannavino was some three levels below lab director at the time. That caught the attention of Blackjack Bertram, who was Cannavino's boss four or five layers up the line at the time.

Cannavino had met Bertram a year earlier under testy circumstances. Some of Bertram's staff had called in Cannavino to see whether he'd handle a small project for Bertram. Cannavino looked into it and decided the project would fail, so he refused. Bertram's staff members hauled him into Bertram's office and, according to one person who was in the room, said, "This jerk won't take the job."

Bertram asked why.

Cannavino said, "It probably won't work, and I won't go through the motions for anybody."

Bertram said that he had a lot invested in the project personally and was sure it would work.

Cannavino said, "You're so good, why don't you do the goddamn job yourself? "

Bertram glared at Cannavino and said, "Get out of here."

A year later, though, Bertram decided he couldn't lose Cannavino to Conti. He gave Cannavino a huge promotion himself, to lab director in Poughkeepsie.

As Conti continued to ascend the ladder into IBM's senior circles, he pulled Cannavino along with him. In the mid-1980s, by age forty, the kid without any college experience was running IBM's mainframe business, which accounted for about half of IBM's revenue and two-thirds of its world-beating profits.

Cannavino did well enough that Jack Kuehler, soon to be president of IBM, decided to put him in the PC job at the end of 1988, at the still-young age of forty-four. Putting a mainframe guy in the job meshed with IBM's idea that mainframes were the center of the universe and the real trick with PCs was to integrate them better into the mainframe world. The job was also a test to see whether the young hotshot had enough of the right stuff to straighten out a mess. Cannavino initially balked, but Kuehler talked him into taking the job.

Cannavino quickly got promoted again, becoming general manager of the group including PCs and workstations in mid-1989. This time, another fluke opened the way. Dick Gerstner, whose appointment to the general manager's job at the end of 1988 had precipitated Bill Lowe's departure, lasted only a few months in the job because of a medical misdiagnosis. Gerstner had such severe lower-back pains that he found it hard to fly and often had to lie down on the floor at work. He frequently resorted to conducting business from his bed at home. The pain became so debilitating that Gerstner couldn't handle it anymore, so he retired early. What the doctors missed, though, was that the core problem was Lyme disease, a painful disease carried in deer ticks. Once the problem was diagnosed correctly years later and was treated, Dick Gerstner's back problems became manageable, but he was long retired by then. In the meantime, Cannavino had easily won the spot that Lowe had salivated over for years. Cannavino had gained considerable new standing.

By the late 1980s, Cannavino was remarried to a programmer he had met in Poughkeepsie, and, partly through her, had settled into his current work-hard, play-hard life-style. He met his wife, Suzie, when he decided one day to figure out why his engineers kept spending all their available time in one programmer's office. He dropped his work and went into her office. As soon as he saw her, he dispatched the engineers to go finish his work. He stayed with Suzie.

She loved horses and, soon enough, so did he. Now he raises horses on a farm with a two-hundred-year-old farmhouse that they bought in Dutchess County, some forty-five minutes north of his office in Somers, New York. He is the hunt master of a local fox-hunting club, and his idea of a grand vacation is to don his riding boots and go off for a week of riding through the dense brush in Virginia hunting foxes. Cannavino also skis whenever possible and plays enough golf to maintain his twelve handicap. He once decided to play some of the great Scottish courses and, with typical abandon, covered twenty courses in ten days by playing thirty-six holes every day. (Some who play with him wonder whether his handicap is inflated. They say he always seems to be a few strokes better than a twelve handicap, meaning he always wins any wagers on the game.)

Despite all his extracurricular activities, Cannavino continues to maintain the tightest schedule of any senior IBM executive. He is frequently triple-scheduled, meaning he not only has meetings all day long but has backup meetings scheduled in case one of the other meetings falls through and then has backups scheduled for many of the backups.

His schedule is so tight that people wanting to meet him sometimes camp out in front of his office, waiting for him to leave for home—even though that often doesn't happen until 9:00 or 10:00 P.M. and sometimes not until the wee hours of the morning. Cannavino often works so late that he doesn't even make it home; he just sleeps for a few hours at a nearby Holiday Inn. He has finally developed a system where his longtime executive assistant, Susan Fairty, carries his proxy around the world to meetings that Cannavino doesn't have time to attend. Or she walks into a meeting that was to have been run by Cannavino and announces that she is "virtual Jim"—a nerdy term that means that, for the purposes of that meeting, she is Cannavino.

Cannavino takes considerable work home with him, to the point of creating a lab in his home, where he sets up numerous competitors' PCs so he can tinker with them to see how they stack up against his products. He also sometimes orders machines from his own organization to see how quickly and how well people respond to the order. Cannavino, in his puckish way, once left some lengths of pipe outside the home lab, just waiting until his wife finally asked why they were there.

"Oh," Cannavino said, "those are for the water-coolant system for the mainframe I'm having installed."

As Cannavino moved up the ranks, he developed plenty of admirers. The now-retired Conti, for instance, says he thinks Cannavino is the best executive at the company and should have been named to succeed Akers as chairman. Favorite subordinates, benefiting from Cannavino's strong sense of personal loyalty, repaid him in kind with something approaching devotion. One aide, Dick Guarino, talks about a time when Cannavino's main team of people had been traveling for weeks, working on a tough issue, and were worn down. Guarino was feeling particular pressure because he was about to get married, but he was being distracted by work. At the end of one day, Cannavino announced that he was going to throw a bachelor party. He asked everyone to leave the room. When they came back a few minutes later, they found a huge pink cake set up in the middle of the room. Everybody groaned, wondering how Cannavino could be so tacky as to have a scantily clad woman jump out of a cake in this day and age. Sure enough, the top of the cake popped off—and out jumped a fully clothed Cannavino.

Those not part of the favored inner circle, however, sometimes had a different view of the man. Some complained about the size of his ego—even in a company where, at that level, everybody had a huge ego. When Cannavino ran the mainframe business, he set up an office in Somers that was bigger and fancier than Akers's office. People going to see him said they were off to see the "king." When he went to run the PC business, some of the mainframe folks counseled their counterparts there that they'd do fine as long as they learned to bow and scrape.

Those who worked in other parts of IBM, especially marketing, found Cannavino hard to stomach. His peers in the marketing organization complained that he had to take over any meeting he attended. No one else could ever have a good idea. He wouldn't pitch in and help them deal with a customer problem. He also showed up late for a lot of meetings because of his overscheduling, and when he did arrive, he often went off on some long story that didn't seem to have anything to do with the meeting.

Cannavino developed a prickly management style, which annoyed some people. One young executive sent to accompany him for a day as part of his training tells of watching Cannavino in action during some annual review meetings. The executive, Jnan Dash, who has since left IBM, says Cannavino told him on the way into the meetings, "You're going to see people try to bullshit me all day long. My job is to catch them at it." In the first session, after a young man made a lengthy presentation about how well his part of the business was doing, Cannavino thundered, "I don't believe a goddamn word that you just told me. Start from the beginning, and this time cut the shit." Then he turned to Dash and winked.

Even those who liked Cannavino found him terribly demanding. His attitude seemed to be that as long as he and his assistant, Fairty, were working late into the night, so should everybody else. He sometimes even took a subordinate into a health club with him—where Cannavino, who used to be forty pounds heavier than he is now and who used to smoke as much as four packs of cigarettes a day, spent considerable time trying to control his weight. Cannavino would go to it on the StairMaster, sweat pouring off him, while some guy stood next to him in a suit taking notes as wheezing obiter dicta were issued.

Whatever people thought of him, though, IBM was looking for someone to blast through the cultural gridlock that had paralyzed the PC business for so many years—and this seemed to be the right guy.

As Cannavino settled into the PC job in 1989, he spent the first six months or more in ignorant bliss. He just ran around fixing some of the obvious problems with the PC business's processes, confident that he was improving things. It wasn't until well into 1989 that Cannavino realized he had some more serious, strategic problems that demanded attention, in particular ones concerning his relationship with Gates and Microsoft.

When Cannavino began really investigating the relationship, he considered just bagging the whole thing. He began to look through the code the two companies had produced for the OS/2 operating system and what he saw appalled him. There was none of the discipline he was used to seeing in the software written for IBM's mainframes, where detailed notes inside the code explained what it was trying to accomplish and where programmers produced lengthy manuals providing further documentation. When Cannavino looked into the process used to produce the software, he decided it was out of control. He had also seen all the reports about the scads of bugs in the latest version of the OS/2 software. And, by the way, no one was buying it.

But Cannavino decided his hands were tied. IBM had made one of its grand commitments to customers that they could build huge strategic computer networks with OS/2 as the core. IBM guaranteed that it would be a good system and that software applications taking advantage of it would be widely available. He couldn't break those commitments. Not only did IBM's most valued customers in big corporate data-processing departments stake their careers on IBM's ability to deliver what it promised, but senior IBMers often put their own reputations on the line on something like OS/2. Anytime anyone ever raised the possibility in a senior executives meeting that he might kill some project, three or four people always protested: "Wait a minute, I just visited XYZ Corp., and I promised that we'd keep improving that project because it's strategic." No senior IBMer ever wanted to be embarrassed in front of a customer. Having seen how the press clobbered IBM when it gave up on the PCjr years before, senior IBMers also weren't anxious to get creamed again by acknowledging defeat on OS/2.

There was a more subtle pressure on Cannavino, too, an arcane accounting procedure that IBMers don't like to acknowledge has any effect whatsoever on their thinking. The procedure at IBM means that only a quarter of the cost of developing a piece of software is treated as expenses in the year those costs occur. The remaining costs are amortized, with IBM accounting for them as expenses in the three following years. The theory is that the substantial up-front costs of developing software should be spread out over the many years during which the software is sold. The result is sometimes different. Here was IBM spending perhaps $150 million a year developing OS/2. Because the company had been spending that kind of money for years but deferring a lot of those costs, Cannavino had perhaps $225 million of costs stored up, waiting to hit him. If he continued the OS/2 project, he could take them gradually. If he killed the project, though, he'd have to take them all at once. That would destroy his results and give IBM a nasty little write-off.

Deciding he had to go forward with OS/2 in 1989, Cannavino considered doing it on his own, but he found that Gates had been too cagy to allow that. Gates had made sure that Microsoft wrote most of the key parts of the OS/2 software. That way—as Cannavino discovered—if IBM ever tried to make a clean break, it would find that it had to start pretty much from scratch on parts of the code that were not only important but were so complicated that it might take IBM programmers a couple of years to get up to speed, a frightfully long time in the PC business.

Cannavino decided he had no good options. He couldn't kill a lousy operating system, and he couldn't get rid of a partner he didn't like or trust. So he temporized. Over the next two years, he tried for any little edge he could get over Microsoft. He got none, though, from the hardheaded Gates. All Cannavino produced was a stalemate, which doomed OS/2 and let his arch-enemy Gates take over the world.

By 1989, Windows had been a nonevent for years, and it was beginning to seem as though it might not complicate Microsoft's relationship with IBM too much even though Windows seemed to be competing with the jointly produced OS/2. Microsoft had actually cut its Windows staff back to a skeleton crew as small as one programmer in 1987 and early 1988, while Ballmer whipped the two hundred or so people on the OS/2 team to get a version of OS/2 out by the end of 1988. Even once a few more people found their way back onto the Windows work in mid-1988, OS/2 remained the hot project. Microsoft's best programmers say they all wanted to work on OS/2, and they did (even though IBMers have long suspected that Gates hedged his bet on OS/2 by having a team of his best people going full bore in the background on Windows). At one point, Ballmer asked in a meeting whether Microsoft shouldn't just give up on Windows. Recollections of people at the meeting now differ on whether Ballmer was serious or was just playing devil's advocate, making sure Gates considered all the options; but the fact is that Windows was a low priority for Microsoft through 1987 and well into 1988. There was good reason, too, because Windows wasn't selling. Microsoft claimed it had sold 500,000 copies by the end of 1987, but the vast majority had been given away, and many weren't even being used.

Windows began to resurface as an issue, though, in mid-1988 because of a whim. Microsoft had hired an intern for that summer who knew a University of Arizona professor named Murray Sargent. Sargent was a laser physicist, not a programmer, but he seemed like a smart guy and he had the summer off, so Microsoft decided to go ahead and hire him, too, in a sort of a two-for-one deal. Microsoft's philosophy has always been that the more smart people there are around, the better.

It turned out that Sargent had a little homemade program for debugging software that overcame the sort of problem that had done the most to limit the capabilities of Windows. The problem was that Windows couldn't deal with large amounts of memory. That meant that programs written to run on Windows had to be tiny, which limited their features. Windows also couldn't handle many programs at once. Sargent never would have had a chance to apply his ideas on memory to Windows except that he finished early on what was supposed to be a summer-long piece of work on OS/2. With too little time left for another formal assignment before classes started at the University of Arizona in the fall of 1988, Sargent was told just to go play around with anything he found interesting. He began fiddling with Windows and found that his ideas might solve the memory problem. Sargent showed his work to Ballmer right before going back to teach. Ballmer was excited.

This breakthrough came at a time in 1988 when Microsoft was less than happy with IBM. In the spring of 1988, IBM had joined a group called the Open Software Foundation, enraging Gates. The OSF, which included Digital Equipment, Hewlett-Packard, Apollo Computer, and numerous other companies, had gathered together at a press conference a dozen chief executives representing more computer selling power than had ever been collected under one roof. The idea was to develop a unified version of Unix, an operating system developed by AT&T that many scientists and engineers used. Unix was an excellent operating system and already had a broad-enough base of users in 1988 that Gates worried it could become popular enough to wipe out his dominance of the PC operating-system market through DOS and, down the road, either Windows or OS/2. The only problem with Unix was that every manufacturer selling computers that used the Unix operating system produced its own flavor of Unix. Applications written to run on Unix on IBM's workstations wouldn't run on Digital's workstations or HP's minicomputers, even though all the hardware nominally used the same operating system. That made the Unix world as fragmented as the PC world had been in the late 1970s and early 1980s, when applications written to run on Tandy's PCs wouldn't run on Apple's, Kaypro's, and so on. It was only when DOS came along and made it possible to run the same applications on anybody's IBM-compatible hardware that demand for PCs exploded. Gates, of course, remembered well how great that explosion had been. He worried that if, suddenly, all these hardware giants like IBM, Digital, and HP agreed on a single version of Unix, then demand for Unix could take off the way interest in DOS had. Unix, he thought, could be the most direct competitor imaginable not only to DOS but also to the joint work Microsoft and IBM were doing on OS/2.

Gates had mounted a brief but spirited counterattack against IBM's involvement in the OSF. He had received the news about a week ahead of time, while talking to Bill Lowe one evening at the 1988 spring Comdex trade show in Atlanta. Gates paced and fumed and fumed and paced until an assistant suggested a way that he could go over Lowe's head the next morning. The assistant, John Sabol, had been Terry Lautenbach's administrative assistant at IBM and knew that Lautenbach answered his own phone after his arrival at 7:30 until his secretary arrived at 8:00. Lautenbach was now Lowe's boss's boss, so Gates gave him a try early the following morning. Lautenbach thought Gates's concerns had enough merit that by noon the next day—following some lengthy fax correspondence and a Gates trip to the West Coast to make a previously scheduled speech to an IBM group—Gates was in Armonk to argue his case. He now had to deal with Jack Kuehler, IBM's vice-chairman, who as IBM's most senior technical person had driven the deal with the OSF.

Kuehler met Gates at the front entrance to the headquarters building and walked him down to one of IBM's executive dining rooms. True to the bland decor throughout the IBM empire, these ground-floor rooms, just across from the cafeteria, have plain yellow wallpaper and cupboards along one wall that are covered with an inexpensive-looking dark veneer. The only view from the rooms is of the parking lot in the back of the building, and the voices of people walking by often disrupt the conversations in the rooms. The only sign of privilege was the device, like a garage-door opener, that sat at Kuehler's right hand, which he pressed every once in a while to summon a waiter.

Kuehler argued that IBM needed to give its customers a choice, about whether they wanted Unix or OS/2. Kuehler also let slip that the Open Software Foundation was going to use IBM technology as the core of its version of Unix, letting IBM influence the direction the OSF was going to take and generating sizable payments from the OSF for the rights to the technology. (Kuehler neglected to mention that IBM bullied the OSF into using the IBM technology by saying IBM wouldn't join the group otherwise. As it turned out, IBM had all its standard problems with software and missed almost all its deadlines for delivering the code. As a result, IBM lost out on about $100 million in payments from the OSF, and the OSF used others' software as the basis for its version of Unix.)

"Jack, they don't want your technology," Gates said. "They want your money and your name." He warned that IBM, by helping gather together so many powerhouses to push a version of Unix, was undercutting its own OS/2 efforts. He said that IBM would confuse customers about what was strategic, OS/2 or Unix. "What are you guys up to?" he asked.

Gates got nowhere. He left Armonk angry and confused about IBM's intentions in the spring of 1988. When, just a few weeks later, he heard about Murray Sargent and his way of overcoming Windows's limitations, Gates had no qualms about pursuing the project.

In October 1988, when IBM announced a deal with Next, Steve Jobs's new company, Gates blew up again. IBM paid $50 million for the rights to an innovative operating system Jobs developed and talked about making it available to run on IBM's PCs. That would have endorsed Jobs's operating system and put it in head-to-head competition with both OS/2 and with Microsoft's Windows and DOS. Gates wondered again what his partner was up to and whether he still had a place in IBM's thinking.

By late summer of 1989, with Gates pursuing Windows again and with Cannavino confused about how to deal with his sometime partner, Cannavino and Gates began a series of skirmishes. The biggest concerned money.

Cannavino complained that Microsoft was paying too few of the expenses for developing OS/2. He noted that IBM had considerably more than 1,000 people working on the main part of the project, while Microsoft had perhaps 200. Cannavino said the difference meant that IBM was writing far more lines of the code than Microsoft—in fact, with Microsoft improving some sections of IBM code by rewriting it to make it shorter, IBM once again accused Microsoft of sometimes producing a *negative* number of lines of software.

Gates responded that lines of code was a bogus measurement. Calculated in terms of what each company's software accomplished, Microsoft was doing at least as much as IBM, he said. If it took IBM six or seven times as many programmers to accomplish what Microsoft had, well, that was Cannavino's problem. Gates the penny-pincher always wanted to keep his costs at rock bottom. Gates the former star programmer who believed in the Michelangelo model of programming would also rather put fewer people on a software project than too many.

The fight produced hundreds of foils over the summer as both companies lined up all their supporting evidence and argued their points. Finally, Cannavino and Gates agreed to a joint review by a senior technical person from each company. The two, who weren't involved in the project, would not be told whose code was whose. Both sides waited, sweating it out for months. Then the verdict came in: Microsoft had won. The scientists tried to paint it as not much of a victory. They said the Microsoft code was only marginally better. They also said that the code from both companies had problems. Cannavino seized on this to argue that both companies lost. But Gates and his programmers rejoiced. Not only did this support their feeling that they did better work but the verdict showed that IBM's programming ranks were as overstaffed as Gates had maintained all along.

The companies shortly found themselves in another competition, this one called the Great Hilda Fly-Off. People at both companies had written software to manage files—such as the documents produced in word-processing software. Each company asserted that its way was better. After spending weeks using foils to make their arguments, IBM finally did a test that it said proved its system was faster, then acknowledged under pressure that it rigged the test. When the companies finally agreed on terms for a retest, a group at Microsoft, led by the software's author, Gordon Letwin, gathered in his cluttered office at Microsoft's headquarters, a campus of low buildings that spread out through the pine trees east of Seattle. The group ran the test on their software and found it took fifteen seconds to finish a long sequence of tasks. They started the test on IBM's software and waited nervously.

When fifteen seconds passed, they smiled. Then thirty seconds passed; a minute; a minute and a half. By the time two minutes had passed, the Microsoft group was jumping up and down, throwing manuals in the air and cheering.

IBM actually still tried to put its file system into OS/2. The foils prepared by IBM's technical people showed that the IBM approach *ought* to be faster, and the IBMers stuck by the analysis. An incredulous Letwin complained directly to Gates and Ballmer, who went way over the project manager's head and, armed with the impartial test results, got IBM to back down.

A little additional friction developed when Microsoft hired away from IBM a vice president, Mike Maples, to run its application software business. Gates and Ballmer got permission from Kuehler before talking to Maples, but his defection still left some hard feelings. Maples gave IBM what he thought was two weeks' notice, then went off to lunch and came back, to find his belongings packed up and sitting outside his office. The locks on the office had already been changed. Maples went home and signed onto the IBM system from there so he could send e-mail to colleagues and friends telling them of his decision. The next morning, he thought of a few more people he wanted to inform personally, but when he tried to sign back onto the system, he found that his password had been deleted.

Over the years, lots of senior IBMers scratched their heads over Maples as they saw him earn enough from his Microsoft stock to buy a ranch and generally get rich. His colleagues at IBM thought he was a good executive, but they thought of him as just another guy. In fact, he was so much a part of the IBM bureaucracy that he wrote a chapter in the IBM development manual on how to create software. His colleagues missed the fact, first of all, that he took a chance by moving to a modest-sized company while they chose to remain secure in the bosom of Mother IBM. They also mistakenly assumed that because he was part of the bureaucracy, it must be part of him. It was not. Maples quickly showed people at Microsoft that he understood which parts of the IBM "process" made sense and which ought to be left behind. He did that in a couple of symbolic ways. When he had his first staff meeting, he sent out the agenda electronically a week ahead of time and included "dress code" as one item. All his casually clad programmers thought, Oh, boy, here we go. At the meeting, Maples waited until the very end to say, "Now, as to the dress code. There is none. But I wanted to let you all know that I've spent a lot of money over the years buying white button-down oxford-cloth shirts, and I intend to wear them until they wear out." Everybody laughed. Maples also got himself into a bet with Ballmer about the contributions their organizations would make to the United Way. Whoever generated a lower contribution would have to swim the length of a pond known as Lake Gates on the Microsoft campus. When the contributions were totaled, Maples and Ballmer contrived a way to say that they both lost so both had to swim through the pond's chilly waters one November day. Ballmer played it to the hilt, stripping to a tiny bathing suit, swimming through the waters, and then shivering in a towel at the far end. Maples played his part, too, showing up in his best IBM suit and tie and swimming the pond fully clad—although some sharp-eyed people noticed the top of a wetsuit sticking up over his white button-down collar.

IBM and Microsoft also began fighting over the fundamental direction of OS/2 in 1989. Microsoft insisted that they give up on the five-year-old chip that had served as the heart of the AT. The version of OS/2 aimed at AT-class machines wasn't selling, and the AT's processor was badly enough designed that fixing that version would be tough. Better to move on to machines built around the 80386, Gates argued. Working with the next-generation chip would be easier, and 80386 machines had become incredibly hot sellers by this point. Cannavino disagreed. He still had to live up to the years-old promise that IBM's ATs would be the focus of IBM's hardware and software improvements for ten years. Cannavino also would have had to take a big write-off to cover the costs that had been incurred in developing the AT version of OS/2 but that, because of IBM's accounting system, had yet to appear as costs on his books. He could do without that headache.

With the generals on both sides fighting across a wide front, nobody was focusing much on fixing the clumsy system that had evolved for the joint work—with some seventeen hundred programmers on OS/2-related projects at four sites on two continents. With all those people on the work, coordinating their efforts was so tough that the work made little progress.

Cannavino also did little to address the by-now-obvious problems of overstaffing in his programming operations and did nothing to cut through the bureaucracy entangling his people. Brian Proffit, the manager of the OS/2 version being worked on through this stretch, complains, for instance, about the trouble he had when he tried to redo an important piece of the graphics software. The piece's performance was dismal, and an improvement would increase the speed at which the whole OS/2 product ran applications. But when a group of mainframe programmers found out that he had redone the software on his own, they asserted that they, in IBM's terms, "had ownership" of that sort of graphics. The mainframe group insisted that it should do the software. Both sides "escalated" the fight, which eventually went all the way up to the Management Committee. Weeks later, word came back down that Proffit had lost. The mainframe group assigned the project a low priority, though, and never finished it. Proffit's already-completed work sat on the shelf for three years while people continued to criticize OS/2 for being slow.

As fall 1989 began, the problems with OS/2 became a continental divide for the entire PC software industry. Hundreds of companies from Lotus on down had staked their futures on OS/2 by designing their spread-sheets, word processors, and so forth to run on OS/2. Those applications wouldn't run if the computer user didn't have OS/2, so if OS/2 didn't get its act together fast, the companies were going to have to write off the fortunes they had spent on development. But things were even worse than that. It was becoming apparent that Microsoft was developing its applications to run on Windows. If Windows took off before OS/2 did, then Microsoft, as the only big company with Windows applications on the market, would clean up. Gates and Microsoft already seemed omnivorous. They owned the incredibly lucrative market for PC operating systems and sold more than half the software applications that people used on their Apple Macintoshes. Gates and Microsoft were also a respectable third or fourth in sales of application packages in the IBM-compatible world for all the major software categories—word processors, spreadsheets, desktop presentations, and so on. If Windows became a hit while OS/2 bombed, Gates could wind up dominating the market for IBM-compatible applications, just as he seemed to control everything else in the PC world. He was already a tough competitor, larger than any of his rivals. If Windows succeeded, he might become unstoppable. IBM, having guaranteed that it would make OS/2 work, found itself with a lot of Gates's unhappy software competitors beating on its door. They realized that OS/2 not only needed to succeed; it needed to take off fast.

Cannavino held a series of small meetings in the fall of 1989 with software makers, including Jim Manzi, Lotus's chief executive; Fred Gibbons, chief executive of Software Publishing; Dave Liddle, chief executive of Metaphor; and a few others. By now, things had become personal. Cannavino, who expects absolute loyalty from those around him, felt none from Gates. He no longer just distrusted Gates; he actively disliked him. Likewise, most of the software executives he gathered together resented Gates. The few who didn't resent him hated him. Gates's personal wealth had just crested $1 billion, yet he seemed rapacious to his less fortunate competitors. He used his dominance of the market to drive the hardest possible bargain. He seemed to want to control every part of the software market. Now he appeared to have pulled a fast one, telling everyone else to develop for OS/2 while he developed applications that ran on Windows.

The meetings were fiery. The software executives jumped all over Cannavino, saying he'd better cut Gates and Windows off at the knees. Cannavino had promised that OS/2 would win. Now he'd better deliver. Otherwise, he could forget about ever having any credibility in the PC world again.

Cannavino paced around his conference room, hinting that he had a plan that would crush Gates. The crux of it seemed to be the threat that he could use his rights to DOS to sell it in direct competition with Microsoft. Although IBM had just sold DOS when it was installed on

IBM's own PCs, Cannavino hinted he might start selling through dealers packages that would compete with Microsoft's sales of retail DOS
packages—for people who wanted to install DOS on their PCs themselves. Cannavino might also get clone makers to buy DOS from IBM
for installation before they shipped their machines. All the clone makers
had been buying DOS from Microsoft, and DOS was still by far the
biggest single piece of Microsoft's business, so IBM could have stung
Microsoft with cutthroat competition on DOS's pricing.

Cannavino, in his best Luca Brasi imitation, muttered darkly that
the Windows/OS/2 issue mattered to IBM. He promised to do whatever
he had to to handle Gates. The software executives left hoping that
Gates might soon find a bloody horse's head lying under his sheets one
night.

Cannavino also held a series of meetings with Gates through the
fall, trying to make Gates compromise Windows. Cannavino said little
about what he would do if Gates continued to cross him, but he was
full of menace.

"You think you can sneak around behind my back," Cannavino said
at one point in the early fall of 1989. "But let me tell you, anytime you
try to do business with one of my big customers, even before you're out
the door they're calling me to tell me what you've said."

Then he sputtered through clenched teeth something that became
a refrain: "I wouldn't want to be in your shoes. I wouldn't want to have
to compete with the IBM Company."

Gates says Cannavino "kept saying to us, 'You can't do any more
work on Windows. You've got to wind up your work on Windows.'"
Gates says he worried about what federal antitrust authorities would
think about IBM and Microsoft trying to carve up the market for PC
operating systems—and the Federal Trade Commission did, in fact,
investigate whether Microsoft had acted improperly. Gates adds: "My
lawyers always tell me that if somebody says something like that, I
should knock over my drink [to get everyone's attention] and say, 'Just
remember, I never agreed to that.'"

Cannavino's arguments about the dangers of competing with IBM
left Gates unimpressed. Gates was, however, troubled by the deteriorat-
ing relations with IBM. He also wanted IBM to endorse Windows to
help Microsoft get independent software companies to develop applications that ran on Windows—computer users, after all, cared what tasks

they could perform on their computers, not what the operating system did. While Windows was gathering momentum, Gates wanted to get all the help he could as he led up to the introduction of the next Windows version in May 1990.

"Over the last year, our relationship has been on hold," Gates wrote to Cannavino in October 1989 as he tried to find some way to keep his ties with IBM. "I still don't understand what Microsoft has done to cause such a painful period of waiting."

It was really time pressures that seemed to keep the two talking. With the PC industry abuzz over the obvious friction between IBM and Microsoft, Cannavino and Gates had decided they needed to say something about the state of their relations in early 1989 at Comdex, a trade show in Las Vegas, where all the industry's major players—and some 100,000 other people—gather every year. Both sides kept sending teams of staff people to hammer out issues. Gates and Cannavino often flew off to neutral sites in the middle of the country for one-on-one meetings to break deadlocks.

With time running out, they finally reached a very tentative compromise. Cannavino would give Gates the endorsement of Windows that he had craved all these years. In return, Gates would state that Windows was aimed at low-end personal computers, while OS/2 was the industrial-strength operating system that should be used on more powerful PCs.

The compromise came too late to allow for a full-fledged contract, which made both sides a little nervous. Both decided to go ahead, however, assuming that things went well at a final meeting Sunday morning at the Hilton Hotel in Las Vegas. Gates, Ballmer, and a few other Microsoft executives spent all day Saturday and much of the night pounding out details of their version of the compromise with IBM. While Gates the billionaire takes commercial flights whenever possible —flying in coach class—this time he and his executives worked so late, they couldn't find a commercial flight that would get them to Las Vegas from Seattle in time. They chartered a small plane and, with storms covering the West Coast, took what turned out to be a terrifying ride. The pilot kept trying to rise above the turbulence, but the wings iced up, so he kept dropping lower to the ground, where it was warmer— and where the mountaintops were. The whole flight was up and down, with plenty of knuckle-whitening bumps along the way. Worse, the pilot didn't seem to know where he was going. One member of the group, trying to make chitchat, asked the pilot how many times he'd flown to Las Vegas. "Once," he replied. No one, of course, got any writing done on the IBM compromise during the flight, but Gates did manage to stay lost in thought throughout. He, alone among those on the flight, doesn't remember it as anything out of the ordinary.

Once everyone arrived in Las Vegas—the IBM executives, as usual, having flown in on one of the comfortable corporate jets—the Microsoft and IBM people held their meeting at the Hilton. Things went well. The compromise held. So everyone then went off to a dinner that had been arranged with twenty-five top executives from the biggest PC software companies. The dinner became a turning point in the history of IBM's PC business and that of the whole industry.

The dinner had been arranged hastily, once it appeared that a compromise was possible, but IBM worked the dinner hard. A senior PC executive called and personally invited each of the software executives. For each executive who came, IBM had one of its senior executives attend the dinner as a sort of handler—glomming on to the software executive, sitting next to him at dinner, chatting him up. (These handlers were standard IBM practice with potential customers. Someone attending an event for customers usually found an IBMer sidling up to him or her at the coffee machine during a break. The IBMer would be roughly the same age as the potential customer, and as the two talked, the customer would find the IBMer shared several of his or her outside interests. The customer would also discover that the IBMer knew an astonishing amount about him or her, creating an impression that would usually have the customer going back into the meeting with a warm glow.) IBM also planned the seating carefully, making it clear which executives were considered friends and which were seen to be too close to Microsoft. The tables were arranged in a U shape, with Cannavino and Gates next to each other at the bottom of the U, IBM's friends along the Cannavino leg of the U and Microsoft's friends along the Gates leg.

The dinner struck everyone as odd right from the beginning. So many restaurants had already been booked by other companies arranging big Sunday-night dinners at Comdex that the IBM organizers could find room only at Chateau Vegas, a place that was tucked in behind the convention center and that, because of its garish red-and-black wallpaper, made some of the executives think they'd walked into a bordello. The room was too small for the sixty people there, meaning people sat on top of one another. The ceiling seemed to be four and a half feet high, so many people felt claustrophobic. Gates and Cannavino occupied a sort of booth at the head of the table that made it hard for them to stand up and speak. A noisy air conditioner at the far end of the table dripped on those underneath and drowned out most of what Gates and Cannavino said. A sound system worked only intermittently. Dinner consisted of plates piled high with steak, chicken, and lobster, far more food than anyone could eat and more than anyone even cared to look at. The IBM handler sitting next to Fred Gibbons of Software Publishing was so drunk that those around him kept watching to see whether he'd fall facedown in his mound of food.

Cannavino and Gates talked briefly to lay out the compromise. They stuck pretty much to the script, but neither could quite bring himself to go all the way. Cannavino never really endorsed Windows, and Gates never completely said that he would curtail Windows development from then on. Both bristled at what they saw as the other's evasions.

Questions were invited. There were only a few, but they were telling. One person asked Cannavino point-blank whether he was endorsing Windows. Cannavino fudged. He was sort of saying yes, but he never came right out and did it. Gates and Ballmer looked at each other and Ballmer muttered under his breath, "Oh, fuck." As he watched Gates, he says he could see that "Gates was pissed. He was pissed, pissed, pissed."

Gibbons, an IBM ally, stood up and said, "Bill, you walked into my office a while back and told me I should be developing applications for Windows. Are you now walking into my office and telling me I should be developing applications for OS/2 instead?"

Cannavino assumed the answer was going to be yes. Instead, Gates gave a long, complicated answer that indicated he thought software developers should do applications for both Windows and OS/2.

Dave Liddle, sitting next to Cannavino, tried to clarify in order to hold the compromise together. "Okay, Bill," he said. "But if you were advising the people in this room about how they should spend their development dollars, you'd suggest they spend them on OS/2, right?"

Cannavino waited, assuming that he'd finally hear a simple yes. Instead, Gates said, "The people in this room are all the heads of their own software companies. They're all bright people who are fully capable of making up their own minds. I wouldn't presume to tell them how to run their businesses."

Cannavino fumed. The software-industry executives who had met with him ahead of time were stunned. Microsoft wasn't going to cut off Windows, they thought. Instead, it seemed determined to make Windows succeed, and it now seemed that Windows would become popular long before OS/2. Microsoft's applications designed to run on Windows would then clobber those companies who had been focusing their development on that nonevent, OS/2. Cannavino had seemed to think he could bring Gates to heel, but the software executives suddenly realized that Gates had become too powerful even for IBM to handle.

"That's when I knew the game was over," Gibbons says. "The numbers were on the scoreboard, and Microsoft had won." Manzi of Lotus got up and walked out, annoyed.

When the dinner broke up and some people gathered around Gates, Cannavino tried to shove through the group and reach him to demand an explanation. But a Gates assistant headed Cannavino off, promising that they'd all get together to talk later. Gates, in the middle of a crowd, wandered off, oblivious to Cannavino's heated concerns.

When the software chieftains went outside, they found that the IBM organizers had slipped up. A long line of limos waited outside to take the IBM executives back to the Las Vegas Hilton but there were no cars for anyone else, and the restaurant was out of the way enough that taxis were hard to come by. The IBM executives trooped out, piled into their limos, and drove off, leaving an important group of potential allies stranded on the curb. Several gave up and hiked back to the Hilton. They gathered in the bar to hash through what they had just witnessed. Finding a group of reporters camped out there, they lamented in front of them about how the IBM-Microsoft compromise had fallen apart.

Throughout the next day, Monday, Gates and Cannavino struggled to patch up their differences. They settled into a trailer in the parking lot behind the convention center, where Cannavino had a mobile office —complete with a big desk, plush carpeting, a bathroom, several phone lines, and room for several assistants. Cannavino didn't want his executives to miss out on the comforts of home while they worked at the trade show, so he had outfitted eight lavish trailers and had them driven cross-country to Las Vegas from New York. Gates spent the day and most of the night meeting with people, sometimes just with Cannavino and sometimes getting caught alone with as many as nine IBMers. When he left the trailer shortly before dawn Tuesday, it seemed that the compromise was back in place.

Cannavino still wasn't convinced. He didn't quite see what all the fuss was about Windows. To a mainframe guy like Cannavino, Windows felt like a toy operating system. Cannavino assumed customers wanted something solid, something that wasn't glitzy, something that felt like a mainframe—in other words, something like OS/2. So Cannavino didn't want software developers or customers thinking he was endorsing Windows, despite the compromise he had worked out with Gates. In the late morning, some of Cannavino's handlers began running him through a series of mock questions they thought might come up at the press conference that afternoon. The first question was, of course: "Aren't you really saying that you're endorsing Windows?"

"Hell, no!" Cannavino exclaimed.

One of the questioners said, "It looks like a duck, it walks like a duck, and it quacks like a duck, so it must be a duck"—an IBM expression that, in this context, meant that Cannavino certainly seemed to be backing Windows.

Cannavino was astonished. He glanced around the room at his fellow IBMers and said that if even one person might interpret his comments as support for Windows, then perhaps he should cancel the press conference. Even once Cannavino left his trailer and started walking through the convention center, he told his assistants he wasn't sure he should proceed with the event. When they arrived at the entrance of the conference room, they discovered just how many people wanted to hear Cannavino's position on Windows. The room was supposed to hold only 140 people, but 800 showed up to watch the fireworks—all jockeying for position as they tried to cram into the room. Some of Cannavino's staff had to call security guards to keep the restless crowd under control. Some reporters from major news organizations never did secure a position inside the room. (A public relations person representing Microsoft pleaded with IBM to clear out some of the numerous IBMers who were taking up seats, to make room for reporters. But IBMers, seemingly feeling there's safety in numbers, always have dozens of staff people at press conferences, so IBM wasn't giving up any seats.) Cannavino shoved his way through the crowd as he approached the door.

Gates, coming along a few minutes later, saw the huge crowd in the hall and mused aloud whether he and Cannavino should just hold the press conference in the corridor where there was much more room. When Gates reached the podium, Cannavino, arms crossed and a scowl on his face, stood fifteen feet away. Cannavino seemed to want as much distance as possible between himself and Gates. Even when Gates invited him to the podium, Cannavino never got closer than six or seven feet. The two adhered to their script on the compromise—with Cannavino offering halfhearted support for Windows and Gates holding out the prospect that OS/2 was the future—but things fell apart once the questions began. The strain became apparent, just as it had to those who had attended the dinner two nights before. Of course, the first question was whether IBM was finally committing itself to installing Windows on its hardware and encouraging software developers to write applications that ran on Windows. Cannavino swallowed hard, shifted his weight, and gave a rambling four-hundred-word nonanswer. When someone followed up with a question to try to pin Cannavino down, he responded with a longer equivocation.

Cannavino left the press conference sure he had artfully avoided any public commitment to Windows, but he seemed to be the only one in the industry with that impression. Cannavino had done irreparable damage. He had lost face with the software industry. He unintentionally pushed them to abandon OS/2 and embrace Windows, thus helping to ensure the demise of OS/2 and the success of Windows.

Cannavino also left the room thinking he retained at least modest control over Microsoft, but he was alone in that opinion, too. Many of the reporters covering the conference had been at one of the bars in the Hilton two nights before, listening to executives from independent software companies grouse about how Gates had run roughshod over Cannavino at dinner, so the reporters knew that Gates had bested Cannavino. Everyone else in the industry, outside of IBM, decided, too, that by late 1989 Gates had become too successful and too powerful for IBM to handle. Once Windows became a hit in 1990, Gates made so much money and took such control of the direction of the software industry that he became unstoppable.

NINE

I t was a rite of passage for marketing hotshots at IBM that they'd be sent through Blackjack Bertram's product-development organization for a year so he could put them through their paces. A fresh-faced young man or woman, eager to meet the boss, would be summoned into Bertram's office.

"You fucking marketing people!" Bertram would thunder, cigar still in his mouth. "You think you can prance on through here on your way to becoming president of the IBM Company! Well, I don't give a shit about your careers! You fuck with me and I'll have your ass!"

The young executive would then stumble bewildered out of Bertram's office.

Bertram—always "Jack" to his face and always "Blackjack" behind his back—used to bludgeon people all the time because it was the only way he found he could get to the truth. IBMers' habit of insisting everything was super grated on a smart engineer like Bertram. There had to be problems, he knew. That was how the world worked. So if someone didn't confess to a problem the first time, Bertram pressed him until he did. His crotchety manner, so unconventional for an IBMer, inhibited his advancement for a while, but over time it won him mythic status. He had as wide a following as any executive has had in IBM's recent history.

That was particularly true among the engineers, where Bertram groomed an entire generation of IBM senior engineers. He amazed other engineers not only with his good instincts but also with his attention to detail. He needed just three or four hours of sleep a night, so, especially if he was on the road, he'd wake up at 3:00 A.M. and go wander the plant floor in, say, Santa Teresa, California, at a facility that reported to him. Bertram would see how smoothly the manufacturing operation was really running—and not have to rely on someone's foils to tell him what the manufacturing problems were. Then if someone in charge of the manufacturing operation tried to hide a problem at a meeting later that morning, Bertram would challenge him with all sorts of detailed information that, to people in the room, he seemed to have pulled out of the air.

Marketing executives, the traditional enemies of engineers inside IBM, marveled at how Bertram not only did his job developing products but kept better track of customers and their problems than most marketing people could. Bill Grabe, a former senior marketing executive, says it was always dangerous to be in a meeting with Bertram. Grabe might stand up and say, "We have a problem at Boeing. The problem is . . ." Then Bertram would say, "That's completely wrong. I was just out at Boeing yesterday, and the real problem is . . ." Bertram would, of course, be right.

Even the lawyers respected Bertram, and the IBM lawyers didn't like anybody. The lawyers had to jerk Bertram into line now and then, keeping him from trying to beat up on competitors the way he'd beat up on young marketing executives. But Nicholas deB. Katzenbach, once IBM's senior lawyer, says that Bertram was one of the smartest and most forceful executives he's ever met.

After years of bruising people's feelings, then slowly winning them over by proving himself right, Bertram was finally awarded a senior vice presidency. But then he became ill. By 1986, Blackjack was dying.

He had Jillian-Barre syndrome, the so-called Yuppie disease, which typically tired people out and was very painful but wasn't supposed to be a killer. Still, the fifty-six-year-old Bertram found himself bedridden most of the time and slowly slipped away.

Before he died, though, he conspired with Jack Kuehler, an executive vice president at the time, and Ralph Gomory, the head of IBM's research operations, to do one final thing. Bertram detested hearing how IBM had blown it in the workstation business, inventing the technology that others used to create the industry but missing the opportunity because of bureaucratic inertia and what he saw as blatant stupidity. Bertram wanted IBM to try again. As usual, he also had a plan. He wanted the operation based in Austin, Texas, figuring that no one from headquarters would want to visit there, so people wouldn't meddle with the project. He wanted the researchers in Yorktown Heights who had designed a promising chip actually to get off their butts, get out of their labs, and go build it. When Kuehler, who was Bertram's boss, made one of his regular visits to see Bertram in the hospital, where he was struggling to breathe through a respirator, Bertram sprang another surprise, too: He wanted Andy Heller to run the project.

Heller was a well-known renegade at IBM. The husky, bearded Heller wore open-necked shirts and cowboy boots, even when in the rarefied air at headquarters at Armonk. He had a huge voice that either could be a lovely, classically trained tenor if someone caught him at the piano in a hotel bar at a conference or could be just a weapon that he used to intimidate an opponent. Heller loved to argue. He once got so mad at what he saw as the pomposity of IBM salesmen that he took his motorcycle up to the fifth floor of a sales branch and rode it through the halls. Heller was one of the wildest of the "wild ducks" IBM has ever seen. (The Watsons used to say they liked having wild ducks around because it was important to have some people who wouldn't fly in formation. The term is still used around IBM, but much less so, because most of the wild ducks decided they weren't welcome any longer and flew elsewhere.) Heller was essentially told as an egotistical young scientist that if he could really make as many research breakthroughs as he thought he could, then he could go ahead and say anything he liked to anybody. Heller fulfilled his end of the bargain and proceeded to hold his bosses to theirs: He mouthed off all over the place. He charged into Chairman Frank Cary's office to give him a job evaluation and generally tell him off. Heller marched into Senior Vice President Spike Beitzel's office and accused him of endorsing a technology approach that Heller advised was "a bag of shit." (Beitzel's response was: "Son, if you give me a bag of shit, and I find I can sell it at a profit, I'm going to ask you for two more.") Heller became the youngest scientist in IBM's history to be named a fellow, giving him the right to go off and do whatever research intrigued him. Now, in 1986, he desperately wanted to try to do a workstation for IBM, even though he was a researcher and had never developed a product before. Bertram, who had served as a second father to Heller, bringing him up through the ranks and trying to shield him from getting into too much trouble, thought Heller should get the chance.

Kuehler gulped when Bertram told him he wanted Heller to have the job. But he looked at Bertram, lying there in a bleak hospital room, hooked up to a respirator and probably dying, and Kuehler said he'd see what he could do. He knew he'd have a tough time because all of IBM's management knew what a hard handle Heller was, but Kuehler was a member of the Management Committee and had a lot of pull, so he managed to sell Chairman John Akers and the other MC members on the idea.

Gomory, IBM's senior scientist, who, like Bertram, reported to Kuehler, made an impassioned speech in front of the researchers at Yorktown Heights in mid-1986, asking for volunteers to do hard time in Austin for a few years. Bertram helped line up a few key people, including IBM legend John Cocke, who had generated scores of key innovations but had never before agreed actually to develop a product. Bertram then summoned the core group to his hospital room and told them to ignore Gomory's flowery talk. Their real marching orders were: Come back *with* your chip, or *on* it.

Heller's wife turned out to be the final roadblock. She didn't want to move to Austin. So Bertram, who was friends with both Heller and his wife, called her. He said, "Look, you don't understand. Andy is going to do this with you or without you." She caved in.

"It was impossible not to grant the wish of a dying man," Heller says, "at least not a man like Blackjack Bertram."

By early 1990, IBM finally got its workstation.

The technology behind the workstation got its start all the way back in the 1960s, when Cocke had a seemingly simple idea about chip design. He began noticing how infrequently processors performed many of the complex tasks they were built to handle. He wondered whether a chip would operate more efficiently if he junked the complex operations and relied on a few simple instructions. (A chip of that era would be able to carry out instructions that would be like telling someone, "Drive to the supermarket," "Drive to the office," "Drive to the ball game," and so on. Cocke wondered whether it wouldn't be better just to include a few instructions the equivalent of "Drive," "Stop," "Go left," "Go right," and so on. It turned out that using a few instructions was far faster. This new breed of chip became known as a RISC chip, for reduced instruction set computing.) Cocke continued developing the idea through the early 1970s and generated increasingly spectacular results, but no one outside the research community paid much attention. All IBM's businesses were booming so no one sought a radical shift in technology. Besides, Cocke's numbers were almost too good to be believed. He was talking about computers that were twenty, forty, sixty, even eighty times as fast as those IBM had on the market.

By the early 1980s, Cocke found a sponsor in Bo Evans, who was one of the several most senior technologists at IBM, before Kuehler became the dominant force in technology in the mid-1980s. Evans, an unpleasant man known for his willingness to challenge everyone's assumptions, concocted a scheme to redo IBM's product line, top to bottom, based on Cocke and his new RISC technology. Everything from a PC on up through a mainframe would be built around a single version of the RISC chip. The result could have been profound. IBM, as RISC's inventor, would have led its competitors in taking advantage of the huge increases in power RISC could provide. IBM's development costs would have come down because it wouldn't have had to develop different processors for each family of computers; it would have focused just on developing the basic RISC chip, spreading the costs across all its families of machines. IBM would have done its own PC chip, meaning it wouldn't have had to watch Intel become a PC giant at IBM's expense. Nor would IBM have had to put up with Digital Equipment's taunting in the mid-1980s; IBM would have had as unified a set of products as Digital did when it proclaimed that "Digital Has It Now!"

Evans pushed the RISC idea hard but succeeded mostly in making people mad. The chairman in the early 1980s, John Opel, didn't want to impose a technological vision on the whole company. He wanted each individual business to make up its own mind. The minicomputer business was interested because it had such a hodgepodge of product lines, none of which talked to one another very well. The typewriter people liked the idea, too. But the mainframe technology people didn't trust such a new type of chip and thought some of Cocke's numbers must be fudged; they couldn't believe he was getting the huge increases in power he claimed. Besides, mainframe sales were soaring, so people in that business didn't want to take a chance. Likewise, the PC business didn't see any reason to endanger its incredible early successes.

Evans pressed his point so often and loudly that Opel finally blew up at him in a Management Committee session. He coldly said that everyone knew what Evans thought on the subject, so would he just shut his mouth. The room fell silent. Opel seldom lost his cool. A few months later, Evans left the company, having essentially been fired, even though Opel, in the IBM tradition, tried to obscure that fact. With him went one of the final voices questioning the assumptions being made by IBM's senior executives.

The minicomputer project using RISC did become a hot project. It acquired cachet internally because it attacked such a hard problem— developers said combining all these minicomputers into one machine was akin to taking a sports car, a luxury car, a station wagon, and a van and combining them into one appealing, all-purpose vehicle.[1] IBM assigned four thousand people to it for more than three years, making it the biggest development project since the death in the 1970s of Future System—the overly ambitious attempt to jump way ahead of the whole industry, whose collapse was IBM's Vietnam, making it cautious about big projects. But the minicomputer project, code-named Fort Knox, fell victim to IBM's "process." Rather than set up a single development team in one place, IBM let each of its existing minicomputer groups do pieces of the development at their own facilities. That not only meant tons of flights around the country and scads of meetings to keep everyone up to date on what everyone else was doing but also meant that each minicomputer group remained insulated from the rest. Each insular group insisted on dominating the project, convinced that the personality of its minicomputer should provide the core personality of the new minicomputer. When meetings were held to try to resolve the problems, the IBMers, taught that it was wimpy to give in, "nonconcurred" and "escalated" their fights as far up the management chain as they could. Together with IBM's standard problems developing software, the fragmented development approach ensured that remarkably little progress was made.

The weary quip among developers became: "We highly endorse the multisite development approach. We wish all our competitors would use it."

Fort Knox was finally killed in 1985 after more than $1 billion of wasted effort.

Although IBM often seems to be a bottomless pit of development resources and money, the Fort Knox project siphoned off so many people that little additional RISC work got financing. The one other project that was pursued through 1985 was a much smaller one in the typewriter business, where developers were trying to produce a word-processing system that would tie together entire departments. The typewriter business figured that was the only way to head off Wang, whose word processors were still popular in the early 1980s.

By focusing on existing businesses—typewriters and minicomputers—IBM missed what turned out to be the biggest opportunity for RISC technology: workstations. The reason is that the IBM system makes it easy to do better versions of things that have been done before but almost impossible to do anything new. That's true even for trivial matters such as the color of shirts people wear and product names, so it's all the more true for new machines, like workstations, that could curb the earnings from computers made by profitable and powerful existing businesses. Nobody saw the possibilities for workstations because nobody was looking for them—the sort of problem that dogged IBM over the past decade in every part of the business.

IBM also missed the workstation market because it focused on the wrong competitors. To the extent that IBM worried about rivals at all in 1985, it looked over its shoulder toward its three largest Japanese rivals—Fujitsu, Hitachi, and NEC—which were trying hard to compete on IBM's mainframe turf but which weren't coming up with new categories of products, such as workstations. IBM should have been focusing more on the thousands of small competitors that were appearing, especially American start-ups such as those that created the workstation market—just as IBM's PC nemeses were start-ups Microsoft and Compaq and modest-sized Intel. Apollo, on the East Coast, came to market with a workstation first, in 1980. It was followed a couple of years later by the company that would give IBM the most problems in workstations: Sun Microsystems.

In the past, IBM always reacted fast enough to take over any markets it missed the first or second time around. But Sun was a new breed of company, moving so fast it wouldn't be so easy to catch. Sun was founded by four young Californians—a Berkeley Ph.D. student, software whiz Bill Joy; recently minted Stanford MBA Scott McNealy; hardware tinkerer extraordinaire Andy Bechtolsheim; and venture capitalist Vinod Khosla. Thinking that IBM and the other established computer companies had become the industry's version of Muzak, they built Sun around a rock-and-roll personality. Each year on April Fool's Day, engineers organized a practical joke that tried to outdo the prior year's. One year, some senior manager found his car floating in the middle of the pond in front of Sun's building. Another year, McNealy, a golfer, found a putting green inside his office, complete with sand trap and water hazard. One year, all employees showed up, to find that the whole Sun headquarters had been shrink-wrapped in a huge sheet of plastic.

McNealy, who became chief executive, set the tone by saying in public most anything that came into his head. When, in early 1993, IBM was searching for a new chief executive, McNealy was quoted as making the crack referring to President Clinton's marijuana episode. "Scratch me off the list" of potential chief executives, McNealy said. "I inhaled." When IBM hired Lou Gerstner from RJR Nabisco, McNealy said that was great because Gerstner could change the company without having to change IBM's initials. From now on, they'd simply stand for International Biscuit Maker.[2]

Perhaps most important, as Sun began to grow in 1983 and 1984, it adopted a slash-and-burn style of product development that—very much unlike IBM's—quickly tried to render obsolete all existing products, even Sun's own. The approach often left Sun vulnerable. It might replace its entire product line in a single year, so if anything went wrong, Sun's profitability got hammered. But the approach also kept Sun's competitors scratching their heads, wondering how to deal with this company that seemed to have total disregard for consistent profitability. Digital Equipment couldn't keep up; neither could Apollo. Hewlett-Packard started sliding away, until it acquired Apollo. IBM spent years trying to respond. Meanwhile, Sun just kept growing. (The only time Sun hit a long bad patch was when it got talked into buying an IBM mainframe on the theory that it was growing so fast, it needed a mainframe to manage all its orders and other back-office functions. Sun had so much trouble with the mainframe that it lost control of its business for the better part of a year.) Sun's success did as much as anything to pick up the pace of change in the computer industry, making manufacturers give up the comfortable seven-year life cycle typical of mainframes and adjust to the furious one- to one-and-a-half-year life cycles that were coming in the workstation and PC businesses.

Once Sun and Apollo hit the streets with their workstations, it took IBM a while to accept that there really was a market for the machines. Workstations are essentially PCs on steroids—with faster processors, with more memory, with bigger screens that have vastly greater ability to generate moving images, and with connections that make it easier to hook workstations up in networks. Workstations turned out to be coveted by scientists and engineers, in particular because they could run CAD/CAM software—which stands for computer-aided design, computer-aided manufacturing. This allowed designers to play with realistic-looking images of potential products on their screens without having to go through the time-consuming process of having a machine shop build a prototype. But salesmen like to sell to existing customers —it's easier than making cold calls to find new ones—and the salesmen who ran IBM didn't have much experience with scientists and engineers as customers, so IBM didn't see the incredible need for CAD/CAM. IBM also figured that, over time, its PCs would become powerful enough to handle the work that workstations were doing.

John Opel, chairman into 1986, didn't wake up to the problem for so long that IBM didn't get a workstation on the market until January 1986, almost six years after Apollo's pioneering product hit the market and four years after Sun's debut. The IBM product was awful. When IBM finally began development of a workstation in 1984, it didn't have a suitable processor available. The Fort Knox RISC project might have provided a good processor, but it was collapsing amid all the internal bickering about what direction to take. The chip being used in the typewriter business's project was a couple of years out of date, so it was slower than chips that had been developed more recently. The chip had also been stripped of its so-called floating-point capabilities, the capabilities that made the RISC chip so blindingly fast in doing the calculations that engineers and scientists needed to do. IBM tried to graft some floating-point capabilities back onto the chip. But the marketing people running the workstation business decreed that the work had to be done in just a few months, lest Sun and Apollo be left alone for too long. The result was slop. Although IBM had invented RISC fifteen years earlier, the RISC chip IBM finally brought to market in the RT PC in January 1986 was hopelessly underpowered.

IBM hoped that it could at least freeze the market. In the past, customers seeing IBM jump into a new market assumed that IBM would quickly catch up. They would worry about buying from an upstart competitor because it might disappear once IBM brought its full force to bear on the market. But that didn't happen this time. The need for processing power was so great that the RT bombed, and customers kept snapping up Sun and Apollo machines.

IBM then tried its standard trick, throwing so many resources at the RT's problems that it expected to quickly get a much better machine out the door. The RT did, in fact, improve, but Sun and Apollo just wouldn't stand still. In 1987 and 1988, IBM kept bringing out new versions of the RT, but those would get IBM only to where its competitors had been the year before. IBM was always a generation behind. In the technical world, the RT became as big an embarrassment as the PCjr had been in the consumer market.

Even as IBM continued insisting that it would make the RT succeed, once Bertram made his dying wish about a new type of workstation in 1986, IBM put the RT on a back burner and pursued Bertram's project, code-named America. When Bertram died, the project's main sponsor became Kuehler, already an executive vice president and on his way to becoming president, making him the highest-ranking nonsalesman in IBM's history and the dominant force in setting IBM's technology direction from the mid-1980s through 1993. Kuehler looked the part of the senior executive, with his conservative suits, short, straight hair, and big glasses. But, as an engineer who never had the personality beaten out of him in sales school, he came across as very different. Instead of making severely formal presentations using lots of foils, Kuehler just jotted down a few notes and extemporized. He never assumed the arrogance that marked so many of the former salesmen, who had seen themselves as bravely serving in the front ranks as IBM battled its competitors. If Kuehler needed to talk to some senior executive in Armonk and found the executive talking with someone, Kuehler always apologized. He usually introduced himself to anyone he didn't recognize, even though everyone knew who he was. When meeting with people, he might take his suit coat off, throw it over the back of a chair, and cheerfully say, "Let's pretend we're Californians." Or, seeing someone he didn't even know that well, he might call out in his folksy way, "Hey, Jones, how the hell are you?"—to which the appropriate response was, "Fine, Kuehler, how the hell are you?" When Kuehler became president in 1990 and complimentary stories appeared throughout the national press, he sent handwritten notes to the reporters, thanking them for their kind words.

Kuehler had none of the tolerance for staff work that occupied so much of IBM; he had one staff job in his career—for eleven months—and hated it. While so many of IBM's senior executives came from the Midwest or Northeast, Kuehler came from the heart of Silicon Valley, where in his younger days he often rented a plane for a day so he could land it on a beach and go play volleyball. Kuehler had a broader agenda than most of his salesmen colleagues, taking it on himself to try to save the U.S. semiconductor industry. It was Kuehler who in 1982 arranged for IBM to invest in Intel, helping save it from disaster. It was Kuehler who in the late 1980s got IBM involved in several consortia to pool semiconductor technology among U.S. companies as a way of trying to avert Japanese dominance. It was Kuehler who made sure IBM helped a U.S. company, Silicon Valley Group, finance the purchase of a key producer of semiconductor manufacturing equipment from Perkin Elmer rather than let a Japanese company acquire the Perkin Elmer division. Kuehler also testified frequently before Congress to try to raise the federal government's concern about the waning dominance of the United States in semiconductors.

In the early 1990s, toward the end of his career, Kuehler occasionally got dinged by IBMers for not standing up enough to his boss, Chairman John Akers, and warning Akers that IBM needed to change radically if it was to avoid the enormous troubles it faces today. Kuehler also seemed to rely too much on the traditional IBM approach of phasing out old technologies as slowly as possible and bringing new ones to market gradually so they didn't disrupt sales of profitable older machines. But in 1986, he backed the workstation market completely. He told the workstation group that they could do whatever they liked, then provided what IBMers call the "air support" in Armonk to make sure that no other part of the company interfered with the work.

Kuehler gave Heller, the project's leader, twenty "gold badges" in 1986, meaning that Heller could scour any business that reported to Kuehler—which was about half the company at this point—and hire any twenty people he wanted to form the core of the thousands of people who eventually became involved in the project. Heller relied heavily on his old friend Cocke, who had come up with the RISC concept so many years before and who had, in the early 1980s, spotted several bits of work in the IBM research community that he thought could be pulled together in a phenomenally fast workstation processor.

It took long enough for Kuehler to fight the battles in Armonk that it wasn't until 1987 that work really began. But once the renegade Heller got going, he charged through IBM the way he charged through everything else. When IBM's main chip plant in Burlington, Vermont, wasn't delivering prototypes of his chips to him as fast as he wanted in 1988 and 1989, he climbed all over them. Heller says the people there finally got fed up and asked for an audience with Akers and his Management Committee. Heller found out about the meeting at the last second and chartered a plane to make sure he got to Armonk in time. He marched into the MC meeting to confront the Burlington group. Burlington said that it had started out taking 120 days to fabricate some of Heller's key chips for him. That was now down to eighty-seven days, they said, putting them near the theoretical minimum turnaround time of eighty. What, they wanted to know, was Heller so upset about?

Heller says Akers turned to him and said, "What about it?"

Heller says he told Akers, "John, I have a great idea. I'm going to save you three billion dollars a year. If Burlington is so far behind in its technology, let's just close it."

Akers was not amused, Heller says. Akers stopped the meeting and pulled Heller out into the hallway to chastise him for ten minutes about not being a team player. Akers said he wanted Heller to work things out with Burlington.

When they went back into the meeting, Heller says, Akers turned to him and said, "Okay, Andy, what do you say now?"

Heller says he told Akers, "John, I just had another idea. Companies like Texas Instruments and National Semiconductor don't seem to be burdened with Burlington's knowledge about what the theoretical minimum time is for this process. They must just be too stupid to realize that they shouldn't be doing things in a lot less than eighty days. So I'll just buy my chips from them."

Akers was still not smiling. He stopped the meeting again, hauled Heller outside, and lit into him again. Heller says Akers threatened to fire him unless he became more of a team player and cooperated with Burlington.

This time when they went back inside, Kuehler intervened before Heller could get himself into even more trouble. Kuehler suggested that Burlington keep making Heller's chips but that Heller be allowed to send as many people as he wanted to Burlington to try to find ways to speed up the process. With a little nudging, Burlington soon got the chip-making process down to twenty-seven days. Heller says Akers never did acknowledge that Heller had a point. (It's hard to know exactly what happened between Heller and Akers. One Management Committee member of the time says he doesn't remember the exchange Heller reports. He says Heller was indeed on Burlington's back and had horrible fights with the people there, but the MC member says Kuehler always refereed those battles before they got to the MC level. The MC member also says that Heller's various bosses tried to keep him away from Akers because they were afraid Heller would say something silly and outrage Akers. Heller stands by his story, and it certainly seems like something he might do. The story also fits what numerous former IBM executives describe as Akers's personality. They say he hated hearing bad news and couldn't abide having people stand up to him. That became even more typical of him after a few years in the top job, as he acquired an increasingly regal manner.)

Heller benefited from having so many of the original research team on hand, so work on the main chips went quickly in 1987 and 1988. There was no need to keep flying people back and forth between Austin and Yorktown Heights for meetings. There were none of the misunderstandings that occur when researchers follow the normal IBM "process," sending development and manufacturing engineers designs covering square yards of paper and wishing them luck in interpreting the designs in exactly the right way. When Heller had a problem to solve, he just pulled people into his office in the wee hours of the morning and chewed on them until they produced a solution. Still, problems developed—mainly, of course, in software. Heller was going to miss his hardware deadline of early 1989 by a few months, but, as usual, the software was well behind that.

Heller wanted to announce the machine anyway, to let the world know that IBM had a screamer of a workstation ready to go and that everybody else's hardware was a generation behind. He'd confess that the operating system wasn't yet ready for prime time but would promise to have it finished in a few months. In the meantime, he'd give customers a preliminary version so they could begin writing applications.

The MC didn't buy it. They said he couldn't announce a machine that still required so much work. Heller felt they were being chicken.

He thought the MC didn't want to announce the machine so soon because it was so powerful that it would cripple sales of IBM's established minicomputers and mainframes. (IBM's official position by late 1988 was that its product strategy was a free-for-all in which any division could make products that competed with any other IBM division. In fact, this was far from true. Akers discouraged salesmen from marketing Heller's workstation as a replacement for more expensive minicomputers until mid-1991, and, in general, competition among the different product lines was still managed pretty carefully up to the day Akers stepped down in early 1993.) Heller was ordered to tell his people that the product wasn't being announced because it wasn't ready. Heller refused, saying that was a lie and that he wouldn't lie for anybody. The MC didn't budge. Heller quit.

Akers took the opportunity to strip the workstation unit of its autonomy and fold it back into the rest of the business in late 1988, in a group together with the PC division being run by the newly arrived Jim Cannavino.

The workstation group continued plugging away but kept running into problems, so the planned introduction date kept slipping later and later into 1989. Bob Montoye, who designed a key part of the workstation chip, says that even once they thought they were ready to start manufacturing the machines in preparation for a late 1989 introduction, a glitch in the main processor meant that only a handful of all the chips they produced actually worked properly. After weeks of chip making, in late November 1989, he still had only nine processors that passed all IBM's tests. The group began wondering whether the hardware wouldn't turn out to be the main problem, after all.

Finally, after poring over the square-yard sheets of flimsy paper that contain the drawings of chip layouts, Montoye saw the problem. Two of the hundreds of thousands of transistors on the chip were a thousandth of a human hair too close to each other. Unless IBM got lucky in the manufacturing process and mistakenly placed the two transistors ever so slightly farther apart, the transistors would interfere with each other. That was enough to make the chips unusable. Montoye immediately fixed the problem. Within days, IBM had hundreds of usable processors. Soon, that became thousands. The hardware was back on track, and the announcement was cleared to go ahead in February 1990.

Montoye found himself having to justify the change for months afterward. Although everyone acknowledged that he should be congratulated for solving the problem, some of the midlevel executives in the workstation business and some bosses in manufacturing argued that he shouldn't have been allowed to make the change without filing all the appropriate documentation. Montoye said it could have taken weeks for him to get the change approved, but that didn't stop the arguing. For months, he got e-mail demanding that he file for approval just so people could say he had followed the established procedure.

When the workstation was announced in 1990, it stunned its competitors, who had seen IBM miss so often with the RT that they thought it would never get a workstation right. The new machine, called the RS/6000, was almost twice as powerful as the next-most-powerful workstation on the market. The part of the chip that handled scientific calculations was five or more times as fast as competitors'. IBM had also learned from the AS/400 experience and had carefully set up customers and software developers. As a result, lots of good software became available quickly to run on the RS/6000, and several big customers had already signed up. The RS/6000 not only did well among technical people, who were the traditional workstation market, but also wowed many of IBM's traditional customers such as brokerage houses, which installed networks of RS/6000s to help their traders follow subtle trends in financial markets.

At the introduction in February 1990, IBM bragged that it would capture the biggest share of the workstation market by 1994. Early results seemed to back IBM up. The RS/6000 was available in large volume for only the final six months of 1990, yet it became a $1 billion business. That grew to $1.8 billion in 1991 and $2.5 billion in 1992, within striking distance of market leader Sun.

IBM, through a deal with Motorola in 1991, also announced plans to make a low-cost version of the RS/6000 processor and use it to generate a line of powerful PCs. IBM even decided to sell the processors to outsiders, meaning it was finally moving to head off Intel's dominance of the market for PC processors. An IBM-Motorola chip-design facility was set up in Austin, establishing a collegial atmosphere freed of the IBM bureaucracy. Technical people wanting to solve a problem often went outside and played some volleyball while they cleared their heads and talked through an issue. Some people bought some freshwater sharks to place in the pond in front of the IBM-

Motorola facility, partly to have some fun and partly to remind everyone that their PC and workstation competitors are man-eating sharks. With everyone focusing more on substance than process, the IBM-Motorola group soon found itself ahead of schedule with the new versions of the RS/6000 processor.

Still, IBM had some technical problems along the way that limited the workstation's momentum. Problems with the operating system continued for several months into 1990 as IBM once again found itself struggling to produce good software. The problems limited early sales of the machine. The IBM group also found it hard to get out a less expensive, less powerful version of the RS/6000, which is where most of the sales were. The inexpensive version was initially planned for 1990, but IBM had never been very good at producing chips cheaply. It never had to be. As long as IBM stayed on the technological leading edge and made increasingly powerful chips to drive its mainframes, customers didn't pay much attention to the price. The low-end workstation first slipped into early 1991, then to late summer, then to early 1992, and finally to spring 1992. It took so long that engineers, making a play off the RS/6000's code name, America, said the new machine should be called Vietnam. It began while America was still great, they said, and it took forever to get out.

The America project turned out to be frightfully expensive. IBM lost more than $500 million on the business in the first two years. And, while the business was supposed to become profitable in 1992, it was still in the red because IBM decided to invest so much money in producing a line of PCs based on the RS/6000 processor.

While the RS/6000 work is one of the biggest success stories in recent years at IBM, showing what the company's technological strength allows when a group is cut loose from the bureaucracy, the project also came so late in the development of the workstation and PC markets that its impact will be minimized. Less than nine months after IBM began high-volume shipments of the RS/6000, Hewlett-Packard responded with machines as powerful as IBM's at a much lower price, forcing IBM to cut its prices as much as 60 percent. HP took advantage of some defections of key technologists from IBM in recent years, notably Joel Birnbaum, one of Cocke's key collaborators in the development of RISC, who helped HP's workstation people pursue some of the same ideas that led IBM to the RS/6000. Sun has fallen behind in terms of pure power, but it has such good software and is so entrenched that it has gained market share, not lost it, since the introduction of the RS/6000.

The IBM line of PCs built around the RS/6000 processor could come along and shake things up, giving IBM a way of making its PCs more powerful than its competitors' and letting IBM regain from Intel much of the lucrative market for PC processors. But it would have been a lot easier to try to push a new processor into a market before customers became so accustomed to Intel's processors that most people describe their PCs primarily based on the type of Intel processor they contain. IBM had plenty of opportunities to take control of the market for PC processors, back when Don Estridge decided not to try to put a RISC processor in his PCs in the early 1980s and when Bill Lowe frittered away the opportunity to do customized versions of Intel's processors in the mid-1980s. IBM expects to have PC-like machines based on the RS/6000 out by late 1993, but even IBM doesn't see much happening fast. IBMers say it won't be until a better PC version of the RS/6000 chip comes out in mid- to late 1994 that they expect anyone really to notice. That means machines in 1995, and who knows how long it'll take to get interesting software to run on the machines? It could be 1996 or later before inexpensive PCs built around the RS/ 6000 processor make much of a splash. That means IBM *might* retake some control of the huge market for PC processors *fifteen years* after it introduced the PC.

In the meantime, IBM continues to face important defections as people get frustrated or take one of IBM's many "come one, come all" offers of severance packages. Heller left in frustration to start a company financed by IBM's most hated competitor, Fujitsu. If he succeeds, he will produce an exceptionally powerful machine in late 1993 or 1994 that will be aimed directly at both IBM's workstation and mainframe businesses. Cocke developed heart trouble and retired. Montoye took a severance package and went to work for Heller at HAL.

Montoye said he and many of his friends who worked on the RS/ 6000 referred to the buyouts as IQ tests. The test IBM posed was: "We'll give you a mess of money if you'll leave IBM and get a better, higher-paying job elsewhere. Are you bright enough to take it?" All his friends, Montoye says, passed the IQ test.

TEN

Jim Cannavino looked foolish in early 1990. He had given Bill Gates's Windows what was intended to be a tepid endorsement in late 1989, but everyone in the industry, including Cannavino's bosses, had seen the endorsement as far broader than Cannavino had, and he had seemed to get nothing in return. Gates hadn't slowed Windows down at all in favor of OS/2—quite the reverse. Cannavino didn't even have any rights to use or resell Windows, because all the hard feelings that resulted from the IBM-Microsoft dinner debacle at the fall Comdex show had prevented the companies from reaching any kind of formal deal. Cannavino needed to get something, anything, from Gates.

Gates was more than willing to talk. He still wanted to hang on to his most important partner, even if he was beginning to have problems with Cannavino. Gates also wanted IBM's full support for his new release of Windows, called Version 3.0, which was coming out in May 1990. That announcement seemed to Gates and Cannavino to be a good venue for telling the world about IBM's plans for Windows— which Gates hoped would include IBM's preloading Windows on many of its PCs and which Cannavino hoped would get Microsoft to think of Windows and OS/2 as more of a family, so that it would encourage people who started out using Windows to move quickly on to using its more powerful big brother, OS/2. In addition, Cannavino still hoped to get Gates finally to give IBM a better deal on the division of operating-system royalties. So Cannavino and Gates began a long series of meetings in early 1990 to try to get a deal done. As Microsoft began preparing materials for the May announcement, the public-relations people wrote things that would be announced by a "mystery guest," who they hoped desperately would be Cannavino.

This time around, both sides appeared to be ready for a radical shakeup. Although it's not generally known, even at IBM and Microsoft, Cannavino was ready to give up all responsibility for the development of OS/2, essentially admitting that IBM couldn't hack it and that Microsoft ought to be the one in the personal-computer operating-system business. Cannavino was going to take all his OS/2 programmers and have them work on multimedia applications, which combine video, still pictures, animation, sound, and text in ways that may lead to new methods of educating children, making presentations in business, and so forth. The IBM programmers would at least have had a chance to make an impact in multimedia, rather than pouring their efforts into OS/2, which turned out to be a bottomless pit. And progress in multimedia applications could have helped all makers of PCs, because those applications require manipulating so many images at high speed that they soak up as much power as a PC can provide. If multimedia applications become popular, IBM and its hardware competitors will all sell lots of fast new hardware.

Cannavino was so close to shooting his OS/2 development operation that he made Gates and Steve Ballmer swear they wouldn't start rearranging Microsoft's programming staffs to accommodate the change. He worried that some smart programmer at Microsoft would guess what was going on and tell someone at IBM, spreading panic through Cannavino's programming operation in Boca Raton, Florida.

If Cannavino had gone through with his plan, he would have saved the $150 million or so he was spending each year on OS/2 and could have spent the money to better purpose. OS/2 would have been freed of the nutty development structure that had so many programmers at so many sites on two continents reporting to two separate and sometimes warring managements. Gates would suddenly have had lots of incentive to make OS/2 work. Even if OS/2 continued to fail, Gates was going to give Cannavino enough rights to Windows that he wouldn't be shut out of Windows's good fortune. Gates and Cannavino would have been partners again.

The plan might have worked, but it didn't. The two didn't trust each other. They couldn't quite seem to close the deal. Cannavino, as an ex-mainframe guy, still didn't see that a limited operating system like Windows could be a best-seller, while Gates saw that it would be one, so the two had such different feelings about the value of rights to Windows that they couldn't reach an agreement.

As May 1990 approached, Cannavino and Gates tried the brute-force approach, holding numerous one-on-one meetings and getting all sorts of staff people involved. Then Cannavino had an accident. Although his friends have always assumed he'll maim himself someday while careering through the woods on a horse at full gallop chasing the sound of hounds in the distance, Cannavino actually hurt himself on a tennis court. He twisted a knee and tore some cartilage. Cannavino was in obvious pain. He kept attending all the meetings, but he seemed distracted. With the May announcement of Windows fast approaching, he seemed to Gates and Ballmer to be feeling pressured to make a decision fast yet didn't seem to feel comfortable making such a momentous decision while his mind wasn't concentrated on the issue.

After Gates and Ballmer made no progress at one session in Cannavino's conference room in early May, they had to head home but agreed to continue the discussions from there via a videoconferencing system. That didn't go well, either. Ballmer and an assistant left on a later flight than Gates and ran into a freakishly late winter storm that forced their plane to land in Cleveland. After hours of waiting, they finally made it as far as Detroit but had to sleep on the floor of the airport that night while waiting for an early flight the next day. When it came time for the videoconference to start that next day, Gates went off to a neighboring company's offices, where he had leased time on the videoconferencing equipment. But Ballmer and his staff member had yet to land at the Seattle airport, and the meeting couldn't start until they arrived an hour late. Gates and Cannavino turned the sound off on the equipment but left the video on. They spent an hour doing make-work, able to see each other on their TV monitors but not saying anything. It was looking like any sort of deal was fated not to happen.

By the end of the videoconference, it seemed that the ill will had pushed Cannavino and Gates further apart. Cannavino agreed to fly out with a team of people two days later to see whether they couldn't try one final time. The whole group actually arrived at their offices that morning in early May with their bags packed, expecting to leave in the middle of the day. But when Cannavino limped into the office, he called everyone and said he'd decided to give up. The trip was off.

Cannavino continued to dump money into OS/2. He gave up the chance to make a splash in multimedia. He gave up any rights to Windows, which became a runaway best-seller. All his attempts to put together a software strategy fell apart because he couldn't figure out how to deal with Gates.

The pressure on Cannavino to deliver better results was accelerating, too, because problems in the mainframe arena had made 1989 a disaster for the whole company. Through most of the 1980s, customers' demand for mainframe processing power had risen a steady 35 percent or so a year. Even though technological improvements meant that IBM and its competitors cut prices about 20 percent each year, that still left IBM with 15 percent growth in revenue each year. Nice work, if you can get it, especially for a company that was already the fourth-largest industrial company in the United States. Confident that this could continue, IBM expanded its use of an approach referred to internally as the "golden screwdriver." The concept was an old one, stemming from the days when IBM sold mechanical sorting devices, but IBM had updated it in a very profitable way. If a customer ordered a mainframe that was the smallest machine IBM offered, the company might actually ship the customer a machine that was twice as powerful and that contained twice as much memory. IBM would simply include a couple of lines of software on the machine, which kept the processor from using the extra memory and made it run at half its true speed. Assuming the customer did eventually decide he wanted a faster machine with more memory, IBM received a windfall. It simply sent out a technician, who shooed everyone out of the room lest someone figure out exactly what he was doing with his "golden screwdriver." The technician merely erased the couple of lines of software that were slowing things down, then left the customer a bill for a few million dollars. By the late 1980s, IBM had so much extra capacity already installed at customer sites and just waiting to be activated that the company appeared to be capable of coasting for a long time even if growth in demand slowed.

And as of 1989, Akers still didn't believe the mainframe growth was slowing. He had pushed the idea that he could sustain growth at least approaching the historical 15 percent level even with PCs going great guns and seemingly starting to cut into mainframe sales. Akers insisted the spread of PCs would, in fact, sharply increase the demand for mainframes. That was because in IBM's mainframe-centric view of the world, the mainframes would serve as the hubs for huge networks of PCs, acting as storehouses of information and generally playing traffic cop, shuttling data between PCs. But it was turning out that Akers was wrong.

As recently as the early 1980s, customers would have installed mainframes in the middle of their networks just because their IBM salesmen told them that was the right way to go. No longer. Customers had finally asserted themselves, becoming familiar enough with the technology that they had seized control from computer manufacturers and were going to determine the direction the industry took.

This should have been no surprise. Plenty of things that had seemed technologically complex had, over the years, become so much less threatening that they had become mundane. Cars in the early 1900s were seen as so complicated to operate that manufacturers assumed each one would require a chauffeur. Televisions in the early days were the stuff of magic. Someone from the manufacturer had to install it in the buyer's home. To align the picture, he maneuvered a wand in front of the screen. IBM had seen this sort of familiarity take over its type-writer business, where salesmen in the 1940s and 1950s personally took each electric typewriter out of its wooden crate, installed it at a customer's office, and instructed the user on how it operated. The salesmen spent so much time hand-holding that they could usually sell only a dozen or so of the imposing devices a month—anyone selling at least ten made a nice living.

Mainframes obviously seem more complicated to the general public than typewriters, cars, or televisions, but not to the huge technology operations that companies had been building for decades to run their computer operations. Huge consulting businesses, trade press, and technical publications had sprung up, too, making more technical knowledge available to a corporate computer operation than any small team of blue-suited IBM salesmen could hope to possess. By the late 1980s, the customer had come of age.

The customer's new comfort level meant new choices. Rather than always buying mainframes from IBM, customers could now take a hard look at compatible machines made by Hitachi and Amdahl. These mainframe clones had been around for some fifteen years but had done far less damage to IBM than PC clones had. IBM had always been able to convince important customers that either their mainframe clone might break down at an inopportune time or that some whiz-bang technological trick that IBM had up its sleeve would soon make the clones obsolete. Because mainframes are at the core of most big businesses, the computer managers didn't dare take a chance on having a problem develop that would mess up the payroll department or shut down the order-entry system. Besides, more than half the heads of big corporations' data-processing departments were IBM alumni, so they were inclined to go with IBM. Some of the technical concerns waned during the 1980s as Hitachi and Amdahl developed excellent reputations for quality. Corporate customers also saw that IBM hadn't managed to make PC clones obsolete and wondered why the mainframe world should be any different. In addition, computers became such a big part of most companies' expenses that chief financial officers began to get more involved in computer purchases as the 1980s progressed, and these hard-hearted numbers guys had no loyalty to IBM. They were loyal only to the lowest price. By 1989, IBM found that customers were no longer always doing what they were told.

"The line always was that nobody was ever fired for buying from IBM. Well, I know that's not true anymore because I fired the guy," Bill O'Neil said in 1989. O'Neil, who was then a senior technology executive at Drexel Burnham Lambert, said that someone came to him with a lame proposal to buy some IBM equipment. When pressed on the reason, the subordinate said he'd recommended the IBM computers because he thought IBM was a safe choice. The hulking, bearded O'Neil, who towered over his employee, said he told the guy, "Wrong," then made a noise like a game-show buzzer and said, "Game over. Next contestant, please."

Some people in the computer industry began circulating a joke on electronic bulletin boards that showed how out of touch people thought IBM had become. The joke had the pilot of a small plane and his ten passengers lost in a heavy fog at night in Atlanta. The plane's radio and all its instruments had been knocked out by lightning. The pilot finally saw a man standing in the window of a tall building, rolled down his window, and shouted, "Where am I?" The man in the building shouted back, "You're in an airplane." The pilot banked sharply to his left and landed at Atlanta's airport a few minutes later. A passenger, stumbling wearily out of the plane, said to the pilot, "It's miraculous that you landed us here safely, but how in the world did that man in the window help you?" The pilot replied, "Oh, that's easy. What he said was completely correct and totally irrelevant to my problem, so I knew he had to be in the IBM building."

In the late 1980s, as Amdahl and Hitachi showed customers that they could match IBM's quality, IBM went from more than a 90 percent share of the market for IBM-compatible mainframes down to less than 80 percent—with each ten points of market share accounting for about $4 billion in revenue and several hundred million dollars in earnings.

The whole mainframe market also began to grow more slowly as customers adopted what they called a "surround" strategy. IBM has always counted on the fact that customers are reluctant to rewrite all the software that they have produced to run on their mainframes. It's expensive and time-consuming to rewrite the millions of lines of code that go into payroll systems, accounting programs, and so on. It's also dangerous. Mainframe software handles the core operations of major businesses and government agencies throughout the world, and a single typo in any of those millions of lines could either corrupt the information the computer generates or paralyze operations by crashing the system. The risk of rewriting software tended to keep customers from dumping their expensive mainframes in favor of a collection of PCs or minicomputers, which would have required a total redo. But many customers had decided they would simply surround their mainframes with smaller, more cost-effective minicomputers and PCs that would handle all the new applications the user wanted to develop. That way, users wouldn't have to monkey with their existing software. They also wouldn't have to buy any more mainframes.

IBM's "golden screwdriver" approach had given it a little room to coast in the late 1980s, but even that couldn't hide the problems for long.

Akers should have seen the changes coming. In fact, he did. The study he had commissioned in 1987 had predicted that mainframe revenue growth would quickly slow to 5 to 6 percent a year, from the 15 percent rates that had made IBM so fat and happy. But Akers never did adjust. He talked about keeping expense growth to perhaps 6 percent a year, but it never quite happened. IBM's overhead, the prime target of cost cutting, was still 30 percent to 35 percent of revenue each year, nearly twice the percentage at its Japanese look-alike competitors Hitachi and Fujitsu and five or six times the percentage at IBM's PC competitors. IBM still employed some 390,000 people in 1989. IBM's luxuriant bureaucracy still allowed for people to spend most of their weeks in meetings, flying all over the country to fight turf skirmishes.

Still, Akers thought he had acted decisively to head off the problems that hit IBM in 1989, so he became frustrated as they persisted. He knew he was off to the worst start of any IBM chief executive ever and he began to think about what his place would be in history when he retired in a few years. Akers knew that historically IBM had accounted for half of the entire computer industry's revenue and that, under him, that figure was now down to less than a quarter of the industry's revenue. He worked himself into a fighting mood. He decreed that the market-share losses would stop.

In fact, the one thing that his decentralization in early 1988 had accomplished was that it gave the sales force more freedom to interpret orders such as Akers's 1989 edict that losing market share would no longer be tolerated. Salesmen now had much of the control over pricing that had previously been reserved for senior management, and they realized, even if Akers didn't, that competitors' products were now so similar to IBM's that the only weapon IBM could use to stop market-share losses was lower prices. The salesmen used their weapon. They began a price war that gave customers discounts as high as 50 percent and that eventually rendered list prices meaningless. Buying a mainframe started to include as much wheeling and dealing as buying a used car.

Customers talked about their "million-dollar coffee mugs"—they had found that if they had a coffee mug from Amdahl or Hitachi on their desks when an IBM salesman came calling, they could get $1 million knocked off the price of a mainframe. George DiNardo, who was an executive vice president at Mellon Bank in the late 1980s, says that he once got an IBM salesman to slash a price on a mainframe by pulling a Japanese sword off his bookcase, waving it above his head, and shouting, "Hitachi!"

With mainframe prices plummeting and nothing else able to take up the slack—not even the still highly successful AS/400 minicomputer business—IBM's earnings plunged in 1989. Akers gave up on the year in early December, announcing he was going to cut ten thousand jobs and taking a big write-off. He made sure the write-off was big enough to give him a cushion going into 1990—some securities analysts estimate that the write-off let him take in 1989 above $1 billion of expenses that he otherwise would have had to account for in 1990.

Then Akers adopted his best fighter-jock attitude and, knowing he would have to dodge plenty of flak, called a meeting in December 1989 to address the hundreds of unhappy securities analysts who had been recommending IBM stock and the scores of reporters who were beginning to smell blood. Akers looked pale and haggard—his mother had died a couple of days before the press conference—and came across as far less positive than normally. But when one analyst asked whether top management should be taking some responsibility for IBM's problems and whether Akers could assure the group that he wouldn't be calling a similar meeting a year later to explain similar write-offs and job cuts, Akers glared at the analyst for several seconds before responding. Having humiliated the analyst, he then said essentially that the question was stupid. Of course things were under control.

"I believe that a management team is measured by its ability to deal with problems," he said sternly, "and I believe we are identifying the problems and dealing with them."

Sensing that he finally had to do something about getting IBM more into the profitable software business and out of the hardware business, where it was taking a beating, but not knowing quite how to do it, Akers authorized a series of scattershot attempts in 1989 and 1990. He let one executive invest half a billion dollars in software companies. He let others try what turned out to be the last of IBM's "all things to all people" software strategies. Akers let Cannavino revive his PC business's attempts to publish PC software. Akers even let another executive try a couple of ways of turning IBM on its head, having teams of IBM programmers focus on solving customers' software problems and making any hardware sales an afterthought.

All attempts failed, for all the usual reasons.

The investments in software companies were the brainchild of Ned Lautenbach, the younger brother of senior vice president Terry Lautenbach. Ned was known as a reasonably smart executive with a strong analytical bent—he was a Harvard MBA at a company that had few MBAs at its senior levels. He would say little during meetings with his peers, then, after seeing which way the wind was blowing, would lay out a five-point program that summarized the feelings of the group. People who worked for him described him as a decent guy who sent flowers or a handwritten note if someone did good work. But those who worked in other parts of the business describe him as cold, even hostile. Certainly, the small, owlish Ned had none of the easy charm of his husky, gregarious brother Terry. When one of Ned Lautenbach's peers presented a customer's problem and tried to get different parts of the business to pitch in to solve it, Lautenbach refused unless the project somehow made him look good.

Ned Lautenbach had done well as he moved up through the U.S. sales force, but he had made a hash of his prior assignment in the mid-1980s. He had been responsible for the PC business's relations with computer dealers during the time Bill Lowe ran the PC business, and Lautenbach had managed to alienate just about everybody with his heavy-handed tactics aimed at keeping dealers from selling non-IBM equipment. When Compaq came along and took the opposite tack, helping dealers in any way possible, the dealers were so mad at IBM that they did everything they could to sell Compaq, thus contributing greatly to its success. Given his failure in the mid-1980s, his peers found it hard to understand how he had been promoted in the late 1980s to run an important software business that included 33,000 people. Akers seemed enamored of Lautenbach and every once in a while said something such as, "That Ned is really something, isn't he?" Lautenbach's colleagues nodded, of course, but they left the room wondering what Akers saw that everybody else missed.

Lautenbach thought it was time IBM stopped sitting on the sidelines watching all the little software companies in the industry get rich while IBM got nothing. He figured that IBM had essentially created Microsoft and Gates but had nothing to show for it, while Gates was on his way to becoming the richest man in the United States. In fact, by this point, Gates's multibillion-dollar personal net worth would have been enough to pull off a leveraged buyout of IBM, if the go-go days of easy financing had survived the end of the 1980s. Lautenbach could also point to scores of other software companies that he argued had benefited from IBM's creation of the PC industry and from the company's expensive efforts to keep the markets for mainframes and mini-computers growing. He argued that IBM need merely study each type of software carefully so it could identify what IBMers called the "best of breed." IBM would invest in that company, giving it IBM's blessing and supposedly ensuring that it would grow rapidly. And by selling good software, IBM would help sell its hardware. Holding equity in the software maker would also mean that IBM would benefit as the software maker did, so IBM would never again have to kick itself for missing out on buying a hunk of Microsoft or whatever.

The problem was that IBM turned out not to be much better at picking the "best of breed" among software packages than it was at writing the software. Nobody will ever confuse Microsoft with Policy Management, American Management Systems, Easel, Digital Interactive, or the dozens of other companies that absorbed half a billion dollars of Lautenbach's money in 1989 and 1990. (IBM was also turning out to be as poor a stock picker when it came to its own stock as it was when buying others'. Akers stepped up a program in 1989 and 1990 to buy back IBM stock, insisting that the stock had fallen so much that it had become undervalued. He wound up spending some $6 billion on IBM stock over the years, at prices averaging $119 a share. That is nearly two and a half times the price of IBM's stock in mid-1993, when it hovered in the high forties, so, at least on paper, IBM has lost $3.5 billion buying its own stock.)

Part of the problem, too, was that IBM smothered the smaller companies with affection. These were companies that had been financed with maybe a little venture capital or even just with somebody's credit card for a while and that still looked to keep their head counts as low as possible. Suddenly, IBM would get so enthusiastic about their software that it would send dozens of people to learn more about it or to learn how to sell it. Easel, for instance, found itself with twice as many IBMers in its offices as Easel staff members and didn't quite know what to do. The little companies had to hire people just to act as liaisons with IBM, keeping the multitude of IBM businesses happy. Over time, the whole focus of the little company shifted subtly to that of managing its relationship with mammoth IBM. No longer would the company focus on doing the software that caught IBM's eye in the first place.

IBM's bureaucracy is like a "giant pool of peanut butter we have to swim through," says Donald Coggiola, senior vice president of Policy Management.

When Lautenbach's investment strategy bogged down and the rest of his software work seemed to be producing little, he was replaced in 1991 by Bernard Puckett, who quickly spun off as many people as he could to other parts of the business and cut his organization to 7,000 from 33,000. But Lautenbach was actually promoted out of the job, not demoted. He was sent to run IBM's enormous Asian operations, which would give him the international experience he needed to make a serious run at the top job. (After producing one of the worst years the Asian operations have seen, Lautenbach would, in fact, get one more bump up the ranks. He wound up on the Management Committee, supervising all IBM's international operations, and became one of the two internal candidates considered to be most likely to succeed Akers. Once again, his peers wondered how Lautenbach kept failing upward.)

Shortly after Lautenbach began his career as a stock picker, IBM announced in May 1989 another in its smorgasbord of software strategies. This one was designed to tie together all the work people do in their offices. The project was the brainchild of Joe Guglielmi, a dark, good-looking man who always wore severely starched, monogrammed white shirts and could come across as a caricature of the IBM salesman. Like Cannavino, Guglielmi had joined IBM as a technician right out of high school. Guglielmi worked his way up through IBM's marketing branch in his hometown of Syracuse, getting his degree at Syracuse University at night, then moved up through IBM's sales organizations. It was because Guglielmi—often referred to as Joe G. because people have trouble pronouncing his last name—joined IBM at such a young age that he picked up all of IBM's language and culture as his own. Guglielmi became known for his IBM-speak, giving long, jargon-full nonanswers to just about any question from a reporter. When the reporter challenged Guglielmi and said he'd just dodged the question, Guglielmi would acknowledge that perhaps he hadn't been clear. Then he would lower his deep voice even further and, in his most sincere marketing tones, give the same nonanswer. When he traveled, he always had a limousine around, even if it was just to take him a few blocks from a restaurant back to his hotel. Guglielmi took three or four staff people with him to handle his schedule and write down whatever he wanted them to do. He had absorbed all of the mindlessly bureaucratic habits that are part of the IBM culture. He became the embodiment of the idea that IBMers don't want to be rich, they want to be important.

The software project, called OfficeVision, was Guglielmi's bid for the big time. He had proposed that IBM figure out how to tie together all the types of software people used in offices—word processors, spreadsheets, data bases, desktop publishing, desktop presentations, electronic mail, and so on—in a way that let them share information seamlessly. That way, someone working on a document in a word processor could instantly e-mail it to someone else. Someone doing some desktop publishing could tie his newsletter to a spreadsheet so that if someone changed the numbers in the spreadsheet, they would automatically be changed in the newsletter. It was a grand idea. But it turned out to be too grand. The software never quite worked.

When Guglielmi sold the MC on the idea for OfficeVision in early 1987, he put together a huge team of people to spend four months studying what needed to be done, but they kept getting pulled in every direction imaginable as all parts of IBM seized on OfficeVision as a strategic project they needed to control. Earl Wheeler, who ran IBM's software business, insisted that OfficeVision needed to follow his SAA architecture to the letter. Cannavino's PC people said it was obvious that OfficeVision—or Office, as it was known internally—had to be built on top of OS/2. Other parts of IBM insisted on certain electronic-mail standards. And so it went. Once the project got rolling, it involved fifteen hundred programmers, a mind-boggling number. Those programmers were backed up by additional armies, too, of product planners, financial experts, and forecasters. The OfficeVision groups were spread out at nine sites—a ridiculous number—at IBM facilities around the world, ranging from Sindelfingen, Germany, to Dallas, Texas.

As always, IBM tried to meet 99 percent of customers' needs with a product; even the PC industry had found that a 75 percent solution was far better. Even if it was possible to meet 99 percent of customers' desires in a single product, it took far too long to bring it to market. And, as was the case with OfficeVision, it usually wasn't possible to have one product be all things to all people.

In the end, OS/2 turned out to be the biggest problem for Office. To tie everything together, Office required the so-called Extended Edition of OS/2, which included not only the basic operating system but also an IBM data base and communications software. But those weren't ready, even though IBM had been working on them for more than two years by the time work on Office began in 1987 and more than four years by the time Office was announced. (When Bill Lowe had been quizzed at the PS/2 and OS/2 announcements in April 1987 about why only IBM, and not Microsoft, was working on the Extended Edition pieces, he had replied condescendingly that they were very complicated. Only IBM, he said, had the necessary expertise to do such complex data base and communications software.) Guglielmi tried having his people work off preliminary versions of Extended Edition in 1987 and 1988, but Cannavino's programmers kept getting pulled in so many directions that Extended Edition continued to change. Guglielmi finally decided to do something on his own that duplicated the capabilities of Extended Edition, but his hordes of programmers got tangled up in the problem, too.

When it came time to announce OfficeVision in May 1989, Guglielmi went ahead and promised that he could soon ship the version of OfficeVision designed to let people share work on PC networks—the version most customers wanted—even though so much work remained to be done. But the network version of Office soon began missing its schedule. It went from a planned shipment date of mid-1990 to late 1990. In late 1990, IBM said there was another delay but didn't even estimate what a new date might be. A few months later, IBM meekly said it hoped Office would be ready soon.

Guglielmi compounded his development problems by trying to charge far too much for OfficeVision. Rather than adopt the PC model of keeping software pricing low to create the greatest possible volume, Guglielmi decided Office was such a huge project that IBM would charge about fifteen thousand dollars for the software and hardware each person needed in order to use it. Even though the all-important network version of the software wasn't initially supposed to be available until a year after the May 1989 announcement—and, of course, didn't come close to meeting its schedule—Guglielmi still hoped customers would buy the hardware necessary to run the software or at least buy the mainframe and minicomputer versions of the OfficeVision software. Customers were just going to have to trust IBM that the important network version of OfficeVision would be as good as IBM promised and so plan ahead for its arrival. But customers weren't willing to do that any longer. They decided to give the competition a try or at least wait to see what happened.

In the past, in the mainframe world, Guglielmi might have had time to recover because of IBM's near monopoly. But in the PC world, IBM faced real competition. Lotus came out with Notes, which did much of what Office was supposed to do. Microsoft was also pushing what became the new wave of software strategy. Rather than trying to do everything at once, Microsoft did a little at a time. It produced a good word processor, a good spreadsheet, a good desktop-presentation package, and so on. It also built into those applications ways of sharing information with each other. Microsoft then encouraged other software companies to build those capabilities into their software. That way, customers could go merrily along spending most of their time worrying about the basic PC applications—spreadsheets and word processors— yet soon enough could share information across their PC networks in the ways that IBM envisioned would be possible with Office.

With IBM's development problems continuing well into 1991, now two years after the OfficeVision announcement, and with customers losing interest, Akers took the project away from Guglielmi. IBM soon announced that OfficeVision had been "stabilized," which in IBM- speak meant that no more work would be done. OfficeVision was stable in the same way a dead person is stable.

Cannavino contributed to IBM's software smorgasbord in 1989 with a plan that resembled one that Don Estridge had sponsored way back when. Cannavino set up a small business, called Desktop Software, to find good PC applications that someone else developed and published them under IBM's logo; in effect, IBM would provide its seal of approval to someone else's software and take a cut of the revenue in return. This small business would also develop applications on its own.

Cannavino turned the responsibility for developing the business over to Fernand Sarrat, an engaging man with bright, wild eyes who was known for relishing the perquisites of the executive life at IBM as much as anyone ever had. His administrative assistant would run out of the room to find a soda at the slightest sign Sarrat was thirsty. The assistant would also collect Sarrat's dry cleaning or whatever. The assistant—an out-of-towner being run through headquarters to get some grooming—decided to live near Sarrat so he could drive his boss to work every morning. Sarrat was sometimes kidded by his peers for living well when he traveled on business, but he just laughed it off. Sarrat, who came from a wealthy family and had plenty of money apart from his hefty IBM salary, said that he didn't put in for all his expenses. "Even IBM couldn't afford my real expenses," he said.

But Sarrat never got the business going. He managed to find a few marginal products, but that was all. Software companies didn't rush to do business with Sarrat because they had seen that IBM didn't have any influence in the PC software business. Its only successful PC product, a word processor called DisplayWrite, had done well only among big-iron customers who had used DisplayWrite on their mainframes. Little software companies had also seen how IBM could smother its partners, as had happened with some of Ned Lautenbach's investments. Many big software companies used their size to attract small developers looking for a large company to take their products to market. The little developers were willing to give up a share of their revenue in return for access to the big company's marketing forces. But IBM, the largest and most visible software company of all, couldn't seem to do what Microsoft, Borland International, and other software developers did all the time.

Sarrat almost got his business going when he spotted the Paradox data base well before its owner, Borland, made it a best-seller. Sarrat hoped to buy a significant piece of Borland in 1990 as a way of cementing the relationship, then build a business that used Paradox as the core product, linking together all the other applications he would acquire. After extensive secret negotiations, he worked out a deal to buy around 10 percent of Borland's stock for ten dollars a share. But he needed approval, first from Cannavino, then from Akers and the Management Committee. Sarrat ran into trouble when Wheeler and his mainframe software business objected that Sarrat would be endorsing a data base product that didn't fit with IBM's mainframe scheme. By the time Sarrat appealed to the MC and won approval weeks later, Paradox had made a breakthrough and Borland's stock price had risen. Borland's asking price for the stock went way up. Sarrat decided it would be too hard to push the question through all the layers a second time, so he dropped the idea. Borland stock soon hit eighty-seven dollars a share, meaning IBM passed up a gain of hundreds of millions of dollars on what would have been a minuscule investment. Once again, picking stocks turned out not to be IBM's game.

When Sarrat tried having people develop applications internally in 1990 and 1991, he had no better luck. He told people they were supposed to go off and think like entrepreneurs. He organized groups of three or four people and told them to think of good products. The problem is that nobody at IBM knows how to think like an entrepreneur. Nobody thinks that it would be a lot of fun to work around the clock, sleeping under his desk, living off diet Coke, taking a huge chance that would either make him fabulously wealthy or leave him out of work and penniless. Besides, someone putting in phenomenal hours and producing a hit product at IBM wouldn't get wealthy—he'd just get a pat on the head and a bonus of maybe a few thousand dollars. The first thing one of Sarrat's groups did, long before it was close to having a product, was ask him to approve spending half a million dollars a year on exhibition space to show the eventual product to customers. The attitude seemed to be that the little product group would look important if it had a showroom, and that IBM was so big that half a million dollars wouldn't matter to anybody. Sarrat shot down that idea and lots of others like it, but people just didn't seem to understand what being an entrepreneur meant. As much as Sarrat and others talked at IBM about taking chances and being more entrepreneurial, IBMers didn't get the message. They were used to playing it safe. They didn't know *how* to take risks.

Sarrat really got himself in trouble when he decided to act like an entrepreneur himself. Akers and others had been preaching for years that each business had to stand on its own, that people could do whatever they wanted even if it meant stepping on someone else's toes. Then Sarrat decided that the smart thing to do would be to develop applications that ran on Microsoft's Windows, rather than on OS/2. That didn't sit too well with anyone. IBM had promised customers that OS/2 would do everything Windows did, and more, so the MC couldn't let some part of IBM run off and help the enemy, Windows. The MC cut off Sarrat's funds in 1992. He sold all the rights to the software that he had acquired and shut his business down.

The most radical approaches IBM could have taken in software in 1989 and 1990—and the ones most likely to have worked—were being pushed by Bob Berland, a bald, tough-talking New Yorker. Berland was the most passionate IBM executive that outsiders had ever seen. He'd believe in some strategy so strongly that when he'd go off to industry conferences, he'd grab people in the hallways to pull them into his room and browbeat them about some idea he had. He didn't dance around issues, trying to come up with the safe way to respond. If he thought IBM had messed up, he'd say so. If he thought someone was giving him or IBM a hard time unfairly, he'd say that, too.

In 1986, for instance, Akers gave a keynote speech at a big software conference at a resort in the hills above Phoenix, Arizona. The speech was just twenty minutes of platitudes about how IBM hoped to work with software developers. The speech underwhelmed the audience so much that John Imlay, chief executive of Management Science America, a big software maker, had a baboon brought up on the stage later and asked it what it had thought of Akers's speech. It yawned, then spat on the floor; the audience erupted in cheers. Long after Akers had hopped back on his corporate plane and jetted off, Berland was still around, working the conference, saying that, yes, IBM had had its head up its rear end for years but insisting in his booming voice that the developers needed to give IBM another chance because now it finally had something to say.

The grandest of Berland's ideas came to be called the Enterprise Alliance. The concept was that instead of first sending a bunch of people to a customer to push hardware, IBM send in a team of programmers. They'd talk to the data-processing customer about what new applications he was trying to develop or how he was trying to smooth over existing problems with his information systems. Then the programmers would propose ways of speeding the process and offer, for a modest fee, to do a piece of necessary software within thirty to ninety days. At the end of that time, customers were usually impressed. These data-processing customers were generally swamped with requests from other corporate departments for software development, so seeing the IBM programmers do some work as fast as they did was an epiphany. The customers typically then either hired IBM to do all the programming for a substantial fee or at least bought from IBM the sorts of programming tools—debuggers, code generators, and so on—that IBM's people had used to do the work so quickly in the first place. Either way, when it came time to buy the hardware to run the new software, the customers leaned toward IBM. In any case, Berland argued, if IBM could speed up the pace of software development and finally cut into the years-long backlog of requests for software at most companies, then the demand for everybody's hardware would increase as companies found they needed more hardware to run all this new software.

The Enterprise Alliance idea caught some attention inside IBM in 1990 and gradually grew to include several hundred people, but Berland always had trouble changing things inside IBM because he lacked a traditional power base. He was a vice president, one of the thirty to forty at IBM at any given time, but he was a minister without portfolio. He could go off and make deals on IBM's behalf with software companies, but he didn't have a ton of people reporting to him—the traditional measure of power at IBM. He was allowed to go off and stir things up in IBM's dealings with outside software companies, but he had to work to sell his more radical notions, and the MC bought few of them. Berland became a sort of voice crying in the wilderness, warning that IBM had better turn itself upside down and focus on software if it wanted to continue its unparalleled successes.

Then he got sick. The fifty-year-old Berland suddenly started having headaches in mid-1990. He began to mumble. Finally, he went to a hospital on Long Island, New York, for a CAT scan and got the shocking news: He had a brain tumor—a big one.

There was a chance that surgery would help, so the doctors operated, but once they saw how completely the tumor had worked its way into Berland's brain, the lead surgeon gasped. Berland wouldn't know it for months, but the doctors knew then that he had no chance.

Once Berland began to recuperate from the initial surgery, he got IBM's president, Jack Kuehler, to install a terminal in his hospital room. Even though Berland was weak, he spent hours a day at the terminal keeping track of his projects. He also sent dozens to hundreds of e-mail messages, urging people to change the way they did business. As the months went by, the messages became increasingly desperate.

Berland kept his IBM discipline to the end despite his mounting frustration. When a reporter called once at the hospital to wish him well, the two talked for just a few minutes and only about his health. Yet as soon as he hung up the phone, Berland called a public-relations person just to confess that he had held an unauthorized conversation with the press.

The closest he came to disloyalty, even while dying, was in his rough sense of humor. When a visitor once asked how he was doing, he griped, "I'm constipated." Then he laughed and added, "Just like IBM."

He died a month later, in July 1991.

In mid-1990, Cannavino still hoped to make progress in operating-system software by bringing Microsoft into line. Having failed when he tried to bully Microsoft before the 1989 Comdex trade show, then having failed when he used brinksmanship to try to get Microsoft to make concessions before its May 1990 Windows announcement, Cannavino now tried the silent treatment. Following the breakdown of the talks with Gates in early May, Cannavino and his main lieutenants simply didn't return any phone calls or letters from Gates and his principal aides for more than six weeks.

Finally, in desperation, Gates had a florist deliver to Cannavino a box that looked as if it contained long-stemmed roses. When Cannavino opened it, he found a bunch of olive branches. He chuckled.

Cannavino appreciated the gesture enough that he sent Gates a long letter saying he thought they had some real opportunities to work together. But Cannavino also laid out some conditions he thought had to be met before they could proceed, the most important of which concerned the division of royalties between the companies from their joint operating-system work. Gates replied, and the talks were suddenly back on in the summer of 1990.

Gates recognized, though, that he needed to get around Cannavino somehow if he was going to reestablish a real relationship with IBM, and he was almost desperate to do that. Gates worried, in particular, about Novell, a big company that owned the market for software that helped PCs communicate with one another when hooked up in networks. Gates worried that, while he owned the desktop market, Novell's ownership of the network market would keep Microsoft pent-up. (That's because corporate computer operations are arranged in a hierarchy, with PCs on the bottom and mainframes on the top. Gates controlled the desktop software business, but he wanted to grow beyond that, eventually becoming the heart and soul of corporate computer networks. To pull off that grand plan, he needed to build from his strength in the PC business, first gaining control of the market for software used in local networks of PCs, then moving on to take control of the market for software used to let PC networks communicate with mainframes and with other networks of PCs over long-distance phone lines. If Novell kept Gates from gaining control of the software for PC networks, his plan would be thwarted.) IBM was languishing even more than Microsoft in the PC-network software, so Gates thought he and IBM might be able to gang up on Novell. Given his tattered relationship with Cannavino, Gates called Cannavino's boss, Kuehler, to see whether maybe the two of them shouldn't talk. Kuehler said, in effect, Sure, come on out and we'll have lunch.

Kuehler, of course, immediately called Cannavino, who didn't like the fact that Gates had gone over his head. Cannavino decided he would keep the lunch from happening until Gates caved in on numerous issues concerning the structure of the IBM-Microsoft relationship. Once Gates realized the lunch was being held hostage, he got his back up.

"It's like I was supposed to bend over just for the chance to have lunch with some guy from IBM," Gates says.

So just a few weeks into their rapprochement in mid-1990, Cannavino and Gates were already at loggerheads again, and they fought their way through a tough summer. Cannavino's lateness for meetings began to drive Gates and Ballmer nuts. They once flew across country for a five o'clock meeting but found Cannavino unavailable. They were ushered into his conference room and told he'd be a while. One of them went out for what turned out to be horrible Chinese food, and the two plus an assistant just sat there for nearly three hours, picking at the food and staring at the walls. When Cannavino finally arrived, he laid out some of IBM's priorities. When it came time for Gates to respond, he listed a few things that Microsoft believed were important for the relationship; then, unable to restrain himself, he said coldly, "We also believe in being on time for meetings. . . ."

Cannavino started one meeting by talking for twenty-some minutes about his new car, apparently trying to establish rapport with Gates, whose interest in fast cars had been widely reported in the press. Gates just stared at him, not saying a word through the whole soliloquy. Gates's assistants insist Cannavino might chat for two and a half hours of a three-hour meeting about nothing in particular, then Cannavino would talk business for half an hour, accomplishing little.

Gates says the monologues used to drive him nuts. "I kept wanting to say to Cannavino, 'We need a shorthand because these meetings are taking too long. Every time you say, "thirteen," I'll know that what that means is that all you want to do is what the customer wants. And for

every one of these other gibberish slogans, we can also get little numbers. There are a lot of small integers available. We'll just tighten these
meetings up. You know, Cannavino, if you want to talk about how
you're going to save the U.S. educational system, okay, we've heard that
story. That's a good fifteen-minute one. That can be number eleven.
If, Cannavino, you want to give that speech about how you've cut
manufacturing overhead and how you've done such a great job running
things and how you're such a tough guy, that one we can give a little
shorthand, too, because you're getting good at that little speech.' "

Gates also complains that Cannavino closed most meetings without
making any decisions. "When you sit in these meetings and you're
trying to discuss something and you're trying to make a decision, you're
trying to make judgments on behalf of customers about where technology is going to be and where you should invest," Gates says. "To have
someone, after all these hours, say, 'Well, we'll do whatever the customer wants,' it's so irritating. And they think every time they say that,
it really means something."

Cannavino's staff says lots of the time at the start of meetings was,
in fact, taken up by arguing over what they called dubious assumptions
by Microsoft. Ballmer might come in and write on the white board
in Cannavino's conference room such things as, "No one is writing
applications for OS/2." Accepting that assumption meant accepting that
OS/2 had flopped and that Windows was the way to go, so Cannavino's
assistants say he spent as long as necessary batting down the false
assumptions before he let the meeting proceed.

When negotiations bogged down, Cannavino and Gates resumed
their series of one-on-one meetings at neutral sites around the country.
(The meetings were not, however, really one-on-one. Cannavino never
went anywhere without his assistant, Susan Fairty, who lived near Cannavino, well north of his office, so she could drive to work with him in
the morning and who was so closely in tune with her boss that anytime
he went on one of his diets, the petite Fairty also walked around the
office snacking on diet bars. From the start, Gates had always believed
in numerical parity with IBM, lest IBM use numbers to dominate their
meetings, so he brought along one of two assistants.) This time, though,
the meetings just seemed to make things worse.

Cannavino blew up at Gates at one point and said, "You may think
I'm an idiot, but I'm not, and I'm not going to let you make me look
like an idiot again."

For his part, Gates complains about how little got accomplished even though he tried to sit patiently through Cannavino's monologues. "I'm really very good at this stuff," Gates says. "I know how to be somebody's son. You know, 'Yes, Dad.' But seven hours goes by and you haven't really talked about anything. You haven't decided anything."

Cannavino's posturing also irritated Gates. He says Cannavino once said, "I have to get approvals for these things, but someday, when I run this company, I won't have to get approvals." Gates adds, "This guy's not shy about his abilities."

One meeting, in Minneapolis in the late summer of 1990, really set Gates off. The meeting took so long that Gates missed two flights out and almost didn't make it back in time to address a PC user group meeting that night. After the meeting, a still-angry Gates told a group of people, "That asshole Cannavino! He never did get around to saying anything meaningful. All he wanted to talk about was how he had just come back from a trip to Japan, and he thought I should look into Japan because there would be lots of good business opportunities there. Fuckin' A! I've been in Japan a helluva lot longer than he has. I should have been telling *him* about the business opportunities there!"

With Cannavino and Gates still so far apart in the summer of 1990, the plan for a Kuehler-Gates lunch in late August got called off at the last moment. Cannavino still insisted that he and Gates needed to do a version of OS/2 that corrected the flaws in the version that the companies had been selling in 1989. The version was tailored for machines built around the Intel processor used in the now-ancient IBM PC AT, which became available in 1984. Gates argued that they should give up on AT-class machines because they were yesterday's news—or, more aptly, 1984's news, not 1990's. But Cannavino still couldn't give up on the promise IBM had made to its customers back in 1984—that it would continue to tailor any advances in software so they could be used on AT-class products. Both agreed that the division of labor on OS/2 meant it was guaranteed to fail, but they argued about how to reallocate control. Eventually, IBM and Microsoft hammered away at the issue long enough to decide that IBM could go ahead and do a better version of OS/2 for AT-class PCs. IBM would also take the lead role on a more advanced version, aimed at PCs designed to use the more advanced 80386 chip. Microsoft would take the lead on an even more advanced version, built to take advantage of even faster processors that, by mid-

1990, seemed to be coming soon. Cannavino and Gates even agreed on a way for IBM to get limited rights to Windows and for the royalty structure to be rejiggered in a way slightly more favorable to IBM.

It wasn't easy. As they came close to an agreement in September 1990, the IBM and Microsoft staffs butted heads all day long at a Holiday Inn in White Plains. The hotel was on the edge of a rough section of town but seemed to be out of the way enough that the staffs didn't expect to be spotted by any reporter or nosy executive from a rival company. Gates flew in for a meeting with Cannavino that started at 7:00 P.M. They holed up in a conference room for hours while a half dozen members of Cannavino's staff paced outside, wondering what was taking them so long. Finally, Cannavino and Gates emerged. But they still couldn't agree. They just needed to get out of their tiny room. They repeatedly paced the length of the brightly lighted hallway, well after midnight, while Cannavino's staff tried to read their body language. It didn't look good. Cannavino, an emotional sort who tends to hug people, tried to put his arm around Gates to act like the wise older brother. Gates recoiled. When the two locked themselves into their meeting room, though, they quickly settled. Cannavino grabbed a Magic Marker and wrote the six remaining issues on the white board on the wall. "I'll give you these three issues," Cannavino said, "if you'll give me these three." Gates said that was fine by him. In September 1990, three and a half years after Bill Lowe had first started trying to negotiate a new arrangement with Gates, IBM and Microsoft finally had an agreement.

Gates summoned Ballmer and a couple of lawyers from their hotel rooms elsewhere in White Plains, where they had been waiting by the phone. They pored over the tentative deal until nearly 4:00 A.M., then grabbed a couple hours of sleep and drove the few miles up the road to Armonk for the signing early the next morning. As the tired Gates stood waiting for Cannavino on the orange carpet outside a little office Cannavino keeps at corporate headquarters for use on his frequent visits there, Gates said he was hungry and asked for some cereal. Someone got some, and the tired Gates began shoveling it down. As he did, he looked around and saw how old the PCs were on secretaries' desks and in the cubicles he could see into. While Microsoft employees generally have the latest and greatest PC equipment, most of the machines Gates could see in Armonk were either comparable to the original PC or to the XT, which came out in 1983. That meant the newer of the machines were seven years old.

"Jesus," Gates said, "this tells me more about IBM than anything I've ever seen."

Both sides portrayed the September 1990 agreements as a breakthrough that finally headed off any possibility of a divorce. However, the strains were evident even before the agreements were signed. IBM trusted Gates so little and thought his command of the press was so great that someone on the IBM side had already leaked to the trade press the gist of what was going on, trying to put a spin on things and portray the deal as an IBM victory. Cannavino and his assistants didn't trust Microsoft to wait even a day to go public with their version of things, so the assistants arranged to have Cannavino call a series of reporters at home on Sunday afternoon to announce a deal that wasn't signed until the following morning.

Cannavino quickly became even more suspicious when Ballmer managed to kill immediately all work at Microsoft on the two versions of OS/2 that IBM now controlled. Cannavino thought, for one thing, that Ballmer should have kept people in place for a while, to help their IBM colleagues ease into the work. He also knew that it would take his software people weeks to months to reallocate the two hundred people Ballmer moved around, so he figured that Ballmer must have been planning the changes well in advance of any agreement with IBM, confirming his worst fears: that Microsoft must not have been working hard on OS/2 in the months leading up to the September 1990 agreement. Cannavino simply couldn't believe that anyone could move as fast on personnel issues as Microsoft just had.

Still, the peace held for more than two months, until Microsoft held its annual conference for software developers. Ballmer invited an IBM representative to attend the conference and sent the Microsoft slides for the conference to IBM ahead of time, which got him a testy call from Lee Reiswig, a Cannavino senior software executive. But neither Ballmer nor Reiswig anticipated the fallout that the slides would produce. As the Microsoft conference progressed, Cannavino and his main assistants got more and more calls from software executives saying that Microsoft had backed off its commitment to OS/2 and was pushing Windows. The callers couldn't point to anything precise. It was more like instead of saying, "OS/2, OS/2, Windows," Gates and Ballmer were saying, "Windows, OS/2, OS/2." But, as suspicious as Cannavino was of Gates, that was all he needed to set him off again.

Things got worse in early January 1991. When it looked like *The Wall Street Journal* was going to do a tough story on the IBM-Microsoft relationship, a public-relations person for Microsoft tracked Ballmer down and warned him that he'd better call the reporter fast to respond. She tried to push him into action by sending as part of her e-mail message her guess on what the *Journal's* headline might say and what the first couple of paragraphs of the story would look like. Ballmer, trying to be responsible, called Reiswig and warned him that he, too, should call the reporter. In the process, though, Ballmer referred to his PR person's version of the headline and lead paragraphs in such a way that Reiswig thought he had a copy of the *Journal* story, not understanding that the subject of a story is never, ever sent a copy of the story in advance. Deeply suspicious, Reiswig called his PR people and demanded that they, too, get a copy of the story. When they tried to tell Reiswig that he needed to understand how closely newspapers guard the contents of their stories before publication, Reiswig shouted, "All I understand is that they have a copy of the story and you don't!" He became even more wary of Microsoft's growing power.

Things then blew up later in January 1991 when a story in the national press said Microsoft had given up on OS/2 and was devoting all its attention to Windows. The story was very premature. Microsoft was beginning to question the future of OS/2 but still had lots of its good people plugging away at it as hard as they could. Cannavino, Reiswig, and the others were fully prepared to believe the article, though, given all that had happened in their dealings with Microsoft. They felt that they'd been had. Even worse for Cannavino, the story appeared the morning of an IBM board meeting where IBM's operating systems strategies were going to be presented to directors and where Cannavino was a featured speaker. Everyone in the room wanted to know what was really going on and how Gates and company had pulled such a fast one on IBM.

Ballmer, at a Microsoft senior management meeting in January 1991, noted that stories were appearing in newspapers, stating that IBM and Microsoft were now going to battle to the death. He wondered out loud, "Are we really at war with IBM?" He didn't know it yet, but they were.

ELEVEN

IBM remained so insular in the late 1980s and early 1990s that its headquarters staff often didn't even seem to know who the other major players in the industry were. An intermediary for Jim Manzi, chief executive of Lotus, one of the biggest PC software companies, complains that when he called Chairman John Akers's office in 1990, no one seemed to have even heard of Manzi. Akers's administrative assistants were supposed to be the best and the brightest of IBM's younger generation, the highest of the hi-pos, and Manzi was well known even outside the computer industry—he had, for instance, recently been on the cover of *Business Week*. Yet when Manzi's intermediary called to try to set up a meeting with Akers, he found himself explaining at length.

"What was that name again?" the administrative assistant asked Manzi's go-between. "Manzi?" he repeated hesitantly after the caller said the name. "How do you spell that? And what company is he with again?"

Terry Garnett, a senior vice president at Oracle, another huge software company, says he had a similar experience several times when he tried to reach President Jack Kuehler and found himself dealing with Kuehler's supposedly hi-po administrative assistants. They didn't seem to have a clue what Oracle was.

By the end of 1989, Jim Cannavino thought he had recognized the problems caused by this insularity and could do something about them. He began forcing his product-development teams to investigate how other companies did things. Cannavino also hoped to get his development teams to work faster by making them smaller. Cannavino decided that a project to develop a laptop computer for introduction some time in late 1990 would be his test case.

Cannavino was trying to reenter a market where IBM had flopped in the mid-1980s with its Convertible laptop and where IBM had been a nonfactor as the market grew to be several billion dollars a year, so he tried to re-create the experience of the original PC team in 1980. He put together a group so small and stationed so far in the back of IBM's Boca Raton facility that visitors usually had to struggle to convince the IBM receptionist that the group even existed. Visitors would then wander through long corridors and eventually reach tiny offices in the back of the facility, whose windows looked out over a swamp. As often as not, the visitors found that some alligators had crawled out of the swamp to sun themselves outside the laptop group's offices. One alligator always appeared right before trouble hit, so he became known as "Murphy," as in Murphy's Law. And as Cannavino would learn to his chagrin as 1990 progressed, Murphy appeared a lot.

The laptop project unfolded at a cocky time for IBM. After five mediocre to poor years, IBM's 1990 was terrific. Momentum built as the year progressed, convincing everyone at IBM that what they saw as the incredibly tough restructuring of the prior years had finally led them into the promised land. When IBM's investor-relations manager finished a conference call with securities analysts, describing a terrific quarter IBM had in 1990, he couldn't help but vent the frustrations that had built up for years: "This earnings release," he said, "is dedicated to all the pessimists on IBM."

Nineteen ninety was great partly because the AS/400 continued to kill the competition, letting IBMers gloat as Digital Equipment unraveled. In addition, a stronger U.S. economy and some sales programs gave the United States its first strong performance in years. But 1990 also benefited from things that IBM management should have recognized as unsustainable, starting with the huge 1989 write-off that made 1989 absorb hundreds of millions of dollars of what should have been 1990's expenses. The mainframe group had also used some financial legerdemain in early 1990 to get customers to continue buying the current line of mainframes by promising huge price breaks on new ones becoming available in 1991. That certainly helped 1990, but Chairman John Akers shouldn't have been fooled into thinking he could maintain 1990's mainframe sales pace. IBM's 1990 also benefited because a new line of disk drives introduced toward the end of 1989 gave the company several months' advantage over competitors—a burst of revenue that obviously wouldn't last into 1991 or 1992.

Still, Akers took 1990 as vindication of his restructuring and decided the big problems were behind him. He gave up on attempting major changes and began merely fine-tuning. In particular, he ordered all his business units to start selling parts in the original-equipment-manufacturer market, meaning that companies could now buy from IBM and resell under their own labels anything from a PC part like a disk drive all the way up through an entire mainframe. The original-equipment-manufacturer, or OEM, push came partly because Akers and Kuehler wanted to head off the Japanese in Europe. Japanese companies had started out as parts suppliers to some computer makers there, then eventually bought the troubled companies. Witness, Akers and Kuehler said, what had just happened in 1990 when Japan's Fujitsu—the company IBM most hated—bought control of ICL in Britain. Fujitsu now had a way of selling all its products in Britain, a market that had been largely closed to it before and that IBM had dominated. As usual, though, IBM's biggest competitors in the OEM market turned out not to be the huge Japanese companies. Instead, IBM's main rivals were the host of small companies—such as disk-drive makers Seagate and Conner—that needed to be aggressive about cutting prices and that were faster at adopting new technologies than their larger, more bureaucratic Japanese rivals.

Akers thought that having IBM sell parts would force internal suppliers of parts to keep up with outside suppliers, so the PC business, for instance, wouldn't have to pay far more to buy parts from within IBM than competitors spent when they bought from other suppliers. The OEM sales would also generate needed research and development money. The IBM chip business, for instance, was finding it increasingly hard to justify the hundreds of millions of dollars needed to build plants to make the cutting-edge memory chips that U.S. policymakers consider to be crucial in helping the United States compete technologically with the Japanese. Akers and Kuehler hoped selling excess chips —and striking more joint ventures with other chip makers—would help cover the costs of those plants.

Still, IBM found it hard to change its thinking. Someone at IBM's research facility in Almaden, California, for instance, still had to go through all the bureaucracy that had been in place since the federal antitrust case had preoccupied IBM through the 1970s if he wanted to line up a research contract with an outside company. The researcher had to get approval from Almaden's lawyers, from lawyers at research headquarters in Yorktown Heights, and from lawyers at corporate headquarters at Armonk. Any veto could kill the planned contract. Approval could take two years.

Akers and Kuehler also discovered that IBM had been so insulated for so long that it couldn't just throw open its doors, say, "We're here," and expect to have a multibillion-dollar business overnight. Everything about IBM was different, down to the way it drilled holes in its circuit boards and to the fact that it made square chips while everyone else made rectangular ones. IBM needed to learn to drill holes, configure chips, and do a million other things in unfamiliar ways before it could expect to make an impact in the OEM business. Even then, nobody was going to buy an IBM PC disk drive just to have one in their machines. IBM had to win on its own merits, and it would find itself besting its little competitors only some of the time.

Besides pushing on the OEM front, Akers also decided to begin a Quality program, joining a host of American companies adopting Japanese ideas about the need for measurable results in all business processes and for constant improvement in those results. The eventual aim was to reach a nirvanalike state called Six Sigma, in which a company would be making fewer than 3.4 mistakes per million products made, calls answered, and so on. Akers started out with the best of intentions. He had someone calculate that IBM spent $2.4 billion a year fixing problems with products; had those problems never occurred, that $2.4 billion would have dropped right down into IBM's profits. Akers also said, correctly, that IBM was frustrating customers with, for instance, bills so confusing that the customers sometimes paid IBM to help them decipher the bills. Akers assumed that pushing Quality would solve such problems and keep customers happier.

To give the Quality program a high profile, Akers put Steve Schwartz in charge of it. Schwartz was not only a senior vice president; he was also well known as the hero of the AS/400 development project. In addition, Schwartz was a well-traveled executive who knew enough people that he could cut to the heart of a problem quickly. He had an un-IBMish, cut-the-crap manner that kept people from hiding behind IBM's procedures. Schwartz was also an old friend of Akers, giving him unusual access. Akers pulled Schwartz aside and told him that the Quality program was to be their legacy to IBM. They had both been at IBM for thirty-some years and both were due to retire at the end of 1994. Akers told Schwartz he thought the Quality program could have IBM's earnings, revenue, and stock price setting records again by the time they retired.

While Akers spoke out on few issues, he even talked publicly about what the Quality movement could do to reinvigorate American business and held IBM up as an example of how other companies should run their businesses. He also continually talked up Quality inside IBM to make sure IBMers knew that this wasn't just another program du jour of the sort IBM had repeatedly pushed and then dropped over the years.

The problem was that Quality made progress in fits and starts. Teams of people figured out ways to simplify bills and cut bureaucracy. But the teams themselves formed a shadow bureaucracy. Just about everybody was in some kind of meeting each week on Quality, not counting the days of Quality training that everyone had to take. When IBM focused on a little detail like the messages people left on their answering machines, it beat the detail to death. IBM hired Bob Newhart at considerable expense to prepare a training film on phone messages. Then IBM handed out brochures on "the five secrets of success for a winning greeting." Just to make sure everyone paid attention, IBM put together a group of phone police who spent their days calling people's phone mail to check on their messages. Offenders got a sort of citation sent via e-mail, with a copy sent to their bosses.

Akers was convinced that the Quality program really would take IBM to the next level. "This has captured the imagination of IBM people much more than I ever thought it would," he said. "Now people are wandering around thinking about how to conduct their business perfectly. It's astonishing. It's the best thing to ever happen to us."[1]

But the heavy-handed approach gave the troops mixed feelings at best about Quality—known at IBM as Market-Driven Quality, or, given the need for an acronym, MDQ—and its obsession with the Six Sigma measurement. "Six Sigma Equals Heil Hitler," one person wrote on a form requesting anonymous feedback on the Quality program. Another employee complained about how IBM was continuing to cut back on its number of employees and wrote that MDQ really stood for "Move, Die or Quit." An underground employee newsletter stated that MDQ must mean "Management-Driven Quest (for bigger bonuses)."

The Quality program solved some problems but also got IBM focusing on the wrong issues. Akers was trying to fine-tune an engine that was so old and beat-up, he should have been ripping it out and replacing it.

With Akers and Schwartz pushing Quality in late 1989 and 1990, Cannavino began experimenting a bit more with his development organization. His first attempt at a new approach came with a home computer called the PS/1. The prospect of doing another home computer scared such senior executives as Akers and Kuehler to death. IBM had taken such a beating over the PCjr years before that nobody was all that anxious to risk repeating the experience, even if it made good business sense. But a group in Lexington, Kentucky, had won approval for a home-computer project in 1988, shortly before Cannavino arrived in his job, and he decided to see it through.

He designed the project to mimic the original PC operation. People in the group were moved away from the center of things, to a warehouse in a remote corner of the IBM Lexington site, deep in the rolling hills of Kentucky bluegrass horse country. The group was kept to about a dozen people. These employees self-consciously tried to flout IBM convention by, for instance, wearing suspenders. The team came up with a solid lineup of three machines in 1989, known as Bluegrass Good, Bluegrass Better, and Bluegrass Best. But demands from other parts of IBM then hit the project so hard that it developed what its leader, Tony Santelli, has referred to as double vision.

First, Bluegrass Best was taken away from the PS/1 group. The machine was supposed to be a hot "multimedia" machine aimed at people who wanted videogamelike graphics and sound in their home computers. Not a bad idea, and at the planned price of about three thousand dollars, it could have been a hit. But an IBM group in Atlanta that developed software and specialized computers for grade schools and high schools insisted to the Management Committee that Bluegrass Best was the kind of machine it needed to expand rapidly in the schools market. The education group won the battle that ensued. It then took the three-thousand-dollar machine and, getting carried away with all the offers of technology from inside IBM, jazzed it up with some avant-garde multimedia capabilities that generated enthusiastic reviews in the trade press. In the process, though, the education group doubled the machine's price, forgetting that schools have notoriously little discretionary money to spend. Cutting the price in half by stripping out technology would have made more sense than doubling the price. In the end, IBM sold few units of Bluegrass Best.[2]

Bluegrass Good and Bluegrass Better stayed with Lexington in 1989, but the executives running the PS/2 line feared them as competitors and mounted a campaign to cripple them. PS/2 executives reasoned that if Lexington was allowed to introduce such high-powered machines at cheap enough prices to sell them through department stores to home users, then few would want to buy a more expensive PS/2. The PS/2 line already had enough trouble. The PS/2 executives' campaign was the kind of pressure that every IBMer from Akers on down had been insisting for years had long disappeared, but the habit was hard to break. Those groups with profitable products still held extraordinary sway over those trying to bring out new machines and almost always won the fights over how much the new guys could take on the old guys.

The PS/1 group eventually emasculated their machines. They decided to put the old AT processor in their machines, even though it was six years old and even though many of IBM's competitors used a more powerful processor, a version of the Intel 80386, in their inexpensive introductory machines. Some of the PS/1 models came with black-and-white screens, at a time when the whole market was well on its way to requiring color screens. Anyone wanting to improve a PS/1 model by adding memory, installing a larger hard disk, or adding a circuit board to allow the PS/1 to be hooked up into a network found that the machines had been designed to be difficult to upgrade, lest someone actually decide to buy the Bluegrass machines instead of PS/2s for their office.

Under pressure not to be too aggressive, the PS/1 group also overpriced its machines. When the group announced its machines in mid-1990, they cost more than the entry-level machines of rivals even though competitors' PCs were more powerful. The PS/1 team even convinced themselves that their list prices would stick because people going into a Sears would prefer the IBM brand name to those of clone makers such as Packard Bell and Epson. Michael Shabazian, an IBMer who had been involved in the original PC and who was now running a big dealer chain, Intelligent Electronics, says IBM representatives insisted that the PS/1 wouldn't sell at a discount even though that's how the K Marts of the world sell everything and even though all PCs were selling at 25 to 30 percent discounts off the manufacturer's suggested retail price at this point. In fact, an IBMer told Shabazian that Sears had promised him it could sell the PS/1 at a 10 percent premium *above* list price.

"I told him he was nuts," Shabazian says.

The discounts began almost immediately. Within a year, Sears and everyone else were selling the PS/1 at a 50 percent discount.

When the announcement of the PS/1 came in mid-1990, Cannavino did avoid the trashing the PCjr took, but he didn't impress anybody, either. The general reaction was that—surprise, surprise—IBM had come out with another mediocre home computer that seemed to be designed mainly not to hurt sales of any other products. The most innovative thing about the announcement turned out to be the way Cannavino dressed. The stage in the art gallery in the basement of the IBM building at Fifty-seventh Street and Madison Avenue in Manhattan was set to look like a home office. After the lights went up on the stage and went down in the audience, there was about a thirty-second pause when nothing happened. People in the audience began shuffling their feet, uncomfortably wondering whether someone had missed his cue. Then Cannavino entered the little office through a side door, wearing a *sweater*.

Cannavino puttered around in the office for a few seconds, then looked up as though he had just noticed the audience.

"Oh, hi there," he said. In a joking reference to the fact that a last-minute delay on the PS/1 had produced some stories saying it was behind schedule, Cannavino then added, "Some people might say I'm a little late. But I think I'm right on time."

Nobody knew it at the time, but Cannavino's little stunt led to a whole new version of the dress code at IBM. Cannavino and his executives soon used costumes all the time, whether they were ski suits or cowboy hats or various T-shirts. He decided he liked the relaxed look, so his employees soon started wearing sweaters while working the floor at trade shows—official IBM sweaters, to be sure, and carefully color-coded to indicate what part of the PC business employed the person. Eventually, Cannavino declared that sweaters were acceptable for daily wear to the office, ending the blue-suit era at least in the PC world. So at least the PS/1 announcement in mid-1990 was remarkable for something, if not quite what Cannavino had in mind.

The indifferent reception to the PS/1 in 1990 rippled through another grand venture of IBM's, too, because Cannavino had used the PS/1 to try to pump some life into an information service called Prodigy. This service allowed people to dial into a central computer through a modem and enter an electronic community in which they could buy things at a sort of shopping mall, check out news headlines, send mail to anyone on the system, or participate in discussions held on electronic bulletin boards. Prodigy began life in the early 1980s as an IBM-Sears-CBS joint venture and became an IBM-Sears project when CBS decided it was a bad idea and got out in 1987. The project continued to lose some serious money in the years following the CBS pullout, but Cannavino hoped to expand Prodigy's base of users greatly in mid-1990 by preloading each PS/1 with Prodigy's software and giving each PS/1 buyer a few months' free use of the service. Everyone on up through Akers hoped that when hundreds of thousands of people bought their PS/1s, they'd get hooked on Prodigy and finally turn it from a money-losing mess into a huge business. When things didn't quite work that way, Prodigy had to fall back and regroup.

Prodigy had been started back in the early 1980s at a time when seemingly every computer company, every telephone company, and every newspaper had decided that the home was the new information frontier. After a few years of wasting money, just about every computer company, every telephone company, and every newspaper decided that maybe the home wasn't such a great market, after all. But a few companies hung on, and the IBM venture distinguished itself by having a couple of novel and good ideas. For one thing, Prodigy (called Trintex back then) figured out that home users wanted to pay only a fixed fee per month, not have the clock ticking as they ran up fees based on how many hours they were at their PC. Prodigy also made the PC the center of its strategy, avoiding the mistake many of its competitors made when they used the TV to display whatever information a user was gathering. (The competitors' mistake became immediately apparent the first time some real user tried to tell his kid to stop watching cartoons so Daddy could call up a stock quote. The battle for hegemony that followed quickly showed who controlled the television set—or ran the household, for that matter.)

But Prodigy made plenty of mistakes, too, mainly because IBM, the dominant personality, didn't have a clue how to run a start-up venture. One senior IBMer made a smart, visionary speech in front of Prodigy's management, saying they should base their plans on powerful technologies that would be available in a few years. That meant they wouldn't have to worry about tailoring their software for the slow machines then prevalent, such as the Apple II and the original IBM PC, which had been around since 1981. Then Akers looked at the Prodigy business plan and thought, Wait a minute, where's my revenue stream? Do I really have to wait three years to start getting a revenue stream out of this? So the Prodigy people began worrying about tailoring their software to the IBM PC and the Apple II.

"IBM walks into the future looking backward," said one of the IBMers who was involved with Prodigy at the time but who quickly left in frustration.

Prodigy was so slow when it ran on those underpowered computers that it drove users nuts, and few people bothered. In addition, the work sucked up development time that could have been spent more profitably. And dealing with the primitive machines then in use forced the programmers to go through some contortions in their code that made the Prodigy software slow even when more powerful computers came along.

IBM also imposed its deep-pockets mentality on Prodigy. While most start-ups scraped for pennies, Prodigy added people and equipment as fast as possible because they would probably be needed down the road. When Prodigy needed to do some software to generate IDs for users, one programmer could have done the simple job in a few months, but Prodigy hired eight. They got the work done a few weeks faster than it would have taken one programmer, but then they sat around because there wasn't anything else for them to do. No one worried about that. Prodigy, supposedly a start-up, even had its own management training school. IBM did, so Prodigy should, too. The deep-pockets mentality meant that Prodigy soaked up money at a rate that eventually caught even the attention of IBM and Sears.

Having IBM as a parent also forced Prodigy into making some weird decisions on what computer hardware to use. In the early days, Prodigy let IBM dump on it a bunch of Series 1 minicomputers—the same Series 1 that had given Don Estridge fits before he took over the PC project—even though they were hopelessly underpowered. The problems Prodigy had with the machines meant that its network always seemed to be running at capacity and that users always found the system slow.

Prodigy misjudged the market by assuming it could get people to give up their catalogs and buy their clothes, their sporting goods, their furniture, and just about everything else through Prodigy. But the stick-figure drawings that would appear on someone's computer screen didn't quite summon the same response that a glossy color picture of a tanned model would in the Lands' End catalog. Because buying was lower than expected, so were the revenues Prodigy had hoped to generate by letting companies advertise at the bottom of users' screens.

People wanting to send e-mail messages or correspond on electronic bulletin boards lapped up Prodigy because they could pay one set price, but Prodigy managed to annoy those users, too. First, it raised the price for anyone sending more than thirty e-mail messages a month. Some users complained, and a few even tried to organize a boycott, but the price rise was a perfectly defensible business decision, so the boycott generated no publicity and wouldn't have hurt the venture. Then the IBM-like, Big Brother part of the Prodigy personality appeared. Prodigy cut off the boycott organizers' access to the system. Suddenly, this became a censorship issue that generated broad publicity and embarrassed Prodigy nationwide.

As the issue unfolded, the debate focused on a point that bothered many of the bulletin-board users who had turned out to be Prodigy's biggest market. The world of bulletin-board users is generally an intellectual free-for-all where people write the most outrageous things to one another. Much of the early use focused on sex—just as 900 numbers, videocassette rentals, and most other new technologies seem initially to focus on sex. Bulletin boards had even produced a new class of publication called "zines"—short for magazines—many of which took as their starting point the idea that Captain Kirk and Mr. Spock of "Star Trek" fame were secret lovers and then built a whole world around that premise. All this sex stuff made Prodigy and its IBM parent uncomfortable. (In the early 1980s, IBM had planned a bold move into the consumer-electronics market by forming a joint venture with MCA called Discovision, which would make laser-based devices that would play movies stored electronically on platters that looked like large compact discs. But IBM had all its normal problems coordinating its efforts with those of a partner. IBM executives also never adjusted to the idea that someone might be at home watching a dirty movie that was being played on a piece of equipment that bore the IBM logo, so IBM killed the venture. Discovision sold its patents in the late 1980s.) Prodigy censored anything that didn't meet its family-values test. Some Prodigy users began circulating the phone numbers of competing bulletin-board services—although not on the Prodigy boards, because Prodigy would censor that, too.

The censorship stuff eventually became amusing in 1991 and 1992. One user tried posting a note about a "Franklin Dime" on a coin-collector bulletin board, but the censor wouldn't post the note. Prodigy forbids using full names of people, and the censor thought Franklin Dime was someone's name. Another user raised an unholy stink about what he said was an incredibly anti-Semitic note someone had posted. Prodigy was by now so defensive about its censorship policies that it defended this note, apparently on the assumption that if it had cleared the censors, it must be okay. Prodigy appointed as its spokesman on the issue an executive with the German surname of Heilbroner—Herr Heilbroner, he came to be called. The issue became a full-fledged uproar in newspapers nationwide until, after a couple of days, Prodigy executives finally realized they had never let the offending comments be posted on any bulletin board. They were clean, after all. But they still looked foolish.

By the time CBS had decided to pull out of Prodigy in 1987, IBM and Sears were nervous enough that they looked for another partner. The partner wouldn't even have had to put up any money to buy in, even though IBM and Sears had pumped several hundred million dollars into Prodigy by that point. The partner would only have had to pay its one-third share of the future losses. IBM and Sears estimated they would generate losses of $1.2 billion until Prodigy turned profitable sometime in 1992, though, so they got no takers. Losses like that may not have been real money to IBM or Sears, but they were to plenty of other companies. And what if Prodigy took longer than expected to turn profitable?

It did. By the end of 1992, the losses were continuing, with no end in sight. Prodigy started raising prices and putting bulletin-board users on a clock, getting away from the original low-fee idea that looked like the one thing about Prodigy that held promise. Prodigy also cut four hundred of its eleven hundred jobs. Rumors circulated inside Prodigy that those were just the beginning. The rumors also had IBM and Sears trying to find a telephone company interested in taking Prodigy off their hands. Failing that, the rumors said, IBM and Sears might just shut the thing down.

With the PS/1 having failed in mid-1990 as a test of Cannavino's hardware design concepts, he turned his attention fully to his laptop project. He wanted the project to let the world know that after a bit more than a year in the job he had fundamentally changed the way the PC business developed its products. The laptop would show that IBM could bring out products as fast as anyone and make them as good as anybody's, Cannavino said.

He decided to proceed deliberately, though, because he didn't want to repeat the humiliating failure IBM had had when it built the Convertible laptop in the mid-1980s. Before Cannavino would try a ten-pound laptop, he decided to do a twenty-five-pound portable, just to get developers used to the idea of cramming a PC's parts into a small package.

Cannavino had decided that much of the PC business's problem was that it wasn't spending enough time talking to customers in advance of the start of development, so he had the portable group speak to hundreds of customers. The group then did some slick design work and came out with a portable that won every prize imaginable—right as customers decided that portables were far too heavy and that they would never buy another one because they really needed laptops.

Despite the failure of the portable, Cannavino still insisted that talking more to customers was the key. What if, he was asked, customers didn't know enough to ask for what they really wanted? They hadn't known a portable was possible until Compaq, looking at the technological possibilities, gave one to them. Customers hadn't known a good laptop was possible until Compaq looked ahead at what technology would allow and gave them a good laptop. For that matter, had any customer told Sony that what he really wanted was a tiny radio and cassette player, maybe in a few different colors and styles, possibly one of which would be waterproof and maybe with a clever name like Walkman?

How, the questioner wanted to know, would Cannavino guarantee that while he was preparing a world-class laptop some competitor wouldn't be out there exploring the technological frontiers and coming up with a new and better type of machine?

Not to worry, Cannavino said. Customers know what they want.

He also figured that if he built enough raw speed into the development process, that would protect him. If he got it wrong the first time, he'd do another version and get it right. So Cannavino had the laptop developers focus heavily on learning how competitors accomplished their development and on moving as rapidly as they did.

Cannavino turned the project over to Bob Lawten, a midlevel executive who had managed the portable's development and who had received credit for the good reviews it garnered. Lawten got the approval for his business plan over Christmas 1989 and, not one to waste any time, immediately called together his team—which, like the original PC team, was composed of a dozen people. Lawten didn't want to disturb his family, gathered together for the holidays at their vacation home on the New Jersey shore, so he stepped outside to a pay phone just off a deserted beach and put together his first conference call while being buffeted by the wind and the sand on a bitter December day.

Lawten pulled out all the stops on this one. He took advantage of IBM's design capabilities in Japan to have people working around the clock. His group in Boca Raton worked on a problem for a twelve-hour day, then sent whatever they produced to their counterparts in Japan. The Japanese put in another twelve-hour day on the problem and had their results waiting when the Boca group arrived for work the next morning. The pace was so fast in early 1990 that the excited laptop designers in Boca wanted the product's code name to be KAP, for "kick-ass product." (They settled on the name Aloha, which they chose because they wanted to say hello to the laptop market, but it actually turned out to be more of a good-bye.) Some of the marketing people spent so much time away from Boca, flying around the country to find out what customers wanted the product to be, that when one employee took his three-year-old daughter to work and said he wanted to show her his office, she asked to see his airplane.

The Lawten group, like the Estridge group, bought lots of parts from the outside—in this case, mainly from Western Digital—so Lawten set up a sort of war room at Western Digital's offices on the West Coast. The room was a sweatshop, like the room where Microsoft had done its initial development on the IBM PC in 1980 and 1981, because it had to be kept locked. But it was a good location because it was in a time zone between Japan and Florida. Lawten sometimes walked into the office, to find that his operations were held together by two fiber-optic cables and a pair of ears. There would be one person sitting in the empty office and coordinating all activities by holding two phones up to his ears—Boca would be in one ear and Japan in the other.

The group sometimes got going so fast, they looked like the Keystone Kops. One time, someone carrying all the product plans set his briefcase down in an elevator while visiting an office in a building mainly occupied by a competitor. When he briefly got distracted and walked out of the elevator, the doors closed behind him and the product plans disappeared. He grabbed a couple of his colleagues, who all stood there watching the elevator board to see where the elevator stopped. They all knew that the project could be killed if someone got hold of the plans at such a sensitive, early stage, so they sighed with relief when it stopped on only one floor and quickly came back down. But the elevator was empty. The group fanned out through the building and spent an anxious hour hunting for the briefcase before finding it unopened, removed from the elevator by a Good Samaritan for safekeeping. When a member of the laptop group did a videotape for the manufacturing operation on how to assemble a laptop, he concluded by holding the finished product up in front of the camera, at which point the laptop started smoking.

The Lawten group adopted as its mascot Jud McCarthy, a nerd's nerd who rather enjoyed having the work spread across so many time zones because it meant he could get an answer to any question at any hour of the day and was pretty likely to wake someone up in the process. McCarthy had glasses as thick as the bottom of a Coke bottle and seemed to subsist on Coke and popcorn through the entire process— that is, when he wasn't drinking his peculiar version of rosé wine, which he made himself by mixing red and white wines, or eating days-old leftover food. The laptop group became famous for essentially holding other organizations hostage when, say, some lawyers wouldn't sign an agreement or some other business unit wouldn't agree to provide parts at a price the Lawten group could live with. The laptop group would just order a few pizzas—they had trained the local pizza delivery boys how to find their way to the back of the Boca facility. Then they'd negotiate for thirty-six hours, forty-eight hours, or whatever it took to make the food turn green and to get the recalcitrant people across the table to decide they'd better give in or they might never get to leave. At that point, the iffy food would get set aside either until some janitor stumbled across it or McCarthy decided it really looked okay and finished it off.

With everybody so jazzed about working hard, the process hummed through most of 1990, leading up to a planned October introduction. Based on the products coming out from competitors, it looked as if Cannavino was going to be first to market with a new, fast processor and with a big hard drive, a crucial requirement in the laptop market. Maybe Cannavino was right. Maybe the customer did know what was right, after all.

Rather than go through the normal sequential process—where the development people finished their work, then handed things off to the manufacturing people, who figured out how to make the product and then called in the marketing team—Cannavino let everyone go at it at once. Manufacturing broke the usual protocol and actually built the first prototypes so its people would know what kinds of tools might be needed to build the real thing and could get started working on them. Manufacturing also had a little workshop set up off the factory floor so that someone could grab a problem part and tinker with it right there to see if a slight alteration made the part easier to fit into the tiny computer. Normally, any sort of change would have required weeks of paperwork and layer upon layer of approval. Cannavino and the Lawten group patted themselves on the back for taking such a risk. (Their self-congratulation points up one of the most glaring problems that IBM developed over the years. Its executives focused mainly on how much they were reducing the number of bugs in their software or whatever —but in comparison with what it had been at IBM before, not in comparison with competitors. If anyone at IBM ever focused on competitors, it tended to be on where the competitors were at that moment, not where they would be in a year or two. Saying that IBM had rid itself of its slow sequential development process was perfectly true and was no doubt a risk for the IBMers who'd abandoned it, but the claim wasn't terribly relevant. Compaq had abandoned the sequential process years earlier, so it was already on to other ways of cutting development time. IBM needed to try something more radical if it didn't want to run constantly behind. Dan Mandresh, a securities analyst at Merrill Lynch, likes to say that IBMers always thought they were playing the golf course. As long as they knocked a stroke or two off their score every year, they were happy. What the IBMers didn't seem to get was that they were actually competing against the other golfers and that some of the others were pros who were also spending plenty of time at the driving range improving their scores just as fast as the IBMers were improving theirs.)

Murphy the alligator began to show up more often as fall 1990 approached. A problem appeared in a chip and seemed to defy solution. There was no backup. The announcement had to be delayed from October 1990, when the laptop would have been way ahead of the pack, to February 1991, when it would be about even. Then Lawten's manufacturing operation discovered defects in a tiny connector used in assembling the delicate screen. The laptop group eventually learned that they had been victimized by fate: The connector supplier's key manager had had a stroke and his chief deputy had quit. Thus, Lawten had to push back the announcement one more month, to March 1991.

In March, Cannavino registered his disappointment by moving the base for all his portable PC development work to Yamato, Japan. The move disappointed the U.S. contingent, who began distorting the name of the top Japanese PC technology executive: Nobuo Mii, whose name is pronounced "Knobby Me," became "Knobby Knees." When he came to the United States and took an IBM course in Boca Raton to improve his public speaking, he was told to read a Lee Iacocca speech trashing the Japanese.

With the laptop announcement upon him, Cannavino began to fight the standard battle with the marketing group over pricing. He wanted to price his laptop at five thousand dollars, which would have been very aggressive. He liked that idea. IBM had bombed so badly with its laptop before that he wanted the world to know IBM was back. But his marketing counterparts refused to risk leaving any money on the table, as usual. They brought out their foils to insist that they could sell the initial production run at six thousand dollars. The only comparable machines on the market sold for more than that, so why give up that extra one thousand dollars per machine?

Cannavino countered that his competitors would obviously lower their prices as soon as IBM's machine came out. His marketing counterparts said, in essence, Well, okay, then we can always lower our prices, too.

Cannavino got angry. Why not just go with the lower price right away? he asked. Whatever price was announced was the one people would remember, he said. If competitors then made a splash by cutting their prices, people would think of IBM as selling a much more expensive machine. They'd think, IBM blew it again. He also worried that it would take IBM too long to respond with lower prices. It could take sixty to ninety days to get a price change approved. Many had to be personally approved by Kuehler. The fight escalated, but the Management Committee agreed with the marketing group. It wasn't IBM-like to set aggressive prices. That cut into profits.

Sure enough, when the machine came out at six thousand dollars, competitors cut their prices to less than five thousand within days. Cannavino got permission to respond and actually underpriced his competitors, but no one noticed. People saw IBM's as a six-thousand-dollar machine, so customers thought, That IBM, why can't it get a laptop right?

Within months, IBM had cut the price all the way to $3,500, but few people cared. The continual price cuts began to be seen as a sign of weakness. With every cut, someone would write a story saying that the machine was such a dog, IBM was having to slash prices yet again.

Part of the problem was that right at the time the laptop came out in March 1991, the bottom fell out of IBM's financial situation. With the whole financial world focusing on the awful results IBM was forecasting for 1991, no one really wanted to focus on an IBM laptop, even if it had turned out to be technically elegant.

The real problem, though, was that Cannavino had been wrong. Customers hadn't known what they wanted. They hadn't known that it was possible to take all the capability IBM was building into its ten-pound laptop and put it in a six-pound, so-called notebook, computer—that is, customers hadn't known until Compaq showed them a notebook computer. Cannavino had built people exactly the laptop they said they wanted, but they all went off and bought the Compaq machine, the one they hadn't seen, the one that had been built because the technology had made it possible and not because some customer council had approved it.

Although Cannavino had planned to use a strong laptop to catapult himself into the market for what he called mobile computers, he had managed to enter the laptop market right as it was fading, just as he had hit the portable market exactly as it was disappearing. Cannavino stepped up development of some notebook computers, but they, too, were delayed. They didn't reach the market until 1992 and were "me, too" products when they got there.

A Cannavino assistant said that by the end of 1991, IBM's plan for the world of portables, laptops, and notebooks was in the worst shape it could possibly be in.

TWELVE

With Jim Cannavino deciding in early 1991 that he finally had to declare war on Bill Gates and Microsoft, he first did an uncharacteristic thing: He considered giving up. He was spending $125 million a year on OS/2, yet nobody seemed to want it. Meanwhile, a million people a month were buying Gates's Windows. Maybe, Cannavino thought, he should just save everybody a lot of trouble and admit that Gates had won this round.

Cannavino had some of his staffs look into the issue. They recommended he keep going. Cannavino took the issue up with Joe Guglielmi —late of the OfficeVision debacle and by now Cannavino's senior marketing person on OS/2. Guglielmi agreed that they couldn't afford to give up. The two then scheduled time with Chairman John Akers, President Jack Kuehler, and the others on the Management Committee to make their case that OS/2 should survive.

When Cannavino and Guglielmi walked into the sacrosanct corner of IBM headquarters where the MC meetings are held, they found Akers seemingly siding with Gates. Akers had always had a cordial relationship with Gates. He had been the one to invite Gates onto the United Way national board, having Gates join as his mother was leaving. Several IBMers say Akers even once asked Cannavino and some of his main staff members why when talking to the press were they being so abusive toward Mary Gates's boy, Bill? Akers also had made a visit out to Microsoft while on vacation in late 1987 that Gates describes as the high point of the IBM-Microsoft relationship. Akers, after visiting family in Oregon, went up to Microsoft to have a day of briefings on what Gates and his people were up to. Akers had dinner with Gates and his parents and seemed to take a personal interest in the visit (at least as the father of a marriageable daughter who seemed to keep bringing home young men he found somehow unfit; Akers kept asking questions about one young Microsoft executive, wondering how Gates found people like that, while his daughter never did). The October 1987 stock-market crash came just days after their meeting, seemingly putting the U.S. economy on the brink of collapse and giving Akers plenty of more substantive issues to confront, so the two didn't manage to conclude any business. But Gates and Akers always seemed to feel warmly toward each other. Why, Akers was now asking Cannavino and Guglielmi in early 1991, should IBM keep spending all this money on OS/2 when customers seemed to want Windows?

Standing at the podium in the MC room, with Tom Watson, Sr.'s portrait glaring at him from the back wall, Cannavino acknowledged that maybe IBM shouldn't. But he said he thought there was about a 60 percent probability that it should. He also said that if IBM proceeded with OS/2, it had to do so alone, because Microsoft was clearly going to do everything it could to promote Windows and cripple OS/2. Speaking faster as he warmed to his topic, Cannavino said he thought that IBM should continue with OS/2 partly because it could make real money in personal computer operating systems, even though the market was a relatively small $600 million a year and IBM, through OS/2, had almost no market share. Cannavino also raised the whole issue of setting standards. If Microsoft controlled the market, then it, not IBM, would decide when to build capabilities into the operating system that would let software developers build video, for example, into their applications. If IBM decided that multimedia applications were the wave of the future, could it really wait for Gates to make multimedia possible?

Kuehler had become Cannavino's most ardent supporter, helping ensure that he could avoid IBM's bureaucracy as much as he wanted and pay a low share of corporate overhead, even though Cannavino's weak financial results in 1989 and indifferent numbers in 1990 shouldn't have warranted any special consideration. Although some of Cannavino's peers running IBM's various national marketing groups and running the different product groups had begun to complain by 1991 that Cannavino was getting special treatment, Kuehler was still aggressive on Cannavino's behalf behind the scenes—when reviewing the plans of IBM's other businesses, Kuehler would demand, "What are you doing for the PC business?" So Cannavino already knew that he could count on Kuehler's support, and, by half an hour into the presentation, Akers was leaning toward agreeing to keep working on OS/2, too.

The clincher was when Cannavino said he needed a bigger operating system like OS/2 to help him sell faster hardware. This was the old IBM approach, in which the company would try to cram something down customers' throats not because they needed it but because IBM needed to have them buy it. The final consideration on OS/2 wasn't going to be whether customers really wanted the new capabilities of OS/2. What mattered was that IBM needed to get customers to use software that ran slowly, so it would soak up more of the horsepower of the machines on the market. Otherwise, why would customers have to buy faster, more expensive machines from IBM?

Cannavino acknowledged that he had a hard sell ahead of him. He also said that Akers and Kuehler shouldn't underestimate how powerful Microsoft had become and how hard Gates would fight. But Akers bought the idea. When Guglielmi ended their presentation by taking one final shot at Gates, Akers closed the meeting by saying, "Go get him!"

Cannavino and Guglielmi flew out of the MC room, ready to bring down Gates. A month later, when Steve Ballmer was in Armonk for some meetings with IBM's OS/2 marketing people, still thinking the companies were working together, Guglielmi cornered him and loudly chewed him out for what Guglielmi felt was Microsoft's deceit on its Windows plans. The fire in IBMers' eyes didn't last, though, at least not long enough to keep Cannavino from having to spend three months doing all the staff work necessary to announce his new OS/2 strategy in April 1991. Microsoft had enough contacts inside IBM that Gates found out what Cannavino was up to in plenty of time to counterattack.

Gates and others at Microsoft prepared for the IBM announcement in April by blitzing reporters, consultants, and securities analysts with information about the failings of OS/2. Microsoft publicized each milestone that Windows passed, noting that it had sold some 13 million copies in the first ten months after the Windows 3.0 announcement in May 1990, while OS/2 had only sold 300,000 copies in the years since its April 1987 introduction, almost none of which were actually being used.

Gates's comments about the 300,000 copies of OS/2 actually got him a payment of several million dollars from IBM as a sort of hush money. IBM had been saying that 600,000 copies had been sold, because it was counting some 300,000 that had been given away to big accounts that bought memory boards from them. As far as anyone could tell, those 300,000 copies of OS/2 had never been used. They also hadn't been paid for. As a result, IBM had never paid Microsoft the several million dollars in royalties it would have been due on a 300,000-unit OS/2 sale. But when Gates began excluding those units from his version of how many had been shipped to date, IBM quickly came up with a royalty check covering 300,000 additional units, on the condition that Gates would now use 600,000 as his official total. Gates did—but he also told a couple of reporters the real story, finishing with a smile and saying that he'd have to insist, of course, that the reporters use the 600,000 number, too.

Once Cannavino was ready to make his OS/2 strategy plain, he put together a typically grand presentation. He arranged for two full days of formal briefings in a hotel ballroom, one with major customers and one with reporters, consultants, and securities analysts. He brought in the heavy artillery, too. Akers and Kuehler made the initial presentations and swore to everyone there that IBM was behind OS/2 as much as it had ever been behind anything. They said that by the end of 1991, Cannavino would deliver a new version of OS/2 that would blow away anything currently on the market. They said OS/2 would run DOS applications better than DOS did and Windows applications better than Microsoft's Windows did—"Better Windows than Windows" became the rallying cry. Akers and Kuehler promised that Cannavino would make sure that plenty of other good software applications were available, too, to take advantage of some of the features of OS/2. Akers made a show of going up to various executives involved in the OS/2 effort and collecting the place cards that were in front of them. The message was that Akers was going to remember just who was responsible for OS/2. Akers said he'd give the name tags back once they got a great version of OS/2 out the door.

Customers, in particular, walked away impressed. Akers and Kuehler were putting not only IBM's reputation but their own on the line. If IBM didn't deliver a great product by the end of 1991, the two of them would personally be in trouble.

Now all Cannavino had to do was deliver.

Akers had begun really feeling the heat in March 1991, and he was determined to make sure that everyone else felt it, too. Following a great 1990, he had convinced the board to give him and his senior management team raises of around 35 percent plus stock bonuses, which meant their total compensation more than doubled. Akers had continued patting himself on the back through the board meeting at the end of February about how well things were going. Then, suddenly, two weeks into March 1991, Akers had to announce that the first quarter was turning into a disaster and that it wasn't clear when things would turn around.

In fact, one of the negotiators involved in IBM's sale of its printer and typewriter business in Lexington, Kentucky, says that Akers rushed to complete the sale so he could record a gain in the first quarter and avoid having to report a loss. The negotiator says Akers could have held out for more money if he had been willing to take his time.

Akers managed to convince the public at large that he had been concerned for a while because of the Persian Gulf War and the general weakness in the U.S. economy. He said he had been watching things carefully since December. But the board knew better. Securities analysts, partly following guidance from IBM, had started 1991 predicting record earnings for the company of more than $7 billion. Instead, Akers was on his way to a loss of more than $3 billion. Akers had a lot of explaining to do.

Perhaps the only thing that allowed Akers to keep running the company as long as he did following the March 1991 debacle was that Frank Cary had to retire from the board that same month because he had reached age seventy. The former chairman still held such sway and still had enough gumption and enough knowledge of the business that he was probably the only board member who could have single-handedly forced Akers out. And Cary was by now furious with his former administrative assistant. Cary had been willing to cut Akers some slack in the mid-1980s, figuring that the early problems had to be blamed on his predecessors. Then Cary had been sucked into believing that Akers was getting his arms around the problems, especially when

1990 looked so good. But once Akers announced that he had big problems just two weeks after assuring the board that everything was great, Cary had seen enough. Cary had been angry enough about having to leave the board of the company he had done so much to build— he called the mandatory retirement age "statutory senility." After the earnings disaster, though, golf partners and friends say he spent 1991 and 1992 grumbling about how he thought "Johnny [Akers] would have had things fixed by now." Cary, who had appointed most of the IBM directors, stayed in close touch with several of them and with most of IBM's senior management team throughout 1991 and 1992, but without a seat on the board, he didn't have much leverage to apply to Akers.

Akers mounted a campaign with the board. Month after month, he dispatched the corporate jets and helicopters to go collect his directors from around the country so they could gather in the MC boardroom in Armonk and hear him explain that IBM's real problem was the weak world economy. Akers also lectured about how all IBM's competitors had problems, trotting out numbers concerning Digital Equipment, Unisys, occasionally Hewlett-Packard, and some of the PC companies. Given how IBM typically had a former chairman or two still on the board and given how much IBM emphasized tradition, Cary's departure meant that board members now looked to former chairman John Opel for leadership. But Opel wasn't one to rock the boat. As 1991 wore on, the board as a whole decided that Akers was doing a fine job.

Akers increased his jawboning of his senior executives, but he never seemed to discipline anyone. The mainframe business was in trouble, but nothing ever happened to the recent boss of the mainframe business, Bernard Puckett, who had used some financial tricks to make 1990 successful, but at the cost of making 1991's and 1992's mainframe results anemic. Puckett had already moved on by the time the business fell apart in 1991, and, safe in his new promotion as the head of a huge IBM software group, he never had to suffer any consequences for the problems he left behind. Far from it; he soon was named a senior vice president and became one of the leading candidates to succeed Akers. Cannavino's business was in horrible shape, but he remained very much in Akers's favor. Several other businesses were turning in indifferent results, but nobody ever went after the senior executives who headed them.

In late April 1991, Akers called together his top twenty managers to scream at them, setting in place a series of events that would cost him the support of most of his senior managers and just about everyone lower down in the company. Akers had decided to jot some notes on a couple of sheets of paper in his kitchen before the meeting, and the longer he sat there staring at the walls, the more he decided his team had let him down. When he gathered together his managers in the Management Committee room in Armonk, he had them seated in rows of chairs like schoolchildren and proceeded to review them, one by one, embarrassing them in front of their colleagues. He singled out almost every business for scorn in a way that was tough for the executives to take. They thought of themselves as a team and saw Akers as part of it, too. Certainly, he had approved every major action any of them had taken. Yet here he was yelling about how *you* have failed *me* here, and *you* have failed *me* there. It wasn't *we* have a problem and *we* have to solve it. It was all *you, you, you* and *me, me, me.*

Akers said that in Europe the "indigenous competitors are flat on their face—ICL, Phillips, Olivetti. The business benefits should therefore accrue." He built to a yell: "Where are they?"

He said that IBM Japan had been losing market share for a couple of years, then bellowed, "Stem the tide!" Akers warned that losses of market share made "me goddamn mad. I used to think my job as a sales rep was at risk if I lost a sale. Tell salesmen theirs is at risk if they lose one."

Akers built to a stirring conclusion by taking apart the U.S. marketing effort. He noted that he had added five thousand people to the U.S. sales force but revenue hadn't budged. "Where's my return for the extra five thousand people?" he roared. "Where's the beef? What the hell are you doing for me?"

The executives sat there and took it because they had no choice. They even acknowledged that he had the right to be unhappy. Some people certainly weren't doing their jobs. But then Akers committed the cardinal sin among senior IBMers, who are trained to keep their mouths shut at all costs. Akers went public.

The day after he chewed out his senior team, he happened to be scheduled to address twenty people in Armonk as part of one of IBM's most prestigious management-training classes. Akers was still angry from the day before. He also had decided that part of his problem was that his messages got filtered too heavily before they got out to the troops in the field. IBM had always been like the Marine Corps: If the top guy said, "Right, face," everyone turned right immediately without a moment's thought. But Akers felt as if he'd been screaming, "Right, face" for years, yet most of the company had either never heard the order or were still trying to decide whether to obey. So as long as Akers had some young hotshots in from the field, he strode into the small conference room they'd been using at IBM's training center and used the same notes to deliver the same message that he had to his management team the day before. He figured that maybe the young executives would carry the word back to their departments about how deeply unhappy their chairman was.

One of the eager beavers took Akers at his word when he said he was tired of having his messages filtered. The exuberant executive took copious notes, then wrote them up on his terminal and sent them via electronic mail to everyone in his department. But things didn't stop there. All of IBM is hooked up electronically, so the Akers memo quickly got passed on to other departments, then to others, until, within a couple of weeks, everyone in the company had a copy. How many copies each person had received became a measure of how well connected the person was—a senior marketing person in New York said he received more than thirty copies in just a few days.

Soon, copies leaked to a couple of newspapers, and once those stories were published, it seemed that the whole media world picked up the memo. It was probably a sort of voyeurism. It had always been so hard to see inside IBM, with its layer upon layer of bureaucracy ensuring that any feeling was obscured by the time something was said to the public, but here, finally, was a way for people to see what happened inside this important company when the executives had their blue suit coats off, those red ties loosened, and those white starched collars unbuttoned.

The publicity caused more of an uproar than IBM had ever seen. The IBMers in the trenches acknowledged some of the points but felt humiliated by some of Akers's comments about how he was tired of having people "hanging around the water cooler" gossiping and that he felt people ought to start fearing for their jobs. Akers now adopted a bunker mentality, urged on by his vice president of communications, Mary Lee Turner. Turner is a tense sort who admits to once having had a sixteen-cup-a-day coffee habit. When she once tried to cut back, she had to dash out in the middle of an opera at the Met in New York to go to the bar and ask for five cups of coffee, which she drank one after another. As if the coffee isn't enough caffeine, she is also a chocolate fanatic. In college, breakfast often consisted of two Bufferin and a can of Hershey's chocolate syrup. Coming from marketing, where IBMers are used to finding customers amenable to having messages broadcast at them, Turner never figured out how to deal with a cantankerous, increasingly skeptical press. When things were going well in 1990, she had begun to open up, arranging a series of off-the-record meetings between Akers and reporters to build relationships and provide some context for the things he was doing. But those had stopped abruptly in March 1991 when he announced the earnings problems. Now, even though Akers could be extraordinarily good at defusing the hostility of the press or of groups of employees, he decided just to lie low and hope that no one would notice how bad things had become at IBM. The once-thick-skinned Akers was becoming jumpy.

In the absence of any guidance from the top, some lower-level IBMers organized an electronic bulletin board for people who wanted to discuss Akers's comments. The bulletin board carried some of the standard IBM earmarks. No one was allowed to include any excerpts from the original Akers memo, for instance, because someone had marked it "IBM Confidential"—even though the memo had been reprinted in most every newspaper in the world by that point. But the bulletin board was remarkable mainly because of how it broke with IBM's closemouthed tradition and produced hundreds of thousands of computer lines of comments from thousands of people. The comments showed a company deeply at odds with itself, complaining about what people called the "Big Gray Cloud" of managers who couldn't seem to see out of their cloud well enough to know what was really going on in the world.

"People would stand and watch without comment as an IBM manager tossed thousand-dollar bills off the nearest bridge, [fearing that a challenge] could be 'a career-limiting move,' " one wrote, expressing a lot of people's concerns that subordinates were afraid to tell their bosses about problems.

One writer said that he and everyone in his area had vowed to speak their minds if they ever got to see a senior executive, but then, en masse, "painted the walls nice and shiny" when senior vice president Carl Conti came to visit. The writer added, "By the way, Mr. Conti looks very young in person!!!"

"At this rate, IBM will soon go the way of the railroads, [which] also had stodgy managements and employees who prided themselves on being 'company men,'" another wrote.

"We have a vast hierarchy of management whose singular talent is that of career advancement," still another said.

One IBMer used a parable: "The U.S. Secretary of State was a guest at Moscow's May Day parade. Wave after wave of machines of destruction rolled by: missiles, tanks and artillery. Then came the Red Army in precision formation. . . . Finally, there was a large group of what appeared to be civilians trudging behind the army in some disarray. The Secretary turned to his host . . . and asked, who were these civilians? 'Those are the middle managers of the Soviet economy. You have NO idea the damage they can cause!'"

Many of the IBM writers, of course, went after Akers.

Complaining about the huge raise Akers got in early 1991, while the rank and file had been getting tiny raises—if they got anything at all—one wrote that the ordinary IBMers "will pull together long after John Akers has retired and hired an accountant to figure out what to do with all the stock he owns."

Another wrote, "Rumor has it that Mr. Akers doesn't even have a terminal/workstation. I don't understand how he can even pretend to understand our business."

Numerous people griped about IBM's vaunted processes, which seemed to strangle everything.

Referring to the Big Gray Cloud as the BGC, given IBMers' love of acronyms, one wrote, "I've heard a lot of talk about process . . . but I haven't seen anything to suggest that our planning cycle is close to a process—unless repeatable chaos counts as one. It seems to me to be based on wishful thinking and task forces—someone in the BGC decides we need product X at time T and commissions a task force to design it. Six months later it gets killed and the same 'process' gets repeated—only now we're six months further behind the competition." The writer was a programmer who said her last four projects had been killed.

"It takes 6–12 months to get a contract approved," another wrote. "To get capital equipment takes at least a year, to get a new development project takes at least a year to be approved, to get a fix approved takes months, to develop a new version of a product takes over one year." In one of the most telling points anyone made on the bulletin board, the person added, "Unfortunately, if we use the processes in place to solve this problem, it will take years."

Some thoughts were whimsical, suggesting that maybe IBM ought to change its original THINK sign. Given the changes IBM was going through, they suggested a new sign: Perhaps RETHINK, or THINK AGAIN, or maybe THINK SOME MORE. One proposed that the THINK signs just be altered by writing underneath the word *think*, the words *or thwim.*

But many people were heartbroken about the changes going on at IBM.

"IBM has always been a special place," one wrote. "When it abandons its Basic Beliefs, it will become just another GM, AT&T or Exxon."

Another complained about the ranking system that was being used to fire employees. "We are NOT grades of lumber," he wrote.

Several concluded by asking whether anybody out there in the Big Gray Cloud was listening. Eventually, some senior executives began reading parts of the bulletin board and found it informative, but Akers, who wasn't comfortable using his terminal, did not. Akers never did respond, losing him a lot of credibility with the troops. Turner, his spokeswoman, didn't do him any favors, either, when she was quoted as dismissing the discussion on the bulletin board as "idle chitchat." Most of those people thought they had been debating ways of returning IBM to its core ideas, such as respect for the individual, and of finally finding a way to return IBM to the position of respect they were sure it deserved.

When business didn't improve as the year progressed, Akers stepped up the pressure on people to leave. He also finally took steps that should have been taken years before, enforcing a rating system that had become meaningless and suggesting that those at the bottom of the rating system seek their fortunes elsewhere. IBM had long had a system where people were rated on a scale of one to five, with one being the highest and five meaning the employee was in real trouble. But grade inflation had occurred. Almost no one was ever rated a five. In fact, almost no one was ever rated a four. Everyone seemed to be a three— sort of like a gentleman's C—or better. Now, Akers was going to cut the scale to a one-to-four rating but insist on a bell curve: 10 percent of any manager's employees would be ones, 40 percent would be twos, 40 percent would be threes, and 10 percent would be fours. Half the fours would be in an odd category called four-check. Anyone who stayed in that category for long either had to take a severance package or would be fired. The time given for low performers to turn around was also cut from months to a few weeks. The line around IBM had been that people given strict performance standards to meet to avoid being fired were on the "measured mile"; now they were said to be on the "measured hundred yards."

The rating system shocked IBM to its core. It's hard to imagine, given that IBM was undergoing such trouble and given that plenty of companies fire weak performers, but IBMers just couldn't imagine that they could be fired.

Things didn't start out that way. Tom Watson, Sr., had laid off a few people once. Tom Junior never laid anyone off, but he fired loads of people, often on no notice. Frank Cary's staff once recommended he lay people off just to show them he'd do it and get rid of this notion of lifetime employment. While he never did, he often told people that IBM could maintain its no-layoff tradition only as long as the business went well, and he kept a tight lid on employment—IBM's head count was about the same at the end of the 1970s as it is now, after more than 100,000 people were hired in the 1980s and then shown the door. But all those caveats about whether full employment could last were swept aside with the euphoria of the early 1980s. A temporary worker expressing surprise at the lack of typing work and wondering whether she shouldn't be moved to a different employer would be told just to bring a book to work and read during her shift the way everyone else did.

Akers's rating actions also offended people because they bumped up against the sacrosanct idea of respect for the individual. IBMers had been used to a long, slow judicial process that allowed for numerous appeals of any discipline, but now there was a rush to judgment because Akers needed to get rid of people fast. The process became sloppy. Most of the middle managers charged with sorting out the winners from the losers were afraid that their jobs were going to be eliminated as part of the push to cut bureaucracy, so they were spending more time looking over their shoulders to see when they'd be cashiered than they were worrying about the people who worked for them.

Some IBMers began to refer to Akers by a variant of his name—instead of John F. Akers, he became John Fakers. He talked tough, but he hadn't removed a senior executive in three years. Lots of people began to wonder whether Akers could last. He had only three years left until he hit the mandatory retirement age of sixty, and rumors began to surface monthly that the board was about to push him out. So, while people took the rating program very seriously, they didn't pay much attention to what Akers said anymore. IBMers, like members of the civil service, decided that maybe they could outlast the current guy and see what the new guy wanted to do.

By late 1991, to regain any kind of credibility, Akers had to fire a top guy. Results had been too bad for the entire management team to avoid taking the fall. Too many lower-level people had been shown the door. Akers needed a scapegoat. It didn't take long to find one: George Conrades.

Conrades had always stood out. While all IBM executives were supposed to be polished, Conrades took that to an extreme. Tall, lean, with blond hair, chiseled features, and a low, silky voice, he came across more as an anchorman than as an executive. He accentuated the effect with tasseled loafers, pocket handkerchiefs, and suits that dared to have a hint of color in them beyond blue. On first meeting, he could have that same treacly smile that so many IBM marketing people have as they're about to go into their pitches, but he also had remarkable antennae; thirty seconds into a conversation, he might realize he was bombing and shift to a completely different, more genuine approach.

As a rising young executive, he had the audacity to form a little band that had some fun, often at IBM's expense. They wrote one song to the tune of "Don't Step on My Blue Suede Shoes" but called it "Don't Step on My Wing-tip Shoes." Conrades played drums—at least until Akers became Conrades's boss and told him the band had played its last number.

Other senior IBMers may have concentrated on their golf or raised horses or taken up flying in their free time, but Conrades rode his Harley. He talks lovingly of the time he and some other senior IBM executives made what he calls the ultimate sales call. They were trying to sell some AS/400 minicomputers to Harley-Davidson and somehow concocted a scheme to wrap the sales call around a motorcycle trip from Harley headquarters in Wisconsin to Rochester, Minnesota, where the AS/400s are built. Conrades says he and several other senior executives got to ride with dozens of Harley-Davidson people to the Minnesota border, where a local Harley group met them and escorted them into Rochester. By the time they hit Rochester, the group numbered in the hundreds. Police were spontaneously stopping traffic so the group could thunder through. Conrades and the rest of the blue-suit group were loving it. (A year later, Conrades and one of the other executives rode their bikes down to a Harley rally in Florida. By then, the two of them and all the other senior IBMers on the ride had left the company. The Harley executives said, "What in the world happened? Did that ride get people in trouble?")

Conrades was also unusual because he stood up to Akers, always carrying himself as though he might be the next chairman. For a long time there, the race to succeed Akers—a race that was always upper-most in senior executives' minds even though the favorites changed every year—had seemed to narrow to Conrades and Mike Armstrong, who had done an admirable job turning around IBM's European business in the late 1980s after leaving the job running the group that included the PC business in 1986. So Conrades always felt that he should speak his mind no matter the circumstances.

The Conrades-Armstrong competition had devolved into an amusing little sideshow, in which both would attempt to make the other look bad, although trying hard to keep things light and friendly. In 1991, when Conrades was responsible for IBM's U.S. operations and Armstrong had a spot on the Management Committee overseeing all international operations, they took turns baiting each other. One would find a way of asking a question in a Management Committee meeting that would put the other on the spot. He'd look across the room, to see his rival's eyes light up with surprise, then start to burn. After the one on the spot would confess that he didn't have a solution, the other would say, "Actually, we've found XYZ to work nicely." They'd be terribly civil in front of Akers, but as soon as they got back to their offices, the loser in the battle for position would call the winner and say, "You asshole! Why the fuck didn't you tell me you were doing XYZ? I'd have done it, too, and we'd have all been better off." The winner might say, "Actually, I stole the idea from one of your businesses," and then just chuckle and say, "Every man for himself."

Conrades wasn't known as the greatest strategist in the world. He didn't come across as technically adept—even though he had majored in math and physics in college. He also didn't understand development very well. When he was briefly general manager of the PC and workstation businesses, he was known for making fast decisions on development issues, but that was mainly because he'd make them so often—

he'd decide something in the morning, then change his mind by the afternoon, and maybe change his mind again by the next morning. He didn't use a PC much, at least not willingly. Kuehler once told Conrades that he had to start using a PC because Kuehler did most of his communicating via e-mail with those who reported to him. Conrades said that was fine, but when he started sending e-mail to Kuehler, it was too perfect—formatted properly, every word spelled correctly—so Kuehler knew that Conrades still wasn't touching his machine. Conrades's secretary was typing the e-mail for him.

But Conrades was a great leader. He could take an issue and boil it down to its essence, then explain to people in simple terms what they needed to do to tackle the problem. By the time he finished, people not only understood what they needed to do but were ready to charge a machine-gun nest to do it. His colleagues call it a crime that no way could be found for him to stay at IBM. They also say that there were more obvious candidates as scapegoats, if Akers had based his decision strictly on performance. The first phone call Conrades received the morning that his demotion appeared in the newspapers in November 1991 was from former chairman Cary, livid that Conrades had been pushed aside. But Conrades was a bit too outspoken for the increasingly insecure Akers and, as someone who had been seen as a possible heir, he had also been a threat. Conrades had to go.

Conrades had actually had a couple of warnings in the fall of 1991 that he was in trouble, but he couldn't bring himself to believe them. The first was very subtle. He was playing golf with Kuehler, and Kuehler asked innocently what Conrades thought of Cannavino. Conrades had no use for Cannavino. He thought Cannavino's products were awful and that the results he had posted were an embarrassment. Conrades also thought Cannavino was out for himself rather than for the good of the whole company. He complained about how Cannavino had to dominate every meeting he attended, and how he talked on and on at the start of most meetings about some silly issue or other and never pitched in to help another part of the business. Kuehler was surprised. He had apparently been trying to enlist Conrades in a campaign to get IBM's senior executives to support Cannavino. Conrades realized that he was committing a faux pas by attacking Cannavino, but he couldn't help himself. He could no longer expect any support from Kuehler.

The second warning came when Conrades attended the October 1991 wedding of a daughter of Terry Lautenbach, who was Conrades's boss at the time. Conrades and Armstrong wound up in a corner, giving each other a good-natured hard time over a glass of wine or two too many. As they talked about IBM's problems, Armstrong sighed and said, "George, the only thing I know is that you and I will never get a chance to fix them."

Conrades, understanding that Armstrong was predicting neither would ever succeed Akers, puffed out his chest and said, "Don't be so sure about that."

Armstrong had decided that Akers was going to pass over both of them because they were only five years younger than he was, and Akers wanted to give the top job to someone who would have a longer tenure than they could. Armstrong didn't explain his reasoning, but when Conrades said, "Mike, do you really know that neither one of us is getting the job?" Armstrong replied, "I mean it. I really know."

"You're trying to tell me something, aren't you?" Conrades said.

"Yes," Armstrong replied.

Conrades couldn't get himself to take that warning too seriously. He and Armstrong had competed too long for either to take anything the other said at face value. (In fact, Armstrong didn't know for sure about their fates, but a couple of weeks after the wedding, Akers did call Armstrong into his office to say Armstrong was being passed over. Armstrong responded that he was going to look for another job, and he left IBM in early 1992 to run Hughes Aircraft.)

When it finally came time for Conrades to be demoted in late 1991, it was left to Terry Lautenbach to do it. Lautenbach had approved Conrades's major strategy, a revamping of the U.S. sales force, which was just beginning to be implemented, but Akers told him to take Conrades out, so he did. Lautenbach called Conrades into his office and delivered the news.

Conrades protested, but Lautenbach said there wasn't anything he could do. Conrades marched down the hall to Akers's office. He said Akers obviously had the right to do whatever he wanted but said he didn't understand. The mainframe product line had been caught in an awkward transition in 1991, waiting for new products to become available. The disk drives sold with the mainframes had huge quality problems. The PCs were way behind the times.

"Tell me those are marketing problems," Conrades told Akers angrily. "I just want to hear you say it."

Conrades added that Cannavino had been in his job three years and his results stank. "By the same logic you're using with me, why isn't he gone, too?" Conrades demanded.

No reply. Akers just glared at him, getting a bit red in the face. Toward the end, Akers's naturally ruddy complexion began to look more and more like the rash that would break out on GM Chairman Roger Smith's face when he was under pressure and that Smith eventually cited when he resigned. But Akers wouldn't budge.

The next day, Conrades had been scheduled to present his business plan to the Management Committee for the following year—and he shocked everyone by showing up. The MC had assumed he'd send a subordinate. Instead, Conrades made a passionate presentation for an overhaul of the U.S. business. He then went about his business for the rest of the week. One consultant, Bob Djurdjevic, who met with him on Thursday of that week, later told reporters that either Conrades didn't know of his demotion at that point or was the greatest actor in the history of the world. That would make Conrades the greatest actor in the history of the world. He had known for two days.

When the hour for Conrades's public execution arrived, Lautenbach again was the one who pulled the trigger, at eight o'clock on a cold Monday morning in late November 1991. Ordinarily, the passing of power at IBM requires pomp and circumstance. Hundreds of people are summoned into a ballroom to cheer the departing executive and welcome the new one—especially if the executive position is as high as Conrades's was. This time, though, Lautenbach just called together the two dozen people who reported directly to Conrades. Lautenbach walked into the room with his head down and said, "George is out and Bob is in"—a reference to Bob LaBant, a former Conrades assistant who had been running IBM's AS/400 minicomputer business. "That's it," Lautenbach said, and he walked out.

As the senior marketing executives milled around after the short meeting, trying to fathom one of the most shocking demotions in IBM's history, word spread that Conrades wasn't just losing his 110,000-person U.S. sales force organization and being given a staff job where he would have 50 people reporting to him. Conrades was now going to report directly to his old rival, Armstrong.

Armstrong immediately called Conrades and said, "George, you have to believe I had nothing to do with this. I didn't even know this was going down." Armstrong then asked Conrades what his plans were for the future.

"Actually, I'm going to leave," Conrades said.

"Whew!" Armstrong answered back. "Then the world *is* still round."

The rank and file seemed to welcome that Akers had finally pushed out a top guy after years of seemingly just beating on lower-level employees, but the U.S. operation wondered what had happened to its inspirational leader. In Conrades's place in late 1991 was put LaBant, an Akers favorite who had had a suspiciously smooth climb up through the marketing ranks and who was unlikely to pose the threat Conrades had. After a series of sales jobs, LaBant had suddenly found himself running the AS/400 minicomputer business. It was an easy job, because LaBant's predecessor, Steve Schwartz, had already solved the problems dogging IBM's minicomputer business and had established the AS/400 as a huge success. LaBant just had to keep things rolling, and he did. Somehow, though, his work with the AS/400 convinced Akers that LaBant ought to have the Conrades job running the huge U.S. sales force, the most senior marketing job in the company.

LaBant is an intense sort, without the easy way with words that normally distinguishes the top marketing people at IBM. He once had the honor of introducing Akers to a group of senior IBM executives but managed to drop the cards he had arranged in the wooden speech box that most IBM executives use. Akers was the one person who really and truly needed no introduction, but LaBant, rather than just wing a few words, fumbled around with the cards in front of several hundred senior executives as he tried to get them back in order.

Despite his intensity, LaBant is a friendly man who seemed to be almost a mascot for more senior people as he climbed through the corporation. LaBant—sometimes affectionately called "Boo Boo"— managed to recover from the introduction debacle, for instance, when someone later said something about preparing to address the group the next day. LaBant said, "You'll know where to stand. Just look for the brown stain on the floor." When LaBant got his big break and took over the AS/400 minicomputer group, he would kid about getting the honor of making frequent trips in the winter to his main facility in Rochester, Minnesota, where workers in the rural area tend to start work before the sun comes up and where the cold winds sweeping the plains make things so frigid that tow trucks have to patrol the parking lots every evening to jump-start all the cars whose batteries have died. LaBant says he was once walking down a street toward a parked car, not knowing that people in Minnesota may have their cars rigged up to start up for a few minutes once a day. When the engine sputtered to life with no one in the driver's seat, LaBant says, he thought he'd found himself in a B horror film and just about killed himself trying to dive into a snowbank to get out of the way.

As much as everyone liked LaBant, though, they described him mainly as a good implementer who would always do what he was told, plus a little more. Ever the salesman trying to exceed his quota, LaBant would make his numbers in the AS/400 minicomputer business just a tad better than promised, or when he was told to cut four to six thousand people from the U.S. sales force, he made sure he found a way to cut seven thousand. But when even his friends were asked what would qualify him for one of the top jobs at IBM, they would pause and say, "Well, he's an awfully nice guy."

With the rest of IBM seemingly collapsing around him in the summer of 1991, Cannavino buckled down to fulfill the oh-so-public promises he'd made about OS/2.

Most of the responsibility fell on Lee Reiswig, a rumpled-looking man who had started at IBM without any formal technical training but who had somehow become a manager in an IBM software operation and had gradually worked his way up. Reiswig could have been derailed in the mid-1980s, because he was one of the people most involved with the TopView disaster. But Reiswig, who was known for being good at keeping track of who was headed up and who was headed down in the political battles at IBM, managed to escape the blame.

With OS/2, Reiswig got off to a reasonable start in mid-1991. Even though he was known as one of the proponents of the rigid software process at IBM, he had figured out that the company had too much process, too many programmers, and teams that were too big. So he went about shrinking the numbers of people and the size of the teams. Reiswig, who was always popular with his programmers, also tried to build more spirit into the teams than had been there before. The dumpy Reiswig proclaimed himself the "Blue Ninja" in the battle against Microsoft. He wore a "Blue Ninja" T-shirt at trade shows while doing demos and sent e-mail, even to senior executives, that was signed,

"The Blue Ninja." When things got off to a rocky start on the new round of OS/2 work, rather than criticize from a safe distance, Reiswig moved from the Armonk area down to Boca Raton, where the work was being done. (Reiswig was one of the executives whose name tags Akers had collected back in April 1991 so he'd know who to go after if OS/2 flopped.)

Reiswig also tried to incite his programmers by using comments made by Gates and Ballmer, much the way football coaches post nasty comments from opposing players on bulletin boards. The biggest fuss came when Ballmer was widely quoted as saying that there was no way IBM could build top-notch Windows capabilities into OS/2 by the end of 1991, as IBM had promised. Ballmer was quoted as saying that if IBM proved him wrong, he'd eat a floppy disk. The IBM programmers tacked a floppy disk up to a wall, which carried the acronym SBD, meaning Steve Ballmer diskette. That was the one Ballmer was going to have to eat.

The IBM programmers still found things heavy-handed at times, despite Reiswig's attempts to lighten up. For instance, Reiswig at one point made fifty-hour weeks mandatory. Some of the programmers, who had been working eighty- to ninety-hour weeks, took that as an insult. They said that if IBM wanted to play those sorts of penny-ante games, then they'd work exactly fifty hours a week. Progress on OS/2 actually *slowed* after extra hours became required. An apocryphal memo began circulating among the IBM programmers about a rowing race that had supposedly taken place between IBM and Microsoft. Microsoft had one coxswain shouting orders while eight people rowed, the memo said. IBM had eight coxswains shouting orders while one rowed. Microsoft won big. So IBM launched several task forces to do some coxswain/oarsmen analyses and decided after several weeks that the problem was that the oarsman wasn't rowing hard enough. When the race was rerun and Microsoft won big again, the oarsman was fired.

After a month or so, though, Reiswig figured out what was going on and removed the requirement. Hours soared, and the OS/2 project became one of the most engaging in the history of IBM. Some programmers moved into their offices. Others moved into hotels near the Boca Raton facility rather than have to commute home every night. Spouses and kids came to the office for lunch on Sundays just to have a chance to see their programmer parents and spouses. Workers in the cafeteria began noticing that lots of the programmers were wearing the same clothes for several days in a row and figured out that they were working through the night. So the workers—who were employed by a contractor, not IBM—began volunteering extra time to make sure that there was hot food in the cafeteria twenty-four hours a day. Reiswig had the cash register pulled out and decreed that food in the cafeteria would be free for the remainder of the project.

The IBM programmers realized that they had only one more shot to make OS/2 work. Windows was so far ahead that another failure would doom OS/2 even in their eyes and their bosses' eyes. Lots of these people had been working on OS/2 in some form or other for six or seven years, and they were determined not to let that effort go to waste.

With Microsoft out of the picture as a potential partner on OS/2 by mid-1991, Reiswig and Cannavino turned to a little software company named Micrografx for help on the graphics piece of the operating system. Micrografx had been founded by two Texan brothers who decided in the very early days that Windows was going to be significant and so came up with some graphics software that would work with Windows. The two, Paul and George Grayson, flew off to a conference to corner Gates and learn more about Windows. Then, on the way home to Austin, Texas, they stopped in a bar, where they did some of their best thinking. Striking up a conversation with a guy who turned out to be a programmer, they hired him. The Graysons didn't really have any money, so they financed the company with a credit card, running up bills as large as they could get away with. Even once the company became established, the two men in their late thirties would fight just as they had as kids—bystanders once had to keep them from going at it on the floor of the Comdex trade show. Believe it or not, this is how good software is often developed. On the strength of a single idea and some quick execution, the two staked their claim to a corner of the PC software market and built bigger fortunes than any of the IBM executives, who wouldn't think of taking a swat at a colleague in the middle of a trade show.

Reiswig's association with the Graysons went more smoothly than the IBM-Microsoft relationship, but it had its rough spots, because IBM, despite all the changes it had made to its software process, still had far too many people and was far more bureaucratic than its smaller, nimbler competitors. It's been said that IBM's way of crossing a hundred-foot gorge is to have one hundred people jump on one foot each, and that way of thinking still hadn't changed enough. IBM's part of the OS/2 work was about two-thirds of the new code, while Micrografx's was a third, yet IBM had nearly one thousand people working on its portion, while Micrografx had fifty. IBM continued to insist on the accuracy of its foils, even when reality insisted otherwise. George Grayson says, for instance, that one bit of translation that was going to have to occur in the graphics portion should theoretically have been a simple thing that wouldn't have slowed the software at all. But Micrografx had learned the hard way in doing similar programming earlier that the one bit of translation would ricochet through the whole program, causing thousands or tens of thousands of similar bits of translation to have to occur. That would slow the whole operating system appreciably. But his contacts at IBM refused to admit that a problem existed, because the foils said it shouldn't. IBM proceeded on the assumption that everything was fine until, months later, it finally gave up and reversed course.

"We said, 'Take that chart and shove it you know where,' " George Grayson says. "They believed their charts more than they believed reality."

A corporate IBM policy also managed to bollix things up late in 1991, right as the OS/2 team was working itself into a final frenzy to try to meet the all-important December 31 shipment deadline that IBM had announced so publicly. For years, IBM had been letting people carry over into future years any vacation days they didn't take. By the time many people retired, they might have a year's worth of vacation saved up, giving them an extra year of salary. But with business slowing, IBM's corporate headquarters mandated that people take all their vacation each year or lose it. People with days in the bank had to use ten extra days each year—no exceptions. So there were hundreds of programmers down in Boca Raton working more enthusiastically than anyone had ever seen and crashing toward a deadline, and their managers informed them that they had to go on vacation. Many fought back, and some won a reprieve, but lots of programmers just disappeared during December rather than forfeit weeks of vacation. George Grayson of Micrografx says the vacation problem meant that the better version of the OS/2 graphics didn't make it into the version of OS/2 that was to be shipped at the end of the year, contributing to complaints about the slowness of the software.

With the end of the year fast approaching, Reiswig and Cannavino had some reason to feel good. Their programmers had come up with a clever trick that solved the biggest problem with running on the OS/2 operating system the applications that people had written to run on Windows. But as outsiders began to get a peek at the software and as word filtered out into the trade press, Reiswig and Cannavino discovered that the trick wasn't good enough. Given the approach the OS/2 team was taking, any application running under Windows was going to take up the whole screen. With just Windows on the PC, the same application could be limited to a small part of the screen while other windows were also open—so someone could grab numbers from a spreadsheet, put them in a letter, and double-check everything against an incoming fax or whatever. Reiswig and Cannavino had claimed they would have better Windows than Windows in OS/2. Public opinion now told them this wasn't it.

Rather than risk having the product shouted down, Reiswig and Cannavino announced late in 1991 that OS/2 wouldn't make it on time, after all. IBM got trashed in the press. A spate of stories said the problems showed that IBM really couldn't do software and questioned whether IBM would ever get a decent version of OS/2 out the door. The Steve Ballmer diskette came down off the wall in Boca Raton.

Reiswig and Cannavino tried to convince the world that they had pulled the product simply to improve it, not because they were late. They actually shipped a few customers a version of OS/2 on December 31, 1991, just so they could say they had finished something on time. But the Boca team kept running into problems as 1992 began. They thought they might cut corners by not doing "beta" tests—giving copies to lots of customers to see what bugs popped up when the software was used in the real world. But the trade press got hold of that and suggested that IBM was going to ship a shoddy product just to meet its new deadline, March 31, 1992. The product was supposed to be handed off to manufacturing in mid-February, so lots of copies would be in customers' hands and in stores on April 1. But getting Windows applications to run on OS/2 was turning out to be far more complex than IBM had bargained for. The handoff to manufacturing slipped to late February, then to early March, and finally to late March.

Cannavino was, by now, big on symbolism. So on March 31, even before the final version of OS/2 was done, Reiswig gathered the development team in Boca, announced that OS/2 was going to be a huge hit, and smashed a window with a sledgehammer. (IBM was partly retaliating for a bit of fun Microsoft had had at IBM's expense. When Microsoft held a company meeting in early 1992 in the Seattle Kingdome, Ballmer drove in in a red Corvette with WINDOWS printed on the car doors. The crowd of more than ten thousand roared. Someone then followed him into the stadium in a car with OS/2 written on the doors. The car was an Edsel. A pack of Harley-Davidson motorcycles then stormed in, with one eventually pulling out and circling the stadium while the song "Leader of the Pack" played over the public-address system. When the motorcyclist took off his helmet, it turned out to be Gates. Cannavino wanted to respond by buying a red Corvette and smashing its windows, but he was talked into some less expensive stunts.) When Cannavino spoke to a PC users group in New York the night of March 31, the lights were turned down for his grand entrance and a film clip was shown of Cannavino skiing down a hill, jumping off a mogul, and, with the help of some special effects, smashing through a window. When the lights came up, Cannavino walked onstage wearing a ski outfit, crunching broken glass under his boots as he came. He held in one hand a package containing diskettes and manuals, which he proudly held up as the first copy of the final version of OS/2. OS/2, he announced, had finally arrived.

In fact, Cannavino didn't hold the first copy of the latest version of OS/2 in his hand. Problems had come up at the last minute, and some programmers had to work through most of the night of March 31 to fix them. IBMers now acknowledge that OS/2 was actually finished on "March 32."

Things didn't get any better from there, either. Cannavino had publicized the March 31, 1992, deadline so much that those who were interested went to their stores April 1 to look for it, and it wasn't there. The programmers had been so late that there hadn't been time to make any copies. It was mid-May before IBM managed to get many copies to customers. Then it turned out that Cannavino's marketing people had badly misguessed what percentage of people would want OS/2 on five-and-a-quarter-inch diskettes and what percentage on three-and-a-half-inch diskettes—so Cannavino was left to try to sell the idea to the press that the higher-than-expected demand for five-and-a-quarter-inch diskettes was really a good thing because it meant a certain segment of the population turned out to be more enthusiastic about OS/2 than he had thought.

By spring of 1992, with things going badly on OS/2, the PC business was in disarray. Everybody was pointing fingers to assign blame to someone else. Everybody was bickering. Reiswig, Cannavino's senior software executive, and Guglielmi, Cannavino's senior marketing executive, couldn't agree on who was really in charge of OS/2. They held the same rank in the PC business, but Guglielmi was a corporate vice president, while Reiswig was not. Guglielmi assumed that his vice president's title meant he could order Reiswig around, so he'd call meetings and order Reiswig to show up. Reiswig responded by waiting until Guglielmi assembled his entire thirty-person staff in a conference room and then had an assistant stick his head into the room to announce Reiswig wasn't going to make it. Cannavino and Guglielmi shouted at each other over issues all the time. When Cannavino left, Guglielmi usually turned to someone on his staff and said something like, "That moron doesn't know shit about marketing. If I was running the PC business, we'd have things turned around in one minute." Guglielmi seemed to be arguing with everybody. Always a shouter and always profane, he now appeared to be cussing out anybody he could find, always ending by shouting, "Goddamn it! Goddamn it! Goddamn it!" His staff began making fun of him behind his back; someone summoned to see him would tell colleagues, "I'm off to see Joe G.— goddamn it, goddamn it, goddamn it."

When Cannavino and his team weren't arguing among themselves, they fought with the U.S. marketing force. The basic issue was that Cannavino thought he should be able to control the pricing, advertising, and marketing of his products, including OS/2, but in the IBM structure that control belonged to the national marketing forces. When a senior member of the U.S. marketing force, Doug LeGrande, once rolled his eyes at something Cannavino said in a meeting and made a snide remark, Cannavino stopped him after the meeting and blocked his way out the door. The dark, husky Cannavino stood inches away from Le-Grande's face, frothing with anger. Cannavino spoke through clenched teeth and, with each word, thumped LeGrande on the chest with his forefinger for emphasis.

"Don't [thump] you [thump] ever [thump] pull [thump] that [thump] piddly [thump] shit [hard thump] on [thump] me [thump] again [hard thump]," Cannavino muttered.

When LeGrande was once stopped by an IBM staff member who

had been waiting outside a restaurant for a dinner meeting to break up, the staff member asked for approval of a marketing document, then made the mistake of saying that Cannavino had already approved it. LeGrande threw the document down on the sidewalk and jumped up and down on it several times in a sort of war dance, yelling, "No! No! No!" Without reading a word of the document, LeGrande said, "You have my approval for it, and that's all you need. You don't need Cannavino's approval."

Guglielmi, representing the PC business, and Winnie Briney, a fairly senior member of the U.S. marketing force, found in early 1992 that they couldn't stand to be in the same room with each other. Even if one said the most obvious, incontrovertible thing, the other had to contradict it: If Briney said, "Today is Tuesday," Guglielmi said, "Not in Tokyo."

Cannavino's people and those from the U.S. marketing force held dozens of conference calls in the spring of 1992, but they never seemed to talk about anything substantive, such as the competition, for example. Instead, they argued about turf. Some of the biggest fights between the PC team and the marketing group concerned which side would get to start a press conference they were jointly planning. While one side talked, gathered around a speaker phone in a conference room, the other side often put its phone on mute so they could talk among themselves about the idiots on the other end of the line. The marketing people in particular groused about Cannavino. They saw him developing a high profile outside the company and said it was fine for him to go off and charm reporters with notions about changing the way IBM was doing business, but they also griped that he didn't know anything about marketing, which they thought was clearly the secret to IBM's successes over the years. How could he know about marketing? they asked themselves. He was merely a product-development guy.

The bickering in the spring of 1992 came at a horrible time for OS/2 because Microsoft had, to no one's surprise, timed a bunch of ads for Windows to coincide with the announcement of OS/2, and the internal bickering paralyzed IBM as it tried to respond. Cannavino wanted to retaliate with ads right away, but he didn't control advertising for OS/2; the marketing group did, and they had decided the money should be spent late in the year. That was how they'd always done things. The fourth quarter is always the strongest of the year for mainframe sales, so that's when marketing had become accustomed to spending its ad money. Cannavino's marketing people had to go beg for the money right away, lest they get killed by Microsoft. It took several weeks for the issue to get settled and for even some ad spending to get moved up.

As the marketing campaign unfolded, it turned out to be a mess. OS/2 elicited a reasonable reception this time as an industrial-strength operating system that might appeal to some corporations, but Cannavino and the marketing people kept insisting it was something that should be on everyone's home computer. When the end of the year did roll around and the marketing people got to make their Christmas push for OS/2, they sent letters to the trade press suggesting that people do columns essentially recommending this $150 box of industrial software as stocking stuffers—a prospect the trade press immediately ridiculed. IBM also spent some $1.5 million to sponsor the Fiesta Bowl football game, renaming it the OS/2 Fiesta Bowl in the hope that people sitting around swilling beer on New Year's Day would decide that OS/2 was for them. (There will apparently be two more OS/2 Fiesta Bowls, because IBM signed a three-year contract.)

Some of the ads IBM used may have hurt as much as they helped. One showed a pastoral scene with the sun in the background and with names of OS/2 applications written on blocks sticking up from the earth in the foreground. Several people in the industry described that one as the sun setting behind a graveyard. IBM almost really slipped up on the OS/2 logo, too. It spent more than $100,000 on the logo, but the first version—simply OS/2 inside a circle—looked like the international symbol for banning something. The slash in OS/2 was so long that it went almost all the way through the circle, making the logo look like a symbol for No Smoking, No Pets, and so forth, except this time it appeared to be saying, No OS/2.

Cannavino and Reiswig had lost all the momentum to Gates and Microsoft in 1991 and 1992, most critically among software developers. Cannavino would brag about getting a couple of hundred developers to show up for an OS/2 seminar, but Windows would draw in the thousands. Microsoft held a Windows conference in 1991, during which the group had to go from one building to another in downtown Seattle; the organizers discovered that the group was so big, they needed a parade permit. A magazine aimed at software developers and PC users had started out as "OS/2" magazine, then became "Windows and OS/2," then late in 1991 became "Windows."

To try to drum up support, Cannavino, Reiswig, and others at IBM played some games with the numbers. They had their business plan specify that they would ship 1 million copies in the first year, a number they knew they could beat without even trying. That way, they could brag that sales were way above plan. The IBMers let it be known that the real expectation was 2 million, but some executives also whispered to analysts off the record that the number could be as high as 4 million. Four million would have been impressive enough that it got some people's attention, but because the word had been passed off the record, the IBMers knew that they wouldn't be judged failures when the number actually shipped turned out to be far lower.

Cannavino had to do some creative accounting to make 1992 come in on target, at 2 million. Dealers said that about one-third of the people who bought IBM PCs that came with OS/2 preinstalled were paying the dealers to take OS/2 off and replace it with Windows, which meant Gates got a double payment, because IBM paid him a royalty on each copy of OS/2 it sold, and Gates got to sell a copy of Windows, too. Yet Cannavino counted these preinstalled OS/2 copies as sales, even though no one paid IBM for them and they weren't used. Similarly, industry analysts said that another third of the people who bought IBM's PCs with OS/2 preinstalled were leaving OS/2 on the machines but were disabling it so they could run applications on DOS or Windows. (Cannavino couldn't even get his retired mentor, Carl Conti, to use OS/2. Conti, a former senior vice president who ran the group that included mainframes, has a powerful PC he uses at home, but he disabled the OS/2 because it was just getting in the way.) Cannavino's accounting still treated these disabled copies of OS/2 as sales, even though, again, the people who bought them were merely buying a piece of IBM hardware and wouldn't have paid another cent for OS/2 if it had been optional. Between those two categories of users, some 600,000 to 700,000 people who had copies of OS/2 weren't using them. IBM gave away some 700,000 more copies to all those who had bought earlier versions of OS/2, yet it counted those freebies as sales. The copies that IBM actually shipped to new customers in 1992 and that were in use seemed to total just 600,000 to 700,000 out of the 2 million Cannavino claimed. And just about all of those were given away as part of the sale of an IBM PC or were sold for less than one hundred dollars, about a 50 percent discount off what was supposed to be the real price of OS/2.

One way to look at how well OS/2 really did is to look at how many applications packages designed for OS/2 have been purchased. The answer is not many. Only 1 percent of all software application packages sold for use on personal computers in 1992 were designed for use with OS/2. That's about the same as in 1991, even though IBM supposedly sold many new copies of OS/2. Applications designed specifically to run on Windows, by contrast, accounted for 38 percent of all PC software sales in 1992.

Cannavino bragged that the new version of OS/2, called 2.0, had done far better in the first nine months of its life than Windows had and he insisted that OS/2's technical advantages would give it plenty of momentum going into 1993. In fact, OS/2 was nowhere. The broad base of consumers being targeted for OS/2 couldn't have cared less whether OS/2 was "fully 32-bit" or about the other techie stuff IBM was emphasizing about OS/2. Microsoft was selling more Windows copies a month than IBM would sell in a year, and no amount of yard markers carrying OS/2 logos at the Fiesta Bowl was going to change that. Cannavino certainly could have made waves about OS/2 being off to a faster start than Windows if he had been back in 1985, when Windows first appeared, but he was making his comparison more than seven years after Windows got its head start. The claim sounded hollow.

By the end of 1992, Cannavino and his predecessors had spent more than $2.5 billion developing and marketing OS/2 and applications, such as Office Vision, that were to run on top of OS/2, yet they had less than $200 million of revenue to show for it. (Cannavino has publicly disputed similar numbers. He insists that OS/2 is profitable, although he is clearly ignoring the money that was pumped into OS/2 in prior years and declines to explain how he arrives at his numbers.) With OS/2 flopping and IBM struggling in hardware, the very term *IBM-compatible* started to fade. Some people began referring to the machines as "Windows-compatible" or, somewhat more frequently, "Intel-based," because the type of Intel chip used as the processor in a PC did so much to determine the speed at which the machine operated. Even those people who stuck with IBM as the standard-bearer sometimes called the machines "IBM-like" or "IBM-style."

Cannavino may have thought he had made a clean break from Gates, at last, when he proclaimed his OS/2 strategy in April 1991, but he shouldn't have. Gates had outmaneuvered him one final time, and Cannavino had to figure out how to deal with that.

Almost as soon as IBM began talking publicly about putting Windows into OS/2 in 1991, a Microsoft lawyer called an IBM lawyer and suggested that maybe they ought to talk about that. IBM clearly had the rights to OS/2 and to Windows, but the Microsoft lawyer said IBM was going to have to pay a double royalty. IBM would have to pay Microsoft its standard royalty on OS/2. IBM would also have to pay its standard royalty on Windows because it was going to include all the Windows code in each copy of OS/2. The IBM lawyer didn't care much for that idea.

The IBM developers also soon questioned whether Microsoft had lived up to its end of the bargain concerning a piece of software that was crucial for Windows to run properly. The IBMers argued that Microsoft had been extremely late in providing IBM with the software and had done a poor job. Some of Cannavino's assistants complained that they ought to sue. After some meetings with Microsoft staff on the issue, they left a conference room at IBM's building in Somers, New York, saying they'd love to get their hands on Gates's scrawny little neck and heave him through the window.

Gates and Cannavino were at it again.

Their staffs argued the points through most of 1991 without making any progress. Gates and Cannavino didn't even talk through this stretch because Cannavino's distaste for Gates had finally grown to the point where he couldn't face him. Cannavino did manage to send Gates a message in mid-1991; while out jogging on the streets of downtown White Plains one Saturday, Cannavino bumped into a Gates assistant named Tony Audino. They said hello, but then Cannavino began to work himself into a lather. Standing there in his sweatsuit with his Walkman in his hand, Cannavino blistered Audino for what he saw as Gates's attempts to line up customers by sneaking behind IBM's back.

When Audino reported back to Gates, Gates said, "Geez, I can't even get the guy to return my phone calls, and you get forty-five minutes with him."

In a remarkably understated letter that said, "The 1990s are certainly proving to be turbulent," Gates appealed to Akers to intervene.

Cannavino separately decided to see whether Akers and Kuehler could do something about his problem with Microsoft. Akers's office contacted Gates and told him that he would finally get the high-level audience he thought he had arranged in August 1990, when he was supposed to have had lunch with Kuehler. When Gates arrived in Armonk in late October 1991, he found a place that felt very different from what it had just a few years before. So many jobs had been wiped out that the parking lot was almost empty. (Akers had actually considered having most of the asphalt ripped up and the area sodded over to send the signal that those staff jobs were never coming back, but then he decided he shouldn't be spending any money on capital projects at headquarters.)

Gates walked though some concrete pilings in front of the main entrance; they had been placed there to keep people from driving a car bomb into the building. He went into the foyer, which had been tacked onto the front of the building so that anyone with a hand-carried bomb would be able to blow up only the reception area, not a major part of the building. Gates sat down to wait for Akers to meet him and, picking up that day's papers, realized he was in trouble. Ballmer had been quoted in a story about OS/2 and had said of IBM, "It's always nice when a competitor screws up."

Akers met Gates and took him to the executive dining rooms. Kuehler joined them. Sure enough, they had read the papers that day, too.

"I'm tired of reading about the IBM company and the Microsoft company in the press," Kuehler said. "I'm tired of reading about how the IBM company and the Microsoft company can't get along. Can't we agree to at least have our disagreements in private?"

"Hey," Gates said, "nobody would meet with us. We weren't sure whether you wanted us to negotiate with you through *Computer World,* or was it *PC Week?*"

Gates also complained that IBMers had made personal attacks on him, such as a report in the press that one wanted to put an ice pick through Gates's head.

"Well, you said stuff that shouldn't have been said," Kuehler replied. "You said IBM hasn't made any money in the PC business."

"You're right," Gates conceded, "I did say that, and that's hearsay."

"You shouldn't have said that," Kuehler said.

"Okay, I won't say that anymore," Gates replied.

After things settled down a bit, Kuehler started talking about the Clarence Thomas hearings, which had stretched into the wee hours of the morning the night before. That put Gates at a bit of a loss. He still didn't own a TV and had been too busy to read the papers much for the previous several days. Gates felt lucky that his father, a lawyer, had followed the hearings with fascination and had described some of the high points in a phone conversation the day before. Gates faked his way through some chatting about the hearings. He didn't really want Akers and Kuehler to think he was the only person in America not up on Anita Hill.

When Akers, Kuehler, and Gates finally got down to business, Gates launched into his plans—a long list of things he thought IBM and Microsoft could accomplish together.

Akers and Kuehler just watched in silence.

When Gates finished, Kuehler said softly, "What happened to OS/2, Bill?"

Gates started to explain, but Kuehler said, "We're not interested in that. License us that Windows code."

Gates said, "Well, I'm not going to just give away that code."

"If you ever want to work with the IBM Company," Kuehler said, "then I want your partnership back."

"Well, we didn't have much of a partnership there for a while," Gates said. "We can do a lot of good things together. We can have a good relationship. But as for a partnership . . ."

They talked some more, but all they could agree on was that both sides should stop saying nasty things about the other in the press.

Akers escorted Gates back to the front of the building, where a car was waiting. On the way out, Akers said, "It's really sad the state of affairs the IBM/Microsoft relationship has come to." Gates responded in kind. They actually talked mostly about the United Way, whose salaried professional chairman had just been thrown out for using his position to make himself and friends rich. Akers had the real problem, because he was the national volunteer chairman of the United Way, but Gates, as a board member, needed to confront the problem, too. They stood outside in the cold, leaning up against Gates's car, and talked pleasantly for several more minutes. Then they shook hands and said good-bye. This would be their last meeting.

Once the heavy executive artillery decided it couldn't make Gates cave in on royalties, Cannavino turned to the really big guns: his lawyers. About nine months later, they carried the day.

The lawyers decided that IBM held hundreds of software patents that everyone in the software business, Microsoft included, was violating. If Gates wanted to talk royalties, they told Microsoft, then let's talk royalties. Gates eventually agreed to pay IBM some $20 million to get the rights to those patents.

With the royalty issue finally settled, Gates decided to take Kuehler at his word: He wanted to try again to talk business with IBM. Members of Kuehler's and Cannavino's staffs separately decided that it would be good to have one more face-to-face meeting with Gates, because the agreement on the Windows royalties marked the final issue outstanding between the companies. Once those papers were signed, the divorce between IBM and Microsoft would be final and the division of property set. Cannavino could no longer deal with Gates, so the matter was left to Kuehler, who asked Gates to join him for breakfast in October 1992 at the IBM building in Manhattan.

Gates decided that he would try to soften up Kuehler by bringing along the royalty check for $20 million. He would make some joke about how that was a lot to pay for breakfast, but if that was what it cost . . .

Kuehler was unimpressed, and the breakfast got off to a bad start. They were dining in the Tom Watson, Sr., library, which IBM had transferred to the top of the forty-two-story building, right next to the boardroom. The library conjured up the flavor of the man and his times, with its dark-stained bookcases and old tomes and with the official portrait of Tom Senior glowering down from high on a side wall, just below the original THINK sign. It is an impressive room, but Kuehler was waxing a bit too nostalgic for Gates's taste as he described the room in detail.

"I was thinking, What, am I supposed to be overwhelmed?" Gates says. "I mean, I'd eaten in the room five times before. I thought that maybe I should be the one giving the tour."

Things warmed up after a few minutes. Gates said he was on his way to Washington, D.C., to receive an award, so Kuehler said, "That's nice. Maybe I should nominate you for the National Academy of Engineering medal."

But when Gates launched into his standard medley of work he wanted to do with IBM, Kuehler just smiled.

"We'll have to see about that one, Billy," Kuehler said repeatedly.

Kuehler never quite said it, but he clearly felt that IBM had created Microsoft and Gates and that much of that wealth should have belonged to IBM. It rankled Kuehler the businessman that IBM had let that happen. It annoyed Kuehler the gentleman that Gates and his colleagues seemed so ungrateful.

"You've done pretty well for yourself, Billy," Kuehler said a couple of times.

When the breakfast ended, Gates decided that he'd never be allowed to work with IBM again. The relationship that had begun twelve years earlier with a vague discussion about a tiny piece of language software for a nonexistent machine and that had blossomed into the defining relationship for the entire PC industry had finally ended.

In the intervening years, Microsoft had gone from thirty-two people to twelve thousand and was still growing as fast as the construction crews could throw up buildings on the Microsoft campus among the evergreens of the Pacific Northwest. Microsoft's earnings had gone from less than $1 million a year to more than $500 million, on their way to $1 billion. Microsoft had come from nowhere to be one of the top ten companies in the United States in terms of the value of its publicly traded stock. Depending on the day, Microsoft's stock value often exceeded IBM's. Gates had become the richest man in America.

IBM had gone from being one of the world's most profitable companies in 1980 to a 1992 so horrible that it would post the largest loss that any company had ever seen. The number of employees had dropped by 40,000, and the cuts felt even worse because IBM had added tens of thousands of jobs in the 1980s, then wiped out all those jobs and was going to continue to shrink from there. IBM's stock had fallen some 30 percent, to levels not seen since the mid-1970s, when IBM was much smaller.

By the time IBM finally cut off Gates, those stories that talked about dominance of the computer industry discussed IBM in the past tense. The most powerful figure in the industry was the mop-haired guy with the dirty glasses who was walking away from the IBM building and toward his car at the corner of Fifty-seventh Street and Madison Avenue.

THIRTEEN

IBM began to think the unthinkable in February 1991. A bunch of Jim Cannavino's engineers from the workstation part of his product group got together in a conference room in Somers, New York, to discuss whether they should sign on to the corporate plan to generate revenue by selling raw technology to other companies. It so happened that President Jack Kuehler attended the meeting. The president of all of IBM wouldn't ordinarily go to such a brainstorming session, but Kuehler, an engineer, had taken a particular interest in the IBM workstation. Now, as the engineers wondered aloud about what other companies might want to buy the IBM workstation's central processors to power their own workstations or personal computers, Kuehler committed what could only be considered heresy: He suggested that he call IBM's implacable enemy, Apple.

Apple had actually been trying to get to know IBM for a year. Michael Spindler, Apple's new president, decided he wanted an introduction to Kuehler in early 1990 just to see what kinds of business dealings might be possible. In the intimate world of Silicon Valley, Spindler soon discovered that he could use Regis McKenna as an intermediary. McKenna is a white-haired, grandfatherly sort, but he has a glittery presence in Silicon Valley because he has concocted daring marketing campaigns that have helped so many start-ups get established, beginning with the strategies that let Apple catch the public imagination with the Apple II and that positioned the Macintosh as "the computer for the rest of us." As Silicon Valley's marketer to the stars, McKenna—whose business card lists his title as "Himself"—seemed to know everybody. When Spindler asked whether McKenna knew anyone out east at IBM headquarters, he learned that politically active McKenna even knew Kuehler well because Kuehler had stayed involved in a college friend's political career after moving away from his native California.

After McKenna arranged a call, Spindler and Kuehler merely talked by phone long enough to decide they could overlook the IBM/Apple stereotypes and actually deal with each other. In the fall, Spindler tried again, to see whether Kuehler would sell him IBM's workstation processors for use as the basis for a new, more powerful line of Macintosh personal computers than Apple thought it could build if it kept relying on Motorola's processors. Kuehler demurred. He still considered the processors to be among IBM's crown jewels, not for use by outsiders. But when IBM's workstation group changed its position in a Somers conference room in early 1991, Kuehler thought he'd find Spindler receptive.

He was right. Apple had pursued its interest in a faster processor for its Macintoshes far enough that it would soon have settled on a supplier other than IBM, but Kuehler caught Spindler with a few weeks to spare. The two then initiated a lengthy feeling-out process to see whether buttoned-down IBM and New Wave Apple could really work together. It took a while. Apple's approach is "Ready, Fire, Aim," while IBM's method is, "Ready, Aim, Aim, Aim. . . ."

At the first meeting between the Apple engineers and the engineers at IBM's workstation development facility in Austin, Texas, the Apple contingent showed up for a meeting at IBM wearing three-piece suits that looked as if they'd never been worn before. When they walked into the office of senior IBM technologist Phil Hester, they found Hester and most of his people wearing cowboy boots, jeans, and denim shirts.

"Oh shit," the Apple people said under their breath.

"Gotcha," Hester responded with a chuckle.

Most of the early meetings, in fact, had the Apple people in suits and the IBMers in polo shirts or whatever else they thought would pass for California casual. IBM also often flooded meetings with three times as many people as Apple sent. Some meetings, such as the first one on a possible multimedia project, got so out of control that, as one participant put it, it seemed that the two companies planned a project that "would require more money than God had and that would make more money than anyone had made in the history of the world."

Once things settled down in the spring of 1991, though, the two companies hit it off very quickly. Kuehler and Apple's chief executive, John Sculley, took a liking to each other. They eventually set up video-conferencing equipment in their offices so they could talk face-to-face daily—like George Jetson and Mr. Spacely—even when they weren't traveling to meetings with each other. Kuehler even gave Sculley the ultimate honor: an IBM ID card, meaning he had the same privileges as an IBM employee at any IBM facility worldwide.

Once a couple of months passed and the companies decided they could work together, teams of people holed up at a training facility near IBM's headquarters to pound out the details. Although the companies had evolved a dress-code approach that had people dressing informally at Apple's facilities and wearing suits at IBM's, Cannavino once again used clothes as a symbol. He declared that everyone could dress informally at the IBM center. The message was: Let's not stand on ceremony. Let's just get it done. Cannavino spent most of his time with the IBM negotiating team just to make sure that things kept moving and that he could blast through any brick walls that the IBM bureaucracy threw up. Finally, Cannavino essentially moved into the facility.

All the attention delighted Sculley. He found IBM terribly responsive, despite its reputation, because Kuehler and Cannavino personally intervened anytime anything went wrong. The Apple engineers found that they actually spoke the same language as IBM's engineers, especially those IBMers in Austin, Texas, who had taken advantage of their distance from headquarters to develop a renegade culture.

By May 1991, the companies were rolling. They soon agreed to have IBM make a version of its workstation processor that Apple could use in new Macintoshes to make them much more powerful than existing Macs. IBM enlisted Motorola's help in making the chip because Motorola knew more about making chips inexpensively than IBM did. IBM and Apple also teamed up on two major software ventures. One was for a next-generation personal-computer operating system that both hoped would blow Microsoft out of the water. The other would focus on multimedia software designed to make it easier for people to use video, sound, and graphics on their personal computers.

An Apple executive did commit a faux pas by letting on to the press that Apple and IBM were talking, which turned so much attention on the talks that it kept the pressure on and forced the sides to redouble their efforts at security. They thought they could avoid scrutiny by meeting well away from their headquarters, and to avoid causing suspicion, they never met more than once in the same place. All the attention kept people spooked, though. One IBM staff member says he took one trip to various sites around the country, including Apple headquarters and the IBM Austin facility, and found messages waiting for him from a *Washington Post* reporter at every hotel.

The companies reached a preliminary agreement by July 1991, then built toward a formal agreement in early October. Things moved along well enough that they booked time in the ballroom of a San Francisco hotel and arranged for satellite broadcasts around the world. After a difficult, final negotiating session the day before, the IBM, Apple, and Motorola executives all essentially signed off on the deal. But then the Motorola executives sprang a surprise. Their corporate bylaws didn't allow them to sign a contract until forty-eight hours after the negotiations were completed, just to give them time to make sure they were doing the right thing. The Motorola people wanted to proceed with the announcement, but Cannavino would have to be willing to do so without a signed contract. Cannavino was apoplectic.

After a couple of hours of scrambling, he convened a meeting in his hotel room at midnight California time. The announcement was supposed to hit the wire services in five hours—8:00 A.M. eastern standard time—and he didn't know what it should say. His staff advised him that IBM shouldn't announce the Motorola part of the deal without a signed contract, but they weren't sure how Motorola would react to being excluded from the big event set for the morning. A public-relations person finally suggested a bit of brinksmanship.

He revised the main press release to exclude Motorola's name and include some language saying that IBM hoped to find a company to manufacture the processors Apple was going to buy. Included in the language was a vague suggestion that IBM was talking to several companies, implicitly threatening Motorola with the loss of their business if it couldn't find a way to sign by morning. An army of secretaries then went through and deleted every reference to Motorola from the whole packet of press releases.

Cannavino took the press releases off to the Motorola suite at about

1:00 A.M. The Motorola executives got the hint and woke up their bosses back home in Arizona and Chicago. By 4:00 A.M., they were ready to sign. That left the PR people barely enough time to issue the press releases to the wires, but the announcement got out on time at 5:00 A.M.

People jammed the ballroom the next morning, October 2, 1991. Everyone in the industry remembered well how snooty Apple had been when IBM came out with its PC, taking out full-page ads that purported to welcome IBM to the world of small computers and that claimed credit for having created that world. Everyone in the industry knew well how that ad had set the tone for a decade of mutual disdain. So it fascinated the securities analysts, the consultants, the customers, the reporters, and even the Apple and IBM employees to be able to sit there and watch Sculley, Spindler, Cannavino, and Kuehler make nice.

Some of the IBMers joked that as they sat there up front and looked at the stage, they could see the entire sweep of history. There on the one end was Spindler, hulking, big-browed, surprisingly inarticulate. He represented Neanderthal man. Next to him was Cannavino, with his curly hair and goofy grin. Cannavino represented a step up the evolutionary ladder. Next came Kuehler, the clean-cut, articulate, professional engineer. He represented modern man. Finally came Sculley, the wild-eyed marketing guy who had begun establishing himself as a visionary. He represented future man.

As the IBMers scanned the stage, they hoped that the association with Apple would wake some people up at IBM and help lead them into the future. The potential was certainly there. If IBM could redesign its workstation processor well enough to meet the needs of PC makers—reducing the chip's power consumption and output of heat, for instance—and Motorola could manufacture the processors cheaply enough, IBM could recapture the huge market for PC processors it had ceded to Intel. If the operating-system project succeeded, IBM could at last slow down hated Microsoft and regain a lot of the earnings that had been going Microsoft's way since OS/2 flopped and Windows took over the world. If the multimedia piece worked, IBM could push the world toward highly visual uses of computers, which require so much processing power that they would push consumers to buy a whole new generation of more powerful machines and generate billions of dollars of new hardware sales. Only one question remained, a question that never would have troubled IBM in the 1960s or 1970s, when it built a reputation for being as tough-minded and efficient as the Marine Corps. The question was whether IBM could pull it off.

Even as Cannavino and Kuehler were glowing at the Apple launch event in October 1991, Akers was worrying. Nineteen ninety-one was proving to be such a disastrous year that Akers was gradually realizing he hadn't cut costs nearly enough and that simply declaring the company would be more entrepreneurial wouldn't make it happen. By the end of November, Akers decided he had to reorganize yet again, cutting tens of thousands of additional jobs and taking another huge write-off.

The idea behind this reorganization was essentially the same as it had been back in 1988 when Akers announced his prior reorganization to end all reorganizations. Akers wanted to decentralize further. That way, decisions would be made by people who were lower in the organization but who knew more about their individual markets than the people at the top. The decisions would also come faster because those making them wouldn't have to seek permission from so many people beforehand. Akers decided that this time he would go even further than he had before. He would break the company up into thirteen units, forming what he would call a loose federation of companies. Most of the units would be product groups—such as the PC business, the disk-drive business, the mainframe business, and so forth. But Akers also set up a marketing business that would buy products from units such as the PC business and then resell them. Akers also said that even centralized service functions such as personnel would contract with other parts of IBM to provide their services and be free to sell their services to other companies. Over time, the companies would report separate financial results. Akers would also consider selling part or all of any of the businesses.

With the plan set, Akers now had to sell it. Despite his withering glare and assertion in December 1989 that everything was under control and that he wouldn't soon have to apologize to investors again, now two years later he was about to find himself in a room full of securities analysts, trying to argue that this time he fully understood the problems and finally really did have things under control.

Akers took the offensive. When he took the stage in the ballroom at the gleaming, recently refurbished Macklowe Hotel in midtown

Manhattan, he trumpeted his moves as a fundamental redefinition of IBM. His senior people began referring to the new IBM. The press began talking about the thirteen new units as the Baby Blues.

The idea Akers was working toward made a lot of sense. The reason Silicon Valley companies had been clobbering IBM for years—while the feared Japanese had been doing much less well—was that they had had the kind of freedom and responsibility Akers was now trying to build into IBM. The Silicon Valley companies had owner-managers. The person at the top owned enough of the company that making the company succeed would make him rich, maybe filthy rich. He wanted to be filthy rich. He would do anything necessary to be filthy rich. If that meant taking a chance or pinching pennies or working ridiculous hours and sleeping under his desk, he'd do it. And once he'd made his fortune, he'd do whatever he had to do to keep it, even if it meant firing a few friends. The Silicon Valley companies that had been eating at IBM didn't contain people who were any smarter than those at IBM. Most of the people didn't even start out being more entrepreneurial than their counterparts at IBM. The Silicon Valley companies were just driven by a purer emotion than IBM was: greed.

At IBM, people wanted to be important, not rich. Executives wanted big staffs, lots of employees, access to the corporate jet, a title. People down in the trenches were conditioned to want security. Neither security nor the desire for importance translated well into greed.

Akers now suddenly wanted to build some greed into the IBM system, but the culture was going to make that awfully hard. Akers couldn't just start paying people what they were worth. A brokerage house could go ahead and set up commissions that might pay some obscure currency trader $10 million in a year, but IBM's civil service–like salary structure was too carefully calibrated to let someone get even a few tens of thousands of dollars outside the bounds of his or her salary range. Trying to give people the kind of potential for an earnings windfall that existed among start-ups would have blown IBM apart. So when Akers decided to pay just about everyone in the company bonuses based partly on how their business unit did, the most he could bring himself to have hinge on that payment was 3 percent of the person's salary. That translated to maybe a couple of thousand dollars a year, hardly enough to make someone want to take the kind of entrepreneurial chance that might cost him his job.

Akers couldn't even sort out what the real performance of the business units was. He acknowledged that it would take years to phase out the centralized accounting system and give each business its own financial statement.

As much as Akers tried to tell people to think for themselves, he also couldn't quite bring himself to cut them loose. He was too much a product of the culture. He had been trained since day one to think that when he moved higher up in the organization than someone else, that meant he was a better executive and therefore made better decisions. So now that he was the top guy, having fought for decades to get to the top, was he really going to tell people who worked for him several levels down in the PC business that they were better equipped to make a decision than he was? No. Instead, while Akers ostensibly welcomed change, demanded change, he kept the anachronistic Management Committee together. It still made decisions on internal disputes, and that still allowed the old-line businesses to undercut whatever their younger brethren tried to do, even though Akers had decreed that would no longer happen.

Akers couldn't bring himself to break from the company's paternalistic past, either. He tried to stick with the full-employment policy, which told employees, in essence, "If you do your job, there will always be a job for you." Guaranteeing jobs worked splendidly when IBM was expanding so fast over the decades, because the growth gave IBM the chance to hire all the new people it needed. But by late 1991, IBM was shrinking, not growing. The computer market had changed so much to emphasize PCs rather than mainframes and to require strength in services rather than the ability to sell hardware that IBM needed to hire tens of thousands of people with specialized skills in new programming languages, in consulting, and so on. IBM also needed people who had worked in other companies and who had fresh ideas. But IBM's full-employment policy was keeping the company focusing on taking care of its existing employees rather than on finding fresh blood.

Cannavino led several heads of the thirteen new IBM business units in arguing to Akers in late 1991 that the one thing they really needed was their own sales forces. Competitors had cut into the business units' profit margins so much that they could no longer afford the luxury of paying 35 percent of their revenue each year to finance IBM's sales force. The business units also didn't think they were getting enough out of that money. They said the idea of the generalist salesman who could sell all IBM products had been washed away. IBM just had too many products, and customers were demanding too high a level of technical knowledge for any little group of generalist salesmen to provide. Akers turned them down. He had grown up in that sales force. He couldn't tear it to shreds.

Akers still didn't seem to think in December 1991 that IBM needed to do anything radical.

"We think 1991 was an aberration," he said. "These are pretty unusual times," he added, before predicting that IBM would return to its normal growth in 1992.

Akers was asked at the time of the reorganization whether his plans weren't just the start, with lots more work to be done in coming months to decentralize IBM. No, Akers said. The basic problem was solved. Now it was just a matter of implementing the new organization.

Well, then, he was asked, wasn't this reorganization just trying to put in place the same thing he had tried to put in place four years earlier? Akers acknowledged that it was. He was just trying to make it all sound as impressive as he could, because he wanted IBMers to take him seriously this time.

Employees didn't seem to be buying it, though. When asked what they thought of the reorganization, IBMers rolled their eyes and said, "Which one?"

As Akers began implementing his reorganization, he had an excellent example of successful decentralization that he knew extremely well— IBM's Lexington, Kentucky, operations, which he had agreed to sell to an investment firm in August 1990. Although the operations were quickly building a sense of entrepreneurship into longtime IBM employees, Akers bristled anytime anyone even mentioned Lexington. People talking about what came to be called Lexmark always said it showed how well things could go once the strictures of IBM's bureaucracy were removed. Well, Akers was the boss of that bureaucracy, and he wasn't sure it was so bad.

Lexmark had begun as one of the most charming of IBM's businesses decades earlier because its typewriters were sold to real people, not to faceless corporate data-processing departments. The marketing people amused themselves with all sorts of gimmicks. One once had an all-white electronic typewriter made for Tom Watson, Sr., to present to the Pope in the 1950s. Someone once decided that customers ought to be able to order typewriters in any color so they could fit in with an office's decorating scheme. So unpainted typewriters flowed down the manufacturing assembly line with a patch of cloth or some other color sample taped to their sides, just so the painters could be sure to match the color exactly. Typewriters ordered by the University of Tennessee once went down the line with an orange UT banner sticking up from them—a serious affront in Lexington, the home of arch UT rival University of Kentucky. The assembly-line workers decided to go ahead and paint the typewriters UT orange but wrote, "Go Big Blue," on the underside of the covers, leaving it to the UT folks to figure out whether that was a reference to IBM or to the University of Kentucky's colors.

The mostly male IBM salesmen in the 1950s and 1960s developed such a reputation for palaver when approaching the primarily female secretaries who were choosing the typewriters that the Lexington operation became known as the Romance Division.

The initial electric typewriters that IBM produced were odd-looking contraptions, with devices built onto the sides that were designed to hold ribbons but that made the typewriter appear to have ears. Once the Selectric came along in the 1960s, though, the typewriter operation became one of IBM's most successful. Customers loved the rock-solid feel of the Selectric keyboard and that they didn't need to worry about having the carriage return, which might knock over a coffee cup or whatever was in the way. The way the little round typing element rotated so swiftly to get in position to strike each character also fascinated people. So customers were willing to pay exorbitant prices for the typewriters—twenty dollars or so for a typing element that cost IBM about a dollar to make. Many customers developed an extraordinary bond with their Selectrics, which continues to this day. Ron Javers, former editor of *Philadelphia* magazine, says that he used to have a PC on his desk hooked up to the office network but that his staff used to insist he turn it on only when he needed to shed extra light on the paper in the Selectric right next to it.

As happened with so many IBM businesses, though, the people in Lexington focused so much on their existing profitable business that they were timid about trying new things and missed several subsequent opportunities. By the late 1970s, competitors were using the new and smaller electronic processors that were being built into Apple's, Tandy's, and other companies' personal computers. Suddenly, IBM competitors' typewriters came with tiny screens and electronic memories, making it easier to correct errors in text and produce batches of letters. But Lexington was slow to react. In addition, PC printers started appearing that used so-called Daisy wheels to print much faster than Selectrics could. Lexington tried to stick with the old Selectric technology. Then Wang came along with its dedicated word processors. Lexington hadn't done anywhere near enough research to match Wang's ability to edit text on-screen before turning it into a letter or to do mail-merge, producing batches of letters that were individually addressed. Lexington was discovering that doing a great typewriter with a solid feel wasn't enough anymore.

When Lexington finally pulled itself together in the early 1980s and tried to get into the PC printer market, it had trouble because the MC couldn't grasp that a printer business needed to be run very differently from even the PC business—because printers had lower profit margins and needed to be sold differently. Lexington then got caught up in Chairman John Opel's fascination with robotics and with becoming the low-cost manufacturer in the early 1980s, so it spent $350 million to automate production of a printer that was about to become outdated. Lexington missed the chance to catch the next wave of PC printers, laser printers, because of one of those painfully common situations where IBM seemed to know too much. Lexington made high-cost, superfast laser printers for mainframe customers and knew that just the mirror that directed the laser beam inside the printer cost several thousand dollars, which made Lexington decide that a consumer printer costing just a couple of thousand dollars was years away. Then when Canon showed that it could build a cheap laser printer and offered to sell the core technology to anyone who wanted it, IBM was too proud to buy it. Hewlett-Packard wasn't too proud; it used the Canon technology to bring out an early laser printer and capture the multibillion-dollar market.

By the mid-1980s, the romance in Lexington had died.

In 1989, IBM came out with a couple of decent laser printers, but they were too little, far too late. Just slapping the IBM logo on a product wasn't nearly enough to dislodge a dominant competitor like HP that had good technology, a great reputation, and excellent relations with dealers. When the laser printers didn't pick things up, rumors started circulating that the eight-thousand-person facility would be sold or closed. Soon, barely a week went by that a rumor wouldn't circulate through the plant about how a team of Japanese executives had supposedly been spotted on a midnight tour of the facility to see whether they wanted to buy it.

Akers had, in fact, begun talking with Clayton Dubilier, a small leveraged-buyout company known for turning around technology businesses and for caring more about the people involved than most of the slash-and-burn leveraged-buyout businesses that sprang up in the 1980s. Akers decided by the summer of 1990 that he wanted to do the deal, then learned that even the chairman of IBM couldn't just order something to happen and expect it to occur.

A senior Akers lieutenant, who was the boss way up the line for the people who ran the Lexington operation, told the Clayton Dubilier partners that they could get certain rights to IBM's patent portfolio that were crucial for future products. But then Don Gogel, a Clayton Dubilier partner, found himself in a negotiating session with some junior lawyer who told him he couldn't have those rights.

"Wait a minute," Gogel recalls saying. "The boss of the Lexington operation told us we could have those rights."

"That's too bad," the lawyer said. "Our policy is that we don't give out that kind of right."

"If I'm not mistaken," Gogel said, "the person who gave me the patent rights is the boss for the entire U.S. operation. What he says goes."

"Wrong," the lawyer said. "I don't report to him. I report up through the corporate staffs to somebody else. If anybody is going to overrule me, it's going to have to be my boss. You're going to have to escalate."

Gogel finally blew up. "You don't understand," he said, standing up and leaning across the table. "If you don't give me those rights, I won't write John Akers a check for one point fifty-eight billion dollars, and John Akers will not be happy with you."

The lawyer didn't flinch. "If Akers wants to give you those rights," he said, "he can do that. But I'm not going to unless he or one of my bosses tells me to."

So Gogel had to launch a formal protest. The lawyer made his formal response as part of the IBM escalation process. Weeks later, the issue reached the Management Committee, which agreed that Clayton Dubilier would indeed get the rights.

All sorts of issues eventually made it to the Management Committee, or at least to a level below the MC, because some staff operation at IBM that seemingly had no control over the business in Lexington disagreed—or nonconcurred—with something the business's managers had decided to do. IBM's procurement people found out that some senior person responsible for the Lexington operations had agreed to buy only Lexmark laser printers for IBM's internal use. The procurement group nonconcurred. The issue had to make its way up to the MC. IBM's accounts payable group found that an IBM negotiator had agreed to give Lexmark favorable treatment by paying bills in thirty days instead of the normal sixty. The accounts payable people nonconcurred. Akers found himself having to get involved in that detail, too.

Even as the deal was about to be signed in March 1991 and hundreds of lawyers, bankers, accountants, and business executives crowded into the conference rooms at Clayton Dubilier's small offices in the middle of Manhattan, the escalation process intervened yet again. A manager in the Netherlands discovered at the last second that the deal was going to force him to eat some inventory, so he nonconcurred and the deal ground to a halt. Hours dragged by, and everyone just waited, wondering what the holdup was. As the business day drew to a close in the United States, the situation was even tenser in Europe, where it was approaching midnight. The bankers who had gathered in London to sign off on the $1.2 billion of credit Clayton Dubilier had lined up for the deal had come in on a bank holiday to complete the work, and they were wondering why they had bothered. Finally, a senior IBM executive called the Netherlands, got the nonconcurring manager at home, and said that while the manager had every right to go through the formal process, this time that was just too bad. The Lexmark deal was going to go through, and right now.

Gogel says the deal couldn't possibly have happened if Akers hadn't intervened any number of times to short-circuit the IBM process, sometimes going down six or seven layers into IBM's organization to make sure personally that something was going to happen. When the negotiations finally ended and the deal was signed in March 1991, Gogel was so fed up with IBM's escalation process that he had a board game called

Nonconcur made up and passed out 350 copies to people involved in the negotiations. When he gave Akers a copy, Akers showed he hadn't yet lost his entire sense of humor. He laughed heartily.

Once Clayton Dubilier took control of Lexmark and installed a former IBM vice president, Marvin Mann, as chief executive, one of the first things people at the facility did was take the old IBM development manual and place it in a block of Lucite on the plant floor. Those now in charge wanted everyone there to remember the evil book. But they didn't want anyone to be able to open it ever again.

Mann, a southern gentleman who had been very much a part of the process at IBM, went about dismantling the IBM culture that infused the place. The whole contention system was wiped out. Instead, all the different elements of Lexmark were put on the same team and told they'd all win or lose together. Meetings were cut to a minimum; so was travel. Staffs were so thoroughly wiped out that the headquarters operation for the $2-billion-a-year business consisted of fewer than twenty people on part of a floor in a small building across the street from the train station in Greenwich, Connecticut. The chief financial officer led an unofficial ban on foils, seemingly the only medium IBMers could use to communicate. He said he'd throw anyone out of his office who tried to come in with foils. Even those at Lexmark who still used foils might keep only one around, just in case anyone asked how their part of the business was doing. But no one was any longer spending weeks at a time preparing foils for some meeting.

Real decentralization occurred. An assembly-line worker in Lexington was just four levels below Mann. Under IBM's control, he would have been seven or eight levels removed from Mann, who himself would have been four or so levels removed from the chief executive of IBM. As many people as possible were given their own financial statements, making an assembly-line manager, for instance, focus for the first time on the interest costs associated with all the parts he might otherwise have asked to have stockpiled around the line.

Information was shared with the workers, not hoarded as a trapping of power. John Trisler, who manages the typewriter operation in Lexington now, says that when he learned once at the end of a day that his results for a month had been especially good, he made sure that everybody in his organization knew what the numbers were by noon the next day. Could that have happened at IBM?

"No way," Trisler says. "I'll tell you what. Even I wouldn't have known what those numbers were when I was at IBM. Only somebody two or three levels above me would have had those numbers."

Once the bureaucracy began to disappear and everyone realized that they had to take individual responsibility or wind up on Kentucky's lengthening unemployment lines, people responded by pinching pennies in a way that wouldn't have occurred to them under the deep-pockets approach at IBM. Workers seeing a contractor installing a ramp asked him how much he was being paid. When told he was being paid $25,000, they stormed into their manager's office to tell him he was paying twice what he should have been. Another worker went into a manager's office to say that he needed approval for twenty-six ionizing devices to hang over an assembly line to cut the static electricity in the air. The worker, still remembering his IBM discipline, came prepared to justify the expense in any number of ways. But the manager told the worker he trusted him to do what was right for the business. The worker went off, thought it over again, and decided he could make do with six of the one-thousand-dollar devices.

People began to take risks. One guy working on his own came up with a way that he thought would greatly improve the clarity of the printing from Lexmark's laser printers—to six hundred dots per inch from the standard three hundred. That wasn't really his responsibility, but those who could have claimed "ownership" actually encouraged him to proceed. The manager in charge of developing the next generation of laser printers then agreed to bet his whole project on the untried technology. The whole rest of the printer was going to have to be designed around the assumption that the technology bet would pay off, but the manager went ahead and did it, anyway. The bet paid off, and Lexmark for the first time had something that it could really sell against Hewlett-Packard.

With the old staffs and contention system out of the way in 1991, Lexmark began doing more with less: The printer business doubled the number of development projects under way and cut the development time in half, even though it had slightly fewer people than it had had under IBM. As managers began to turn responsibility over to employees, they found efficiencies that they couldn't have imagined. Trisler let his typewriter-assembly workers design their own product line, and they cut the time it took to build a typewriter from eight hours to a little more than an hour. Another manager initially followed the traditional IBM process. He brought in some industrial engineers to design a new assembly line and assured the manager that they had double-checked with the workers to make sure it met all their needs. The manager called the workers together and took the engineers to talk with them. He told the workers that they, not he, would sign the form authorizing the new assembly line and asked whether they were ready to do so. Nobody was. He said he was going to leave the engineers with them and that nobody was to leave until everybody was satisfied. It took two weeks to hash things out and delayed the start of work on a line that was already behind schedule, but he, like Trisler, got enormous gains in productivity.

Some big costs began to disappear as Lexmark got to deal with its real expenses and stopped having to accept whatever allocation of costs got passed along from corporate headquarters. Lexmark, for instance, no longer had to contribute roughly 10 percent of its revenue to help with a corporate R&D budget that aimed mainly at the high end of the line and couldn't really be afforded by Lexington, with its low-end, inexpensive products in extremely competitive markets.

Most important, Lexmark no longer had to pay 35 percent of its revenue to cover general overhead and the cost of a sales force that focused on expensive, high-profit-margin products and couldn't be bothered selling Lexington's printers and typewriters. Once Lexmark got free of the IBM sales force, it set up a small group to deal with corporate customers, who had been getting little attention from the IBM force. Lexmark also set up a little group that worked directly with dealers; it learned that printers had to be sold very differently from PCs and so tailored its plans accordingly.

All the changes happening all at once upset a lot of the people in Lexington. One likened IBM's decision to sell to the situation of someone who came home and found his wife wanted to divorce him. Even though he might have known the divorce was coming, it was still tough to be kicked out. Another said he knew that IBM had tried hard to make the sale go well and to make sure Lexmark would take good care of the former IBMers. But he said IBM was still like a father who took his young son for a walk, took him up to a strange house, and said, "Son, this house is equivalent to ours, and this man and this woman here will be equivalent parents. So I'll leave you here now. Good-bye."

Even once the change occurred, people at Lexmark said they found it very hard to break their old habits. One engineer said he couldn't even deal with the decision to make Fridays "dress-down days," when people would dress informally. He said that the first Friday he arrived without wearing a tie, he just sat in his office with the door closed, feeling ashamed and hoping no one would come to see him.

Gogel of Clayton Dubilier said Mann told an employee at Lexmark to go off and figure how many people he'd need to handle three functions. The guy studied things for a couple of weeks and came back with a request for sixty people, twenty for each task. Mann said the Lexmark employee didn't understand. Mann had been thinking three people tops, one for each task, and if that meant that the Lexmark staff couldn't generate a lot of the information it used to generate, that was fine. Mann probably didn't need it, anyway. The Lexmark guy responded that that was not how they used to do things at IBM, so he wanted to be sure he had enough people.

But after perhaps six months, people settled down and put their old habits behind them. At that point, Lexmark's results improved much faster than expected. Debt had been expected to total $1.2 billion at the end of the first year, but it was only $900 million and quickly dropped to $700 million. Operating profits were about twice as high as expected. Lexmark became the best example yet of what could happen if some way was found to keep the IBM technology and the skills of its people while blowing up the stultifying culture.

But as Akers announced his latest reorganization in late 1991 and began to implement it in 1992, he stopped wanting to hear about Lexmark. He was under enough pressure without having to hear about how someone else was doing a better job of dealing with IBM's bureaucracy than he was. One former IBM executive who used to be Akers's boss says that when he pointed out to Akers how much it helped Lexmark to have its own sales force, Akers blew up.

"I'm sick and tired of hearing about Lexmark," Akers yelled.

With Akers finishing up his latest stab at reorganization in late 1991 and with Kuehler and Cannavino having announced the agreement with Apple in early October, things began to return to normal around IBM, which means everything began to move slowly. Without Kuehler and Cannavino on call twenty-four hours a day to blast through the IBM bureaucracy, Sculley found that it took months just to find chief executives for the two most important of the joint ventures. It took even longer to get the operations up and going, even though IBM and Apple had already spent six exhaustive months working through all the details of the organizations. The slow start gave competitors time to react and cut the chances of success.

With Microsoft and Bill Gates increasingly dominating the industry as 1992 began, a phrase was coming into use: "Either fix your problems," someone might say, "or just send all your money to Bill." Either IBM and Apple were going to have figured out some way to move rapidly or they might as well just send the money directly to Bill.

Kuehler and Sculley tried to move first on finding someone for the most important joint venture, called Taligent, which was to produce a new type of personal-computer operating system. They seemed to settle on Dave Liddle of Metaphor, a highly regarded industry figure, but he decided that the corporate parents weren't willing to give him the independence he thought he needed, so he withdrew his name. Apple's engineers eventually decided they wanted Joe Guglielmi from IBM. He was a marketing type with little technical background, but the Apple engineers rather liked that; they figured he'd have to leave them alone. They also figured Guglielmi knew enough of the people at IBM and could play the politics well enough that he could keep the IBM parent at bay. But Guglielmi turned the job down. He was comfortable at IBM and could expect a big pension. He didn't want to take a chance on a start-up.

When the weeks dragged on in early 1992 and no other reasonable candidate surfaced, Sculley went to Kuehler and said, essentially, "Look, you said you were serious about this thing, but you can't even get one of your senior people to take one of the top jobs. We want Guglielmi. I think you ought to deliver him to us."

Kuehler then got tough. He told Guglielmi that the Taligent job was his only choice. If he chose not to move to California and take it, well, he wasn't going to be able to stick around, either. Guglielmi no longer had a job at IBM. Under those conditions, Guglielmi decided that it might be a good idea to move to Silicon Valley.

People in the PC industry shook their heads when they heard about the Guglielmi appointment. Not only had IBM and Apple taken nearly five months to find a top person; they had managed to pick a typical IBM bureaucrat for an entrepreneurial job. Guglielmi hadn't even been that successful a bureaucrat lately. He had messed up OfficeVision, and the latest project he had been identified with, OS/2, wasn't doing anything for anyone, either.

When a story in the national press raised some of those issues, Guglielmi blew up. He gathered together nearly twenty staff members for a two-hour conference call, during which he essentially just recited his resume, down to the number of mainframes he estimated he had sold in his career as a salesman. He didn't seem to be asking anyone to do anything. He just wanted to complain about being mistreated. Getting increasingly worked up as the hours dragged on, he finally ended the call by shouting, "I've done more in my career than fuck up Office-Vision!"

It seemed at the beginning that Guglielmi was going to take lots of the IBM bureaucracy with him to Taligent. He made sure that Taligent, supposedly a start-up, began life as a full-blown company. It had 170-some people on day one, including its own human resources department, a controller's department, and so forth. The company grew quickly from there. Guglielmi introduced foils to Taligent. He got fancy offices for Taligent at the edge of Apple's headquarters.

But the relatively small size of Taligent did prevent him from going too far. He complained about not having enough staff to open his mail, handle his appointments, and clear the way for him on business trips, but he also knew he didn't have the budget to go out and hire them. Without so many staff around, Guglielmi found himself having to study problems on his own—and making up his mind on his own, quite quickly. Guglielmi even began twitting his former colleagues at IBM for making decisions so slowly. They'd tell him they were doing better, that instead of taking three months to research some issue and decide on it, they were taking only three weeks. Guglielmi would say that was fine, but they still weren't making decisions instantaneously the way he was at Taligent. Just being out in California seemed to loosen up Guglielmi, too. He wore golf shirts to the office. He drove a Jaguar while wearing his aviator sunglasses and, during the cooler months, a sporty parka.

The joke at the time of the Apple-IBM announcement had been: What do you get when you combine Apple and IBM? The answer: IBM. In fact, the reverse was turning out to be true. The answer was really: Apple. Apple had supplied the basic technology that Taligent was trying to turn into an operating system, and almost every one of the

160 developers Taligent started with had come from Apple. IBM supplied only one or two programmers. Guglielmi asked the mostly Apple programmers to rejigger their priorities a bit after he settled in, but he pretty much left the developers alone. At the beginning, he had even been in a different building doing his thing while the Apple developers went about their business unhampered. With the IBM bureaucracy kept at bay, work proceeded smoothly.

Even if Taligent succeeds wildly, though, it'll be 1995 before it has much of a product on the market. It takes two to three years for software developers to figure out how to work with a radically new sort of technology such as Taligent's product will represent. It also takes PC users a couple of years to start making the switch to new types of software. So even if things work perfectly, it'll be the end of the millennium before Taligent does much to improve the fortunes of IBM's PC business.

And while it'll take years to figure out just how Taligent will do, it's not a sure bet. Every software company around is playing with the sort of technology that Taligent represents, including a company called Microsoft, run by a person whose name Guglielmi can't even bring himself to utter in staff meetings—Guglielmi just refers to Gates as "that guy in Redmond, Washington." The Apple involvement bodes well for Taligent. Apple, after all, did bring the world the Macintosh and has consistently shown that it understands what people want from computers and software. But IBM has blown it every time in PC software, so there's no reason to assume that this time will be any different. As always, it's also hard to bet against that guy in Redmond, Washington. Guglielmi may end up just sending his money to Bill.

When IBM and Apple began hunting for someone to run their multimedia joint venture in late 1991, the choice initially looked like a no-brainer. It would be Bob Carberry, a hyperactive Ichabod Crane look-alike who was a senior person in the IBM PC operation. Press releases were even drawn up announcing the appointment. But Carberry decided, like Guglielmi, that leaving IBM was too much of a risk. Carberry also worried about what would happen to his pension. He declined, and IBM didn't force the issue.

By the end of 1991, it was no longer even clear that the venture, called Kaleida, would survive. Apple was contributing the key technology, just as it had with Taligent, and felt that IBM should contribute more of the funding. Cannavino disagreed strenuously and set his lawyers to work compiling a list of technologies that IBM was contributing to the venture. The IBM and Apple lawyers argued until March 1992, when Apple caved in.

The search for a top executive resumed, but just about every outsider rejected the IBM-Apple overtures. IBM and Apple may have initially convinced the world that their joint venture was the greatest thing going, but they had dawdled long enough that this was now almost a year after word of the ventures first appeared in the press, so reality had set in. Apple and IBM also insisted on treating the ventures as standard corporate product groups. That made it hard to attract the cream of Silicon Valley society, who wanted a real payoff if they pulled off a success. The search dragged on long enough to jeopardize Kaleida's chances.

The search committee had actually had a top-notch candidate, Nat Goldhaber, interested from even before the Kaleida plan was approved in 1991, but he hadn't seemed to fit with IBM's ideas. The husky, bearded Goldhaber was a product of the 1960s, the son of two Berkeley physicists. He studied transcendental meditation with the Maharishi Yogi in India then, at age twenty-three, founded the degree-granting Maharishi University in Iowa, which is still accredited more than twenty years later. Goldhaber got a master's degree in education, then moved to Pennsylvania, where he became the state's "energy czar" and had to develop emergency evacuation plans during the Three Mile Island nuclear plant crisis in 1979. When Goldhaber moved to Silicon Valley, he founded a company that made networking software called TOPS—for transcendental operating system. He made a tidy little fortune when he sold that company to Sun, so he did the 1960s thing and retired to help raise his infant triplet sons. Besides, Goldhaber was a Macintosh fanatic. He so loved his DuoDock, a Macintosh portable, that he began taking it to bed at night.

His wife looked at it one night and said, "It's her or me. Make your choice."

The one business idea that continued to pull at Goldhaber also didn't fit well with IBM's way of thinking. The idea stemmed from his disillusionment with the personal-computer revolution. Like many people in the early days, he saw it as a power-to-the-people movement that would give individuals access to infinite amounts of information in ways that would make society more egalitarian. Instead, he had seen corporations co-opt the PC and turn it into a corporate tool that left business, government, and other institutions just as strong as they had always been. As Goldhaber sat on his boys' swing set high in the Berkeley hills, with the San Francisco Bay sparkling below him, he decided that something else needed to happen to return the PC revolution to its original ideals. He thought that something else could be a standard language for developing and displaying video, whether on computers or on home entertainment systems such as televisions and videogames. Developing a standard would let home entertainment systems play software developed for computers and would let them take on more computerlike capabilities. Because people seem to be willing to shell out hundreds or even thousands of dollars for home-entertainment systems, Goldhaber saw a video standard as a neatly insidious way of getting computer capabilities into homes as part of entertainment systems. Maybe then people would get the access to information, the ability to communicate, the freedom to work at home, and so forth that PCs were supposed to provide.

He had once approached Sculley about a variant of his idea, but Sculley hadn't seemed to be too excited. In early 1991, Goldhaber happened to hear through a friend at Apple about work that seemed to hold similarly insidious possibilities, so he decided to try Sculley again. Goldhaber offered to work as an unpaid consultant on the project, which eventually formed the core of Kaleida. If Apple liked his ideas, it was free to use them. If not, Sculley could tell Goldhaber to get lost. Sculley agreed. Goldhaber insisted on a formal contract, for one dollar, and framed the check. Then he began spending most of his time on the project. The Apple people on the project seemed surprised that Goldhaber just sort of walked in and volunteered his time because he liked their idea, but they went along.

After several months, Goldhaber became more formally involved when he requested that Apple begin paying him a consulting fee and Sculley agreed. Goldhaber had stayed frugal despite his success, and his wife got tired of hearing him wonder whether he should buy some small item. She told him that whatever he wanted to buy would cost less than he would get for a few hours of consulting at Apple, so he should just ask for a salary and stop his agonizing.

Goldhaber dropped out of the project at the end of 1991 when it seemed that the whole thing might fall apart because the IBM and Apple lawyers couldn't agree on terms. By March 1992, he had feelers about whether he might be interested in running the business, but it wasn't until April that he was even asked to go to Armonk to be interviewed, and the whole on-again, off-again process dragged on from there.

He created a stir in Armonk. Carberry, the IBM executive who could have had the job running Kaleida, often suggested that people call him "Dr. Bob," in a reference to his Ph.D., but Goldhaber called him "Uncle Bob." When Goldhaber went for his interview with Kuehler in the tiny conference room attached to Kuehler's office, he took off his suit jacket because Kuehler wasn't wearing his. "That's right," Kuehler said, "we can be informal." Goldhaber laughed. "Mr. Kuehler," he said, "in California, if we wear shoes we're being formal."

Goldhaber told Kuehler, Cannavino, and Sculley that he wanted to start Kaleida off as a real start-up. He didn't want to begin with nearly two hundred people, the way Taligent had. He wanted a couple of dozen. He didn't want any office space from Apple or IBM. He wanted cheaper space, and he didn't want to be anywhere near either parent. He wanted autonomy. He wanted stock in Kaleida. In fact, Goldhaber told IBM and Apple that he didn't want a salary. He just wanted stock.

That stopped everybody. They could maybe agree about starting small, but stock? Negotiations dragged on another three months.

Eventually, the IBM and Apple executives relented and created what they considered to be stocklike units. IBM and Apple held almost all of those units, but Goldhaber got a few for himself and had a pool of units he could parcel out to employees he was trying to attract.

That didn't feel much like a start-up to Goldhaber. He thought the idea was phony and decided the parents were being stingy. He didn't take any of his units. Instead, he put them in a pool that he would hand out to everyone else. He didn't think he could get good people with the small number of stocklike units IBM and Apple had allocated for the pool. He had also received a promise from IBM and Apple that he could revisit the stock issue in a year; he had decided he would either get stock at that point or he'd quit.

Once he got started, Goldhaber tried to make the place feel like a start-up. He took temporary quarters near a nature preserve by the

San Francisco Bay in Mountain View, California. Someone put up an alternative version of the IBM logo in the small lobby—this one a painting with an eye drawn on the left side, with a bumblebee next to it and the letter *M* next to that. The main conference room has a sign on the door that reads, BORED ROOM.

But Goldhaber found it hard to drive home to his employees that they needed to act as though every cent they spent was their own. When it came time to do business cards, for instance, someone used to handling things in IBM fashion spent $100,000 to have a corporate logo done, then found a high-quality print shop and had cards made that cost $1.04 apiece. Goldhaber blew up. Didn't people understand the importance of scrimping on spending? He told people they'd be better off writing their names on Post-It notes and handing out the notes attached to dollar bills. It'd be about as cheap, and those getting the notes would be a lot more likely to remember them than they would after getting a fancy business card. Goldhaber supervised the next order of business cards and made sure his employees knew they cost twenty cents apiece.

When Kaleida ginned up a preliminary version of its software and shipped it off to Apple, IBM, and seventy-five independent software companies, the reaction was favorable. But all the delays in getting the company up and running had hurt. The software didn't go out until more than a year after IBM and Apple made their announcement and more than a year and a half after the companies had pretty much decided to do the venture. The rest of the world hadn't sat by and waited, either. Microsoft and some other companies began pushing an alternative way of doing multimedia applications and, while they still may lose to Kaleida, lined up considerable support that could limit Kaleida's sales.

There was to be one more delay, too. IBMers say that some internal bungling meant that they got off to a months-late start on using Kaleida's software. So even though IBM is paying half the costs of Kaleida, any products using its technology will probably come out at least several months after products from the seventy-five little companies that are getting a free ride from the IBM-Apple work.

It was beginning to look like Sun's chief executive, Scott McNealy, had been right when he said that combining Big Blue with Apple's red would produce only purple applesauce.

FOURTEEN

I n the early 1990s, when Jim Cannavino was working out of his office in
IBM's Somers, New York, building,
with its striking glass pyramids visible
above the hills from miles away, he
managed to keep things going in a neat little triangle. The most important point of the triangle was the conference room, where an over-
flowing schedule of meetings kept teams of people pouring into and
out of the room well into the evening, while other teams waited their
turn just outside the door. The conference room was where all the
real work got done. Just down the hall was the office of a Cannavino
subordinate who collected all the latest IBM gadgets and the latest
equipment from competitors. The office functioned as a toy room
where Cannavino could go tinker. Right across from the conference
room was Cannavino's office, which he kept bare of paperwork and
used mainly as a retreat. As grand as the office was, Cannavino used it
primarily as a high-tech phone booth where he made calls either on his
conventional phone or his fancy new desktop videoconferencing system,
which he used to talk to such industry luminaries as Intel's chief executive, Andy Grove.

At the beginning of each day, Cannavino's assistant printed out his
schedule on a couple of punch cards, reminders of the good old days
when every big company in the world relied on IBM's punch-card
systems for their data processing. Cannavino consulted the cards to
figure out how to keep moving along the legs of his triangle that day.

In early 1992, as Cannavino sat at the center of his universe, he seemed comfortable. "I feel better about this year than I did last year," he told a reporter. "I like my product line better and like the pace I'm moving at." But one afternoon in June 1992, a call from an assistant blew up Cannavino's neat little world.

The assistant called to tell Cannavino about an announcement from Compaq of a completely redesigned line of inexpensive computers. This was just eight months after Compaq's chief executive, Rod Canion, had been forced out, seemingly leaving the company in chaos. The new guy, Eckhard Pfeiffer, had talked about producing less expensive machines, but Cannavino hadn't expected anything anywhere near this fast. The prices were at least as shocking. They were at clone levels, some even below clone levels. Compaq had always traded on its excellent reputation for quality and had used its ability to innovate to price its products at the same level as IBM or even higher. Now here was Compaq with a whole line of products costing some 40 percent less than IBM's.

Cannavino scrambled to react, but it took days of meetings just to formulate a strategy. It took five weeks to respond, even though the initial counter was just some modest price cuts that still left IBM's prices as much as a third higher than Compaq's. In the meantime, Dell, another formidable competitor with a good reputation for quality, came out with its own line of extremely inexpensive PCs. Between the two of them, Compaq and Dell set off a price war that saw prices crash 40 to 50 percent in 1992. Nineteen ninety-one had already been a tough year for PC prices, so having them fall almost in half in a single year put more pressure on PC makers than they had ever seen.

Cannavino was unprepared. Although he had been trying to get costs down, his costs were still so high that he couldn't possibly sell the machines at anything approaching the new levels. He had no development in the works that would let him respond in less than four months. He had to stall for time.

He eventually tried to talk his way out of the problem with his best bravado. When told that Chairman John Akers had promised that Cannavino would respond to Compaq's aggressive moves by September, Cannavino joked, "Did he say what year?"[1]

When Cannavino was being serious, he and other PC executives said, "Watch this space. By the fall, we'll have everything in order. We'll be able to compete with the best of them."

The problem was that saying that much cheaper and more powerful machines were on the way shut down orders for IBM PCs through the summer of 1992. Customers decided that if the machines were going to be that much better and less expensive, they'd just wait. The second quarter was the worst Cannavino had ever seen. The only thing that kept him from getting into a complete funk about that quarter was that the third quarter was even worse.

Nineteen ninety-two was going to be a long year for all of IBM.

Cannavino had seemed to finally be on the verge of some significant innovation in early 1992. It had looked like he might even have been able to twit Microsoft in the process.

Cannavino had been one of the first executives from a big hardware maker to spot the possibilities of so-called pen-based computers. He had been visiting State Farm, a large IBM customer, and had seen a prototype of one of the computers that had been given to State Farm by GO, a start-up that was working on an operating system for the new type of computer. The idea was that users would be able to use a pen to print directly on the screen, and the computer would recognize the characters. This would mean State Farm could have insurance adjusters print on electronic forms while standing in front of a damaged car and have the information go directly into the central computer, eliminating the days it might otherwise take to have all the information keypunched into the system. Users would be able to write letters or notes without knowing how to type. Just being able to use a pen to navigate around on the screen would eliminate the need to fuss around with various keys or with a mouse. A pen felt much more natural to people. Through 1990 and 1991, a lot of the PC industry's pundits were saying that pen-based computers were the most important innovation since the original IBM PC a decade before, and Cannavino seemed to be in the forefront.

Cannavino was managing to irk Bill Gates in the process because he was going to use GO's operating system rather than one from Microsoft. GO was trying to establish its software as the standard for pen-based computers, just as Gates had established DOS and then Windows as the operating-system standards in the mainstream PC world. Jerry Kaplan, one of GO's founders, had a head start on Gates in developing his software, and if IBM came out with a pen-based system that took the world by storm before Gates could counterattack, then Kaplan might be able to use an IBM hardware success to help him establish his operating system as a standard just the way Gates had in 1981 with the original IBM PC. Gates could lose out on the exciting new world of pen computing.

In setting up his pen computer project in 1990, Cannavino engaged in a little subterfuge to avoid having a fight with any of the managers of his product-development teams. At a meeting of the executives running the teams, he said he wanted to finance the pen project but didn't have any more money in his budget. He asked whether anyone had any projects that they'd be willing to kill. It was a silly question. At IBM, prestige depends on how many people an executive has working for him or how much money he controls, so no one willingly gives up any people or money.

After a pause, though, Kathy Vieth said she'd be happy to kill some projects to make room for the pen work.

"Everybody thought I was nuts," she says.

What no one but Cannavino and Vieth knew was that he had already asked her to run the pen project. She was merely eliminating work in a budget that she would turn over to someone else, in order to create a new budget for herself.

But once work got underway, Cannavino began letting his advantage slip away, partly by bungling his relationship with Kaplan and GO.

Kaplan was a classic Silicon Valley entrepreneur who just didn't mesh well with IBM. The prematurely gray Kaplan would slouch around, wearing blue jeans with the seat hanging so low, his pants always seemed to be about to fall off. He'd sleep late. He didn't care much for process but loved new ideas. Kaplan had previously co-founded a company specializing in artificial intelligence, an idea that turned out to be ahead of its time but that was a noble effort and made Kaplan a sizable sum. Later, Kaplan did a piece of software with Lotus founder Mitch Kapor that attempted to create a whole new class of software called personal information managers. It, too, didn't do well, but it generated enormous attention as an inventive attempt to move personal computers into a whole new class of business tool. By the late 1980s, Kaplan had decided that the industry had talked long enough about the possibilities of handwriting recognition, so he decided to go off and try to make the technology real.

Kaplan immediately ran into IBM. IBM's research labs had done some of the pioneering work in handwriting recognition. In fact, a year before Kaplan began considering building a prototype of a pen-based computer, an IBM researcher in Yorktown Heights was demonstrating to visitors a prototype operating system on a prototype computer. As usual, though, the work languished in IBM's lab because no one in the IBM PC business wanted to try anything so radically different as a pen-based computer. The best the IBM researchers could do was publish their results, which Kaplan uncovered as he did his research and tried to figure out how to design his software.

When Kaplan began trying in 1990 to line up hardware manufacturers that would make pen-based computers using his operating system, he got IBM interested in what he hoped would be his defining relationship. If IBM made systems that got him established in the marketplace, then he'd find ways to help IBM design better systems, possibly faster than its competitors. IBM might finally have a strategic advantage in an important part of the PC marketplace. But Kaplan was put off from the beginning. When the IBM business executives came calling, they'd bring along a lawyer and a "corporate conduct" person. Kaplan thought the executives ought to be the ones running the show; instead, they'd leave the room frequently so the lawyer and the corporate conduct person could tell them what they could and couldn't discuss. Even when an IBM PC executive would talk about making a bland presentation on GO to an industry group, he'd agree with Kaplan on what the content ought to be—but then add, "Of course, I have to check with the lawyers first."

The first time Kaplan went to Boca Raton to talk to IBM about a deal, he didn't bring his lawyer, because Silicon Valley etiquette says that's too formal for a first meeting. But when he arrived at the conference room in Boca, he found fourteen IBMers, including several lawyers. The IBMers spent the first two hours using foils just to explain who they were and what organizations reported to them. He eventually decided that everyone in the room had veto power on the project, but nobody had the authority to say yes. Later in 1990, when IBM summoned Kaplan to Boca to face a "technology review board" that would decide whether his technology was worth IBM's pursuing, he walked past the main Boca receptionist, sitting behind bulletproof glass, and found himself ushered into a holding cell, a bare room with cinder-block walls. When he finally was allowed into the auditorium where the board was meeting, he saw two hundred IBMers arranged by rank in semicircular rows behind the board members—it reminded him of Dante and his circles of hell. Kaplan, a droll speaker who talks slowly, usually with the hint of a smirk on his face, was even more astonished when he walked to the podium and found a series of lights built into it. A green light saying, "Go" went on. After nineteen minutes, a yellow light flashed, saying, "One minute." Sixty seconds later, a red light told him to stop. Clearly, Kaplan and IBM were not going to get along.

Kaplan was once asked to fly to Boca a day early for a meeting in 1991. He found that he'd been asked to come early just so he could brief some IBM staffs on what he was going to say at the main meeting the following day. Then he learned that the main meeting was just a briefing, too, for some executives who would then go off and brief more-senior executives. Kaplan kept wondering when his project would reach the ears of IBM executives at a real meeting, where a decision would actually be made.

Kaplan found the internal politics of IBM to be impossible to figure out. He'd set up meetings with IBM Japan in 1990 and 1991 to talk about opportunities for pen-based computers there, but then he'd find the meetings canceled for reasons that didn't become clear until much later. It turned out that Kaplan had naïvely told the IBMers in Boca about the meetings and they had raised a stink internally, contending that they "owned" responsibility for pen computing. IBM Japan had to back down, even though there were possibly greater opportunities in Japan than in the United States and even though Boca wasn't going to do anything about them. Kaplan learned that he shouldn't send anything to IBM in writing. He would invariably get calls from six people at IBM saying they owned whatever topic he was writing about and castigating him for writing to whomever he had chosen. Kaplan also found that any letter he sent was copied and sent around to at least fifteen people, all of whom would then have to be drawn into any future discussions on the subject. Sending a letter was the quickest way of turning a one-on-one conversation into a series of meetings.

As IBM drove Kaplan to distraction, he began cozying up to AT&T in 1992. He had expected to find AT&T to be just as bureaucratic as IBM, because it was equally big, but he found the people at AT&T to be far more decisive and discovered a healthy lack of interest in political games there. AT&T also seemed to have a much clearer vision of the possibilities for pen computing than IBM did.

Cannavino's pen-computer operation had actually done pretty well in 1990 and 1991 on the design of the pen hardware. It took his people several months of paper shuffling to set up a small operation of about fifty people in Boca Raton in 1990, but the group was small enough and focused enough that it moved fast once it got started. The group produced a computer rugged enough so that a UPS driver could have it drop to the floor of his cab without hurting the computer. The IBM group also came up with a new type of screen and a few other things that made its computer at least the equal of anything available at the dawn of the pen computer market.

Cannavino also got lucky for a change. NCR was the one big company that had seen the potential of pen computing well before he had, and it had announced a product in 1991, nine months before IBM did, but then it ran into problems meeting FCC requirements limiting computers' emissions of radio waves. NCR had simply tested what the computer emitted and thought it was fine. But when someone using a pen touches the screen of one of these computers, it turns out that the pen and the person form a large antenna, greatly increasing the emission of electromagnetic waves that can interfere with radio stations' signals. NCR still hadn't won FCC approval by the time GO was ready for its software's launch in April 1992. IBM, meanwhile, had chosen a magnesium cover for its computer solely to make it more rugged and discovered quite by accident that the magnesium cover limited radio-wave emissions. IBM got its FCC clearance even before NCR.

Even though Cannavino was as well positioned strategically as he had ever been in a PC market, things started to fall apart even as GO was announcing its software and declaring that the pen market was now open for business. GO's top executives staged world-class demonstrations of new types of software applications that ran on their operating system, such as a sort of word processor that let a traveling salesman use a pen to modify a form letter and fax a thank-you note to a hot prospect within minutes of leaving the customer's office. The demonstrations, together with a video full of quick cuts and sly jokes, made the crowd of three hundred customers, industry analysts, and reporters feel as though they had just witnessed the dawn of a new age in computing. When it came time for IBM to announce its pen computer in an adjoining room, Kathy Vieth, the executive making the presentation, tried to maintain the enthusiasm, but her script, vetted by the lawyers, made that hard. One of her big points was that the pen computer exemplified IBM's newfound willingness to throw out all the rules, so much so that this was the first product in IBM's history that would be known only by its name, the ThinkPad, and wouldn't carry a product number. In fact, the press release did list the ThinkPad as the 2521. When Vieth built to what was meant to be a rousing conclusion, she delivered in her deepest, most sincere voice the line, "We are firmly on a path toward meeting customer requirements."

That lame line in April 1992 was the high-water mark in IBM's involvement with pen computing. Sue King, the development executive who had led the IBM team, had already accepted a similar job with Apple and left IBM within days. Vieth, a more senior executive who was the force behind the project, took one of IBM's many severance offers over the summer of 1992, leaving to become a ski instructor at Vail. Even the IBM PR person, the only other IBMer in evidence at the announcement, left within months to go to Dell.

Kaplan says that during the summer when he stopped hearing from Vieth or anyone else at IBM, he tried to track them down and found that they were all gone.

When the pen computer market changed its focus later in 1992 and became more focused on helping people communicate while on the move, rather than compute on the move, Cannavino was in no position to move with the market. The price war that Compaq had started in March was hurting Cannavino so much by midsummer that he was having to cut jobs as fast as he could. Yet because he had to follow the standard pattern of letting people volunteer to take a severance package that they had months to consider, he didn't have any idea who was leaving and who was staying. Cannavino had to impose a six-month hiring freeze just to give him some room to see who was leaving and where he needed to hire people to replace those departing.

By the end of 1992, EO, a start-up, came out with a tiny pen-based device that could even receive and send faxes over a cellular modem. Through a link with EO, AT&T set itself up to do very well in pen computing. Even those companies that didn't do anything radical came out with computers much lighter than the six-pound brick IBM announced in April. But Cannavino could move forward only a little bit on his product's capabilities.

By the end of the year, Cannavino had lost any advantage he'd ever had in pen computing.

Nineteen ninety-two was turning into a rout for all of IBM. PCs and workstations had finally become so powerful that they were cutting the legs out from under the mainframe business, yet IBM had nothing around to replace it because the company had squandered all its strategic advantages in the PC business over the years. In 1992, Microsoft and Intel—which had seized the advantages IBM had left for them to take—together earned close to $2 billion, while IBM's PC business lost $1 billion.

The most powerful workstations were now as powerful as small mainframes had been just a couple of years before. Mainframe technology had improved, too—a fact that Akers had always used to argue that PCs and workstations would never quite catch up to what mainframes could do. But for lots of applications, the fact that mainframes were faster didn't matter. Running a garden-variety program such as a payroll application for a corporate department required only a certain amount of processing power. In the past, that would have meant a small mainframe costing perhaps $4 million. By mid-1992, that processing power could be provided by a workstation costing $100,000. There wasn't any need to buy a mainframe, even if it was more powerful. With the economy in trouble worldwide in 1992, even in Japan, the pressure on companies to keep expenses low made it even less likely that someone would pony up the extra money to buy the more costly machine. In the past, IBM would have pocketed close to $3 million of the small mainframe's price as its gross profit—meaning what's left over after the cost of manufacturing. With the workstation, IBM might earn thirty thousand dollars, providing IBM even got the business, which wasn't that likely because IBM had less than 20 percent of the workstation market.

IBM's problems didn't appear right away in 1992 because the most important models in a new generation of IBM mainframes started to become available in late 1991, and demand for the powerful machines was backed up enough that their sales supported IBM through the first half. Akers expected those new machines to carry IBM in the second half, too, because pent-up demand for a new generation of machines had always lasted several quarters in years past. This time, though, the demand petered out after just a few months. After that, IBM entered a void and took its mainframe competitors with it.

A funny thing happens when a mainframe company finds that buyers have disappeared. It tends to cut prices far more than companies in other industries would ever consider. That's because, once the huge development costs have been accounted for and the kinks have been worked out of the manufacturing process for a new machine, a mainframe costs just thirty cents or so to produce for every dollar in its list price. That makes mainframes extraordinarily profitable when demand is strong, but it also gives manufacturers a terribly long way to go in cutting prices before they get to the point where they'd be selling machines for less than the manufacturing cost. Sure enough, as the summer of 1992 turned into fall and no mainframe buyers could be found, IBM and its major mainframe competitors—Hitachi Data Systems and Amdahl in the United States and Europe; Hitachi and Fujitsu in Japan—picked up where they had left off in the price war of 1989. Mainframes began selling—when they sold at all—at a 50 percent discount in late 1992. By early 1993, those discounts hit 70 percent. For IBM, whose elaborate bureaucracy, huge sales force, and very culture was built around the idea that it could make things for thirty cents and sell them for a dollar, the idea of making things for thirty cents and selling them for thirty to fifty cents was devastating.

The problems in the mainframe business mangled computer companies throughout the world in 1992. Digital Equipment and Amdahl laid off thousands more people. France's Bull had another huge loss. Even in Japan, where the competitors to IBM had always seemed to be the strongest, arch-rival Fujitsu reported its first loss ever, and Hitachi might suffer even more than Fujitsu in the long run because, unlike Fujitsu, Hitachi doesn't have much of a PC or workstation business that could take up the slack left by the mainframe operations. If IBM had focused too much on its Japanese competitors, ignoring all the small U.S. companies that would give it fits, then the big Japanese companies had paid too much attention to competing with IBM and were losing out to those same tiny entrepreneurial outfits.

At IBM, Akers was totally unprepared. He had assured securities analysts in late 1991 that the gross margins for IBM as a whole would stabilize around 52 percent, meaning that, for the company as a whole, something sold for a dollar would cost forty-eight cents to make. He said he knew that 52 percent was a horribly low number for IBM, which had become used to gross margins in the 60 to 65 percent range, sometimes even higher. But he said he was a realistic sort—even as he was kidding himself into thinking that the mainframe market would hold up. Akers told securities analysts in late 1991 that he would cut costs so fast, he would have IBM's earnings back to their glory days by 1994, even with 52 percent gross margins, but mainframe prices fell so fast in 1992 that Akers was having to deal with gross margins almost ten points lower than he said he would grudgingly accept over the whole 1992–1994 period. And margins were going nowhere but down.

With a company as large as IBM, a change of ten percentage points in the basic profit margin was enough to produce a startling turnaround. IBM went from a $6 billion profit in 1990 to a 1992 loss of $5 billion, a deficit so big that, at the time IBM reported its results, the loss was the largest any corporation had recorded in the history of profit-making enterprise.

By 1992, IBMers had started joking about the new severance offers that seemed to be coming more often as problems mounted. Using a shorthand, they said the new offer would be a "seven, seven, two, one, and two." That meant that seven years would be added to the retiree's age in calculating his pension. Seven years would be added to his years of service. And as much as two years of salary would be paid. But the IBMer would have only one minute to think about it and would have to take two people with him.

Sure enough, as 1992 worsened, Akers stepped up the pressure on people to take the severance packages and leave the company. He tried to keep IBMers from thinking jobs were being slashed wholesale by consistently underestimating how many were leaving. He would insist that the number was only fifteen thousand, then reluctantly raise that to twenty thousand, then acknowledge that the number might even be a bit higher—when the number was always clearly going to be much higher—turned out to be forty thousand, more than twice the estimate he had made in early 1992. Akers also tried to use IBM's curious language to hide the fact that many of the people leaving were now being fired. The people being fired were referred to as MIAs—for management-initiated attrition. People weren't fired, they were MIAed.

Akers tried to have the personnel department handle the job cuts as humanely as it always had, making sure that everyone whose job was eliminated as part of the cuts was offered another job if he wanted one. But the system could no longer handle this kind of change. Cutting forty thousand jobs was just too many even for IBM to handle.

To those inside, IBM became a game of musical chairs. Every time they thought they had secured a seat, the music started up again, and when it stopped, another seat had disappeared. People spent all spring and summer in 1992 scrambling for seats. Personnel kept trying to find seats for the "boat people," who found that their jobs had been eliminated, but often wound up offering five or six people the same job, hoping like crazy that only one person wanted it.

Bill Russell, a fourteen-year employee in payroll, says he was told that no job existed for him after his position was wiped out. Akers kept insisting that no one was being laid off, that IBM's revered full-employment policy continued, "but if that wasn't a layoff, then I don't know what is," Russell said.

As usual, Akers compounded his managers' problems by making so many of the departures voluntary. He also plunged the company into chaos by leaving the latest severance offer open for months in the United States, so it wouldn't be clear until July 31, 1992, just who was leaving and who was staying.

The personnel department had tried to make the offers as enticing as possible by telling people that they could decide as late as Friday, July 31, and still have a check covering their severance payment by the time they left work that day. Some IBM managers even decided to let people retire up until 11:59 P.M. that Friday by calling a special number —sort of a 1-800-RETIRED.

So many people took the payments that the company barely functioned for a couple of weeks afterward. Salesmen set up meetings with customers for the following weeks, then decided under pressure on that Friday to take the severance package and leave the customers wondering what had happened. Many of those who left were so disillusioned by the way IBM had given them the bum's rush toward the door that they wouldn't help those who stayed when it came to sorting out the problems.

Greg Rusnack, who spent thirteen years in accounting at IBM, says that when someone called him about a box of paperwork, he said, "Oh, that one. I went to a football game last weekend and I must have used that box to start the fire in the grill."

Months later, things still hadn't been sorted out. Sanford Witlin, who left IBM after twenty-six years in accounting, says he called personnel to find out what the final count had been on how many people left in a certain department. Personnel didn't have a clue. Someone finally took a ruler and measured all the paperwork on the desks. The person estimated how many departures there were per inch of height in the piles and offered a guess. Witlin, who says he had to go on tranquilizers toward the end of his time at IBM because of all the stress, said he knew one woman who was declared "surplus"—IBM's way of saying her job had disappeared. Then, when she was offered what was supposedly a new job, she said, "Wait a minute. That's my old job." Witlin said personnel had offered her "the same job, the same location, the same everything. It was total confusion."

By fall 1992, things were out of control. Akers had been predicting that the third quarter would get the company going again, but business died in the last couple of weeks of the quarter. Akers blamed a currency crisis in Europe—just as he had so often blamed IBM's troubles on worldwide economic problems, the Persian Gulf War, or whatever—but the currency crisis abated early in the fourth quarter, so any lost business should have come back to IBM quickly. It didn't. The fourth quarter turned into IBM's biggest disaster ever—it was the first time IBM had ever had a loss in a quarter just based on its operations and not including the effects of any write-off.

The board continued to express its support for Akers, but he had already lost the faith of just about everyone who worked for him. Some employees began circulating a rap song about the man who was now widely called John Fakers. Others circulated a song set to the tune of "Big John." Called "Big Bad John," part of it went like this:

Every morning at Armonk you could see him arrive
In a big fancy car that a chauffeur would drive.
Kind of big in the wallet and narrow in the mind,
And every VP knew how to kiss the behind of Big John.

Big John, Big John, Big bad John.

Nobody seemed to know why John was the boss.
He just never cared about the profit or loss.
He didn't do much except raise his own pay.
Many earn in a year what he makes in a day, Big John.

Big John, Big John, Big bad John.

As Cannavino strained to hold his operation together during the 1992 summer price wars, he fought to keep down what he thought was the most ridiculous of ideas: that IBM should build its own clone.

Marketing people, especially in Asia and Europe, found that they had a hard time selling any big system to customers without cheap PCs. The customers might want an IBM mainframe and might plan to hook hundreds of PCs to it, but the customers didn't want to pay for IBM's premium-priced PCs when they knew that lots of cheap ones were to be had. When Cannavino balked at the idea of a clone, the marketing people began fighting their battle in the press—a tactic that may be common with the federal government in Washington, D.C., but that had never before been seen at IBM. Marketing executives were actually calling reporters and leaking their plans for clones, hoping to get the notion so widely spread that Cannavino would have no choice but to give in and make them.

Cannavino decided to deal with the issue at a press briefing in May 1992 at the Marriott Marquis in Times Square in Manhattan. Cannavino seemed determined. He called Bill McCracken, a senior marketing executive in Europe, who was pushing the idea of a clone, and had what Cannavino told his staff at the time was "a nice long chat" about how Cannavino wouldn't do a clone. McCracken got fed up, told Cannavino off, and refused to attend Cannavino's press briefing. The night before the press gathering, the briefing sessions with Cannavino continued until close to midnight, concluding with one where he had fifty people sitting around a table in a meeting room while he paced around the table. One of those at the table said it reminded her of the scene in *The Untouchables* where Robert De Niro's Al Capone walks around the table carrying a baseball bat, then suddenly bashes in someone's head. She kept wondering whose head Cannavino was going to smash.

At the press gathering, more than one hundred people packed into a low-ceilinged meeting room for a typically overproduced IBM gathering. Not only did Cannavino have a microphone, even though the room was small enough that everyone could have heard him without one, but there were wireless mikes to be passed around by a legion of IBM staff assistants during the question-and-answer period. In the front, up under the klieg lights and near the huge speakers, were several IBMers wearing headsets so they could talk to those in the back of the room—near the IBM TV camera and bank of phones—and stage-manage the production.

Cannavino tried to make light of his problems. He asserted that his operation was the most profitable PC business in the world—even though he was widely disbelieved because the IBM accounting system seemed to be skewed in his favor and though even by his own internal accounting he was on his way to losing a total of $1 billion in 1992. (Carl Conti, who had recently retired as the head of the group that included the mainframe business, said in late 1992, "I don't have any idea whether he's making any money. And that's the problem. Neither does he. I used to say to my good friend Cannavino, 'Jimmy, I'm carrying you. When are you going to get your act together?' ") Cannavino blithely acknowledged that IBM and Bill Gates's Microsoft had done a lousy job on OS/2, then, when a phone rang in the back of the room and disrupted the meeting, he joked, "Someone's shoe phone is ringing. Maybe it's Bill."

Cannavino tried to show off some of the new technology he would have coming on-line, culminating in a videoconference with ex-IBMer Joe Guglielmi in California to show what Cannavino would soon make available on people's desktops through an arrangement with videoconferencing-equipment maker PictureTel. When the big moment came, though, the sound didn't work. Someone tried to restart the system, but the conference still didn't work. Guglielmi just kept moving his lips, but no words came out. Cannavino tried to move on quickly.

Toward the end of the conference, Cannavino casually let slip that IBM didn't intend to do a clone. When pressed on the question, Cannavino said firmly, "The IBM company is not going to do a clone. You want a clone strategy? That's the IBM clone strategy."

But even the head of IBM's PC business couldn't prevent the European and Asian marketing operations from selling clones. Cannavino continued to insist in the weeks following the conference that IBM wasn't doing a clone, but an IBM *subsidiary* was going to do a clone.

Compaq had looked into doing a clone of its own and decided that it would just cheapen the Compaq image, so when Compaq executives were told at a meeting of securities analysts about IBM's plans, one blurted out, "There is a God!"

Through the warm summer nights of 1992, Cannavino kept his staffs plugging away at what he would bill as a relaunch of IBM's PC business. While other American businesses that were shrinking and reorganizing talked about "right-sizing" or "downsizing," Cannavino said he was "capsizing" his business.

His teams kept working routinely until midnight or 1:00 A.M. Sometimes, they'd work so late, they'd just have time to go home and take a quick shower before turning around and going back to work. Cannavino spent a lot of his nights at the Holiday Inn in White Plains. He tried to fire up his staff by telling them about the battles he was fighting with the Management Committee on behalf of the PC business. As part of what he said was an attempt to "get aggressive with corporate" and reduce the corporate overhead costs the PC business had to bear, Cannavino told his staff that at one quarterly review meeting with the MC, "we put up a chart that said we think corporate is too expensive in the following areas." He paused for effect. "At that moment, a nuclear bomb could have gone off, and for a second I thought it would. It was sort of like pulling all the rods out of a nuclear reactor. You find they snap out but don't go in so easily. But after a moment, Akers said, 'They're right.' "

Once Cannavino won the right to duck some of the responsibility for corporate overhead, he turned control of the hardware part of his PC business over to Bob Corrigan, a manufacturing expert who had been on Cannavino's staff for years. Corrigan was a nuts-and-bolts sort who didn't care much for the traditional trappings of authority. He drove himself to work, traveled on his own, carried his own briefcase. He worked hard but left at a reasonable hour to spend time with his wife and five sons. He insisted that his staff do the same. Those who worked for him found him so refreshingly different that some called him "Mr. Morale" behind his back. Once he got expanded authority, Corrigan began refusing to accept just about any bit of corporate overhead that the accounting department tried to assign to him. He refused, for instance, to pay any of the cost of the corporate jets.

"I never get to use them, anyway," he said.

He also made his employees double up in offices in Somers, New York, so he could pay rent on less space. Then he decided that the space was still too expensive. He told the centralized accounting department at corporate headquarters that it had better cut his rent or he'd leave. When the accountants didn't believe him, he took preliminary steps to rent space in a nearby building and told the accountants they had lost his business. They cut his rent.

Corrigan didn't cut any of the nearly ten thousand people in the PC hardware business—a huge part of his expenses—and most of the cost cutting his business accomplished really came about because Cannavino had convinced the MC to shift responsibility for overhead to other business, but he did make some progress. By September, Corrigan was ready to match prices with Compaq or Dell or whomever. He brought out a new line of products, called ValuePoint, that carried low-enough prices that they finally got sales going again after the dog days of summer, when customers were just waiting to see what IBM would do.

Over the long summer, Corrigan had lost so much market share that it briefly seemed that Apple would claim the market-share leadership from IBM in 1992 for the first time since the original PC hit its stride. Even Compaq was running ahead of IBM in some market-share surveys. But ValuePoint picked up enough sales that IBM sold more PCs in the fourth quarter than in any previous quarter, and IBM just pulled ahead of Apple by the end of the year.

With sales picking up in the fall of 1992, Cannavino decided that Corrigan should move into the public spotlight as Mr. IBM PC. But when it came time for Cannavino to unveil his new organization and for Corrigan to take center stage, Corrigan limped through the proceedings because of a knee problem he had developed jogging. (The fiftyish Corrigan, a devoted jogger, says he has the cardiovascular system of a thirty-five-year-old and the knees of an eighty-year-old.) Cannavino's staff tried again in October 1992 at the big Comdex trade show in Las Vegas, where Corrigan was scheduled to give one of the keynote speeches. Corrigan, they decided, needed something glitzy. This was Las Vegas, after all. And he was going to have to stand out somehow at a show where more than 100,000 people jammed into the convention center's aisles each day, where competitors' speeches were sure to be full of dramatic, quick-cut, special-effects video, and where anyone who got bored might wander off to watch show girls in some real spectacle.

Corrigan came onstage wearing a cardigan sweater that was supposed to remind everyone of IBM's relaxed new dress code but that also made the balding, gray-haired Corrigan look grandfatherly, out of step with the fast-paced show and an industry changing at the speed of light. Following the reminders written into the script on his TelePromp-Ters, he smiled often, but he did it by closing his eyes and tilting his head to the side, as though about to slip off into dreamland. Corrigan kept missing his cues. Huge screens on either side of him were lighted up with video designed to have the people on the screen seem to be talking to Corrigan, but one time he finished his part too quickly and had to wait several seconds for the face on the screen to respond. Another time, the face on the screen answered a different question than the one Corrigan had posed. What was supposedly a live demonstration of an IBM PC translating English into Spanish fell apart when a translation was so far off that titters spread among the Spanish speakers in the audience. Then the person doing the demonstration let on that the whole thing had been rigged, saying, "Oh, I guess I pressed the wrong button." The final indignity was that during the whole second half of Corrigan's speech, a clanking noise offstage made it hard even to follow what he was saying.

It was painful to watch. Corrigan left anyone who attended the keynote with the impression that grandfatherly IBM still hadn't figured out how to rock and roll with the rest of the PC industry.

By the end of 1992, Cannavino, through Corrigan, had made some progress in repositioning his business to compete better in the PC price wars. But most of the progress had been a phony kind. When Cannavino won his battle before the MC about how much corporate overhead he should carry, he made his profit-and-loss statement look better, but he didn't cut any real costs. IBM still owned the same number of corporate jets, even if Corrigan didn't have to help pay for them. IBM still owned the same expensive building in Somers, even if Corrigan was paying less for his space there. IBM still had the same size sales force. Those expenses had just been shifted, perhaps to another product group, such as mainframes. But the costs hadn't disappeared.

Cannavino had made just limited progress in getting control of marketing; he still didn't have a real sales force. Cannavino had done some things to make sure he kept pace with competitors in getting to market quickly with the obvious new technologies, such as whatever the latest Intel processor was. But he still wasn't getting to market faster than his competitors or doing anything innovative. Cannavino talked a lot about decentralizing in September 1992 when he "capsized" the PC business, but he really just went from having one type of committee running his business to having another type of committee run it. Before September, if he had wanted to create a product, he'd had to run a gauntlet of thirty people in different product groups and various national marketing forces, any one of whom could have nonconcurred and held things up. By September, he had had that system removed. But he replaced it with an executive board of ten people, who would jointly rule on what the PC hardware and software businesses should do. At Compaq, the key decisions on a product are made by one person; at IBM's PC business, making a decision on anything of consequence still required a conference room.

The IBM PC business had started so well back in 1980. By 1993, though, the result of that business seemed to have little future. IBM had lost all ability to lead the market and innovate ahead of competitors. The PC business had been reduced to one that lost $1 billion in 1992 and that seemed likely to be only marginally profitable at best in 1993 and beyond. Cannavino occasionally expressed the odd idea that price soon would become a less important factor in purchases of PCs. At that point, he figured, people would return to IBM because they trusted the brand name. But he was wrong. By 1993, the problems in IBM's PC business and at the company as a whole had tarnished the brand name. And price will always matter in PCs. PCs are consumer electronics, and buyers will watch price the same way they do when shopping around for a CD player. Cannavino assumes that, because the price wars have forced some PC makers such as Tandy and Epson out of the business, the price wars will abate, but that's naïve. U.S. airlines have been going through a shakeout for more than fifteen years, and numerous airlines have gone out of business. Every year, airlines talk about how the fare wars have finally ended, and every year one of the dwindling number of airlines starts another one. Ask Pan Am how much good it got out of its revered brand name.

FIFTEEN

John Akers was finally in serious trouble in late 1992. After years of one step forward and two backward, he had promised board members that IBM would take another step forward in the second half of the year. Securities analysts, with some guidance from IBM, had begun 1992 projecting a $4 billion profit for the year, but the prospects for any kind of profit began to fade in late September as IBM's business in Europe fell apart. Akers was on his way to a $5 billion loss, missing analysts' early-year projections by an astounding $9 billion. IBM's long-slumbering board began to stir.

Akers had planned a board meeting in Tokyo at the end of September 1992, the sort of overseas boondoggle the chairman of IBM traditionally held every year or so to help ensure the board stayed tame. Akers had expected an upbeat board meeting—if it could even be called a meeting. Dozens of former executives and directors came along on these several-day overseas trips, and all brought their spouses, so any meetings were just chances for old cronies to catch up with one another and see the world at IBM's expense. Instead of just sitting around collecting praise for getting IBM back on track, though, Akers had to start thinking about how he was going to defend himself.

Some former executives suggested that he ought to cancel the festivities. IBM was in enough trouble that spending a couple of million dollars on a board meeting seemed to be in bad taste. Akers refused. The former directors and executives who had been invited then managed to show Akers up by canceling their plans to attend. Only a couple who didn't get the word that a protest movement was afoot attended the sessions in Tokyo.

Even with the embarrassing earnings problems and an unprecedented show of lack of faith by former executives, it still took the board a while to decide it had a real problem. Maybe that's not so surprising, given the makeup of the board. Three-fourths of the members were just window dressing, designed to put some impressive names on the board—presidents of big universities, former U.S. cabinet officials, and so forth. Of the five members of the executive committee, which was where the real decisions were made, four were pals who had no computer-industry experience and who had been on the board for a decade, approving all the decisions that had helped undo IBM. They were Jim Burke, former chief executive of Johnson & Johnson, a pharmaceutical company; Tom Murphy, chief executive of Cap Cities/ABC, a broadcaster; Dick Munro, former chief executive of Time, a publisher; and Steve Bechtel, head of Bechtel Industries, a construction company. The fifth member of the executive committee was John Opel, the former IBM chairman who had had more to do with creating the problems Akers was trying to solve than anyone else had. As the five tried to find odd moments in which to talk privately during the gala events in Tokyo, they felt they had a serious problem but weren't sure how serious. They equivocated about what to say to Akers.

What finally got them going was that in the clubby world of executive America, everywhere these five turned, they found someone wondering why they hadn't done something about IBM's problems. GM's board had thrown out its CEO; why couldn't IBM's? Compaq's chairman had thrown out its CEO and turned around the company; why couldn't IBM's board move? Munro complained to a friend that he couldn't go to any meetings of boards where he was a member without having someone raise the IBM question. Burke griped that he couldn't go *anywhere* without having one of his CEO friends ask him what was going on.

Former IBM chairman Frank Cary had also managed to keep things stirred up. He had been angry with Akers since right before he retired from the board in March 1991, when Akers had announced a dismal earnings forecast just a month after telling the board that things were finally looking up. Cary didn't have a board seat any longer, but he did have access to just about all its members because he had put all five of the members of the executive committee on the board and had appointed most of the other directors, too. Cary arranged the occasional lunch or phone chat with one of them, particularly with Burke, and laid out what he thought IBM's problems were.

Akers still might have avoided culpability for IBM's problems, but barely two months after the late September scare, he had to confess publicly, in early December 1992, that he had missed his financial forecasts yet again. He had expected that earnings would snap back in the fourth quarter, especially in Europe, where Akers had blamed his September problems on a currency crisis that had scared potential customers at the end of the third quarter but that had long since been resolved. But now Akers had to announce that Europe had become worse, not better. He also had to acknowledge that he didn't have a clue as to why.

Akers once again went before the securities analysts and reporters to explain a problem—the second time this had happened in the three Decembers since he'd faced down an analyst who dared to ask what assurance Akers could give that earnings bombshells wouldn't become IBM's annual Christmas present to investors. Akers once again announced a big write-off—this time large enough to give IBM a $5 billion loss, the widest deficit any company had ever reported. (GM and Ford both subsequently reported larger losses because of a change in an accounting rule that didn't contribute to IBM's problems.) Akers once again produced plans to take another huge slice of jobs out of his work force. And he again insisted that everything was under control.

He gathered the analysts and reporters together in a crowded little auditorium in the basement of the IBM building at Fifty-seventh street and Madison Avenue in Manhattan. In the polite way of IBM press conferences, Akers systematically went around the room calling on questioners. When someone asked whether Akers was thinking of stepping aside or bringing in outsiders to help with the restructurings "that seem to be an annual event now," Akers paused and stared at the questioner.

"No," Akers said. "I've not given any thought to stepping aside. . . . The board supports me, and I do not plan to step aside."

Akers started to move on but caught himself and went back to the questioner. "You forgot to tell me who you are," he said coldly.

The reporter identified himself by name and said he was from *Investor's Daily.*

Akers again started to move on but then went back to the questioner a final time. Just in case anyone had missed his iciness, Akers
glared at the questioner and said slowly, "Pleased to make your acquaintance."

Despite the bravado, Akers was about ready to call it quits. One
former IBM executive says that when Akers told him about the latest
job cuts, the write-offs, and the big loss in early December, Akers
insisted that he would see IBM through to a solution, but the normally
cocky Akers didn't even try to pretend that his heart was still in the
fight.

"I watched him suffer under the pressure," Burke said. "You could
feel the stress."[1]

Burke, who had emerged as the most forceful of IBM's directors,
was now talking to Akers frequently. While Burke had been supportive
in the past, he was now suggesting that Akers think about moving on.
Burke told him that the board still thought he'd been doing the right
things. Burke himself thought Akers was right to decentralize and was
moving as fast as the culture would allow. But Burke said Akers now
had a credibility problem too great for him to be effective.

With some nudging from Burke, Akers brought back a couple of
senior IBMers who had retired, Paul Rizzo and Kaspar Cassani, to help
gather better information about sales trends and try to avoid the nasty
surprises Akers sprang on the board in September and now December.
After years of false hopes instilled by Akers and his management team,
the board had finally lost faith in Akers's ability to forecast.

"Fact is, we weren't getting good information," Burke says.[2]

With the Christmas holidays finally at hand, Akers retired to his six-
acre home in Westport, Connecticut, to ponder his future. As an IBMer
might say, he was wondering whether it could be time to transition to
a new environment to solution the problem and advantage the IBM
company.

Lost amid all the bloodletting in December was the first significant
reduction IBM ever made in its hallowed research and development
budget. Putting that budget at 10 percent of corporate revenue was a
matter of corporate honor. That 10 percent figure was also a matter of
national interest, because IBM did 10 percent of the private research
and development done in the United States every year. In the 1980s,
IBM spent an immense $101 billion on capital projects in research,

development, and engineering, about four times what the Reagan and
Bush administrations spent on the Star Wars missile defense project.[3]
In spending all that money, IBM researchers won two Nobel Prizes
in recent years for basic research having implications far beyond the
computer industry. (One prize was for so-called high-temperature
superconductors, which get their name because they conduct electricity
without any loss of energy even at temperatures well above absolute
zero. With previous types of superconductors, it was so expensive to
keep them cold enough to let them function as superconductors that
they existed almost exclusively in labs. But the types of superconducting
materials the IBMers invented can be kept cold enough cheaply enough
that they could eventually produce such marvels as superefficient high-
speed trains that levitate above their tracks. The other Nobel Prize
awarded to IBMers in recent years was for the scanning tunneling
microscope, which lets users see and manipulate individual atoms. The
device could eventually let people build motors or electronic devices
out of just a handful of atoms. The device has already allowed IBM to
pull off one of the cleverest PR coups it ever managed, when a researcher produced the IBM logo out of a couple of dozen atoms and
the image was reprinted in newspapers and magazines worldwide.)
IBM invented the bulk of the major computer technologies over the
years that propelled the whole industry forward. In recent years,
IBM used its chip technology and its financial muscle to save the U.S.
memory-chip industry, generally considered to be a crucial part of any
hope the United States had of competing against Japanese technology.
But Akers decided in late 1992 that IBM couldn't afford that anymore.
He cut the R&D budget to $6 billion from $7 billion.

That budget cut accentuated the sclerosis that had been developing
at IBM's research operations for years and endangered IBM's core
asset: its first-rate technology. The problem Akers exacerbated had its
roots in IBM's success, just like most every other problem at the company. IBM so completely dominated the computer market in the 1960s
and 1970s that it didn't need to worry about being beaten to market
with a technology. That complacency let researchers get away with the
kind of elaborate procedure that cropped up throughout IBM and that
seems to spring up in big organizations. A researcher whose work was
deemed to be good enough to have a patent application filed received
three points. Work deemed good enough to be published warranted

one point. Work that couldn't be published merited no points. (Other scales were used to evaluate a researcher's publication record based on where his articles appeared, with *Physical Review Letters* being the highest and with an exact number of points assigned to every conceivable publication on down to the superspecialized.)

Once the federal antitrust suit hit IBM in 1969, IBM's lawyers moved into the research area and gained a remarkable amount of control even over these exceptionally technical matters—based on the feeling that the lawyers needed to make sure the researchers weren't doing anything monopolistic. The lawyers made the researchers' procedures even more elaborate. Yet because the whole company did so well, the success reinforced the idea among the researchers that they must be doing something right, maybe even that they were doing everything right.

That's pretty much where things stood until 1991, when Akers said he was going to enforce a bell curve on employee ratings. Well, researchers knew better than anybody what a bell curve looked like. If Akers said that the bottom 10% of people in any department would get the bottom ranking and had better start looking for jobs, the researchers knew that at all costs they needed to stay above the bottom 10 percent. Researchers also knew that getting patents wasn't the easiest way to stay above water. Getting a patent filed meant spending six weeks to six months with some lawyer who didn't understand the first thing about the technology. Getting something published, however, didn't require anything beyond what the researcher did to submit his work for review by the lawyers in the first place. IBM may have wanted to secure lots of patents, and it may have tried to get them by giving three times as many points for a patent as for publication of a paper, but researchers faced with an annual ranking knew that patents weren't worth the extra time they took. It was much easier to be moderately clever three times and publish three papers than it was to be really innovative once and get a patent.

IBM managers from Akers on down talked about the importance of getting technology out of the labs and into products. The research system was even set up so that someone inventing something that became key to a product would get enough points to move off the charts in the annual rankings. But transferring technology into products took three to five years. In the meantime, the researcher could find himself at the bottom of the rankings and out of the company. Better just to publish papers. (By contrast, at Japanese companies, which are known for being good at transferring technology into products, the research system is set up very differently. At Hitachi, for instance, the product-development groups essentially contract with the research group for certain technologies. That builds such a strong link that research flows directly into products, unlike at IBM, where a researcher has to cast around for some product group willing to give up on its old ways of doing things and champion a new technology. At Hitachi, as long as a researcher fulfills his part of that contract, he stays in good standing. But Hitachi also encourages researchers to take the long-term view by building additional funds and time into each contract from a development group. The time and money can be used however the researcher likes, and, while there is no penalty for failure, lots of goodies come with success. The Hitachi system seems to make much more sense than IBM's, because good research requires an extraordinary amount of failure. It's similar to oil companies and all the dry holes they drill while looking for the next gusher. For every research project that pays off, ten may fail, and it's nearly impossible to tell which the ten are in advance. A healthy dose of fear would do lots of other parts of IBM some good, but not the research division.)

A short-term mentality set in. When Akers cut $1 billion out of the R&D budget at the end of 1992, that spread the panic even further. Suddenly, every researcher was scrambling to produce some short-term result just to justify the continuation of his work. Akers didn't even force the research group to go through and weed out the less promising projects. All he did was starve existing projects of equipment, travel budgets, and, perhaps most important, postdoctoral students. IBM had always been able to attract some of the best postdocs, young people who provided some of IBM's most innovative ideas. Bob Montoye, who did a crucial part of the RS/6000 workstation's processor, was a postdoc, for instance, when he first worked at IBM. But as of late 1992, the research division could now afford only a handful.

Marc Levenson shows just how wrong things began to go in the research division. Levenson was a young researcher at IBM in 1980 when he found that he could trick light into doing some things that the laws of physics didn't seem to allow. Under normal circumstances, a beam of light can get a little fuzzy around the edges when it is being shined through the tiny slits in a mask being used to make a computer chip. That's bad. The light is used to put a sort of tiny photographic image of circuitry on a chip, so the light beam needs to be extremely precise or some crucial circuit on the chip may not work properly. What Levenson found while dabbling on his own was that a method called a phase shift could keep the light beam nice and pure, no fuzziness around the edges.

That little trick proved to be significant, because the need for a pure beam of light became even greater as the 1990s began. Semiconductor makers were packing so many times as much circuitry on the same-sized slice of silicon that they needed to be able to draw their circuitry on the chips with ever-tinier lines. If not for Levenson's phase-shift trick, makers of memory chips would have had to give up on using light to print images on their chips and would have had to move on to far more esoteric means, such as X rays, many years sooner than now seems likely.

But no senior person in IBM's research hierarchy realized the significance of Levenson's work when he completed his first project in 1981. In fact, no one in the senior ranks saw the work. Instead, when Levenson wrote up his initial research, it was routinely sent to some lawyers for evaluation late in 1981. They looked at it, said it seemed to them as if it could merit a patent in optics, but then said they had met their quota for optics patents for the year. The lawyers decided not to file for a patent. Instead, Levenson published a paper. Levenson improved his technique in 1982. This time, the lawyers thought they might be able to get a polymer patent, since he had implemented his idea in a polymer. The lawyers hadn't met their polymer quota yet in 1982, so they filed for patents worldwide.

When the U.S. Patent Office sent back a question to IBM, however, the lawyers decided the patent application was no longer worth the bother. They dropped it. No one troubled to stop the patent applications in other countries, and Levenson actually won a patent in Japan, home of most of IBM's competitors in chip technology. But in the mid-1980s, when the Japanese patent office sent IBM a question on a minor challenge that had arisen to the patent, the question was forwarded to the lawyers. One of them saw that IBM had dropped the patent application in the United States, so he gave up the patent in Japan.

By the mid-1980s, the Japanese were showing real interest in Levenson's work. IBM, however, was on a different course. It had decided that X rays were the way to go and was using the technological issue to mount a campaign with the U.S. government against the Japanese. President Jack Kuehler noted that the Japanese government and Japanese companies had more than a dozen research centers set up to explore the use of X rays, while the United States had none. He argued that chip technology was becoming so expensive that the U.S. government needed to ease antitrust laws to let U.S. companies band together or needed to help finance the research. Otherwise, technology leadership would pass to the Japanese. Kuehler had IBM build a half-billion-dollar Advanced Technology Center in East Fishkill, New York, in 1990 to explore X rays. He got Commerce Secretary Robert Mosbacher to speak at the unveiling about the importance of maintaining U.S. technological leadership.

Levenson and a colleague, Frank Shellenberg, continued to work on Levenson's technique, but with Kuehler publicly championing X rays as a national cause, no one in research was going to pay much attention. Levenson and Shellenberg had other, main assignments to handle, so they were having to fit their work on Levenson's technique in on the side and had at their disposal only a six-thousand-dollar budget, which they had carved out of their other financing.

After months of trying, they arranged an audience with Paul Low, a vice president in charge of chip technology, and they impressed him enough that he said he'd do whatever he could to help. Levenson and Shellenberg said that all they wanted was a small travel budget so they could go to IBM's chip plants to try out their ideas in a real manufacturing environment. Low said that that would be no problem. But the lines of authority around IBM didn't run quite the way they used to. This wasn't the Marine Corps anymore. When Low added the money to Levenson's and Shellenberg's department budget, their manager decided he'd rather spend the money some other way.

In utter frustration, Shellenberg left in 1991 to go to IBM competitor Hewlett-Packard. Levenson tried to keep at it, but when the research cutbacks really hit IBM at the beginning of 1993, he returned from a trip and found that all his equipment had been taken from his office. Levenson decided to go after a severance offer and left in mid-1993.

IBM's chip manufacturers have now realized that they don't need

X rays or any other tricky new technology until sometime in the next century. Instead, they will use what have become known in the industry as Levenson masks. It's just that IBM doesn't have either Levenson or the in-house technology to do Levenson masks, so researchers say IBM will probably buy rights to the technology from Japan's Toshiba.

Shortly before noon on January 26, 1993, the limousines began pulling up in front of the IBM building at Fifty-seventh and Madison in Manhattan as IBM's board began to assemble. Directors had been fetched by corporate jet or been flown in by helicopter to the heliport on the East River, and now they were emerging from their long black cars at the busy corner for what they knew would be a momentous meeting.

As they got off the elevator on the top floor and headed to the boardroom, they strolled along a wall full of grand windows that gave them a sweeping view of Manhattan in all directions. The kitchen for the boardroom has the one elegant chef in IBM's U.S. operations, so the directors had a pleasant lunch, then settled down to business.

Akers had already warned board members that he planned to talk about cutting the dividend. That would ordinarily have been a huge decision. IBM had *never* cut its dividend, and tens of thousands of investors counted on that dividend to help finance their retirement. In addition, Akers's chief financial officer, Frank Metz, had assured the world only a few months before that the dividend was safe. But business was so bad that it was clear IBM couldn't afford to pay out more than $2.5 billion in dividends each year. After the board approved a dividend cut of 55 percent, Akers then got to the real event. He wanted to talk about resigning.

Although IBM board meetings are always designed to end at a civilized hour so as not to inconvenience the directors, this one began to drag on into the early evening. Some public-relations people were summoned from headquarters and made the hour drive into the city. They were told something was up that would require a press release but not what it was. They sat there, feeling like they were outside the Vatican waiting for the election of a new Pope. But were they going to see a puff of white smoke or black smoke come out of the chimney?

At around seven, the meeting finally broke. As the directors filed out, it became clear that Burke was now in charge, seconded by Murphy of Cap Cities and former IBM chairman Opel. Akers was out.

Burke held in his hand a copy of the press release on the dividend cut, which Akers had taken into the meeting to show the board. He told the PR people that the dividend-cut release was fine, but he said there were some other items, too. He said that Akers was resigning within three months and that Kuehler had given up his title of president. Kuehler would become a vice chairman so that whoever replaced Akers could choose his own president. Metz, the chief financial officer, was going to take the fall for being unable to forecast the problems that hit in the second half of 1992 and for mistakenly promising that the dividend was safe. Metz would quietly take a severance package and retire. Burke suggested that the Akers news and the other personnel stuff be tacked on at the bottom of the dividend press release.

He was gently told that maybe the dividend cut wasn't the biggest news anymore and that perhaps separate press releases were called for. Burke said that was fine but that he wanted to see them before they went out. He then left with the other directors to go to the Park Lane Hotel for dinner. An IBM vice president, Mary Lee Turner, functioned as a courier well into the night. Although the releases were short, Burke fiddled with them until almost one in the morning, repeatedly sending Turner back to the IBM building to have her crew of PR people write a new draft.

First thing the next morning, the world learned that the IBM board had finally done something about its problems. Rumors had circulated for years that Akers was about to go, but they had happened so often that no one believed them anymore. Now it had finally happened.

Akers left with the worst record of any chief executive in the history of IBM. He had succeeded all his life and risen to the top of one of the world's most profitable companies. Comfortable in the security IBM represented, he had begun to think about his place in history. But this was to be it: He was the one who had presided over the unmaking of one of the great corporate success stories of all time.

He was too much a product of IBM's culture to see most of the problems he faced in time to do anything about them. And IBM's culture had become so ingrown that it resisted his attempts to change. He didn't create most of his problems, but it was in his power to solve many of them and he didn't. He wrestled with the problems. He talked about them a lot. Eventually, he articulated what most of the problems were and took tentative steps toward fixing them. But he repeatedly came up a day late and a billion dollars short.

As Akers left IBM in 1993, the core mainframe business was in disarray. Revenue had dropped by double-digit percentages in both 1991 and 1992 and dropped 35 percent in the first quarter of 1993, on its way to another huge drop for the year. PCs and workstations had finally begun to soak up much of the demand that went to mainframes in the past. Customers had become comfortable enough with the technology that they wouldn't pay exorbitant prices for mainframes anymore, meaning that even these behemoths with hundreds of thousands of miles of circuitry inside them were on their way to becoming generic machines sold mostly on the basis of price. The mainframe business was in free-fall. IBM's near monopoly in that business had traditionally provided two-thirds of the company's profits, profits so big that they provided the whole basis for the IBM way of life—the lush bureaucracy, the impeccably trained sales force, the lifetime employment, the respect for the individual.

Akers also left behind in the mainframe business what seems to be a land mine that someone may step on one of these days. That land mine is the IBM leasing business, which Akers had revived in the late 1980s. The mainframe leasing business is like the car leasing business. When someone leases a new car for three years, the person's monthly payments aren't designed to let the car owner recover the entire price of the new car. That would be unfair. Instead, the person leasing the car is really paying just the difference between the price of the new car and what the owner expects it to be worth in three years. If the car turns out to be a lemon and isn't worth much after three years, then the car owner has a real problem. That's what's happening to IBM. Prices are falling so fast for mainframes that IBM's machines will be worth far less at the end of a lease than IBM expected them to be. IBM's leasing executives insist that they've made extremely conservative assumptions about the value the mainframes will have at the end of their leases, but leasing competitors disagree, and if mainframe prices are tumbling so fast that they're astonishing IBM's mainframe executives, how can the leasing people not be surprised? Logic says that IBM will have to take a big write-off at some point because the tens of billions of dollars of mainframes that the leasing business owns aren't worth as much as IBM's books say they should be.

With mainframes unable to support IBM's lifestyle any longer by 1993, there had to be something else around to do it, but there wasn't. The AS/400 minicomputer line had had a great run, but it was going on five years old as Akers left in early 1993, making it ancient by the computer industry's standards. Software had potential, but IBM wasn't any good at writing it. The only real money IBM made in software was in operating systems for its mainframes and minicomputers, and those profits were dropping along with the rest of those businesses. IBM can certainly do more in selling services, but it can't look to services for anything like its historic profit margins. Services are already hypercompetitive and require too many people to be as profitable as IBM's hardware businesses used to be.

IBM's balance sheet was beginning to be a problem, too, because of all the debt the company was taking on to cover the costs of the severance packages it was granting people. IBM poured so much concrete around the world in the early 1980s and hired so many people that it will continue to take on debt, too, as it pays people to leave and gets rid of all the manufacturing capacity and offices it no longer needs. IBM once had the strongest triple-A debt rating, the highest a company can receive, but that rating started coming down a couple of notches at a time beginning in late 1991 because the increased debt made IBM's position less secure. That not only hurts IBM's prestige when it deals with customers but increases its interest payments, a problem that could snowball as IBM continues to take on debt and sees its debt rating slip.

In the past, Japan and Europe could always be counted on to bail IBM out even if it hit a bad spell with one of its major product lines, but no longer. Europe and Japan had been hungrier for computing power than the United States because they hadn't computerized as fast and so were trying to catch up. But now they had caught up. IBM said it planned to cut ten thousand jobs in 1993 out of the ninety thousand it had in Europe—calling into question the fate of plants in Havant, England; Jarfalla, Sweden; Valencia, Spain; and Montpelier, France. IBM's pretax earnings plunged 90 percent in 1992 in Japan, the fifth straight year in which they've dropped. The sun had set on the days when IBM could sell an AS/400 minicomputer in Europe for almost twice the U.S. price.

In PCs and workstations, the one area where IBM had such an early edge that it could have developed a business to succeed the mainframe one, IBM had frittered away all its strategic advantages. It had handed the operating-system business to Microsoft and the processor business to Intel, which together were earning nearly $2 billion a year by 1993. IBM had ceded the application-software business to a host of companies, including Microsoft. The workstation business had gone to Sun and a few others; the laser-printer business to Hewlett-Packard; the disk-drive business to Seagate and Conner, and so on.

By the time Akers left in March 1993, IBM's PC business was starting to brag about a turnaround. Cannavino said it had had its best quarter ever in the fourth quarter, and shipments were on their way to a 40 percent increase in the first quarter of 1993. The business would return to profitability in the first quarter. What the PC business didn't emphasize is that it lost money in that record fourth quarter and that a 40 percent increase in shipments was barely enough to produce a rise in revenue in the first quarter, because prices were still falling so fast. And competitors such as Compaq insist that analyses of IBM's manufacturing costs, its marketing expenses, and its overhead show that someone at IBM must have been playing games with numbers to come up with a profit for the quarter.

Even if IBM's numbers on the PC company are right, this is a business that's going nowhere fast. Can the PC company really replace a mainframe operation that used to produce $4 billion a year in earnings and support the whole IBM lifestyle?

When Akers announced in January 1993 that he was leaving, it created a media circus that hurt IBM's lagging reputation even more. As the search for a new chief executive dragged on for two months, several prominent people withdrew their names from consideration for what a decade ago would have been considered the best job in the whole world of business. The executives didn't seem to feel that the job was worth the risk of failure. After the board selected Lou Gerstner, the chief executive of RJR Nabisco, it became clear that he hadn't been the first choice—although few people realized just how far down the list he was.

Burke, the head of the search committee, told one friend that he was embarrassed to have to recommend Gerstner to the board. Burke said he sounded out several executives he knew outside the computer industry even before Akers agreed to step down, including Jack Welch, head of General Electric, but they all rebuffed him. When Burke gave the executive-search firms two months to find a new chief executive in January 1993, he assumed they'd be able to find someone in the industry who'd jump at the chance. But several of them had ideas the board couldn't accept, such as Apple CEO John Sculley's idea to merge Apple and IBM and sell off big chunks of IBM.[4] Others just weren't interested. So there Burke was, having to recommend Gerstner, who was essentially just a good consultant.

Burke tried to argue to the world at large that Gerstner knew plenty about the computer business because he had bought lots of mainframes while at American Express—but that was like arguing that Gerstner was qualified to run RJR Nabisco because he smoked cigars. Burke also tried to convince people that he had called Gerstner first out of all the candidates—Burke said Gerstner had been code-named Able during the search for that reason. In fact, Gerstner called Burke to volunteer for the job; Burke didn't seek out Gerstner.

The board's search committee interviewed Cannavino as one of the internal candidates for the job. Cannavino, in his cocky way, told them he didn't think they were qualified to choose a successor to Akers because they didn't know enough about the industry. He told them they needed somebody from the industry. Others would no doubt say they could learn, but he said that was like going for brain surgery to a doctor who had never done it before. The doctor might say, "Don't worry; I've read a lot about the operation." But Cannavino said he wouldn't go to a doctor like that. Cannavino kidded that he was having a great time during their search because no chief executive was looking over his shoulder and the corporate staffs were just scared enough that he might be the board's choice that they were inclined to leave him alone. Cannavino told the board to take a couple of years and really think about this. Maybe send a couple of the candidates off to school for a while. He also gave the board a letter of resignation for their use or use by whomever they chose at any time, and he vaguely threatened to quit if he felt ill-used by the board's choice.

When the day finally came in late March 1993 for Gerstner to assume power, those attending the press conference at the New York Hilton found themselves passing a sign that read TRANSPLANTATION SYMPOSIUM as they entered the ballroom. It was actually for a meeting of cancer surgeons in the ballroom next door, but it might as well have applied to the IBM session.

Akers led Burke and Gerstner out of a side door as he marched one final time to the podium to confront a tough audience. A stony-faced

Akers read a short statement, then introduced Burke, who introduced the new guy. Akers retired to a chair at the edge of the stage, where he slumped through Gerstner's brief talk and the question-and-answer session. Every once in a while, when Gerstner got a barbed question, Akers permitted himself a small smile.

Gerstner came across as the hard-nosed management consultant he once was. His theme was, "I'm the new guy around here. Don't ask me what the problems are or what the answers are. I don't know yet." But Gerstner also said he was a quick study, and he assured those in the audience that he had the courage to take the tough steps. Gerstner certainly sent off plenty of signals that he meant to change IBM— starting with the fact that he was wearing a blue shirt.

As they left the meeting, Akers and Gerstner headed in different directions. Gerstner settled into the third-floor southeast-corner office in Armonk, overlooking the apple orchard behind the building. Akers moved into a lonely redbrick building hidden behind a marina in Stamford, Connecticut, where, as a courtesy, IBM would leave him a modest office so he could serve out the remainder of his days with IBM as a consultant at Gerstner's beck and call.

The fifty-one-year-old Gerstner is a street-smart guy from Long Island, with a bit of a New Yawk accent. Short, round-faced, and pudgy, he would be played by Danny DeVito in any movie. Gerstner comes from a family where the parents never went to college but where the four children, all boys, made names for themselves in business. Gerstner, who has an engineering degree from Dartmouth and an MBA from Harvard, had been hot stuff since he hit McKinsey, a management consulting firm, where he became known for digesting huge amounts of information quickly and for sizing up a business problem immediately. He became a partner in five years, near-record time, then became the youngest senior partner in the history of the firm. When Gerstner joined American Express and became the head of its credit-card business, he was known for bringing in outsiders to top spots, even though American Express had IBM's fixation on promoting from within and even though the people Gerstner hired shook up the hierarchy. (Even the language at American Express and IBM was similar. At IBM, people who had the highest ratings and who could expect to be promoted were said to walk on water, while at American Express that kind of person was called a water walker.) Gerstner was also known for aggressively using consumer marketing to push a brand name. He was the one who built up the mystique around the American Express card.

At American Express, Gerstner was known as a deeply religious man. When he checked into a hotel, the first thing he did was locate the nearest Catholic church. When some people at American Express decided to celebrate an executive's fortieth birthday by bringing in a stripper, Gerstner was the only one who seemed uncomfortable. He just sat in a corner scowling. Still, what people at American Express remember most about Gerstner was how much he managed through intimidation, especially at the beginning of his days there. Through the closed door of his office, he might be heard yelling, "That's the stupidest thing I've ever heard! You're an idiot! Get out of my office!" If those in the hall hung around a second, they'd see some red-faced employee shoot out the door.

One subordinate says that knees literally buckled and hands trembled when Gerstner walked into a room. Someone once arranged a dinner for him and some other senior executives on the spur of the moment at an exquisite restaurant in Tokyo, only to find that Gerstner, on a raised platform where everyone at the dinner could see him, wasn't touching his food. It turned out that he just didn't like Japanese food and wasn't blaming the organizer for not knowing, but half the room couldn't touch their food because they were so nervous that he'd blame them for whatever slight was keeping him from eating his dinner.

When Gerstner moved on to RJR, the Winstons to Oreos giant, he showed he was tough enough to hack away at operations so he could bring down the leveraged buyout's huge debt. Gerstner also showed an extraordinary sense of timing. He landed the IBM job right before what came to be known as Marlboro Friday, because that was the day that RJR rival Philip Morris slashed prices on its premium Marlboro cigarettes. That started a price war that drove down RJR's cigarette prices and killed its stock. But Gerstner had just finished negotiating a deal with IBM's board that would pay him $5 million to cover the value of the RJR stock options he had to forfeit to go to IBM, options whose value would have dropped by at least $1 million if the calculation had been done after Marlboro Friday and not right before. Gerstner also got IBM to guarantee that if the RJR stock he already owned fell below a certain amount then IBM would make him whole, a guarantee that seemed likely to be worth at least a further $8 million to Gerstner as of mid-1993.

In his early days at IBM, Gerstner took some decisive, positive steps. He effectively abolished the Management Committee, saying that he didn't believe in rule by committee. Gerstner also tried to forbid anyone from making a presentation to him using foils. For a while, executives didn't know what to do. They could barely speak without their foils. But Gerstner insisted that if someone had something to say, he should just say it. Gerstner, in general, dispensed with the formalities of IBM meetings. He typically blew into a meeting room after everyone was assembled and, without any pleasantries, got started. He asked quick, tough, almost rude questions. Then he wound things up in perhaps fifteen minutes—while the more formal Akers might have let the same meeting go on for an hour and a half. Unlike Akers, who used to enter and leave his office via a rear elevator and was rarely seen around the headquarters building, Gerstner began walking around, sticking his head into people's offices to ask how they were progressing on some assignment he'd given them. Gerstner began using e-mail to communicate with people and didn't bother relaying questions down through the hierarchy; he figured out who was working on some project and called that person directly, even if the person was five or six levels down from him. He also began getting notes from lower-level people through e-mail that told him about problems that previously would have been filtered out by the time they crept up through the hierarchy and landed on Akers's desk as a formal memo. He heard, for instance, about an attempt to make mainframe-operating-system software prices more affordable for a certain class of customers who were avoiding buying mainframes because the price of the software was too high. The attempt had bogged down because so many national sales forces and product-development groups were afraid of what the price cut might do to their profitability. But when Gerstner heard about the plan, he called the low-level manager who was putting it together and told her to ignore the standard formal processes for getting it approved. Gerstner said he would make the plan go through, and he did.

Gerstner heard through e-mail in mid-May 1993 that IBM's disk-drive operation thought its biggest competitor, Hitachi, was going to announce some products on May 25. He sent e-mail to the disk-drive business, asking when some new machines that IBM had in the works would be announced. June 2 was the reply. Gerstner suggested that the disk-drive business move up the announcement, thereby preempting Hitachi. He was told that wasn't possible. When he asked why, he was told that the disk-drive business always announced its products on either the first or third Tuesday of a month. Why? Because that's the way it had always been done. Gerstner made sure the announcement got moved ahead of Hitachi's.

Gerstner also began bringing people in from the outside, just as he had at American Express. In fact, he apparently started bringing in outsiders on the day of his first press conference, even though he didn't take over for another two days—Gerstner's longtime public-relations adviser, Dave Kalis, was walking around at the conference introducing himself as an IBM vice president. Within a month, Gerstner had brought in a Silicon Valley entrepreneur to replace the head of IBM's disk-drive business, the highest-level appointment of an outsider up to that point in IBM's history, with the exception of Gerstner's. Since then, Gerstner had brought in outsiders as the chief financial officer and head of personnel. That will no doubt continue, bringing IBM the biggest breath of fresh air it has ever inhaled.

Gerstner will presumably try to emphasize the IBM brand the same way he built a mystique around the American Express card—and the same way Burke emphasized consumer marketing when he ran Johnson & Johnson. But that will prove to be harder than shortening meetings. IBM still has a good name, but that name has been tarnished, and IBM's products have started to turn into generic computers, sold mainly based on their prices. While Gerstner succeeded in giving the American Express card cachet, that doesn't mean he'll be able to repeat the victory. Soon after he left American Express, premium cards from Visa, MasterCard, and others made the American Express card a commodity, and the cachet disappeared. (Once that mystique disappeared, American Express had its own boardroom coup, an on-again, off-again attempt at overthrow that eventually dumped Chief Executive Jim Robinson.) At RJR, Gerstner couldn't keep the cigarette market from turning into a generic business where only price and not the fancy RJR brand names made a difference.

To really change IBM's culture and speed decision making, Gerstner will also have to do more than try to outlaw foils. The culture is so strong that, in fact, when Gerstner held a meeting of his most senior people in April to have them explain the strengths and weaknesses of their businesses, a meeting he tried to hold without foils, the executives insisted that they couldn't. So they set their entire staffs working on what were supposed to be brief presentations and came up with the standard stack of foils—ten foils that were to be used, then ten foils to back up each of those in case Gerstner had a question, and ten to back up each of those one hundred.

The broad outlines of Akers's decentralization made enough sense that Gerstner will probably try to continue it, especially because Burke, the head of the search committee, believes so strongly in decentralizing. Besides, Gerstner lacks any real knowledge of the computer industry, so he was apparently brought in to run IBM like a holding company of various businesses—more like a General Electric, with its range of divisions producing everything from light bulbs to jet engines, than like the completely integrated IBM of the past. But Gerstner has no particular experience in the computer industry other than the fact that he, unlike Akers, uses one. (Asked at the March 1993 press conference announcing his appointment what brand of computer he used, Gerstner said he had a laptop but couldn't remember who made it. Apparently, laptop brand names don't mean anything to him.) So Gerstner will be able to apply only management consulting dogma to IBM. His choice by the board indicates that it doesn't think there's any grand vision out there that could revitalize IBM the way the movement into computers did in the 1950s, the way the 360 mainframe family did in the 1960s, and the way the PC did briefly in the early 1980s. Without that grand vision and without a breakthrough product, Gerstner will just be fiddling.

The IBM of the future may be profitable, but it will cast nothing like the shadow it has cast over the computer industry and world economy during the past eighty years.

SIXTEEN

Madge Barnett woke up in a pool of blood on the floor of a rest room at the IBM facility in Charlotte, North Carolina, in December 1990. She felt a crowd of paramedics rushing around her, bandaging her wrists, but couldn't quite remember how she got there. Slowly, things came back into focus. She recalled how she had battled to maintain her self-esteem in the prior year as her boss told her she no longer measured up to IBM's standards and pressed her to leave the company. Barnett remembered how she had slowly lost that battle even though she knew intellectually that she had been a standout employee who had merely run afoul of a bad boss. She also felt the pain that had been racking her body for a year as her good feelings about herself wrestled with the equally deep sense that IBM, the company she adored, could never be wrong, even if it was pronouncing her incompetent. Then Barnett remembered the e-mail message she had received from her manager earlier that December day, saying curtly, "Report to me at 1."

When she got that message, Barnett decided she was finally about to be fired. She panicked. As an engineer involved with testing the circuit cards produced in Charlotte, Barnett often had to open packages of the cards, so she always kept a double-edged razor blade around. Today, it was in her car. Unable to face life feeling that Mother IBM had branded her a failure, she walked nervously out to one of the huge parking lots surrounding the eight-thousand-person Charlotte facility and got the razor blade. She hurried back inside to a rest room, trying to get there before she lost her resolve. That's where her memory stopped. The paramedics were now telling her that she had slashed her wrists and was lucky someone had come across her, lying in the middle of the floor, in time to save her life.

In the prior decade, Barnett had been a model employee at IBM; she believed in the company implicitly and received numerous awards for figuring out ways to save IBM money when manufacturing circuit cards. She was such a gung ho employee that she wrote articles for internal magazines, urging IBMers to support, for example, the market-driven quality movement begun by Chairman John Akers; quality should be "a byword not a buzzword," she wrote. But she ran into trouble with her supervisor in 1989, the beginning of the dangerous times for IBM employees because it marked the onset of IBM's really tough years financially. In earlier years, the kind of problem Barnett had with her boss wouldn't have been a big issue. IBM took such care to be fair to its employees that an otherwise-excellent employee who had a problem with her boss would have been moved to a different area, not fired. But by 1989, the company's goal of respect for the individual seemed to have disappeared.

Barnett complained in 1989 that her boss was sexually harassing her and asked for someone from personnel to investigate her claim. Instead, she says, she was sequestered in a conference room with that boss and told to work out her differences with him—a frightening experience, given the power he had over her. She says her boss told her he'd get her fired for raising a stink. With her complaint having been rejected by her boss, Barnett, certain that IBM would always do the right thing, appealed to Akers's office through what's known as an open-door letter. Even though a minuscule percentage of IBMers manage to get a boss's decision overturned through the open-door process, Akers's office said that she was to be assigned to a different manager and given a leave to teach at a local college. But the open-door process at IBM, once the fail-safe means for maintaining respect for the individual, was no longer enforced the way it had been in happier times. Barnett says the general manager of the Charlotte facility revoked her leave and reassigned her to the same manager who she felt had been harassing her.

This same manager told her to fly to the West Coast to pick up a heavy machine tool, which he said he needed right away. Barnett initially said she thought the machine tool's maker could ship it to Charlotte as fast as she could fetch it, but, as a good soldier, she went, anyway. When Barnett returned to the San Francisco airport with the tool in the trunk of her rental car, she found it had wedged itself into a corner. After struggling for several minutes with the one-hundred-pound tool while traffic zipped around in front of the busy airport, the slight, fiftyish Barnett climbed up onto the bumper of her car and pulled up on the tool as hard as she could. The tool came tumbling out. She fell backward, and the tool crushed her thin left wrist against the pavement. Her straining and the fall also tore muscles in her left shoulder and lower back. That accident in 1990 became the start of her real problems.

Her doctors said she needed to be moved into a different type of job so she wouldn't have to spend so much time struggling to use a computer keyboard. Barnett's bosses refused. When her injuries kept her from maintaining her former pace of work, her superiors disciplined her. As 1990 progressed, they demoted her, giving her a job typing data into a computer, even though they knew she had only one good hand. When Barnett fell behind the two-handed typists, she was threatened with dismissal. Barnett began having psychiatric problems.

"When something you respect as much as I respected IBM tells you you're no good, a small part of you has to believe that," she says. "I can sit here and tell you I know that I was a terrific employee, that I can document the fact that I saved that company hundreds of thousands of dollars in real money. But knowing that intellectually doesn't help when I wake up in the middle of the night with my stomach in knots."

After Barnett slashed her wrists in December 1990, her doctors told her to spend a couple of weeks recuperating. Her bosses forced her to count the time as vacation. When she returned in January 1991, she was told that she was on ninety days' probation because she was typing so slowly. She was also told, ominously, that people entangled in as much trouble as she was in with her superiors almost never lasted the whole ninety days before being fired.

"I said, 'I'll make it through those ninety days if it kills me,' " Barnett says. She had two car accidents on the way to work because of back spasms caused by the damage to her lower back, but she made it every day and, even with only one good hand, lasted through the probation. A few weeks later, in April 1991, she was fired, anyway.

Since she was fired, Barnett has won a worker's compensation case against IBM. (IBM's lawyers deny that the company had done anything wrong.) She says she is considering suing the company for additional money but isn't sure she can handle it emotionally. Barnett says she has continued to see a psychiatrist since leaving IBM and still hasn't recovered her self-esteem. She has tried one more time to kill herself.

Her daughter, a bright twenty-year-old who recently won two scholarships to study international law in Europe for the summer, has been torn up by her mother's problems, too. When Barnett took her to the airport in May 1993 for what should have been the most exciting plane trip of her life, the daughter burst into tears.

"Why should I even bother?" the daughter said. "You didn't do anything wrong, and IBM did this to you. How do I know that, no matter how hard I work, something like this won't happen to me?"

IBM's open-door policy stemmed from the days when Tom Watson, Sr., decided the chairman's door should always be open to his employees. Watson himself often walked out the back door of his office in Endicott, New York, and strolled through the plant floor among his employees to get a feel for what was going on. If anyone ever felt he had been mistreated, Watson wanted to know about it. He'd often call those with complaints into his office to talk things over. Watson just about always overruled his managers and sided with the employee.[1] Over the years, the open-door policy became a crucial part of IBM's culture. Employees felt secure that no matter what went wrong in the way they were treated, the chairman would somehow put things right.

But people like Madge Barnett were discovering in the late 1980s and early 1990s that the open-door program had become a charade. IBM became so big over the years that letting employees file an open-door complaint for investigation by the chairman's office simply produced another bureaucracy. The bureaucracy ruled, and the chairman almost always rubber-stamped the decision. As times got tougher, the bureaucracy almost always supported the manager. Bill Warner, a former open-door investigator, says it became clear in the mid-1980s that a fundamental shift had occurred. Originally, the employee was not only innocent until proven guilty but was supposed to have the investigator as his advocate all through the process. Now, Warner says, the employee is presumed guilty. Even when the chairman sided with the employee, the bureaucracy got its way—as people like Barnett discovered.

Ray Lillie, who worked for IBM for thirty-four years in a tool and die shop in Lexington, Kentucky, says that he wrote an open-door letter to Akers in 1989, complaining that his manager had ordered him to falsify data in a report on the reliability of a product so that it would be easier for IBM to sell the product outside the United States. Lillie requested that his manager be investigated. Instead, Akers's office immediately faxed the manager Lillie's letter. He yanked Lillie into his office, demanding to know why Lillie had gone over his head. Lillie blanched. As unhappy as he was, the manager said that Lillie's complaint required a formal response from Akers, because that was what the open-door process called for. So the manager told *Lillie* to write something for Akers to send *back to Lillie*. The manager also, of course, ordered Lillie to reject his own complaint. Lillie wrote a letter, which his boss sent to Akers. Sure enough, Akers signed it and sent it back to Lillie without changing a word. The letter said Akers had conducted a thorough, unbiased open-door investigation and found that Lillie's claim was without merit. The letter ended by saying, "Lexington management is committed to maintaining . . . quality."

Lillie soon found out, as Barnett had, that people who filed under the open-door policy became marked as troublemakers, even though there were supposed to be no repercussions. Lillie says that a few months after his complaint, he was told that his ranking was going to be cut from a two to a four, on IBM's one-to-four scale, where one is the highest. He was also told that he was on his way to being fired. Lillie says the only way he stayed on was through blackmail. He threatened that if his rating was cut, he would tell upper management that he was repairing his bosses' cars on company time. Lillie actually decided that the threat worked well enough that he insisted on having his rating raised to a one.

The whole tenor of management changed along with the open-door policy. While IBM executives always used to speak with great affection about the IBM work force, in the later rounds of cutbacks, some began talking about "clerks and jerks"—as in "Let's do another reorganization to get rid of some more clerks and jerks."

IBMers began to feel they were always being watched. People with weak rankings looked out of their offices, only to find personnel specialists walking by two or three times an hour for weeks, just to observe them. Hourly workers found managers standing by the time clock, noting the times they started and stopped work; a five-minute discrepancy between the actual time and the time on the card was enough to get a low-ranked employee fired. Undercover agents began walking through some IBM plants to make sure no one was sabotaging equipment.

The whole family feeling at IBM, which used to be such a big part of the culture, disappeared. IBM cut out the Christmas parties that used to be held for the whole family. The summer family day was wiped out. The annual regional dinners for twenty-five-year veterans became every-other-year events. IBM eliminated the several-hundred-dollar bonus that most salaried employees got every year right before Christmas, which was ostensibly to cover estimated overtime worked during the year but was really to help cover the expense of Christmas presents. Personnel didn't even allow going-away parties because it didn't want those remaining to empathize with those being pushed out.

In the past, IBM had hired a dozen or more people from many families and helped tie them together. By the early 1990s, IBM was splitting families up. Younger family members sat around the dinner table and argued to their older IBMer relatives that the company needed to change. Many became frustrated and quit. The older relatives waxed nostalgic for the good times and insisted that IBM would be fine if it just returned to its traditional values, such as respect for the individual. The older IBMers just tried to keep from being forced out before they hit age fifty-five and qualified for a pension. One former employee, who was in sales with IBM, says he was one of ten family members at IBM in the 1980s, but IBM forced out several of them in the early 1990s. He says his IBMer wife developed such bad headaches as her boss pressed her to leave the company that she had CAT scans done, then went to a psychiatrist. The ex-employee says he became depressed because he lost his self-respect after similar treatment. "IBM didn't used to be like this," he says. "It was a place where you went to get up, not to get down." Even those relatives who weren't being encouraged to leave generally got angry and quit. Now, only one of the ten family members still works at IBM.

Although IBM used to go to great lengths to accommodate the spouse of someone being transferred, by the early 1990s, someone being moved might wait a year and a half for the spouse to be given a job at the new site. Someone confined to a wheelchair in payroll in Tarrytown, New York, was told that if he wanted to stay at the company, he'd have to take a job on the manufacturing line in San Jose, California. Lee Conrad, the head of IBM Workers United, a group of unhappy IBMers, says that one engineer with twenty-five years of experience was told the only job available for him at IBM was in the mail room.

Employees became fed up. Conrad says one much-decorated employee stuffed all his IBM awards in a box and mailed them to his manager, with the note: "Hope you can sleep at night." Then the employee walked out. One employee wrote on an anonymous morale survey, "Yes, my morale is low. My morale is always low at wakes." Another, responding to a question about IBM's goal of respect for the individual, wrote, "What respect?" He complained of "an 'anything goes' environment where common decency and normal business ethics have disappeared. IBM is a very inconsistent company, making grand public statements on respect, sincerity and sensitivity while practicing oppressive, discriminatory administration at lower levels. It is inappropriate to raise employees' expectations, only to practice 'mill mentality' personnel management."

An IBM employee in Gaithersburg, Maryland, wrote an anonymous letter to top management, stating, "We [IBMers] are LOSERS, and we feel it." He wrote that when he told friends where he worked, he "got that LEPER COLONY look." He said work had pretty much stopped in Gaithersburg, then marveled that the vice president responsible for Gaithersburg continued to insist that everything was going fine. "He needs to put a pane of glass where his belly button is so that he can see where he is going," the employee wrote, "because he surely has got his head up his ass if he thinks everything is working out here!" The letter concluded by saying, "Don't get me wrong. Your money is as good as anyone else's, and until something better comes along or I retire I'll put in my five hours a day and go home."

True Blue, an underground newsletter that sprang up at IBM as the morale sank in the early 1990s, complained that top executives weren't being honest—in IBM terms, they would "talk the talk but not walk the walk." *True Blue* wrote, "Please, please take steps to streamline our organizations. Cut the work force where needed. But don't insult the collective intelligence of the 'cream of the crop'" by saying that a work force that top management always described as the elite of the elite was suddenly full of people who needed to be weeded out because they were incompetent. Just admit that the company is in

trouble and changes need to be made, the newsletter urged. Some ex-
IBM employees began selling T-shirts that have the IBM logo running
down the left side, with the three letters acting as the start of the words
I've Been Misled.

So much had changed about IBM by the early 1990s that longtime
veterans couldn't recognize it anymore and outsiders thought IBM no
longer mattered. Sam Albert, who spent thirty-two years with IBM and
is now an independent consultant, says that in his early days at IBM if
he had mentioned at a cocktail party that he worked there, people
would have started inviting him to lunch. But in 1992, he said at a
meeting of consultants that he made his livelihood now partly by helping little companies get into partnerships with IBM, and one woman
asked, "Who the hell would want to partner with IBM anymore?"

Albert says, "I thought, Whoa! How things have changed! I decided
that maybe I should go back and change my resume to read, 'thirty-two
years with a large computer company.'"

But those who left IBM still found it painful to go, even if they had
done well at IBM, left voluntarily, and found good jobs elsewhere.
These moves aren't just the normal transitions that people make after
they've spent a few years with a company and decide it's time to move
on. Most of these people who were leaving had been with IBM since
college. They lived in IBM towns. They socialized with IBMers. Their
whole identity depended on being IBMers. Don Estridge had turned
down millions of dollars to run Apple in the mid-1980s because he liked
being able to say, "I work for IBM." Thousands of other IBMers would
have made the same choice. Those who've left say they felt as though
they were being kicked out of their homes or being divorced. Jim
Ballasone, who left a senior marketing job at IBM to become an executive vice president at IBM mainframe competitor Hitachi Data Systems,
says that before he left the company, IBM put him and his family
through professional counseling to help them understand that they
needed to think of themselves as more than just an IBMer and an IBM
family. Ballasone says the counselors kept hammering home that he
had to keep saying to himself, "I am not my job."

Some IBMers, leaving under pressure, couldn't handle the transition and went over the edge.

John Dean Kleder, a former lab worker at IBM, drove up to his
former supervisor's house on the outskirts of San Jose in early 1993. He

carefully pulled two cans of gasoline out of the trunk of his car and poured them around the front of the house. He tossed a match into the fumes, jumped back, and ran to his car. Speeding to the IBM complex nearby, Kleder drove his red Mustang through the plate-glass window in the foyer and leapt out of the car. Flinging cans of gasoline around, he lighted them on fire, too. He hopped back in his car and sped off on three tires and one rim, having lost one tire to the broken glass from the reception area's window. The receptionist called the police, who seemed to have Kleder cornered not far from the IBM facility, but then he broke past them onto one of the highways ringing San Jose. By now, he was down to two tires and two rims, and the metal rims were shooting sparks in all directions. But he led several police cars on a merry chase for a few miles. Kleder didn't stop until he was down to one tire and three rims. When he stepped out of his smashed Mustang, he explained that he decided he had to take matters into his own hands because he was sick of the way IBM had treated him.

The unmaking of IBM has probably hurt more people than the problems at any company in history. The human toll starts with the 140,000 IBMers whose jobs have disappeared over the past seven years. That's equivalent to eleven Microsofts and is more employees than all except the very largest companies in the world have in their total work forces. But that 140,000 number is just the start. Including spouses and children who were affected, those job losses disrupted the lives of perhaps 400,000 people—about the population of Pittsburgh. Whole towns have lost their livelihoods, especially in the Hudson Valley. IBM was easily the biggest employer in that area, with ten times as many jobs in some counties as the next-largest employer. With IBM healthy in the early to mid-1980s, unemployment in the area was a low 3 percent, and an air of prosperity convinced people that they had landed in an enchanted woods, with the wizards in Armonk warding off any evil spirits that tried to sneak in. But by 1993, unemployment had more than doubled in the Hudson Valley, to 7 percent, and it was going to rise from there.[2] IBM said it planned to cut six thousand jobs out of the twenty thousand remaining in the area. Those reductions will ripple through this region. Already, retail buying in the area has slowed so much that small stores are going out of business. Some commercial real estate developers have gone bankrupt, too, because IBM stopped needing new space and depressed prices by dumping excess plant and office space on the market. People selling residential real estate began having problems because the housing market died once IBM, which once stood for "I've Been Moved," started to save money by minimizing transfers. School districts wondered how they'd survive once IBM's and IBMers' tax dollars dried up. Charitable donations from IBM and its employees, which had risen 5 to 10 percent a year in the 1980s, began declining in the 1990s. The mood in the mid–Hudson Valley became so depressed that when IBM announced layoffs in the region in early 1993, local officials asked gun shops to close for the day.

The human toll also hit those who had invested in IBM's stock and saw IBM's shares lose $75 billion of value—equivalent to the gross domestic product of Sweden. About half that money came out of the pockets of faceless institutional investors, but they mostly manage pension funds, so their losses on IBM stock have pulled money out of the pension funds of employees at thousands of other companies around the world. The other half of the money was lost by the half million individual holders of IBM stock, most of whom thought of IBM as a classic "widows and orphans" stock that they could sock money into and count on for their retirement. As of 1993, IBM also started paying out $1.5 billion less in dividends each year than it had been.

Charles Kowal invested in IBM for the day when he would make a down payment on a retirement home in Florida. The semiretired fifty-two-year-old sportswear manufacturer made two visits a year to his parents' home in Florida and looked hard during the final year and a half of his search for a boathouse with a view of the Atlantic. He imagined a pleasant lifestyle full of brisk morning swims, aerobics classes at the health club, and visits to the library. But then IBM's stock slid so much in 1992 and early 1993 that he lost thirty thousand dollars and couldn't make the down payment.

"To me, IBM was the bluest of the blue chips," Kowal said. "Now it's turned into a cow chip."[3]

John Strobel, who worked at IBM for thirty-five years, put 10 percent of his salary into IBM stock over the years and planned to use it to buy a retirement home, but he says, "That's not in the cards now." Marie Doty, a seventy-six-year-old grandmother who invested in IBM, says, "I always believed that if you had shares of IBM and General Motors, then you had money. I thought that the world could collapse, but IBM would still go on."[4] When Sally Smith of New York gave her son some money in 1992 to save up for his son's education, she said the gift was really a good-news, bad-news joke. The good news was that she was giving him money. The bad news was that it was in IBM stock.

Tom Watson, Jr., was born in 1914, the year his father took over IBM, so his life has spanned the company's. He was around as his father struggled for the first few years, then, while still a boy, saw his father and the company rocket to fame and fortune. After a personal battle to find his identity and gain confidence, Tom Junior took the company through the next two leaps, getting it into computers in the 1950s and then producing the revolutionary 360 line of mainframes in the 1960s. By the time he left in the early 1970s, the company was one of the defining companies in the history of commerce. Now, at age seventy-nine, "Young Tom" has little to do with the company he did so much to create. The day John Akers announced he was stepping down as chairman, Watson was unreachable on his sailboat somewhere off the Yucatán Peninsula. He's more likely to be flying his plane than he is to be visiting someone at headquarters in Armonk. But it's still hard for him to see IBM fading as he heads into his own sunset years. He has kept quiet about the company so as not to interfere with those running IBM, but he did break that silence in late 1992 in an interview with *The Wall Street Journal*.

"When you see something you love have great difficulties, you are very sad about it," Watson said. "I have every confidence they'll prevail. But meanwhile it's a pretty hard pot of porridge to digest for an old-timer."

NOTES

PREFACE

1. John Markoff, "Campuses Are Hurt by Computer Giant's Woes," *The New York Times,* January 13, 1993, B6.
2. Bureau of Labor Statistics.

1

1. Stephen Manes and Paul Andrews, *Gates* (New York: Doubleday, 1993), 18.
2. Ibid., 21.
3. Ibid., 24.

2

1. James Chposky and Ted Leonsis, *Blue Magic: The People, Power and Politics Behind the IBM Personal Computer* (New York: Facts on File, 1988), 62–63.
2. Stephen Manes and Paul Andrews, *Gates* (New York: Doubleday, 1993), 136.
3. Chposky and Leonsis, *Blue Magic,* 75.
4. Steven Levy, *Hackers: Heroes of the Computer Revolution* (New York: Dell Publishing Co., 1984), 386.

3

1. William Rodgers, *Think: A Biography of the Watsons and IBM* (New York: Stein and Day, 1969), 20–22.
2. Ibid., 11.
3. Ibid., 28–29.

4. Thomas J. Watson, Jr., and Peter Petre, *Father, Son & Co.: My Life at IBM and Beyond* (New York: Bantam Books, 1990), 19.
5. Ibid., 4.
6. Ibid., 6, 33, 38, 80–81.
7. Ibid., 121–23.
8. Rodgers, *Think*, 157.
9. Watson and Petre, *Father, Son & Co.*, 224.
10. Rodgers, *Think*, 100.
11. Watson and Petre, *Father, Son & Co.*, 363–65.
12. Ibid., 290.
13. "The Brain Builders," *Time*, March 28, 1955, 81.
14. Watson and Petre, *Father, Son & Co.*, 311.
15. James B. Stewart, *The Partners* (New York: Simon and Schuster, 1982), 70, 102.
16. J. Greenwald, "The Colossus that Works," *Time*, July 11, 1983, 44.
17. "No. 1's Awesome Strategy," *Business Week*, June 8, 1981, 84.
18. Greenwald, "Colossus," 44.
19. James Chposky and Ted Leonsis, *Blue Magic: The People, Power and Politics Behind the IBM Personal Computer* (New York: Facts on File, 1988), 164.
20. Ibid., 185–86.
21. Ibid., 198.

5

1. Stephen Manes and Paul Andrews, *Gates* (New York: Doubleday, 1993), 316.
2. Michael Killen, *IBM: The Making of the Common View* (New York: Harcourt Brace Jovanovich, 1988), 206–210.
3. Manes and Andrews, *Gates*, 323.
4. Ibid., 361.

7

1. Roy A. Bauer, Emilio Collar, and Victor Tang, *The Silverlake Project: Transformation at IBM* (New York: Oxford University Press, 1992), 21.
2. "How IBM Is Fighting Back," *Business Week*, November 17, 1986, 152.
3. "IBM: More Worlds to Conquer," *Business Week*, February 18, 1985, 86.
4. Bauer, Collar, and Tang, *The Silverlake Project*, 24.

9

1. Roy A. Bauer, Emilio Collar, and Victor Tang, *The Silverlake Project: Transformation at IBM* (New York: Oxford University Press, 1992), 21.
2. Steve Lohr, "Task of Turning Around IBM Is Given to an Industry Outsider," *The New York Times*, March 27, 1993, C1.

11

1. Karen Bemowski, "Big Q at Big Blue," *Quality Progress*, May 1991, 17.
2. Stephen Manes and Paul Andrews, *Gates* (New York: Doubleday, 1993), 409–410.

14

1. Cathy Arnst, "Stand Back, Big Blue—And Wish Me Luck," *Business Week*, August 17, 1992, 99–100.

15

1. John Schwartz, "Available: One Impossible Job," *Newsweek*, February 8, 1993, 44–51.
2. Carol Loomis and David Kirkpatrick, "The Hunt for Mr. X: Who Can Run IBM?" *Fortune*, February 22, 1993, 68–72.
3. Carol Loomis, "Can John Akers Save IBM?" *Fortune*, July 15, 1991, 40–45.
4. *USA TODAY*, April 26, 1993, 1.

16

1. Thomas J. Watson, Jr., and Peter Petre, *Father, Son & Co.: My Life at IBM and Beyond* (New York: Bantam Books, 1990), 16.
2. Cathy Arnst, "Faith in a Stranger," *Business Week*, April 5, 1993, 18–24.
3. *Smart Money*, April 1993, 84–87.
4. Ibid.

BIBLIOGRAPHY

Bauer, Roy A., Emilio Collar, and Victor Tang. *The Silverlake Project: Transformation at IBM*. New York: Oxford University Press, 1992.

Belden, Thomas Graham, and Marva Robins Belden. *The Lengthening Shadow: The Life of Thomas J. Watson*. Toronto: Little, Brown and Company, 1962.

Chposky, James, and Ted Leonsis. *Blue Magic: The People, Power and Politics Behind the IBM Personal Computer*. New York: Facts on File, 1988.

DeLoca, Cornelius E., and Samuel Jay Kalow. *The Romance Division . . . A Different Side of IBM*. Wyckoff, New Jersey: D & K Book Company, 1991.

Ferguson, Charles H., and Charles R. Morris. *Computer Wars: How the West Can Win in a Post-IBM World*. New York: Times Books, 1993.

Foy, Nancy. *The Sun Never Sets on IBM: The Culture and Folklore of IBM World Trade*. New York: William Morrow & Company, 1975.

Killen, Michael. *IBM: The Making of the Common View*. New York: Harcourt Brace Jovanovich, 1988.

Levy, Steven. *Hackers: Heroes of the Computer Revolution*. New York: Dell Publishing Co., 1984.

Manes, Stephen, and Paul Andrews. *Gates: How Microsoft's Mogul Reinvented an Industry*. New York: Doubleday, 1993.

Rodgers, William. *Think: A Biography of the Watsons and IBM*. New York: Stein and Day, 1969.

Watson, Thomas, Jr. *A Business and Its Beliefs: The Ideas That Helped Build IBM*. New York: McGraw-Hill, 1963.

Watson, Thomas, Jr., and Peter Petre. *Father, Son & Co.: My Life at IBM and Beyond*. New York: Bantam Books, 1990.

INDEX